DICTIONARY
OF
MARKETING
AND
ADVERTISING

BUSINESS DICTIONARY SERIES

DICTIONARY OF BUSINESS AND MANAGEMENT

    Jerry M. Rosenberg

DICTIONARY OF BANKING

    Jerry M. Rosenberg

DICTIONARY OF INVESTING

    Jerry M. Rosenberg

BUSINESS DICTIONARY OF COMPUTERS

    Jerry M. Rosenberg

DICTIONARY OF INTERNATIONAL TRADE

    Jerry M. Rosenberg

DICTIONARY OF MARKETING AND ADVERTISING

    Jerry M. Rosenberg

OTHER BOOKS BY THE AUTHOR

Automation, Manpower and Education (Random House)

The Computer Prophets (Macmillan)

The Death of Privacy: Do Government and Industrial Computers Threaten Our Personal Freedom? (Random House)

Inside The Wall Street Journal: The History and Power of Dow Jones & Company and America's Most Influential Newspaper (Macmillan)

Dictionary of Artificial Intelligence and Robotics (John Wiley)

The New Europe: An A to Z Compendium on the European Community (Bureau of National Affairs)

Dictionary of Business Acronyms, Initials, and Abbreviations (McGraw-Hill)

Dictionary of Wall Street Acronyms, Initials, and Abbreviations (McGraw-Hill)

Dictionary of Information Technology and Computer Acronyms, Initials, and Abbreviations (McGraw-Hill)

The New American Community: The U.S. Response to the European and Asian Economic Challenge (Praeger)

DICTIONARY
OF
MARKETING
AND
ADVERTISING

Jerry M. Rosenberg
**Professor, Graduate School
of Management, and
School of Business
RUTGERS UNIVERSITY**

Business Dictionary Series

John Wiley & Sons, Inc.
New York • Chichester • Brisbane • Toronto • Singapore

Copyright © 1995 by Jerry M. Rosenberg
Published by John Wiley & Sons, Inc.

Library of Congress Cataloging-in-Publication Data:

Rosenberg, Jerry Martin.
    Dictionary of marketing and advertising / Jerry M. Rosenberg.
        p.   cm. — (Business dictionary series)
    Includes bibliographical references.
    ISBN 0-471-02503-8 (cloth–acid-free paper).
    — ISBN 0-471-02502-X (pbk.–acid-free paper)
    1. Marketing—Dictionaries.   2. Advertising—Dictionaries.
    I. Title.   II. Series.
    HF5415.R577   1995
    658.8'003—dc20   94-25576

Printed in the United States of America

10 9 8 7 6 5 4 3 2 1

This volume is dedicated, with love, to
Bess
my first grandchild

PREFACE

A creation of commerce over the past two hundred years, marketing and its companion activity, advertising, are usually identified with the nations of the Western world. These fields have captured the imagination of promoters, who attempt to move manufactured goods and evolving services from beginning stages to consumer purchases. Whether it be free markets, managed trade, national control of exports and imports or, for that matter, the concepts of social and not-for-profit agencies, marketing and advertising have profoundly influenced and altered the way our modern life evolves.

Directly or indirectly, people worldwide have been influenced by others who promote and develop tactics for implementing ideas, gathering and processing raw materials, producing and selling merchandise and services, and ultimately distributing these human achievements to distributors, wholesalers, conveyors of services, and then, to consumers. Throughout, whether by broadcasting, print, or other media, the marketing and the advertising of goods and services have become central activities of modern-day commerce.

More recently, traditional approaches have been reexamined and often replaced with newer strategies, and consequently, with new terminology. Globally, the fields of international marketing and advertising not only have expanded but have created a new demand for a greater awareness of overseas forces and a jargon rarely used, nor previously required, by the domestic marketer or advertiser. This situation is changing quickly, however, as the marketing of items and services has become regionalized and has been affected by the recently completed Uruguay Round of the General Agreement of Tariffs and Trade.

To prepare this volume, considerable assistance has come indirectly from authors of books, journal articles, and reference materials. They are too numerous to be named here. On a more personal level, I thank the various individuals whom I used as a sounding board to clarify my ideas and approach; they offered valuable suggestions and encouraged me to go on with this project.

Without the confidence of Stephen Kippur, a friend since the first of my seven Wiley dictionaries appeared in 1978, and presently senior vice president of John Wiley & Sons; Karl Weber, another former editor and now associate publisher; and my newest editor Ruth Mills, this dictionary would never have appeared. Last, but always, there is my wife Ellen, for nearly 35 years the closest of companions, and other supporters Liz, Lauren, and son-in-law Bob, who collectively continue to lend their reinforcement and share my interest in the meanings and usage of words. Once again, I look forward to hearing from readers with suggestions, both for changes and for future entries.

JERRY M. ROSENBERG

New York, New York

CONTENTS

INTRODUCTION

This work of approximately 5,000 entries has been prepared with the hope that awareness of the accepted meaning of terms may enhance the sharing of information and ideas. Though it cannot eliminate the need for the user to determine how a writer or speaker is treating a word, such a dictionary shows what usages exist. It should assist in stabilizing terminology. Most important, it should aid people in saying and writing exactly what they intend with greater clarity.

A word can take on different meanings in different contexts. There may be as many meanings as there are areas of specialization. A goal of this dictionary is to be broad and to establish core definitions that represent the variety of individual meanings thus enhancing parsimony and clearness in the communications process.

Many terms are used in different ways. I have tried to unite them without giving one advantage or dominance over another. Whenever possible (without creating controversy), I have stated the connection among multiple usages.

Commonly used acronyms and abbreviations are included. Foreign words and phrases are given only if they have become an integral part of our English vocabulary.

This work reaches throughout the world, incorporating terms from both government and private-sector organizations, making this dictionary an all-inclusive lexicon of international marketing and advertising.

Among the areas receiving special attention beyond traditional domestic aspects of marketing and advertising are regional trading blocs, other global partners, and the General Agreement on Tariffs and Trade, presently representing 117 nations.

ORGANIZATION

This is a defining work rather than a compilation of facts. The line is not easy to draw because in the final analysis meanings are based on facts. Consequently, factual information is used where necessary to make a term more easily understood. All terms are presented in the language of those who use them. The level of complexity needed for a definition will vary with the user; one person's complexity is another's precise and parsimonious statement. Several meanings are sometimes given—relatively simple for the layperson, more developed and technical for the specialist.

I have organized the dictionary to provide information easily and rapidly, while keeping in mind two categories of user: the experienced person who demands precise information about a particular word, and the newcomer, support member, teacher, or student who seeks general explanation. I have, in most cases, supplied both general and specialized entries to make this work a useful reference source.

FORMAT

Alphabetization.   Words are presented alphabetically. Compound terms are placed where the reader is most likely to look for them. They are entered under their most distinctive component, usually a noun. Should you fail to locate a word where you initially look for it, turn to a variant spelling, a synonym, or a different word of the compound term.

Entries containing mutual concepts are usually grouped for comparison. They are then given in inverted order; that is, the expected order of words is reversed to allow the major word of the phrase to appear at the beginning of the term. These entries precede those that are given in the expected order. The terms are alphabetized up to the first comma and then by words following the comma, thus establishing clusters of related terms.

Headings.   The current popular term is usually given as the principal entry, with other terms cross-referenced to it. Some terms have been included for historical significance, even though they are no longer in common use.

Cross-References.   Cross-references go from the general to the specific. Occasionally, "see" references from the specific to the general are used to inform the user of words related to particular entries. "See" references to currently accepted terminology are made wherever possible. The use of "Cf." suggests words to be compared with the original entry.

Synonyms.   The phrase "Synonymous with" following a definition does not imply that the term is *exactly* equivalent to the principal entry under which it appears. Frequently, the term only approximates the primary sense of the original entry.

Disciplines.   Many words are given multiple definitions based on their utilization in various fields of activity. The definition with the widest application is given first, with the remaining definitions listed by areas of specialty. Since the areas may overlap, the reader should examine all multiple definitions.

AAA: American Academy of Advertising; the professional organization of academics and practitioners in advertising concerned with advancing advertising education.

AAAA: see *American Association of Advertising Agencies.*

AA rating: see *average audience rating.*

ABA: see *area-by-area allocation.*

abandonment stage: the final stage in a product's life cycle, when the profit potential is such that management decides that the best course is to discontinue marketing it. Cf. *milking.*

ABC: see *Audit Bureau of Circulations.*

ABC inventory management: dividing inventories, at the time of purchase into categories A, B, and C, based on relative high or low usage and/or high or low costs.

abeyance order: the request for commercial television time when that particular time slot is not available at the time of the request.

above the line:
(1) *general:* for firms, all incomes and expenses before taxes.
(2) *advertising:* the promotional expenses associated with advertising in one of the media.

above the market strategy: synonymous with *market-plus pricing.*

absence of demand: within a market, the situation where a major segment of the market finds no possibilities of benefits from a product and is completely disinterested in the product. Synonymous with *no demand.*

absolute advantage:
(1) an advantage of one nation or area over another in the costs of manufacturing an item in terms of used resources. Cf. *comparative advantage.*
(2) the advantage enjoyed by a country because it can produce a product at a lower cost than can other countries.

absolute frequency: in marketing research, the number of data elements in a given subunit that has clear boundaries.

absolute product failure: the failure of an item to recover in the marketplace the investment made in its development, manufacture, and marketing.

absolute sale: an agreement between the buyer and seller that there should be no conditions or restrictions affecting the sales transactions. Cf. *approval sale.*

absorption costing: product costing that assigns fixed manufacturing overhead to the units produced as a product cost. See *product costing.*

abstract: an abridged summary of information omitting unessentials.

abuses: in the overseas marketing of products and services; unfair practices by one nation against another following the completion of a trade agreement. Examples are (a) directly or indirectly imposing unfair purchase or selling prices or other unfair trading conditions; (b) limiting product, markets, or technical development to the prejudice of consumers; (c) applying dissimilar conditions to equivalent transactions with other trading parties, thereby placing them at a competitive disadvantage; (d) making the conclusion of contracts subject to acceptance by the other parties with supplementary obligations that, by their nature or according to commercial usage, have no connection with the subject of such contracts. Rectifying such abuses may require the assistance of an international trade court or commission.

accelerator principle: the principle stating that the final consumer demand affects several layers of organizational

consumers. See *marginal propensity to consume.*

acceptance:

(1) *general:* the acknowledged receipt by a shipment's consignee resulting in the termination of the common carrier contract.

(2) *marketing:* a positive reception of a product, brand, or line of products by the public.

(3) *marketing:* an agreement to purchase goods at a stated price and under stated terms.

acceptance sampling: the usage of a given pattern of statistical sampling as part of the inspection procedure of a manufacturing organization that purports to set the acceptance or rejection of specific lots of materials or products. See *decision rule.*

accessibility: one of the four characteristics of a market segment if it is to deserve specific marketing attention. Other features are measurability, substantiality, and uniqueness.

accessible site: a location for a retail store that can be readily reached by customers and employees. Distance is a factor, along with driving time and parking facilities.

accessorial service: a service rendered by a carrier in addition to a transportation service, such as assorting, packaging, precooling, heating, storage, or substitution of tonnage.

accessories: in retailing, items that coordinate with a basic article of clothing to make it more appealing, and therefore more attractive, for the wearer's total image. They include items such as gloves, stockings, scarves, etc.

accessory equipment: portable industrial capital goods used in the production process that require a moderate amount of consumer decision making, are less costly than installations, last a number of years, and do not become part of the final product or change form.

accidental exporting: in international marketing, an export business obtained through no effort of the exporter.

accommodation area: in retailing, the area devoted to providing additional services to customers, such as wrapping of packages, validating parking tickets, etc. Synonymous with *accommodation desk; service area.*

accommodation desk: synonymous with *accommodation area.*

accordion fold: a method for folding an advertising page so that the panels fold alternately inward and outward. See *accordion insert.*

accordion insert: an accordion-folded advertising circular, leaflet, or other advertising brochure that will be bound into a periodical or placed in an envelope as part of a direct-mail campaign. See *accordion fold.*

account:

(1) *general:* a record of all the transactions, and the date of each, affecting a particular phase of a business, expressed in debits and credits, evaluated in money, and showing the current balance, if any.

(2) *marketing:* a customer of a supplier or vendor firm from which the consumer obtains specific materials or services.

(3) *marketing:* a customer with whom the marketer does business.

(4) *advertising:* the client of an advertising agency or an organization that places promotional material directly with the media.

(5) *advertising:* an advertiser.

(6) see *client.*

account classification: the evaluation of retailers or other buyers according to existing and, in particular, potential business.

account conflict: problems created when two directly competing items or services are handled by the same advertising agency. Agencies servicing competitive firms may be in conflict, and often one of the accounts will be withdrawn by a manufacturer.

account executive (AE):

(1) *advertising:* the member of an agency who supervises the planning and preparation of advertising for clients and is responsible for contacts between the agency and the advertiser.

(2) *broadcasting:* a broadcast-station time salesperson who is usually paid a commission on the funds spent by a sponsor for purchasing commercial time.

(3) synonymous with *account representative.*

account opener: a gift given by a bank or other financial institution to a potential depositor opening a new account or adding funds to an existing account. See *direct premium.*

account planning: a means of evolving advertising where the agency research acts as a major part of the creative team; involves personal interviews with select members of the target market. The objective is to design advertising that parallels the concerns and desires of the consumer.

account representative: synonymous with *account executive.*

accounts payable: a current liability representing the amount owed by an individual or a business to a creditor for merchandise or services purchased on an open account or short-term credit.

accounts receivable:

(1) *general:* money owed a business enterprise for merchandise bought on open account.

(2) *advertising:* funds due an agency on client billings.

account supervisor: an advertising agency executive responsible for the work of several account executives and actively involved in client relationships, but not necessarily on a regular basis.

achieved penetration: a marketing measure of the ratio of existing users (or buyers) to current potential users (or buyers) of a product class.

ACI: see *Advertising Council, Inc.*

ACK: see *acknowledgment.*

acknowledgment (ACK):

(1) a statement that a proper document has been submitted.

(2) a written confirmation from a manufacturer to a buyer dealing with the buyer's merchandise order; informs the buyer that the order was received and is being processed, or that any inquiries or complaints are being handled.

A.C. Nielsen Company: see entries under *Nielsen.*

acquisition:

(1) *general:* the takeover of one company by another.

(2) *sales:* a means of expanding a firm's sales by securing other firms, product rights, or technological advances; a means of enhancing corporate growth other than through international expansion.

acquisition budget: money set aside for advertising and promotion in the securing of potential customers.

acquisition cost: the cost to a company of securing business; primarily commissions to agents and agencies.

across-the-board: a broadcast program aired every day of the week at the same time; often also applied to such broadcast activity five or more times per week. Since a program fills in a strip in a broadcast schedule, it is synonymous with *strip programming.* See *media planning.*

action:

(1) *general:* the last step in the communication process, entailing implementation of the communication.

(2) *advertising:* the resulting effort from an advertising agency. Their primary function is to lead to some altered form of behavior, usually to get consumers to purchase a product or service.

action device: part of a marketing promotion to encourage reader involvement through the performance of an action, such as filling out a questionnaire. The concept suggests that greater involvement leads to a higher response from readers. Synonymous with *involvement device.* See *scratch and sniff.*

action plan: synonymous with *marketing plan.*

action program: part of a marketing strategy; steps taken to achieve the plan's goals.

active buyers: in direct marketing, customers whose last purchase was made within the past 12 months. Synonymous with *active customers; actives.*

active customers: synonymous with *active buyers; actives.*

actives: synonymous with *active buyers; active customers.*

active search: the securing of information by a prospect or customers in buying an item or service that lacks sufficient feedback to help in making a buy decision. At this point, the customer who is actively searching for information is highly sensitive to advertising and commercials.

active subscriber: a customer committed to receiving a regular magazine, book, etc., delivery and/or services for a time period.

activities, interests, opinions (AIO): a discipline for understanding consumers' lifestyles and their ensuing purchasing behavior. *Activities* include occupation, hobbies; *interests* relate to community and family; *opinions* deal with issues and politics. Advertisements are often directed to the AIO characteristics of the target group.

activity quota: a measure of the salesperson's success in terms other than sales and the monies generated; includes letters and telephone calls to prospects, offering of demonstrations, visits to potential buyers, etc. Cf. *sales quota.* See *call report.*

act of God: in contractual language, an irresistible superhuman cause, such as no reasonable human foresight, prudence, diligence, and care can anticipate or prevent.

actuals: merchandise and other items available for immediate purchase and subsequent sale.

actual total loss: in marketing, a loss that occurs when an item is totally destroyed or destroyed sufficiently to become useless.

ad: short for advertisement. See *advertisement.*

ad-a-card: a trademark for printed tear-off coupons affixed to advertisements; traditionally placed in newspapers.

adaptation: a design that reflects the dominant feature of a style that inspired it but is not an exact copy.

adaptive-control model: a means for establishing an advertising budget to determine the sales impact of advertising costs. The budget remains flexible and is often reevaluated to allow for the changing marketing situation.

adaptive product: a variation of another offering of the same firm, designed to broaden the company's market share. See *emulative product; multiple brand entries.*

added gravy: revenues resulting from added selling; sales resulting from items used to provide satisfaction from another item, such as linens for outfitting a queen-size mattress.

added selling: the potential to sell more products and/or services to a customer who has just made a purchase. See *added gravy.*

added-value tax: see *value-added tax.*

additional mark-on: an increase in the retail price of merchandise above the price placed on it when it was originally accepted for sale.

add-ons: in retailing, further purchases added to the account of a charge account customer before the previous balance in the account has been completely paid.

address coding method: a technique developed by direct marketers that contains the actual or potential beginning and ending house numbers, block groups, and/or zip codes, and other codes for city delivery service streets.

addressing: one of the costs to be considered, particularly in direct-mail advertising; the manual, mechanical, or automatic inscription of the name and address of the recipient on the face of an envelope or mailing piece.

adequate sampling:

(1) *general:* a test group sufficiently large to reach precision, which reduces the element of chance as a variable affecting the obtained data.

(2) *advertising:* the test group of people to determine which audience adequately represents a market about to be tested.

adjacencies: programs that precede or follow a specific broadcast time period.

adjustment:

(1) *general:* a change in an account to correct an incorrect entry or for some other sound reason.

(2) *marketing:* the satisfying of a customer's claim that a shipment was not as ordered or that the price was improperly charged, by an agreeable financial settlement.

(3) *sales:* the correction of mistakes involving the wrong recording of invoices or wrong dating of purchases bought on open account.

adjustment allowance: appropriate compensation given to a customer to settle a claim or complaint.

admass: high-pressure advertising and promotion in the media to increase sales, with damaging impact on the culture of the society.

administered channel system: a set of relationships in ordering, supply and payment between the producer and channel intermediaries; purports to retain the autonomy of each channel member at the same time allowing informal and lasting organization arrangements to upgrade efficiency and encourage loyalty.

administered price: the price established under situations of imbalanced competition wherein one business has some degree of control. See *price leadership.*

administered vertical marketing: a vertically aligned group of organizations, not necessarily vertically integrated, that performs as a unit to lower the costs inherent in merchandising a line or classification of goods.

adnorm: the percentage of readers of a specific publication who recall a particular advertisement found in the publication; represents a proportion of an accepted norm for advertisements of a similar nature.

adopter categories: groups of persons or firms that adopt an innovation. They are often classified into five groups according to the sequence of their adoption of it: (a) innovators (the first 2 to 5 percent); (b) early adoptors (the next 10 to 15 percent); (c) early majority (the next 35 percent); (d) late majority (the next 35 percent); and (e) laggards (the final 5 to 10 percent). The numbers are percentages of the total number of actual adopters, not of the total number of persons or firms in the marketplace. There is wide disagreement on the exact percentage in each category. See *adoption of innovation.*

adoption of innovation: the process by which an innovation spreads throughout a population. It consists of adopter categories (innovators, early adopters, etc.) and a specific process of adoption by each adopter. See *adopter categories.*

adoption process: the awareness that occurs when a person first becomes aware of an innovation until he or she is willing to accept it; usually in the instance of real things, purchasing them. See *AIDCAS process; awareness; diffusion process; evaluation.*

adoption process segmentation variables: consumer stages that are completed in the process of becoming a regular user of a product and/or service. The stages include awareness, interest, evaluation, trial, and adoption.

ad-slick: a camera-ready advertisement prepared for distribution to firms of an association for placing in the local print media. Ad-slicks often have a blank space where the advertiser inserts an address, telephone number, and other relevant, but brief information. See *dealer listing.*

ad valorem tariff: a tariff based on a percentage of the value of the goods imported.

advance bill:

(1) *marketing:* a bill of exchange drawn prior to the shipment of merchandise.

(2) *sales:* the invoice presented before the items or services itemized have been delivered or carried out. It is usually requested by purchasers for tax reasons.

advance canvass: in advertising, the contacting of retailers prior to the introduction of a new promotional campaign so as to create an emotional high for the forthcoming program and capture support from the stores.

advance dating: the added time allowed by a vendor to pay for goods, enabling the purchaser to receive a cash discount. Such extensions usually are arranged before the goods are shipped. Synonymous with *seasonal dating; season dating.*

advance freight: in international sales, freight paid for in advance. It permits the shipper to endorse the bill of lading with a freight release, and the importer to take immediate delivery.

advance order: the sales order placed sufficiently ahead of the requested date for delivery, thereby often entitling the buyer to a substantial discount.

advance premium: the premium offered to a potential customer by a home-service route firm in the hope that it will be earned by later purchases.

advance renewal: resubscription to a periodical, prior to the termination date.

advantage: in salesmanship, the way an item or service can assist in solving problems or fulfilling needs.

advertise:

(1) *general:* to promote; to solicit, usually without payment (e.g., a radio announcer promoting the qualities of a wine he or she experienced in a restaurant).

(2) *advertising:* applying some form of message or communication to attract

attention of an individual or group to a product, service, concept, institution, etc., with the expectation of some form of behavior or action; usually to purchase the item or service, or gain support for the concept or idea. See *advertised.*

advertised: the promotion of a product or service, without cost (e.g., hearing a radio announcer praise a bottle of wine that he or she experienced in a local restaurant). Cf. *advertisement.* See *advertise.*

advertised brand: the promotion, usually by recommendation, of a brand used by an individual.

advertised price:

(1) *advertising:* the cost to buyers for the item or service presented in a commercial or advertisement.

(2) *broadcasting:* the set price for the advertiser. A formula is often applied combining the time purchase (the volume), the cost to advertise the item or service; and the number of times the commercial is presented.

advertisement (ad): a public announcement or sale offer in a public area or medium, expressed in print, by other visual means, or orally. Major locations of advertisements are newspapers, magazines, and journals, and signs, billboards, radio, and television. Similar to, but not synonymous with commercial. An advertisement is usually paid for. Cf. *advertise; advertised; commercial.*

advertiser: anyone who engages to pay for advertising. See *account; client.*

advertising:

(1) a paid-for nonpersonal presentation or promotion of goods, services, and/or ideas. It is usually paid for by an identifiable sponsor. Decisions involve *what* is to be said and where to *place* the advertising. Cf. *publicity.* See also *promotion.*

(2) often used to include messages promoting concepts and causes; containing three basic objectives: (a) to *inform* consumers about new items, product uses, services available, or other useful information; (b) to *persuade* an audience to buy an item, change brand preferences, or perceive an item or service differently; (c) to *remind* consumers about the need for an item or service as well as where it can be bought.

(3) see *advocacy advertising; aisle advertising; bait advertising; bait and switch advertising; burst advertising; business-to-business advertising; classified advertising; commercial advertising; comparative advertising; comparison advertising; consumer advertising; cooperative advertising; corporate advertising; deceptive advertising; demonstration advertising; direct-action advertising; direct advertising; direct-response advertising; endorsement advertising; end-product advertising; ethical advertising; false advertising; financial advertising; generic advertising; impact advertising; indirect-action advertising; indirect advertising; institutional advertising; keyed advertising; local advertising; mail-order advertising; manufacturer's cooperative advertising; merchandising the advertising; name advertising; national advertising; noncommercial advertising; outdoor advertising; patronage institutional advertising; perimeter advertising; personalized advertisement; POP advertising; positioning advertising; postmark advertising; prestige advertising; primary advertising; primary demand advertising;*

product advertising; product reputation advertising; professional advertising; promotional advertising; public relations institutional advertising; public service advertising; reinforcement advertising; retail advertising; selective demand advertising; shortage advertising; spot advertising; subliminal advertising; subordinate product advertising; teaser advertisement; tie-in advertisement; tombstone advertisement; trade advertising; trade paper advertising; transit advertising; transportation advertising; vocational advertising; word-of-mouth advertising; yellow pages advertising.

advertising agency: a specialized institution that aids businesses or organizations in all phases of promoting sales of a product or service. An agency usually receives a 15 percent commission on the total billing; and the client pays for direct costs on a cost-plus basis. There are *full-service* agencies providing a complete range of creative, production, research, planning, and buying functions; and *limited-service* agencies providing only one service. See also *fifteen and two; full-service agency; sales promotion agency.*

advertising agency recognition: a perception of an advertising agency, based on a medium; its purpose is to gain approval to receive commissions on advertisements placed with the medium by the agency. Factors include creditworthiness, professional qualifications, and clients ready to advertise employing that agency. See *fifteen and two.*

advertising allowance: a discount in price or payment given to a store to help meet the expense of the store's advertising of a product. Such allowances are most often granted when new products are being introduced or when manufacturers are attempting to increase promotion of their products. Cf. *promotional allowance.* See *cooperative advertising; trade promotion.*

advertising appeal: the central concept of an advertisement that communicates to the potential consumer what the advertised item or service provides and gives the reasons it should be bought.

advertising appropriation: synonymous with *advertising budget.*

advertising art: illustrative matter of a creative nature, such as drawings, photographs, layouts, decorative designs, hand lettering, and retouching specifically prepared to use in advertising.

advertising budget: the amount of money an advertiser chooses to spend on advertising in a fixed time period, often one year. Synonymous with *advertising appropriation.*

advertising campaign: the planned use of varying media and advertising methods to solicit acceptance for an idea or item or to increase the sales of a product or service; running for months or as long as several years. Campaigns feature a variety of advertisements on the same theme and sales message. See *campaign.*

advertising contract:
(1) an agreement between the supplier of advertising space or time and the advertiser, providing details of content, cost, and placement of the advertisement. Both parties, once the contract is signed, are bound by these written terms.

(2) an agreement between a supplier and retailer in which the retailer agrees to advertise the merchandise over a fixed time period for a stated amount of money.

Advertising Council, Inc. (ACI): begun as the War Advertising Council in 1941, a not-for-profit organization of advertisers and agencies that designs and controls the distribution of public service advertising programs.

advertising credit: the mention of a store's name in the advertisement of a producer.

advertising effectiveness: a measure of the consumers' recall of advertising messages that they have been exposed to, along with the persuasiveness of the message; often determined at differing stages of the campaign. See *advertising testing; concept testing.*

advertising exposure: the actual presentation of an advertisement to an audience. See *advertising impact.*

Advertising Federation of America (AFA): a federation of member divisions representing different advertising agencies.

advertising goals: see *advertising objectives.*

advertising impact: one of three characteristics in determining advertising exposure and advertising response, the others being reach and frequency. Impact is qualitative and quite difficult to determine. It varies based on the receiver's perception and the sender's context of intent. See *advertising exposure.*

advertising manager: the title given to the individual in the advertising firm with major responsibility for advertising. He or she works closely with the advertising agency and is responsible to the firm's director of marketing or similar titled person. Advertising managers usually report to the firm's marketing vice-president.

advertising media (medium):
(1) various publications, devices, and structures that carry messages to intended recipients (e.g., newspapers, television, billboards, etc). See also *media.*

(2) the classes of vehicle that carry the advertiser's message to its audience. Advertising media are usually categorized into (a) print media (b) broadcast media, and (c) position media. Synonymous with *persuasion vehicles.*

advertising media costs: expenditures involved with placing messages in media. They are related to the length or size of an advertisement, as well as the characteristics of the chosen media.

advertising medium: see *advertising media.*

advertising message: the creative aspect of an advertisement campaign. The purpose of the mesage is to discharge the advertising objectives of the product or service. The message purports to secure the consumer's attention and interest. See *advertising target market.*

advertising models: computerized systems that assist in advertising decision making, by helping to determine budgets, media scheduling, and expectations of sales and profits.

advertising network: the grouping of advertising agencies, noncompeting and independently owned, that share ideas and services in the interest of their clients, and save themselves considerable expense.

advertising novelty: see *advertising specialty.*

advertising objectives: reasons behind an advertising campaign; usually to stimulate the consumer into purchasing a product and/or service. These objectives, once thrashed out, are ultimately translated into specific goals and product positioning.

advertising platform: the main issues or selling aspects desired by an advertiser when preparing an advertising campaign.

advertising quadrangle: from the advertising theory, wherein advertising is examined as containing four parts: the sender or advertiser, the message or an advertisement, the receiver or prospect, and the medium. From the standpoint of marketing theory, the four parts are the product, the prospect, the sponsor, and the channel of distribution. Synonymous with *quadrangle.*

advertising rates: charges for advertising time and/or advertising space. These rates are often subject to a surcharge when a preferred position is secured or are discounted when the advertiser makes volume purchases. These rates are basic costs for air time and space and are traditionally negotiable between the medium and the advertiser.

advertising readership measurement service: a commercial service designed to measure the quantitative or qualitative readership of advertising appearing in any issues of a business publication for the purpose of providing advertisers, agencies, and publishers with some knowledge of the relative effectiveness of the advertising and of the publication in developing interest among readers.

advertising record sheet: a work sheet for monitoring either daily, weekly, monthly, or all three orders for merchandise received as a result of a particular advertisement.

advertising register: one of the directories of national advertisers or agencies published on a steady basis.

advertising research: see *advertising testing.*

advertising reserve: funds set aside by the advertiser to be used in an emergency or special unexpected situation.

Advertising Review Board (ARB): composed of advertisers, agencies, and media specialists, to which advertisement claimed to be misleading or untrue may be referred. With any legal authority, the Board publicizes its decisions.

advertising space: the portion of the total page-space in print (newspaper, magazine, etc.) allocated to advertising rather than editorial and/or news matter.

advertising specialty: a low-cost item (e.g., a ballpoint pen) on which the seller's name, address, and telephone number are printed to promote awareness of the seller's name and location. Synonymous with *advertising novelty; specialties; specialty.*

advertising specialty distributor: synonymous with *specialty distributor.*

advertising stage: see *spiral stage.*

advertising substantiation: documentation provided by advertisers to the Federal Trade Commission to support their advertising claims. This paperwork must show that this data is the basis for the creation of the advertisement.

advertising target market: the specific audience toward which an advertising message is aimed. See *advertising message.*

advertising testing: a means of determining the effectiveness of individual advertisements or full campaigns. Pretesting determines the appropriateness and projected effectiveness before the placement of advertisements; Posttesting determines their impact following an appearance in the marketplace. See *advertising effectiveness; eye camera.*

advertising theme: a major idea behind an advertising campaign as presented to its potential audience. It purports to prove the superiority of the value of the item, idea, or service being offered.

advertising time: the portion of the total broadcasting time given to advertising instead of programming.

advertising weight: the measure of the number of exposures planned or actually completed from an advertising promotional campaign.

advertorial:

(1) a print article produced by the medium's advertising unit and financed by the firm's sponsors. The sponsoring organization pays to be quoted in the text, which appears as editorial material but is referred to as advertising.

(2) an advertisement appearing in layout format to resemble news copy. It can be read as a news column and therefore is a deceptive practice. See *advocacy advertising; reading notice.*

advice note: a supplier's listing of items that is sent to a customer prior to an invoice, either accompanying the merchandise or preceding it, identifying the nature and quantity of the goods but not giving prices.

advocacy advertising: advertising whose goal is the support of a specific idea, philosophy, or course of action on the part of its audience. It intends to induce or discourage particular forms of activity with regard to controversial issues (e.g., a person purchases magazine advertising to attack the availability of handguns to teenagers without proper regulations). See *advertorial.*

advocate channel: an individual communication channel composed of a firm's sales force contracting purchasers in the target market.

AE: see *account executive.*

AFA: see *Advertising Federation of America.*

affective component: the emotional feeling of favorableness or unfavorableness that results from a person's evaluation of an object.

affiant: one who swears to an affidavit.

affidavit: a written, notarized, dated, and sworn statement of the facts pertaining to a financial transaction or civil event. Such a statement must show the name and address of the affiant, must be signed by that person, and must bear the signature of the attesting official (e.g., notary public).

affidavit of performance: a notarized statement in which an employee of a station or network swears that the advertiser's message or program was actually broadcast as ordered. The affidavit is sent to the advertiser or his or her agency along with the invoice of charges as proof of services rendered.

affiliate:

(1) *general:* an organization whose management is connected by contract with that of another organization.

(2) *international marketing:* a unit, either partially or wholly owned by a multinational enterprise. It includes subsidiaries, branches, joint ventures,

and any other legal form implying at least partial control over the entity.

(3) *advertising:* a broadcast station that belongs to or carries the programs of a national network. Affiliates can be independently owned or are a division of a network. Affiliates provide commercial time, and the networks then sell it to national advertisers. Networks desire affiliates to attract large advertisers by securing for themselves large viewing audiences in numerous markets.

affiliated store:

(1) in retailing, a store that is part of a voluntary chain or a franchise.

(2) in retailing, a store under the name other than that of the controlling store.

affiliated wholesaler:

(1) the wholesaler who acts as initiator of a voluntary chain. See *voluntary chain.*

(2) a wholesaler who has an association with other wholesalers utilizing a common trade name for merchandising purposes.

affirmative disclosure: a Federal Trade Commission procedure for regulating advertising. It stipulates that should the information contained in an advertisement be considered inadequate or insufficient by the commission, it can demand that the firm identify limitations of its product or service within its subsequent advertising. This attempts to protect the consumer by providing data for judging both negative and positive attributes.

affirmative dumping decision: the decision that a nation has deliberately marketed products below their fair market value and is therefore subject to antidumping duty orders or other measures.

affixed merchandise: in advertising, items attached to a display in a fixed manner so that the display remains intact.

affordable method: a method of settling marketing budgets based on what a firm can afford to spend.

aforos: in overseas marketing, a customs value for computing ad valorem levies in some South American nations. The customs value is different from market value and is applied to designated classes of imports.

afternoon drive: in broadcasting, the time from 3:00 P.M. to 7:00 P.M. weekdays; a key prime time for radio. See *day parts.*

agate line: in printed newspapers and periodicals, the standard unit of area used to determine the cost of advertising space.

agency commission:

(1) the fee that an advertising agency charges his or her clients for the work completed in choosing and supervising the production work carried out by another firm, such as a film recorder or printer.

(2) the compensation received by an advertising agency from the media for purchases of time or space completed for clients. This commission represents the basic financial structure of the advertising agency business. See *commission; fee basis.*

agency group: see *agency network.*

agency network: advertising agencies separately affiliate to serve as local offices in primary locals to provide appropriate services for other members of the same network.

agency of record: the primary coordinator of an entire program for an advertiser that has secured the services of several advertising firms. The agency of record, who is chosen by the advertiser, then prepares all media contracts and receives payment from the other agencies involved for the media placement of their advertising.

agency produced program: in broadcasting, a program made by an advertising agency as contrasted with a program by an independent production firm, a local station, or network. The agency-produced program is usually brought as a complete package to the network or station, thus allowing the advertising agency to place its client's commercials in the commercial time slots.

agency recognition: acceptance by or having met the highest standards for an advertising agency.

agency reinstate: synonymous with *agent's reinstatement.*

agent:

(1) *general:* an individual authorized to act in behalf of another person, the principal.

(2) *marketing:* a middleman, who does not take title to the goods he or she sells.

(3) *wholesaler:* a wholesaling intermediary who does not take title to merchandise but serves primarily to bring buyers and sellers together and facilitate exchanges.

Agent/Distributor Service: an export/marketing promotion service to industry of the U.S. Department of Commerce's International Trade Administration. Its goal is to locate foreign companies to serve as agents and distributors of American products.

agent's cancellation: the cancellation of an agent's order, either at the customer's request or at the agent's request when payment of a bill is not received. Cancellations are often applied against commissions paid. See *agent's order; agent's reinstatement.*

agent's clearance: synonymous with *agent's order.*

agent's order: a single order, or orders submitted by the subscription agency for fulfillment processing. Synonymous with *agent's clearance.* See *agent's cancellation.*

agent's reinstate: synonymous with *agent's reinstatement.*

agent's reinstatement: a reordered periodical or magazine subscription that had been canceled because the payment was received too late to maintain the flow of subscription. See *reinstatement.* Synonymous with *agency reinstate.*

agent's summary: a report presented with the agency's order that reviews subscription orders for quantity, price of sale, terms, and dollars received or billed.

aggregate demand:

(1) the total spending within an economy.

(2) the total of personal consumption expenditures, business investments, and government spending.

aggregate economics: synonymous with *macroeconomics.*

aggregate supply: the capacity of a country's total resources to produce real goods and services.

aggregation: a marketing method based on the concept that consumers in a particular market are alike. Mass advertising and mass product distribution often result from this assumption, especially when low price is considered the primary appeal leading to the greatest number of consumers.

aggressive philosophy: in consumer behavior, the concept of a firm's attempt to increase market share by engaging in significant competition, utilizing all legal and ethical strategies available. Cf. *passive philosophy.*

agio: in overseas sales, the premium paid for the exchange of one nation's currency for that of another's.

agree-and-counterattack technique: synonymous with *"yes, but" technique.*

agreeing-and-neutralizing technique: synonymous with *"yes, but" technique.*

Agreement on Antidumping Practices: a 1980 international agreement, following the Tokyo Round of GATT, that impacts on international marketing; established conditions under which antidumping duties can be legally imposed by a nation as its defense against what it claims are dumped imports.

Agreement on Customs Valuation: a 1980 international agreement, following the Tokyo Round of GATT, that impacts on international marketing; replaced numerous systems of customs valuation with transparent regulations to afford participating members a fair, neutral, and uniform process of valuing items for the purpose of levying customs duties. The Agreement harmonized numerous goods.

AIDA process: in marketing, a concept of how prospects purchase, based on a series of mental activities. They are Attention, or zeroing in on the salesperson and listening for the presentation; Interest, or desiring further information; Desire, or a need to secure the salesperson's offering; and Action, or placing the order. Cf. *AIDCAS process.*

AIDCAS process: the next step after the AIDA process, to incorporate Conviction, or the conclusion that the salesperson's offering provides benefits as good as or superior to those of any other available offering; and Satisfaction, or the pleasure from the purchase in the belief that the correct choice was made and the expected benefits were received. Cf. *AIDA process.*

aided recall: a method to survey the impression made by an advertisement or other media communication, whereby an interviewer presents an advertisement or other aid to memory. Cf. *diary method; unaided recall.* See *copy testing; recognition.*

AIO: see *activities; interests; opinions.*

air: in broadcasting, the time a program goes over the air waves.

air bubble packing: packing materials made of plastic with air pockets for cushioning.

air check: a permanent record of a broadcast, program, or commercial to determine the quality of production and delivery time or date.

air date: the date when a broadcast program of a commercial is to be shown or heard.

airedale: (slang) a high-pressure salesperson who often dresses sharply, talks fast, and is aggressive in behavior. Cf. *bird dog.*

air waybill: used in global sales; a transport document that covers both domestic and international flights transporting goods to a specified destination. This is a nonnegotiable instrument of air transport that serves as a receipt for the shipper, indicating that the carrier has accepted the goods listed and obligates itself to carry the consignment to the airport of destination according to specified conditions.

aisle advertising: in-store item display to attract attention and make the item accessible to purchasers; usually, the same copy and graphics is used in other promotional efforts produced by the sponsoring product. See *POP advertising.*

a la carte agency: an advertising agency that provides services in parts as needed on a negotiated basis. Synonymous with *modular service agency.*

alien company: when marketing overseas, the incorporated company that is formed and operating under the regulations of a foreign nation.

allied products: in retailing, items associated with one another in the same use category. See *complementary products.*

allocate: to distribute, assign, or allot.

allocation:

(1) *general:* assigning one or more items of cost or revenue to one or more segments of an organization, according to benefits received, responsibilities, or other logical measures of use.

(2) *broadcasting:* the range of wavelengths assigned by the Federal Communications Commission to a broadcast system.

(3) *merchandising:* the lowering of price to a retailer by the manufacturer or wholesaler based on some unique agreement. Traditionally, it is used to compensate the retailer for expenses in marketing the item.

allocation rights: the authority given managers in the area of purchasing to incorporate strategies.

allonge: a paper affixed to a bill on which further endorsements are written.

all-other circulation: the number of copies of an audited newspaper that are sold, excluding those distributed in the city zone (the corporate municipality area) and the retail trading zone (the territory beyond the city zone in which people live who trade in the city to an important degree).

allotment:

(1) *general:* the separation of anticipated revenue among specific classes of expenditure.

(2) *general:* an assignment of pay for the benefit of dependents.

(3) *advertising:* in outdoor advertising, the unit of sale composed of a showing in a given market, often a poster or two based on the market size and its traffic flow.

allowance:

(1) *merchandising:* a deduction from the weight or value of merchandise; a reduction permitted if the carrier does not supply appropriate equipment and the shipper then produces the equipment for use.

(2) *sales:* any price reduction.

all-purpose revolving account: in retailing, the charge account for which the agreement with customers provides that no service charge will be imposed if the account is paid in full within a given time period following the presentation of a statement. Synonymous with *flexible charge account; retail installment credit account; revolving charge account.*

all-you-can-afford method: a technique for evolving a promotional budget where all nonpromotional marketing expenses are budgeted initially, and the remaining funds are allocated to promotional activities.

Alpha test: the testing of a new product in-house, not with potential users (Beta test). The testing may be in a laboratory setting or (as in the case of glues or computers) in some part of the developing firm's regular operations. Cf. *Beta test.*

alternate bundles run: in print media advertising, the printing of two differing versions of the advertiser's message in separate phases of a press run, which are then alternately comingled when bundled for circulation delivery; used to measure the effectiveness of one message over another message.

alternate sponsorship: two sponsors sharing a program, usually each one taking a week. It permits exclusivity for the duration of the sponsorship. See *sponsorship.*

alternate weeks: the advertiser's instructions to a broadcasting medium to run a commercial for one week, then skip one week, and then run it again. After a three-week period, the advertiser pays for a two-week exposure.

alternative media: advertising media that do not fall into clear categories, such as advertisement on shopping mall carts. Alternative media evolved in response to increasing competition by different manufacturers for purchases by consumers. See *media; out-of-home media.*

alternative tariff: when marketing overseas, the tariff containing two or more rates from and to the same points, on the same goods, with authority to use the one that produces the lowest charge.

altruistic display:
(1) a display for items of advertisers other than the ones that pay for the display.

(2) a storewide occurrence for seasonal items including the advertiser's product without specifically naming it.

AMA: see *American Marketing Association.*

ambiguous statement: an advertising method utilizing a statement that can be interpreted in differing ways to mean different things. This may be deliberate on the part of the advertiser, especially when the item or service has no clearly defined target market. Often, consumers who are indifferent or do not possess a strong feeling toward a brand or particular service are attracted to ambiguous statements.

American Academy of Advertising: see *AAA.*

American Association of Advertising Agencies (AAAA): a trade association of leading advertising agencies in the United States; purports to improve standards of advertising by its members.

American goods returned: a provision of the U.S. Tariff Schedules that allows duty-free return of merchandise of American manufacture. The goods must not have been manipulated or advanced in value, except for the packaging of the item.

American Marketing Association (AMA): a national professional organization for persons engaged in the practice and teaching of marketing. It also publishes the *Journal of Marketing,* the *Journal of Marketing Research,* and a twice-monthly newsletter.

American Research Bureau (ARB): a television rating service utilizing both the viewer diary method and an electronic recording and tabulating device, called Arbitron. See *Arbitron; diary method.*

American selling price (ASP): in international sales; the price charged by U.S. producers for goods, used to determine the duty to be paid on a similar item brought into the United States, rather than determining the duty on the actual cost of the item to an importer.

American Telemarketing Association (ATA): an association of telephone marketing businesses and related firms; promotes the use of telephone sales and purports to upgrade the industry's public and private image.

amplification and details: the section of verbal copy of an advertisement that supplements and extends, usually in considerable length, the idea presented by the headline. Frequently follows the subheadline should one be used.

AMS: see *Analytical Marketing System.*

ANA: Association of National Advertisers; a national organization of advertisers, with most members being among the largest manufacturers.

analogy advertising: a commercial that utilizes an extraneous example of one item in a comparison to explain the advertised merchandise.

analysis of covariance: in marketing research, an extension of methods used in the analysis of variance to include two or more related variables. See *analysis of variance.*

analysis of variance: in marketing research, a method for determining whether the differences found in a dependent variable, when it is exposed to the influence of one or more experimental variables, exceed what may be expected by chance. See *analysis of covariance.*

Analytical Marketing System (AMS): one of four systems of a firm's marketing information system. It consists of a statistical bank and a model bank for analyzing marketing information and issues. Deals with new product sales forecasting, choosing a site, sales-call planning, media mix, and marketing mix budgeting.

analytical research: a form of marketing research that focuses on why consumers purchase the products they do.

anchor: as used by consumers to evaluate communications; often employed as a rule-of-thumb concept, such as "the higher the price for an item, the better its quality." An advertiser, aware of anchors used by the target markets, can increase positive reactions and avoid negative ones.

ancillary customer services: optional services provided for customers to increase the noncompetition activities of the sellers; always of a nonessential variety. Some stores do and others do not charge for such services.

ancillary services: see *ancillary customer services.*

Andy awards: awards of the Advertising Club of New York for the best commercial on radio and television, and the best overall commercial from all entrants.

angled poster: a poster placed so that it is viewed by traffic moving in one direction only.

announcement: the second stage of the product launch cycle; used to introduce the product or service to the public.

announcer voice-over: synonymous with *voice-over.*

annual rebate: a discount of approximately 12 to 13 percent granted by the major radio and television networks to sponsors who use network facilities for at least 52 consecutive weeks, and applied to the gross cost of time purchased by advertisers during the year.

anthropology: a branch of social sciences that examines the development of people and their customs. Data from this discipline are used in marketing to avoid mistakes in the use of symbols, cultural themes, and the encroachment into taboos.

anticipation of demand: the requirement for a firm to do consumer research on a regular basis to develop and introduce offerings desired by consumers.

antitrust acts: federal legislation that regulates trade to maintain competition and prevent monopolies. Advertising and promotional allowances are allowed as long as they offer prices for rendered services on an equal basis, and without prejudice, under such legislation. See *consumer protection legislation.*

apathetic shoppers: one of four classifications of consumers; indicates those with little interest in making comparisons. The apathetic consumer is happy to patronize the most convenient store. See *economic shoppers; ethical shoppers; personalizing shoppers.*

appeal:
(1) the motivation of a sales pitch with the expectation that the potential customers will become favorably disposed toward the product or service.
(2) the advantage of purchasing a product or service as given in the sales message for that item or service.

applause mail: letters of praise received by advertisers or broadcasters.

appraiser: one who determines the value of goods.

approach-approach conflict: in consumer behavior analysis, a situation in which a person is drawn toward two potentially satisfying goals, (e.g., to rent or buy a car), that are at least partially incompatible. See *approach-avoidance conflict; avoidance-avoidance conflict.*

approach-avoidance conflict: in consumer behavior analysis, a situation in which a person delays making a decision; may require motivation to resolve this conflict, which involves a goal that can be secured only at a cost. See *approach-approach conflict; avoidance-avoidance conflict.*

approach phase: the part of a sales presentation that includes the announcement and rapid sales work of the seller, the firm, and the product to gain customer interest.

approval sale: in retailing, the sale to a customer where the person has unlimited returns privileges. Cf. *absolute sale.*

apron:
(1) an open area within the store where displays are set, either on freestanding units, or built entirely of items from the floor up.
(2) in outdoor advertisements, the lattice or other decorative finish set below the bottom of the display area.

ARB:

(1) see *Advertising Review Board.*

(2) see *American Research Bureau.*

arbitrary allocation: synonymous with *arbitrary method.*

arbitrary method: a technique for allocating a company's promotional budget where the amount to be spent on promotion over a given time frame is derived from an executive decision rather than from scientific analysis. Synonymous with *arbitrary allocation.*

arbitration: the process whereby parties to a conflict agree to present their dispute before, and have the matter adjudged by, an independent third party, which is not a court of law.

arbitration clause: in international sales; the clause found within the sales contract between an exporter and an importer that specifies the method under which disputes relevant to the contract in question will be settled.

Arbitron: a technique for acquiring television program measurements immediately by means of electronic apparatus placed in multiple homes and connected to a central measurement unit. See *American Research Bureau.*

area-by-area (ABA) allocation: a means for defining the advertising budget, where advertising dollars are assigned to be spent in markets in direct proportion to the advertiser's projected or current product or sales in those areas. Synonymous with *market-by-market allocation.*

area sample:

(1) *general:* a probability sample in which respondents are chosen at random from a complete list of the population in a specific geographic area.

(2) *marketing research:* a random selection of a population in which the small geographic units chosen determine which subjects are included in the selection. Cf. *quota sampling; random sample.*

area sampling: see *area sample.*

area selection: see *area sample.*

area structure: the natural resource specialization based on the anticipated marketing returns on them, leading to a specific location for each institution in the agency structure.

arousal method: a technique of copy testing by which a galvanometer (a machine that purports to measure the changes in electrical resistance of the skin) records the reaction of a consumer subject to an advertisement or radio or television commercial; designed to determine the extent to which an advertising message will influence a consumer before the advertisement is run by recording the changes in sweating in the palms of the hands caused by emotion accompanying the reading or hearing of the message.

arrears:

(1) *general:* monies due but unpaid; a real or contingent obligation that remains unpaid at the date of maturity.

(2) *advertising:* complimentary issues of a magazine sent to consumers whose subscription have expired; permits publishers to meet their rate base, which guarantees the advertiser of the publication an agreed-on circulation.

art director: the senior person working on the graphics side in the creative unit of an advertising agency; usually reports to the creative services vice-president.

articles of mixed status: items manufactured within a free-trade zone of components of more than one status (the product of several factors). Upon withdrawal of the items fabricated within a zone, the finished item is assessed duties in accordance with the status of the merchandise from which it was composed.

artificial obsolescence: the decline in market acceptance of an item because of change in the item or a new version of the item introduced in the belief that it is better for a firm to lose sales of a product to a new one of its own production than to that of a competitor. Cf. *planned obsolescence.*

art service: a firm specializing in the creation of advertising art for use by agencies and advertising departments. See *advertising art.*

as is: items that have no warranty and may be damaged or shopworn.

asked price: the price that is officially offered by a seller.

ASP: see *American selling price.*

aspect ratio: the ratio between the width and height of a television or motion picture screen.

assembling:
(1) *general:* putting together different parts of an article or machine.

(2) *marketing:* the activities involved in gathering supplies or assortments of items or services to assist in sales or purchases.

assessment technique: a means of arriving at an advertising budget by adding a specific, arbitrary amount of money for each unit to be sold. Can be applied as well to the evolution of the budget for the total marketing mix.

asset turnover: the ratio of sales to total assets available.

assigned mailing date: in direct marketing, the date when a list user is to mail a specific purchased list, by virtue of a prior agreement between the list owner and the user. The user cannot mail that list on any other date except with the specific authorization of the list owner.

assimilation-contract concept: a theory that consumers reject an advertisement requiring an extreme attitude shift. Such a message is seen as more extreme than it actually is, further reinforcing the rejection process.

association advertising: a type of horizontal cooperative advertising carried out by trade associations to promote a primary demand for a class of products or services (e.g., milk promoted by the U.S. Dairy Association).

association advertising format: a form of advertisement that conveys its message by setting a relationship between an event, an activity, or an image, and the product being promoted.

Association of National Advertisers: see *ANA.*

assorting: a practice performed usually by wholesalers or retailers to supply an assortment of items (e.g., an automotive supply store carrying hundreds of related items for the car user). It purports to evolve a heterogeneous inventory of products for the convenience of customers. Cf. *sort.*

assortment:
(1) various forms of the same general type of item, such as the depth and width of the merchandise offering. *Depth* is about variety—an array of styles, colors, and prices; *width* is about different product categories, such as towels, hats, lotions to accompany the sale of bathing suits.

(2) relating to specific consumers, the particular combination of items and service seen as needed to maintain or improve their living standard (e.g., toothbrushes and hair spray).

assortment plan: items of one type established to meet the requirements of customers by a determination of inventory levels. See *assortment; basic stock; model stock.*

assumptive close: in sales, a close accomplished without a buyer's verbal agreement. This becomes presumed when the purchaser fails to protest the salesperson's beginning to prepare the order, or to wrap the merchandise.

asymmetrical balance: synonymous with *informal balance.*

ATA: see *American Telemarketing Association.*

at best: in global marketing; the instruction with a buying or selling order indicating that it should be carried out quickly at the best possible price. Synonymous with *at the market.*

ATDONSHINC: as used in the media, anytime day or night, Sundays and holidays inclusive (e.g., when a food store is open for business).

atmosphere: the sum total of the physical characteristics of a retail store or group of stores used to develop an image and draw customers.

atmospherics: external factors from the environment designed to establish a specific mood, or image and/or to stimulate sales. These factors include layout, architecture, colors, and other sensory inputs.

ATR: awareness-trial-repeat: an explanation for the behaviors of a consumer in adopting a service or item. The individual goes from being uninformed of the product or service to becoming a regular user after learning of the item or service's assets and availability (*awareness*), trying the item or service (*trial*), and deciding the trial usage has been beneficial and thus purchasing the item or service again (*repeat*).

attention: the reader-viewer's response to an advertisement.

attention, interest, desire, action: see *AIDA process.*

at the market: synonymous with *at best.*

at-the-market prices: in retailing, prices that are generally the same for all stores within a location. See *market-minus prices; market-plus pricing.*

attitude:
(1) as used in consumer behavior analysis, feelings that express whether a person likes or dislikes objects in his or her environment.

(2) a lasting, learned predisposition to behaving in a consistent way toward a given class of objects or persons. This condition has a direct effect on feeling and action and refers to an aspect of personality that may account for persistent and consistent behavior.

attitude study: see *attitude survey.*

attitude survey: a method for ascertaining consumers' perceptions of products and services, usually by use of questionnaires or interviews.

attribute analysis: a bundle of idea-generating techniques built on the concept that any product improvement is a change in the attributes of its predecessor. Dimensional analysis and the checklist are the most popular techniques.

attribute-based shopping products: products for which consumers get information about and then evaluate features, warranties, performance, options, and other factors.

attribute mapping: in the planning of new products, a statistical means of analyzing a market to find openings for new items. Existing items are placed on a chart and open spaces indicating gaps point to where potential new products can be introduced. Synonymous with *market position analysis.*

auction:
(1) *general:* a unique trading market in which there is one seller and many potential buyers.

(2) *sales:* a means of selling products to the highest bidder.

auction company: a wholesaling intermediary that sells merchandise on an agency basis by means of auctions.

audience:
(1) the sum of people who are exposed to an advertising message delivered by a medium or combination of media. See *reach.*

(2) the target group at which a promotional message is aimed. Synonymous with *target audience.*

audience accumulation: the total net audience reached by an advertisement from all sources of the media. Should an advertising campaign for an item or service run for a six-week period using a combination of media, the audience accumulation is the total number of persons who were exposed to an advertisement or commercial at least one time.

audience composition:
(1) *advertising:* the mix of people, classified by age, sex, or other characteristics, who are reached by an advertising approach. See *customer profile; mix.*

(2) *broadcasting:* the breakdown by program of the listening and viewing audience based on age and sex.

audience duplication: the number of the same listeners reached by two or more programs of the same sponsor; important in media planning. Audience duplication is desired when the advertiser wishes to reach a target audience over and over again.

audience flow: the gain or loss of a broadcast audience during a program or from one program to another. See *holdover audience.* Cf. *share of audience.*

audience fragmentation: separating an audience into smaller groups because of the wide spectrum of media outlets. With more audiences becoming fragmented, broadcast networks are pushed to find new revenue sources.

audience holding index: a means for measuring how well a program keeps its audience interested; measured on a minute-by-minute or 15-minute basis by the researcher. The index is critical because many people start watching a program but soon turn to another broadcast, thereby reducing the audience for the commercial or advertisement.

audience measurement: the determination of audience numbers exposed to advertising in a particular medium. See *rating*.

audience-participation program: a type of radio or television show, the form and entertainment value of which are based on the cooperation of the studio audience.

audience profile: see *audience composition*.

audience rating: the percentage of listeners in the market listening to a specific radio station at a certain time period. See *audience share*.

audience share: the number of listeners of a particular radio station at a given time compared with the station's potential audience. Usually audience share is electronically measured by a device attached to a radio or television, or by telephone interviews or direct mail studies. See *audience rating; share; total audience*.

audience study: a form of analysis to determine the characteristics and attitudes of listeners, viewers, or readers of advertising media. Cf. *media analysis*. See *Arbitron; Hooperating; Nielsen rating; Trendex; Videodex*.

audience turnover: the ratio between the cumulative and average audiences for a specific broadcast.

audimeter: an electromechanical unit used by A.C. Nielsen Company to record station turning of radio and television receivers by tapping a sample of home users. A.C. Nielsen radio listening efforts were discontinued in 1964; the audimeter was first used for television audience estimates in 1950. Cf. *coincidental telephone method*. See *Nielsen rating; share of audience*.

Audit Bureau of Circulations (ABC): an independent nonprofit auditing organization established in 1914 to audit and validate circulation figures for the benefit of its members.

audited net sales: the total amount of sales for a specified period, computed after returns and allowances have been deducted. These totals are circulated by the auditing department of a store and credited to the book inventory of each department.

audition: in advertising, a means by which the advertiser determines the feasibility of sponsoring a specific radio or television program by listening to a trial performance of the program and then deciding if the program meets his or her goals of the item or service.

augmented product:
(1) the core product together with its attendant benefits and services. See *core product*.

(2) an expected product that has been enhanced by a set of benefits that consumers do not expect or that exceed their expectations.

authorized dealer: a middleperson who has received a franchise to represent or sell a manufacturer's products.

automatic group: in marketing research, a reference unit to which a person belongs because of sex, education, race, etc. See *negative group*.

automatic markdown: the lowering of price taken by a retailer according to a predetermined time schedule.

automatic merchandising: see *automatic selling.*

automatic renewal: a means of renewing subscriptions to magazines and periodicals without asking the subscriber's authorization after the initial order. Subscribers are charged for each renewal by credit card number. Publishers using automatic renewal methods are required to keep proof of prior subscriber authorization at the time purchasers first ordered the reading material. Cf. *automatic reorder.*

automatic reorder: an order for staple goods issued on the basis for reaching an established minimum inventory quantity. The reorder quantity is predetermined. Cf. *automatic renewal.*

automatic selling: the retail sale of items or services through machines operated by the consumer utilizing credit cards, funds, or any other authorized method.

automatic vending: a type of nonstore, nonpersonal retailing of goods and services using coin operated, self-service equipment. Examples of merchandise are candy, cigarettes, condoms, sodas.

Automobile Information Disclosure Act of 1958: U.S. legislation that prohibited car dealers from inflating factory prices on new automobiles. This legislation significantly changed the way automobiles were advertised and sold.

autonomous consumption: consumption that is independent of income; the part of total consumption that is unrelated to income.

auxiliary dimensions of a product: those features of a product, other than the item itself, that add to the product's attractiveness, utility, and attraction to the consumer.

availability:

(1) in outdoor advertising, units such as showings or bulletins that a plant operator has open for contract.

(2) the broadcast time offered to an advertiser for sponsorship. Ratings and prices are based on the most recent ratings of the shows, as given by rating services.

available market: people who can afford the item or service, who have ready access to it, and who have shown an interest in using or owning it.

avails:

(1) *general:* the proceeds from a discounted note.

(2) *advertising:* short for availabilities.

average: in market research, the measure of central tendency, showing the middle value around which numbers are grouped. Cf. *mean; median; mode.*

average audience rating (AA rating): one of several kinds of A.C. Nielsen Company ratings indicating the average size of the audience on a minute-by-minute basis. It provides a splendid measure of the size of an audience for a specific advertisement or commercial.

average cost: the sum of all output costs divided by the quantity of production.

average fixed costs: production costs that do not depend on the amount produced divided by the quantity produced. Average fixed costs decline as production grows.

average frequency: the average number of times a consumer or prospect has been shown a commercial in any medium that is part of an advertising campaign.

average gross sales: the dollar amount of gross sales divided by the number of sales transactions that created the gross sales.

average mark-on: the mark-on obtained when the costs and retail prices of several purchases are combined.

average net paid circulation: a measurement of the average number of copies of a magazine, periodical, or newspaper sold per issue; determined by dividing the total number of subscription and newsstand-sold copies for all issues of the period by the total number of issues.

average paid circulation: see *average net paid circulation.*

average profit margin: used to assess the value of a campaign or advertisement. A means of determining the profit margin per item bought by applying an equal proportion of the total expenses of the seller against each item that has been sold.

average quarter hour persons: the number of people estimated to listen at home or away to a radio or television station for a minimum of 5 minutes within a given 15 minutes.

average revenue: the sum of revenues divided by the quantity sold; often presented as an average revenue curve, with quantity plotted on the horizontal axis and average revenue on the vertical.

average stock: the quantity representing the midpoint between the highest and lowest inventory levels for a stated time period. Average stock is calculated by adding each month's opening stock figure plus the closing stock figure for the last month. The total is divided by the number of months being considered.

average variable cost: the cost per unit of production of inputs such as labor, materials, and utilities, which are used in increasing amounts as production increases.

avoidance: used to explain consumer preferences, the administration of a reinforcement that prevents the occurrence of an undesirable behavior.

avoidance-avoidance conflict: used in consumer behavior analysis, a situation in which a person, in moving away from one undesirable path, must move toward another undesirable path. See *approach-approach conflict.*

awareness: in the marketing cycle, the recognition by a consumer that he or she has a need or problem and wishes to have it satisfied. Awareness is the first stage in the adoption process. See *adoption process.*

awareness-trial-repeat: see *ATR.*

baby boomers: in advertising, people who were born in the years immediately after 1945, the end of World War II; in the 1980s and 1990s, a major target audience for advertisers.

back card: the advertising message found on a card fixed to the back of a merchandiser, projecting above the merchandiser to show the communication at eye level.

back cover: the outside back of a periodical or magazine that is frequently read and consequently often sold at a premium. Advertisers prefer this placement and whether or not color is used, pay for this expensive back cover. Synonymous with *fourth cover.*

back dating:

(1) *general:* placing on a statement a date prior to the date on which it was drawn up.

(2) *sales:* commencing a subscription to a magazine or other periodical with an issue prior to the current issue; helps lower back inventory. Synonymous with *back start.*

back-door selling: the deliberate avoidance of the purchasing department by the salesperson, who places a call on people in the department that he or she assumes can use the item.

back end:

(1) following a customer's order, the fulfillment by servicing and delivering of the merchandise.

(2) actions of the consumer after the initial order has been received. Through back end analysis, the seller examines pay up, cancellation rates, and renewal or reorder rates.

back end analysis: see *back end.*

backer card: a form of inexpensive advertising, poster space found on the back of a display; used to secure consumer awareness of an item or to encourage sales at point of purchase.

back-haul allowance: a price reduction to customers who make their own pickups at the seller's warehouse.

backing activities: activities in a retail store that do not directly involve interfacing with customers.

backlighting: a full-color advertisement that has been printed on a translucent sheet instead of on paper stock so that special lighting behind the sheet turns it into a dramatic color slide.

back order: merchandise ordered but not available for delivery because the supplier does not have it in inventory.

back start: synonymous with *back dating.*

back-to-back commercials: two commercials appearing in succession. Two competing products will not appear back-to-back; usually done when a firm buys time to sell two similar or companion items that it manufactures (e.g., curtains and curtain rods). See *competitive separation; triple spotting.*

backup merchandise: items held in reserve at a storage place removed from access to customers but available to employees for restocking purposes. Synonymous with *reserve stock.* See *floor stock.*

backup space: advertising space in a periodical that adjoins an insert (e.g., a coupon, reply card, etc.). Advertisers wanting to use an insert purchase backup space because periodicals and magazines do not sell inserts without it.

backward channel: a marketing channel running backward from the consumer to the middleperson, and, at times, as far back as the manufacturer or producer. Synonymous with *reverse distribution.*

backward integration: a firm's activities for increasing sales and profits by expanding its operations within its industry; usually involves acquiring firms that relate to the company's present business (e.g., a manufacturing company acquiring a supplier to lower costs of materials). See *integration.*

backward invention: in international marketing; product strategy in which firms doing business in developing nations alter, and often simplify, their products to make them more attractive in this new market.

backward market segmentation: identifying segments of a population on the basis of a type of behavior. The principle is that groups having similar behavior will at the same time share attitudes and beliefs and will react homogeneously to marketing promotions.

bad debt:

(1) *general:* the amount due on an open account that has been proved to be uncollectible; any uncollectible receivable.

(2) *sales:* failure of the customer to pay for products or services received. Synonymous with *bad pay.* See *bad pay list.*

bad faith: to mislead or deceive (Latin: *mala fides*). It does not include misleading by an honest, inadvertent, or uncalled-for misstatement. Cf. *bona fide.* See *fraud.*

bad pay: synonymous with *bad debt.*

bad pay file: synonymous with *bad pay list.*

bad pay list: a list of people with a poor credit history who are withdrawn from a customer list, so they no longer receive promotions, advertisements, services, and/or future merchandise. They are purged as people who have a high probability of incurring bad debt expense. These lists can be purchased by advertisers and others. Synonymous with *bad pay file.*

bagman: (slang) the earliest salespeople, who sold from bags of samples in the 18th century. Synonymous with *Manchester Man.*

bailment: in global marketing; the delivery of goods by one party to another, to be held according to the purpose of the delivery, for return or delivery when that purpose is accomplished.

bait advertising: the advertising of exceptional prices or terms for a specified product to attract prospects to a store; potential customers find, however, that it is difficult to buy the product there as advertised. Cf. *bait and switch advertising.*

bait and switch advertising:

(1) a pricing strategy in which a product is given a low price to lure customers into a store, where an attempt is made to persuade them to buy a more expensive model or product.

(2) an unethical and illegal approach in which a retailer advertises a product at a particularly low price with the intention of inducing people who ask for the item to purchase a more costly one. Sometimes the salesperson makes the switch by telling the purchaser that the advertised item is not good or has been sold out. See *switch selling.*

balanced product portfolio: used in setting marketing strategies, the combination of old and new items maintained by a manufacturer.

balanced scale: in marketing research, an inquiry to provide an equal number of favorable and unfavorable category items.

balanced selling: the action of selling all products in a vendor's line in proportion to the sales potential found within a state area, or to the profit associated with the products.

balanced stock: a planned inventory available to customers in proportion to the request for all items they desire in every price range.

balanced tenancy: in retailing, the precise mix of an area's type and number of stores to meet the needs of that community's population.

balance sheet: an itemized statement listing the total assets and total liabilities of an advertising firm to portray its net worth at a particular moment in time.

balance sheet close: a closing strategy when confronted with a prospect unable to make up his or her mind about a purchase. The salesperson prepares a list of advantages and disadvantages for both moving quickly or delaying a decision. If the salesperson has been creative, the pluses outweigh the minuses and become a major reason for the prospect to agree to a transaction.

ballooning: a deterrent to the successful sale of items and services, a price manipulation used to send prices beyond safe or real values.

ballpark pricing: a technique to determine the price for an item by examining the average price level for similar items, choosing a price in this range, and working backward to set the feasibility of yielding at the cost constraint disclosed.

banded pack: items offered at retail that are secured by a tape, string, or plastic film strip and therefore sold as one unit.

Synonymous with *factory pack.* See *economy pack.*

bandwagon impact: the tendency of people to purchase an item because others are doing the same thing. See *law of demand.*

bangtail: a promotional envelope containing a perforated flap that is torn away and then used as an order form. It often used for placing exposed film to be returned for processing. See *syndicator.*

banner:
(1) *advertising:* a large strip of fabric containing an advertisement, product image or slogan, or corporate logo.
(2) *newspapers:* in a layout, a headline running across, or nearly across, the entire page.

bantam store: a community market that remains open in the late evening or on weekends or holidays when other markets are closed. Cf. *convenience goods; depot store; supermarket.* Synonymous with *superette; vest pocket supermarket.*

bar chart: a pictorial graph with bars of varying length to display the relative amounts of the variables or characteristics of interest.

bar code:
(1) *general:* a series of vertical or horizontal parallel lines forming a code that is optically read and interpreted by a bar code scanner. It is used on envelopes and forms for rapid entry of data and for sorting.
(2) *merchandising:* a series of vertical or horizontal parallel lines forming a code that identifies an item, its price, and manufacturer. Electronic cash registers scan the code to register price and prepare inventory figures. See *electronic marketing; universal product code.*

bargain basement: the below-ground-level floor of a store, where special prices are offered on merchandise. The stock often contains low-price merchandise or items not carried on the upper levels of the store.

bargain counter: an area for the sale of discounted merchandise.

bargain hunter: an individual who seeks out the store that is selling items at the lowest possible price.

bargain store: a store that sells merchandise at a submarket price. Assortments and sizes are often limited, and the merchandise frequently is damaged or seconds. See *seconds*.

barnacle brand: a competitive brand that enters and attaches itself to the market in later stages of the product life cycle.

barn-burner wizards: (slang) high-powered salespeople who skillfully push to achieve their stated goals or sales.

barometric price leader: carefully watched by advertisers; a firm that usually interprets best the current economic trends within an industry and is often followed in the setting of prices for the industry.

barometric techniques: a market forecasting technique that uses analyses of past trends to predict the future.

barriers to competition: forces that limit market competition, usually economic or technological conditions that make the entry of more firms to a market more difficult.

barriers to entry: obstacles to creating a new company within a particular industry, resulting from legal or economic advantages enjoyed by existing firms. The greater the barriers to entry, the less competition there is for firms already functioning in the industry.

barter:
(1) *general:* the direct exchange of one item for another without the transfer of money.

(2) *advertising:* trading merchandise and/or services for advertising time or advertising space; used more often during the earliest days of advertising as a means of promoting products and services (e.g., free hotel rooms in exchange for advertising). Cf. *exchange (3)*.

barter broker: synonymous with *prize broker*.

basal skin resistance (BSR): the norm from which changes in emotional response to stimuli such as advertising messages are recorded by means of an electronic galvanometer.

basement store: historically, the basement of a department store containing bargain items; now expanded to mean any place within the store for items sold at budget prices. Synonymous with *budget store*.

base period: a chosen date from the past used in measuring the price index.

base price: synonymous with *list price*.

base rate:
(1) *general:* under an incentive system, the amount guaranteed per hour or other time period.

(2) *advertising:* a one-time rate from an advertising medium prior to offering of discounts. See *open rate*.

base record: a consumers' file maintained by a store, credit agency, etc., with critical information on the person, beginning with name and address.

basic market description: market research done before or immediately after selecting an arena for product innovation charter focus; prepares the firm to innovate in that area.

basic network: the fewest grouping of stations that an advertiser needs to contract so as to the use the facilities of a radio or television network.

basic price:

(1) *general:* the standard published price of a magazine. Synonymous with *basic rate*.

(2) *international sales:* used in conjunction with price supports applying to fruits, vegetables, and pork. Once the average market price is below the basic, or cost of production price, action is taken to support the market by buying in surplus output.

basic rate: synonymous with *basic price*.

basic station: a television station included in the list of network affiliates whose time an advertiser is contracted to buy if he uses the network.

basic stock: merchandise that is in constant demand, thus requiring perpetual inventory throughout the year. See *assortment plan*. Cf. *model stock*.

basing point pricing:

(1) a geographic pricing policy in which the seller designates one or more geographic locations from which the rate that a buyer will be charged is calculated.

(2) to be avoided in the promotion of goods and services, an approach used by an industry whose goal is for all sellers to charge identical prices. The basing point is frequently the location of a plant near the buyer. Such pricing has been declared to be price discrimination in violation of the Clayton Antitrust Act.

battleground map: a map used by the retailer to indicate the geographic location of the flagship and branch stores. Usually, it includes markings for competitor operations.

battle of the brands: the competitiveness between national brands and private brands in an attempt to split up the market. See *brand*.

beachhead: the third phase of the launch cycle. It comes immediately after announcement, and ceases when the product is withdrawn or moves into the fourth (growth) stage. See *launch*.

behavioral economics: an approach to economic research that uses behavioral sciences and findings in explaining and predicting economic behavior, including that of marketing and commerce. The pioneering work is described in the *Handbook of Behavioral Economics* edited by B. Gilad and S. Kaish (Greenwich, CT, JAI Press, 1986).

behavioral researchers: investigators and scientists who use findings from psychology, sociology, anthropology, political science, and other related areas of inquiry to develop concepts and theories pertaining to people, their environment, and their buying behavior.

behavioral segmentation: a market segment strategy resulting from how consumers utilize an item or service and the purchasing pattern they demonstrate; defines consumer groups as to when they make purchases, how frequently they do so, or what product characteristics they are most interested in. Cf. *benefit segmentation*. See *product usage segmentation; state-of-being segmentation; state-of-mind segmentation*.

behaviorism: in advertising, the application of the stimulus-response theory of learning where a stimulus—the advertising message—is repeated over and over again to yield the desired response, such as the purchase of the item.

behavior modification: the increase of desirable behavioral patterns or the decrease of undesirable behavior brought about by using rewards and/or punishments whose efficacy in promoting the desired change has been proved.

beliefs: how consumers feel or think about a product or service that will influence their behavior in making a purchase. Altering beliefs can be a major challenge in promoting a product or service. See *brand awareness*.

believability: in advertising, the plausibility of an advertisement; all components within the range of possibility. A believable advertisement is more effective in most cases, than an unbelievable one, which may raise doubts in the mind of a prospective buyer.

bell cow: (slang) a frequently purchased item whose selling price far exceeds its manufacturing cost; a very profitable item. Synonymous with *blue chip*.

bell-ringer: (slang) a door-to-door salesperson.

belly-to-belly selling: a form of selling where the salesperson confronts the prospect or customer. Synonymous with *nose-to-nose selling*.

below par: at a discount; less than face amount.

below-the-market strategy: pricing by the retailer according to a plan of offering items below usual levels. See *discount house*.

benchmarking:
(1) *general:* comparing the performance of products and processes with those of world leaders.

(2) *advertising:* the creative role of an advertisement or commercial; the standard used for determining how well an advertiser represents a specific client.

benefit:
(1) *general:* a gain or advantage received by an individual.

(2) *advertising:* that which fulfills a need.

benefit market segmentation: see *benefit segmentation*.

benefit segmentation: one of a four-way categorization of the strategies of segmentation; includes the benefits the market draws from products. It helps marketers in determining marketing mix decision. Cf. *behavioral segmentation*.

benefit strategy: a method of salespeople in the opening minutes of contact with a prospect. The salesperson attempts to focus on the rewards and benefits of the product. The benefit is usually specific and concrete, such as the savings of money.

best time available: an advertiser's instruction to his or her client to run a commercial in the best possible available time, which is usually when the largest audience is going to watch or read the commercial.

Beta test: the type of produce use testing that follows Alpha testing and takes place on the premises of intended market users. The procedure may only concentrate on whether the product performs as expected or on whether the performance meets the needs of the user, as perceived by that user, in which case it is called a Gamma test. Cf. *Alpha test; Gamma test.*

Better Business Bureau: a voluntary agency of business executives created to improve business practices and to define fair standards and ethics in the conduct of business activity. The movement to improve conditions began in 1921, when vigilance committees for truth in advertising first appeared in local advertising clubs. Today, there are in excess of 150 local Better Business Bureaus in the United States.

better offer complaint: the complaint of a customer who has found a special offer of a lower price that he or she already paid for the same item or service. Many retailers honor this complaint with a refund or store credit, although they are not legally required to do so.

bias:

(1) *general:* an attitude that influences an individual's feelings, resulting in a leaning toward or away from a particular idea, item, or person. See *Hawthorne effect.*

(2) *consumer research:* the systematic error resulting from the wording of a questionnaire, an interviewer, etc., that suggests one answer over another. See *interviewer bias; prejudice.*

bidding:

(1) *general:* the offering of money as an exchange for an item or service put up for sale.

(2) *marketing:* the making of an offer of price and other details as solicited by a prospective purchaser wishing to, or who is required by law to, get competitive offers prior to placing an offer. Synonymous with *competitive bidding.*

bid pricing: a supplier's fixed price for items or services to be provided covering all the costs incurred and making a predetermined contribution to profit.

big-early, little-late technique: a method of evolving media advertising schedules where the beginning of the campaign is regarded as most significant and therefore allotted the largest amount of funds.

big ticket items: frequently, a reference to merchandise that is large in size and high in price (furniture, appliances, etc.).

big-ticket selling: synonymous with *megaselling.*

bilateral monopoly: a condition that exists when there is only one purchaser for an item or service and the creation of the supply is controlled by one seller.

billboard:

(1) *advertising:* a poster panel in outdoor advertising. Synonymous with *poster.* See *billboard allowance.*

(2) *broadcasting:* the opening routine of a broadcast program, including identification, performer credits, producers, and similar information. See *routine.*

billboard allowance: funds in an advertising budget used for outdoor advertising. See *billboard.*

billing:

(1) *general:* the process of submitting invoices or bills.

(2) *advertising:* the total amount of money charged to clients by an advertising agency. This includes production costs, expenses, media costs, and other service charges.

bill me order: synonymous with *credit order.*

bill of sale: a contract for the sale of goods.

bill to/ship to: instructions to have the invoice sent to a different address than given for the merchandise.

bind-in: promotional pieces, printed on heavy paper, that are bound into periodicals.

bingo card: a reply card for magazine users to indicate from which advertisers they are interested in receiving further information. It is called a bingo card because it features a series of numbers corresponding to advertisements within the periodical and the reader is asked to circle the pertinent number for further information and return the card to the publisher, who then forwards the request to the appropriate advertiser.

biogenic needs: synonymous with *primary needs.*

bird dog:

(1) *general:* (slang) to seek data to assist in studying a firm's position and potential earnings.

(2) *business law:* an individual who is paid to spread fraudulent charges.

(3) *sales:* an individual who is paid to obtain business for a high-power salesperson. Cf. *airedale.*

black and white: an advertisement, appearing in black ink on white paper.

black box: in marketing research, a concept of the inner working that take place between input and output. The black box, or the transformation process between input and output, is said to contain the answer. The black box contains these components: environmental factors—dealing with the marketing messages; personal characteristics—describing interpersonal forces motivating people to buy; and buyer's responses—how and when decisions to buy are made.

black list: in international marketing; a list of individuals and firms of another country with whom the domestic nation forbids commerce by its nationals.

black market:

(1) *general:* buying or selling products or engaging in the exchange of foreign currencies in violation of government restrictions.

(2) *merchandising:* a situation when goods are priced at a high level because they are scarce or unavailable from normal market channels.

blank-check buying: the practice of a retailer placing an open order with a supplier, with requests to be made throughout the season as needed.

blank dummy: the full-size, practical mock-up model of a display. Usually presented with art or lettering.

blanket contract: a negotiated agreement between an advertiser and a medium dealing with all products or services to be advertised. The contract supersedes any arrangements the advertiser may have with an advertising agency. Synonymous with *master contract.*

blanket order: a preseason order to meet expected buyer demand. See *blanket pricing agreement; systems contracting.* Synonymous with *yearly order.*

blanket pricing agreement: a purchasing agreement where the purchaser's orders or anticipated time-period requirements are placed in advance, and the seller agrees to make shipments as requested at the contract price throughout the contract's duration. Cf. *incremental pricing agreement.* See *blanket order.*

blanket rate: the rate applicable from and/or to a group of points. Synonymous with *group rate.*

blanking paper: the paper, usually white, surrounding the perimeter of an outdoor poster. Internal to the border is an advertisement. Cf. *bleed.*

bleed: a technique resulting in the printed area of an advertisement extending to the very edge of a newspaper or magazine page, without the white margin. Serving as an attention getter, the artist is usually given considerable freedom in communicating the advertiser's message. Cf. *blanking paper.*

bleed in the gutter: (slang) an advertisement whose artwork and copy flows without interruption through the center margin of a magazine across the two facing pages; appears without a central line.

blighted area: a factor considered by advertisers, the area in a community or neighborhood that is about to become a slum.

blind advertisement: a want advertisement that lists only the job; the identity of the employer is hidden by utilizing a box number for replies. Cf. *open advertisement.*

blind goods: unusual items that can carry a higher-than-normal margin because of unique qualities with appeal for only occasional customers, who are more interested in filling their requirements than they are in the price.

blind offer: synonymous with *hidden offer.*

blind product test: in consumer research, a test in which people sample various items that are not identifiable to them by brand thus reducing bias or prejudgment.

blind selling: (slang) the selling of merchandise without allowing the customer to examine the item prior to purchase.

blind testing: consumer evaluations of intrinsic qualities of items, taken in a controlled test condition with all brand identification characteristics (packaging, pricing, etc.) removed.

blister package: a type of plastic packaging that permits visual inspection of the merchandise. Synonymous with *bubble wrap.*

block: in broadcasting, a group of consecutive time slots, or the same time period from day to day.

blockbuster: in broadcasting, a program that exceeds estimated ratings and therefore can boast that a larger audience than anticipated watched or heard the commercials.

blocked-out time: time periods during broadcast schedule of a station or network that are not available for sale to sponsors. Such time may be used for the broadcast of public service programs.

blotter: a form of direct advertising consisting of a panel of flexible paper stock, one side of which is made of soft, ink-absorbent paper. The reverse (face) side is usually employed to bear a printed advertising message.

blow in: placing promotional pieces in a periodical with a device that literally blows the pieces between pages. They are unattached and can easily fall out or be discarded by a disinterested reader.

blue chip: synonymous with *bell cow.*

bluefingers:

(1) *advertising:* in the planning strategies of advertisers, people from one family who attain common goals with efficiency and team spirit; for example, relatives who successfully pursue their objectives while receiving pleasure from their togetherness.

(2) *retailing:* friends who spend considerable shopping time together and because of common interests and attitudes, purchase similar styles and items in a particular price range.

(3) synonymous with *jebble.*

blue law: any state or local law restricting business activity on Sunday. Blue laws have been contested as an infringement of individual and free enterprise rights.

blurb: (slang) a brief but highly laudatory statement (e.g., a quotation from a book review) used in further promotional activities. Cf. *testimonial.*

blurring gender roles: a consumer lifestyle in which more men are assuming the once-traditional roles of their wives, and vice versa.

body copy: the primary portions of verbal matter found in an advertisement, as contrasted with the headlines, subheadlines, etc. The length of the copy is determined by the item for sale, the copywriter's method, and the sales concept that is presented. Synonymous with *body text; text.*

body test: see *body copy.*

body text: synonymous with *body copy.*

body type: the typeface used for the major section of text in an advertisement.

bogey: in sales, a standard of performance, such as the volume of sales beyond which a bonus is given.

boilerplate copy: a series of sentences of copy that is standard in all print messages produced by the same advertiser, such as a firm having brochures for each of its products and services.

bona fide: (Latin) "in good faith"; with honest intent. Cf. *bad faith.*

bona fide sale: a transaction where the seller acts in good faith regarding the terms of the sale.

bonded items: in international sales and marketing, items stored in a bonded warehouse to guarantee the government that the tax or duty on the merchandise will be paid on withdrawal of the items.

bonded warehouse: a cost factor for global marketers; goods kept in a government-supervised storage facility where items are stored without payment of duties or taxes until they are removed. See *warehouse.*

bonus circulation: the circulation of a magazine or periodical beyond the circulation number that was guaranteed by the publisher to advertisers. Advertisers benefit from this by having additional readers at no extra cost to them.

bonus goods: merchandise given without extra charge by a manufacturer to a retailer who agrees to purchase a minimum quantity of units in a special deal.

bonus pack: a promotional package that offers the customer more than the regular amount for the regular price; also used by manufacturers as an incentive to buy by affixing a sample size of an item to a full size of the same item. See *twin pack.*

bonus plan: used by continuity marketers to solicit multiple purchases, such as used by the Book of the Month Club, with one free book for every three books bought. Shipping and handling charges are made even on the free item. See *continuity strategy.*

bonus station: a broadcast station carrying commercial network programs without extra cost to the sponsor.

bookends: two 15-second commercials on television for the same item or service, separated by other advertisers' commercials. See *piggyback (2).*

booking:
(1) orders for merchandise accepted on hand as at a given time.

(2) accepting an order for goods to be transported.

booklet: bound printed pages containing an advertisement, instructions on the item's use, or service policy. See *brochure.*

boom:
(1) a time when business expands and the value of commodities and securities increases.

(2) a period of rapidly rising prices and increased demand for goods and services, usually accompanied by full employment.

boomerang:
(1) *general:* in global marketing, an international program to minimize the practice of goods dumping by returning such items duty-free and exempt of quantity restrictions.

(2) *sales:* a technique for dealing with objections. The salesperson uses the prospect's statement of reasons for not buying as the basis of the precise reason for purchasing. Synonymous with *conversion process; positive conversion.*

borax: (slang) inexpensive items that are usually poorly designed and constructed.

border: the line or design surrounding an advertisement.

border barriers: in international marketing, the physical barriers encountered at borders between nations that affect both goods and services. Reducing and eventually eliminating customs throughout an internal market (within national borders) enables the free flow of goods and services.

border tax adjustment: a rebate of sales, value-added, or other indirect taxes paid on merchandise prior to export.

borrow: to receive something from another, with the understanding that the item is to be returned.

Boston Consulting Group matrix: a design that enables a firm to classify each of its strategic business units in terms of the unit's market share relative to major competitors and the annual industry growth rate. The matrix identifies four types of unit: star, cash cow, problem child (question mark), and dog, and suggests appropriate strategies for each.

bottle collar: the cardboard display around the neck of a bottle for carrying an advertisement. Synonymous with *bottle topper.*

bottleneck: operation in a production system whose output sets limits for the entire system's output.

bottle topper: synonymous with *bottle collar.*

bottom-up technique:
(1) *general:* an approach to strategy making whereby the lower levels of the organization push ideas to the top, where strategy is then developed.
(2) *retailing:* a budget technique; the budgeter begins with an estimate of the spending needed to supply each classification, finally arriving at a total for the department, and eventually for the company. See *top-down method.*

bounce-back: to increase total sales, an added offer sent with a self-liquidator. See *self-liquidating premium.*

bounty: in global marketing of goods, added payments offered by a government as an incentive for a specific industry or the export of certain items.

boutique: a shop or part of a store that specializes in merchandise that is new and different. Cf. *salon.*

boutique agency: a small, independent advertising agency that specializes in only one aspect of advertising, such as media purchasing, often on a fee basis.

boutique merchandising: a store organization where related items from a number of departments are brought together in one shop to meet special customer requirements.

box store: synonymous with *warehouse store.*

box-top offer: an offer of a premium based on return of the top of a package or other evidence of purchase. Synonymous with *continuity program.*

boycott: in global marketing, an attempt to prevent the carrying on of a business by urging people not to buy from the firm being boycotted; frequently used on the international scene for political or economic reasons; illustrated by appeals, threats, and so on, to secure redress of a grievance.

BPI: see *brand potential index.*

brainstorming: a process of generating creativity and useful concepts through team or group discussions for solving problems. In advertising, brainstorming aids in the rapid movement from idea to action that forms the basis of the promotional campaign. Cf. *synectics.* See *new product planning process.*

brainwashing: in consumer psychology, a systematic and radical technique of indoctrinating, manipulating, and coercing a person to abandon loyalties, values, etc., and to adopt new ones.

branch house: a location away from headquarters maintained by a manufacturer almost exclusively for purposes of stocking, selling, shipping, and servicing the company's products.

branch office: an office or department of a company at a location away from headquarters. It is a part of the company and not a separate legal entity, as is a subsidiary, an affiliate, or a joint venture.

branch store: a store owned by a parent store. Usually, the parent store is located in the center of the city, with branch stores located in suburban areas of the city or other cities. Cf. *regional store.*

brand: a name, sign, or symbol used to identify items or services of the seller(s) and to differentiate them from goods of competitors. A brand aids consumers in differentiating between items of different manufacturers. Cf. *trademark.* See *battle of the brands; brand generic; manufacturer's brand.*

brand advertising: synonymous with *product advertising.*

brand attitude: consumer opinions toward an item determined by market research to determine what people believe about the item, whether it is fulfilling a need, and to what degree consumers want the product.

brand awareness: realization by a buyer of the existence and availability of a branded product. See *determinant attribute; differential advantages; family brand.*

brand category: a general classification of products and services. Competing items and services that are similar in nature are defined within the same brand category.

brand choice: selecting a particular brand of item from the variety of available brands with similar purpose and content.

brand competitor: an organization that competes with others to satisfy consumers' demand for a specific product.

brand decision process: a sequence of stages (nonrecognition, recognition,

preference or dislike, and insistence or aversion) that consumers pass through in choosing a product brand.

brand development: a means of determining the penetration of an item's sales, traditionally per thousand population. See *brand development index.*

brand development index: the percentage of a brand's sales in an area based on population in that location as contrasted with the sales throughout the country, related to the total U.S. population. See *brand development.*

brand equity: a branding concept that recognizes the marketing and financial value associated with a brand apart from a product's tangible attributes.

brand extension: a competitive strategy involving the application of a market-accepted brand to other products of the firm if doing so will not confuse present customers or lessen the image of the original product or brand; traditionally targeted to a particular segment within the parent brand's general market. Cf. *line extension.*

brand familiarity: the customer's ability to recognize and accept a particular brand of products. Brand familiarity can be separated into brand nonrecognition, brand recognition, brand preference, and brand insistence.

brand franchise:

(1) consumer loyalty toward a particular brand. See *brand loyalty.*

(2) an agreement between the wholesaler or retailer and a brand-name manufacturer giving the former an exclusive right to sell the brand manufacturer's item in a carefully defined location. It permits the

wholesaler or retailer to sell the item in a noncompetitive market and set price limitations as the traffic will permit.

brand generic: the second half of a product's identifying title. Brand is the first half and identifies a specific seller's version; the generic second half identifies the general class of item. For example, Jello is a brand; gelatin dessert is generic. It is not to be confused with generic brands where there is no individual brand. See *generic brand.*

brand image: see *brand awareness.*

branding: the assignment of a brand name to an item or service, thus achieving product differentiation within the marketplace. See *generic brand.*

brand insistence: the extreme of brand loyalty, where the consumer says he or she will accept no substitute item.

brand label: a label that indicates little more than the brand name of the item, the manufacturer, and other information-fulfilling requirements of the law.

brand leader: an item that is considered best in its field or is marketed with that assumption.

brand loyalty: the strength of a buyer's preference for a particular brand, which suggests a refusal to purchase a substitute. Brand loyalty is usually measured in terms of repeat sales and is also reflected in purchases of other items produced by the same company.

brand manager: synonymous with *product manager.*

brand mark: that part of a brand identification that can be recognized but cannot be verbalized.

brand marketing: a technique of marketing each item of a company separately, usually under the direction of a brand manager.

brand name:

(1) *business law:* a name registered with the U.S. government as a trademark to prevent copying.

(2) *marketing:* a word or term that is placed on an item for identification or to be communicated orally.

brand-name bias: a person's tendency to respond to a survey by naming widely advertised brands, often for purposes of giving a good impression, rather than naming the brands that are actually purchased.

brand nonrecognition: the inability of a customer to recognize a brand, even should he or she be able to recognize the product.

brand personality:

(1) the image of an item from the manufacturer's point of view.

(2) how the firm intends the item to be perceived by the target market.

brand position: the ranking of an item in the marketplace as compared with other competitive products.

brand potential index (BPI): a means of predicting product sales in a given market as a relationship between the brand development index and the market development index. The former is the percentage of product sales, the latter is the relationship between the potential and actual item users; used for planning future advertisement budgets.

brand preference: the choice by the consumer of a particular brand over its competitors, usually resulting from a favorable experience with the item. However, if the product proves to be unavailable, the consumer willingly shifts to a substitute.

brand proliferation: the expansion of similar products within a specific line.

brand recognition: the perception by buyers, when confronted with a product, that they have been exposed to that brand name previously.

brand share: synonymous with *market share; share of the market.*

brand standing: bringing together of a brand with an event or concept, such as testimonials in a specific sporting event year after year.

brand strategy: plans and tactics relating to the use of brand names.

brand switching: the selection by a consumer of a product or service different from that purchased the last time around.

brand-switching model: a model that provides a manager with some idea of the behavior of consumers in terms of their loyalty and the likelihood that they will switch from one brand to another.

break: in advertising and marketing, a discount.

break-down approach: allocating the advertising budget to the lines of offerings.

break-down method: an approach to salesforce design in which the size of the salesforce is determined by dividing the forecasted annual sales volume by the expected sales volume per salesperson.

break-even model: a model that shows the basic relationships among units produced (output), dollars of sales revenue, and the levels of costs and profits for an entire firm or a product line.

break-even point: as used to assess the impact of an advertising campaign, the point of activity at which a company earns zero profit. It is reached when total revenue equals total expense. Cf. *break-even pricing.* See *margin of safety.*

break-even pricing:
(1) pricing at a level that will enable a firm to break even.

(2) an approach to pricing in which the price of a unit of the product is set high enough to cover the variable costs of producing that unit as well as the fixed costs of producing the product. Cf. *break-even point.*

breaking bulk: splitting a large inventory of items into smaller quantities as the items move toward the target consumers.

breakthrough opportunity: a marketing situation that provides for a creative company to formulate a new marketing strategy, a new product, or even to evolve a new marketing mix. If effective, it may discourage other potential competitors from entering a similar market.

broadcaster:
(1) a person who delivers or sponsors an announcement, commercial, or program on a network, radio, or television station.

(2) an owner and/or operator of a radio or television station and network.

broad-line strategy: offering by a firm of a large number of variations of the item. See *limited-line strategy.*

broad market: a market situation with a large number of segments of widely different characteristics. See *narrow market.*

broad price policy: sets the overall direction and tone for a firm's pricing efforts and makes sure pricing decisions are co-ordinated with the firm's choices regarding a target market, an image, and other marketing-mix factors. It incorporates short- and long-term pricing goals.

broadside: a single sheet of advertising literature of comparatively large size printed in one or more colors on rather heavy white or colored stock, folded at least once, and designed to deliver a forceful impression by virtue of its size and bold display of type and illustrative matter.

brochure: in merchandising, a booklet that is printed on quality paper and features copy of the manufacturer's product, service, etc. Cf. *booklet.*

broker:
(1) a person who prepares contracts with third parties, as with a freight broker and customs broker, on behalf of a principal.

(2) a wholesaling intermediary whose primary function is supplying market information and establishing contacts to facilitate sales for clients.

brokerage:
(1) found in global practices, the fee or commission charged by a broker.

(2) in the United States, a brokerage firm.

brokerage allowance: the commission paid by the seller in a transaction to the broker who arranges the sale; usually a percentage of the selling price.

brood hen and chick method: the categorizing of branch retail stores as part of chains, with tight merchandising controls. Cf. *brood hen concept.*

brood hen concept: the maintenance of close communications by the retail buyers at the parent store with their branches. Buyers receive requests for items and respond at their discretion. Cf. *brood hen and chick method.*

brown goods: retailers' nomenclature for television sets and radios. Cf. *orange goods; red goods; yellow goods.*

BSR: see *basal skin resistance.*

BTA: best times available.

bubble wrap: synonymous with *blister pack.*

buckeye: (slang) a crude-appearing advertisement that is sloppy, lacking both balance and clarity.

budget: a critical factor in the successful organization of an advertising agency, or any other venture; an itemized listing, and frequently the allotment, of all estimated revenues a business anticipates receiving as well as a listing, and frequently the segregation, of all estimated costs and expenses that will be incurred in obtaining those revenues during a stated time period.

budget-book sale: the contracting by the customer for a specific amount of money to be paid back on a regular basis with a small carrying charge. A book with coupons is used as cash within the store.

budgeting: the process of determining and assigning the resources required to reach market and advertising objectives.

budget store: synonymous with *basement store.*

buffer stock: merchandise kept on hand to prevent a shortage resulting from an unexpected increase in demand for the items. Synonymous with *reserve stock.*

build strategy: the policy of increasing promotional funding to increase a product's market share; affects the future of the product.

build-up method: a method for arriving at national forecasts for individual regions and then aggregating the regional forecasts.

bulk discount: a reduced charge for quantity or multiple purchases. Synonymous with *volume discount.* See *discount.*

bulk mail: second-, third-, and fourth-class mail, including parcel post, ordinary papers, and circulars.

bulk sales: substantial quantities of a publication bought for redistribution.

bulk warehouse: see *warehouse, bulk.*

bullpen: the art department located within an advertising agency where creative artwork and related matters are attended to. Although more expensive than using freelancers, it provides for reliability, continuity for a firm's products or services, and consistency.

bundled pricing: an offering of a basic product, options, and customer service for one total price.

bundle of benefits: a concept that consumer or industrial users do not purchase things as such, but instead purchase the benefits that those items are expected to offer. Cf. *bundle of services.*

bundle of services: a concept favoring leasing rather than owning of equipment based on the theory that the purchase of a machine can be thought of as the purchase

of the number of yearly services that the equipment is expected to provide during its lifetime. Cf. *bundle of benefits.*

burden: synonymous with *overhead.*

buried offer: synonymous with *hidden offer.*

buried position: that place on a publication page where an advertisement would be bordered by other advertisements; also, a bottom corner inside of a page with advertisements at the top and side. It is usually considered an inferior place for an advertisement.

burst advertising: where the advertisement appears for only a short time, such as a week, with a "burst" of exposures. Used to accompany new-item introductions or to coincide with special promotions. See *saturation.*

business advisory services: industrial services that include management consulting, advertising agency services, accounting services, and legal services.

business analysis: the stage in the new-product planning process that considers such criteria as demand projections, cost projections, competition, required investment, and profitability for new products.

business cycle: frequently considered during an advertising campaign, any interval embracing alternating periods of economic prosperity and depression.

business domain: that sector of a market that a company targets as its business environment; often defined in terms of a line of products.

business ethics: as applied in the preparation of commercials, socially accepted rules of behavior that place pressure on business executives to maintain a high sense of values and to be honest and fair in their dealings with the public.

business publication: synonymous with *trade magazine.*

business-to-business advertising: advertising directed at purchasing officials and other decision makers instead of the general consumer. Businesses advertise in their own trade publications. Cf. *consumer advertising; trade advertising.*

busy: (slang) a print layout where the elements are excessive and resist each other, thereby detracting from the advertiser's intent.

buy at best: to bid higher and higher prices without any limit until the required quantity is bought.

buy-back agreement: a provision in a sales contract stating that the seller will repurchase items within a specified time period, usually for the selling price, if the purchaser is transferred from the area. Synonymous with *product buy-back agreement.*

buyer:
(1) *general:* an individual who acquires goods for purposes of making a profit, usually as the result of a resale.
(2) *retailing:* an executive responsible for purchasing merchandise to be sold in a store.

buyer for export: in international marketing; a middleperson responsible for purchasing goods in the domestic market outright and then attempting to sell them globally.

buyer readiness stages: in purchasing a product, the stages a consumer passes through, ranging from awareness to completion and purchase.

buyer-seller dyad: the rapport developed between the customer and the salesperson, often based on close and detailed communication.

buyer's market: a market characterized by low or falling prices, occurring when supply is greater than demand and buyers tend to set the prices and terms of sale. Cf. *seller's market.* Synonymous with *loose market; soft market.*

buyer's over: a situation of more buyers than sellers.

buyer's surplus: the difference between what a buyer pays for an item and the amount more he or she would be willing to pay for it.

buying allowance: a lowering of price on given items offered by a producer to a purchaser as an incentive to buy the goods.

buying by description: a decision to purchase based on a verbal and/or visual presentation of the item. Usually, to be satisfactory, the customer has strong feelings of confidence in the business under consideration.

buying by inspection: a decision to purchase that follows the examination of the actual items to be purchased.

buying by sample: a decision to purchase following the examination of a representative sample or portion of the item.

buying by specification: the submission by a store of specific requests for delivery rather than the purchase of standard merchandise available from the manufacturer.

buying center: all the individuals and groups participating in the buying process that have interdependent goals and share common risks.

buying committee: a group of buyers, often chain stores, that decide by committee on the items that will and will not be purchased.

buying criteria: the requirements of a firm evaluating suppliers of a product or service.

buying direct: the purchase of goods from the manufacturer, bypassing any middleperson.

buying distribution: a concept related to channels of distribution emphasizing that the price paid to gain channel support must reflect not only the marketing job expected of the channel but also the competitive environment that the channel services.

buying error: the failure to match purchases with demand; often leading to a markdown so as to move the merchandise out of the store. Cf. *selling error.*

buying incentive: a premium of additional items, a discount, or a gift, available to prospects should they purchase an item or service.

buying intent: the measurement of a prospect's intention to buy an item or service.

buying loader: a manufacturer's gift, such as a discount or a premium, to a retailer as a bonus for buying the manufacturer's item. See *dealer loader.*

buying off the peg: the purchase of ready-to-wear merchandise, to be taken home or delivered immediately thus involving no adjustments or alterations.

buying power: synonymous with *purchasing power.*

buying signals: verbal and nonverbal cues from a prospective customer that he or she is ready to make a purchase. See *close.*

buying specialists: employees of organizational consumers who have technical backgrounds and are trained in supplier analysis and negotiating.

buying structure of the organization: the level of formality and specialization used in the purchase process. It depends on the organization's size, resources, diversity, and level of specialization.

buy national: a growing appeal to restrain imports from other nations, especially when public procurement practices are at stake. The concept resists the international marketing of goods and services because each competing country claims that the other nation(s) discriminates against foreign competition.

buy-or-die message: promotional material focused on inactive direct-mail customers telling them that unless they make a purchase they will be purged from the mailing list.

buyout:

(1) *general:* the purchase of all the assets, stock, and so on, of an ongoing organization.

(2) *general:* the purchase of the interest in a firm that is owned by another.

(3) *broadcasting:* a one-time payment to talent appearing on radio or television that buys all rights to the performance in that commercial. It tends to be quite economical for the advertiser.

by-line:

(1) *general:* a printed article, often in a newspaper or magazine, that gives the author's name.

(2) *advertising:* in advertising copy, an endorsement by a celebrity or other well-known individual.

CAD: see *cash against documents.*

call: to demand payment of a loan secured by collateral because of failure by a borrower to comply with the terms of the loan.

callback: the technique used by a sales representative on a second or subsequent effort to induce a potential customer to buy. Cf. *user calls.*

call bird: to increase store traffic, incorporating lower prices on items not usually bought in large quantities that are shown in windows or advertisements of the retailer.

call credit: credit given for the price of an item when merchandise is picked up from a customer and returned to the store.

call planning: a telephone sales planning method used by salespeople; involves defining the goal of the call and devising a selling strategy.

call report: a salesperson's record for his or her supervisor identifying calls made to potential or real customers during a stated time period and/or within a specified market. It tells when a meeting occurred, and what was talked about. Synonymous with *conference report; contact report.* See *activity quota.*

call station: an area at which a pickup and delivery service is available, although there are no warehouse facilities.

call system: in retailing, a system of compensating a salesperson, at least in some aspects, on the basis of the amount of business he or she finishes.

call to action: that portion of an advertising message directing the consumer what to do as a result of receiving the advertiser's message, such as call an 800-telephone number to place an order, return a coupon, etc.

campaign: in advertising, a series of advertising communications or promotions, scheduled for a given time period, and connected by a central theme, common goals, etc. In principle, each step along the campaign adds a new, constructive element. See *advertising campaign.*

campaign basis: movement toward a marketing goal without concern for its relationship with the total business system.

campaign plan: see *advertising campaign; campaign.*

canalization: the building by an advertiser or salesperson on an association, perfection, anxiety, or data possessed by a prospective or real customer. It results in a major shift in behavior.

cancel:

(1) *merchandising:* a customer's request to cancel an order or stop service. Synonymous with *kill; kill bad pay.*

(2) *advertising:* to terminate an advertisement or contract.

canned presentation: a prewritten and usually memorized presentation by a sales representative, spoken sentence for sentence, with little or no deviation.

cannibalizing the market: a reference to the result of introducing a new product that, instead of creating greater sales, cuts into existing sales of the item it is intended to replace. Cf. *enhancement.*

canvass:

(1) *general:* to count or examine.

(2) *sales:* to call on prospective customers in person or by telephone to sell merchandise or services, to determine interest, or to gather information. Cf. *cold canvassing.* Synonymous with *territory screening.* See *preapproach.*

capability survey: in purchasing, the inspection of a prospective vendor's operation to secure answers to issues dealing with quality control, capacity to finance and manage, quality of technology, etc.

capacity:

(1) *general:* one of the three elements of credit.

(2) *packaging:* the volume of space within a container or other space, expressed in units.

(3) *marketing:* the ability of a factory or firm to produce results at a given level.

capital:

(1) the amount invested in a venture.

(2) a long-term debt plus owners' equity.

(3) the net assets of a firm, partnership, and the like, including the original investment, all gains, and profits.

capital account:

(1) an account maintained in the name of the owner or owners of a retailing business and indicating the equity in that business—usually at the close of the last accounting period.

(2) balance of payment items not included in a current account.

capital consumption allowance: synonymous with *depreciation.*

capital goods: items ordinarily treated as long-term investment (capitalized) because of substantial value and life (e.g., industrial machinery). Synonymous with *durable merchandise.*

capital intensive:

(1) characterized by the need to utilize additional capital to increase productivity or profits.

(2) requiring a high concentration of capital relative to labor per unit of output; also used to describe products manufactured by such processes.

capitalize:

(1) to include in an investment account expenditures for purchase or construction of property.

(2) to divide income by a rate of interest to obtain principal.

caption:

(1) *general:* the explanatory text accompanying a drawing or photograph.

(2) *advertising:* a word, phrase, or sentence describing the visual element of a print advertisement. Synonymous with *cutlines.*

captive audience: people exposed to commercial messages while passengers on carriers whose use of media they cannot control.

captive market: purchasers who have little latitude in choosing the vendor of a product or service. Consumers purchase these items because they are the only ones available through vendors in a particular location.

captive product pricing: a pricing technique of product manufacturers who require supplies, accessories, or additional devices for operation. The major product is moderately priced to attract customers, while the supplies, etc., are given significant markups (e.g., camera film prices are kept low, while processing prices are high).

captive rotary: a set of outdoor advertising locations used primarily for one advertiser with different items to expose to the marketplace.

captive warehouse: see *warehouse, private.*

carbon-copy concept: in sales, the theory that the training of new salespeople is best carried out by their emulating and memorizing the methods of proven salespeople.

car card: advertising poster displayed in buses, trains, and subway cars.

card rate: the cost for advertising in a publication or a broadcast network or station as published on the rate card for that publication or network.

carload: as applied in global marketing, the amount of a commodity or product that can fill a freight car, or the amount that is sufficient to be treated as a full car.

carnet: in international marketing; a document of international customs that permits temporary duty-free importation of specific items into certain nations. See *covered under carnet.*

carriage trade: (historic term, rarely used today) the class of rich customers who expected and received superior services for their willingness to pay higher prices for merchandise and services.

carrier: in international marketing, an individual or organization that is engaged in transporting products or people.

carrying charge: in merchandising, a charge added to the price of merchandise to compensate for deferred payment.

carryouts: items bought in a store that are not shipped but are taken from the store by the customer. Synonymous with *take-withs.*

carryover effects: the influence exerted on the sales of future periods by present-day marketing expenditures.

cartage: the charge for pickup and delivery of a shipment.

cartel: a group of separate business organizations that have agreed to institute approaches to altering competition by influencing prices, production, or marketing; rarely as effective as a monopoly.

cart wrap: the printed advertising message composed of paper that is designed to wrap about the cart in a store. See *case wraparound.*

case: a container used for goods sold at wholesale rates (e.g., a case of canned tuna).

case allowance: the discount that a wholesaler or manufacturer gives to a retailer when items are bought by the case. Usually, the larger the number of cases bought, the greater the discount.

case wraparound: a sales promotion item created to be placed around the case of merchandise. See *cart wrap.*

cash acknowledgment: a notice sent to a cash buyer mentioning the receipt of an order. Often, cash acknowledgments are accompanied with new information about merchandise and prices of substitutes for out-of-stock items. It is used primarily when a delivery is delayed.

cash against documents (CAD): in global marketing, the payment for goods on presentation of documents evidencing shipments.

cash-and-carry wholesaler: a wholesaler who demands that the buyer must pay when he or she picks up merchandise, without credit, or the wholesaler will not make delivery. Cash-and-carry wholesalers frequently deal in fast-moving (e.g., perishable) items, such as bakery goods. See *truck jobber.*

cash before delivery (CBD): a requirement to pay prior to delivery of goods. Synonymous with *cash in advance.*

cash budget: a schedule of expected cash receipts and disbursements.

cash buyer: a customer who pays by forwarding cash, check, or money order with his or her order.

cash cancellation: canceling a cash order; requiring a refund. Traditionally, such cancellations occur because of customer dissatisfaction with the item or service.

cash card: a card given by a retailer or store owner to a customer to guarantee a discount for cash payment. It is a substitute for credit cards. Some merchants give cash-paying customers up to 8 percent discount.

cash cow: products that enjoy comfortable profits and whose excess earnings are used (milked) to support other divisions, or weaker selling products.

cash discount: a percentage deduction from the selling price permitted by the seller for merchandise sold on credit, to encourage prompt payment of the invoice covering the goods or services purchased. Synonymous with *sales discount.*

cash flow: the reported net income of an advertising agency, plus amounts charged off for depreciation, depletion, amortization, and extraordinary charges to reserves, which are bookkeeping deductions and are not actually paid out in cash. Knowledge of these factors results in a better understanding of a firm's ability to pay dividends.

cash in advance: synonymous with *cash before delivery.*

cash incentive: any promotional method to encourage customers to pay when they order in return for a free-complementary gift. The gift usually is less expensive than the cost of sending another bill and waiting for payment.

cash on delivery (COD): a method of making a purchase with the expectation that the item(s) will be paid for on delivery. Synonymous with *collection on delivery.*

cash order: an order accompanied by the required payment. See *cash buyer; cash with order; credit order.*

cash position:
(1) a measure of the financial viability of an advertising agency; the percentage of cash to the total net assets; the net amount after the deduction of current liabilities.

(2) the ratio of cash and related assets to liabilities.

cash refund offer: a rebate offered by the manufacturer of an item to the customer. Once merchandise is bought, the manufacturer returns a portion of the purchase price in exchange for a label or other proof that a purchase has been made. Cash refunds are used for low-cost packaged items as well as for expensive goods such as cars or refrigerators.

cash-register-tape redemption plan: synonymous with *tape plan.*

cash sale: the surrender of cash at the time of sale.

cash terms: an agreement to pay cash for bought items, often within a given time period.

cash with order (CWO): payment for goods in which the buyer pays when ordering and in which the transaction is binding on both parties. See *cash order.*

catalog(ue): printed material that identifies items for sale. In most cases, the merchandise is described and prices are given; sometimes, a photograph or drawing accompanies an entry. See *mail-order wholesaler.*

catalog buyer: a person who makes a purchase from a particular catalog.

catalog merchandising: the promotion of items for sale in a catalog.

catalog plan: synonymous with *price agreement plan.*

catalog showroom: a discount store at which customers review catalogs and then place orders and wait for delivery.

categorical technique: a marketing strategy for evaluating the sources of supply. The purchaser maintains a record of all vendors and their products based on a list of characteristics to which performance evaluations are assigned as more experience with the supplier is acquired. This technique leads to a more efficient operation and usually lowers costs.

causal research: marketing that zeroes in on cause-and-effect relationships within

the marketplace; for example, the impact of advertising in the selling of a product or service. The value of causal research is that it illustrates the interrelationship of variables in a given marketing situation. Cf. *cause-related marketing.*

cause-related marketing:

(1) a promotional campaign devoted to raising awareness or generating funds for an event or social cause.

(2) the association of a specific product or brand with a particular event, cause, or activity, thus producing increased sales in combination with good will. Cf. *causal research.*

caveat emptor: "let the buyer beware" (Latin); merchandise sold without a warranty by the vendor, the purchaser taking the risk of loss due to defects. Cf. *caveat subscriptor.* See *warranty; without recourse.*

caveat subscriptor (venditor): "let the seller beware" (Latin); unless stated otherwise by the seller, his or her liability to the purchaser for any alterations from the written contract. Cf. *caveat emptor.*

CBD: see *cash before delivery.*

cease and desist order:

(1) *general:* a demand by a court or governmental agency that a person or firm cease an activity.

(2) *advertising:* an order from the Federal Trade Commission to stop a particular advertising activity or unfair method of competing that violates an FTC or other federal regulation. See *Federal Trade Commission.*

celebrity testimonial: found in advertising utilizing the recognition of a celebrity to promote a product or service. Usually serves as a promotion of both the celebrity and his or her cause or product being promoted. See *spokesperson; testimonial.*

CE Mark: used to promote and sell goods from the European Union; a system for marking goods. In this approach to industrial standards, member states agreed on governing principles for the CE mark, which indicates a product's compliance with technical regulations. The CE stamp, important to exporters, signifies a product's conformity to Community rules on technical harmonization.

centerfold: synonymous with *center spread.*

centers of influence: people of high social or business standing through whom a salesperson seeks to find qualified buyers. Centers of influence are people such as bankers or lawyers who exert power or authority over others.

center spread:

(1) *newspapers and other printed magazines:* the center pages, providing an unbroken surface to the printing of an advertisement. Synonymous with *centerfold.* See *spread.*

(2) *outdoor advertising:* synonymous with *double-page spread.*

central buying: a popular approach in chain stores whereby all purchasing is done through a central or main office. Shipments of merchandise, however, are usually made directly to the branch stores of the chain.

centralized purchasing: a system by which a department or unit is authorized to procure, handle, or store all supplies, materials, and equipment required by some or all of the other departments or units of a company.

centralized sales organization: an organization possessing the overall sales function that is concentrated at the highest levels of management. Cf. *decentralized sales organization.*

central market:

(1) the geographic area with a significant concentration of suppliers, where both buyers and sellers can meet to interact more efficiently.

(2) the location where a large number of the major suppliers or manufacturers of a given item or service may be found.

cents-off coupon: a coupon that entitles the holder to a discount on merchandise at the time of purchase. The buyer submits the coupon to the retailer, who returns it to the manufacturer, wholesaler, or a clearinghouse. As many as 150 billion coupons are distributed each year in the United States. See *coupon.*

certificate: any written or printed document of truth that can be used as proof of a fact.

certificate of inspection: a document certifying that merchandise (such as perishable goods) was in good condition immediately prior to shipment.

certificate of manufacture: of importance to international marketers; a statement signed by an exporter that goods ordered by the importer have been finished and set aside for shipment. This document is used with a letter of credit for the benefit of the exporter.

certificate of origin: in international manufacturing; a certificate declaring that goods purchased from a foreign country have indeed been produced in that country and not in another. Under most multilateral trade accords, traders are required to submit duly completed certificates of origin to their international counterparts to claim full or partial exemption from customs duties.

certification: an administrative task that awards a product a certificate if it satisfies special tests.

certification mark: a symbol, word, or other imprint used in marketing European goods to indicate that a product or service meets the sponsoring organization's highest standards of safety and/or certification (e.g., the "E" found on items cleared by the European Union).

chain discount: a series of discounts based on an earlier discount for the same item (e.g., a chain discount of 40 percent, 5 percent, and 5 percent is the same as one discount of 45.85 percent, from the list price of the item).

chain markup pricing: a form of demand-based pricing in which final selling price is determined, markups for each channel member are examined, and the maximum acceptable costs to each member are computed; extends demand-minus calculations all the way from channel members back to their suppliers.

chain prospecting: prospecting by a salesperson who wants the names of one or more prospects from each one that he or she approaches. Cf. *endless chain.*

chain ratio method: a method of sales forecasting in which a firm starts with general market information and then computes a series of more specific information. These combined data yield a sales forecast.

chain store:
(1) two or more stores, usually in different locations, being operated by the same organization.

(2) a retail organization that consists of two or more units under a single ownership.

chain store law: synonymous with the *Robinson-Patman Act of 1936.*

chamber of commerce: traditionally, a national trade-promoting organization servicing its members with information and reports on increasing international sales and trade. Complaints by consumers relating to advertising are often brought to this institution.

channel:
(1) *general:* in the communication process, the style of transmission. It can take the form of oral or written communication.

(2) *marketing:* a channel of distribution. See *channel of distribution.*

channel behavior: activities of cooperation and conflict between people and firms that make up a manufacturer's channel(s) of distribution. See *channel of distribution.*

channel captain:
(1) a channel member that is able to influence the behavior of the other members of the channel.

(2) the manufacturer, retailer, or wholesaler who dominates and controls a channel of distribution, usually setting a distribution policy that others follow.

channel change: the relationship between channel of distribution members in conflict.

channel fit: the degree to which a newly introduced item can be distributed through a channel of distribution already in use by the manufacturer of the new product.

channel functions: the functions completed by some member of a channel: marketing research, buying, promotion, customer services, product planning, pricing, and distribution.

channel interdependency: the members' relationship where each decision and activity affects the decisions and activities of other channels of distribution members.

channel leader: a channel member that dominates the market and may influence or control decisions.

channel length: the levels of independent members along a channel.

channel management: the activities involved in anticipating and understanding the sources of channel conflict and trying to eliminate or minimize them.

channel members: those participating in the distribution process.

channel number: the number of different marketing channels used by one marketer. Influenced by geographic areas and the size of purchasers.

channel of distribution:
(1) the interrelated network of people and firms for delivering goods from the manufacturer to the consumer. Intermediaries assist as merchant middlepeople who take title to goods and then resell it, and as agent middlepeople who do not take title to goods but serve as brokers.

(2) the route a product follows from an original grower, producer, or importer to the last consumer. Often a middleperson

is used (e.g., automobile manufacturers sell to car dealers, who then sell to consumers). See *channel behavior; channel fit; distribution.* Synonymous with *market channel; trade channel.*

channel power: the influence of one member of a channel of distribution over another.

channel width: the different outlets or individual companies employed at each level of the channel of distribution, where selling through almost any wholesaler or retailer occurs in a given area.

charge: in sales, to purchase for credit without making an immediate payment; usually to pay following billing.

charge account: a means of making sales on credit to retail customers. The various types are as follows:
(a) *open (30-day) account*—an account in which the store accepts the customer's promise to pay for items bought, usually within 30 days of purchase.

(b) *revolving account*—an account in which the store sets the maximum amount of money the customer may owe at any one time. The amount is determined at the time the account is opened and is based on individual income and credit rating.

(c) *budget (flexible) account*—an account in which monthly installment payments are based on the size of the customer's account balance, and interest is charged on the unpaid amount.

(d) *coupon credit plan*—an account in which the customer is given credit coupons that may be used in the store as cash. Payment for the coupons is made over a period of time, usually 6 months. This plan eliminates the need for a monthly billing.

charge buyer: a person who makes a purchase on credit to be billed at a later time. Synonymous with *credit buyer.* See *credit order.*

charges forward: a system whereby the purchaser pays for merchandise and shipping charges only on receipt of the goods or, following receipt of goods, when a bill arrives.

charging the top of the rate card: the ability to attract new advertisers to a medium at a one-time rate resulting from the demand, which exceeds the capacity of the medium to accommodate.

charging what the traffic can bear: an expression suggesting that the seller asks the highest price that he or she believes the market will bear (people will pay).

cheap jack: (slang) an individual who sells merchandise rapidly by unorthodox approaches, including using unoccupied stores to set up his or her goods.

checkerboard: the layout grid provided for space utilization of advertising in a periodical or magazine. Space is usually sold at the half-page rate.

checking copy: a copy of a publication delivered to an agency or advertiser to verify the inclusion of an advertisement as requested. See *tear sheet.*

checkout counter: the location where items bought are checked and paid for; frequently used by an advertiser for displays.

check question: in sales, a carefully phrased question designed to elicit an answer from a potential customer that will provide some clue as to the progress being made toward a buying decision. See *trial close.*

cherry picking: buyer selection of only a few items from a vendor's line, rather than buying a complete line or classification of merchandise from any one source. Synonymous with *hi-spotting.*

China eggs: (slang) people who at first appear to be good prospects to purchase an item or service, but who fail to become customers.

chi-square test: used in marketing research as a means of estimating whether a given set of data differs from expected values to such a degree as to be evidence of the operation of nonchance factors. It is the sum of the quotients obtained by dividing the square of each difference between an actual and an expected frequency by the expected frequency.

choice criteria: critical characteristics used by a firm's purchaser when evaluating merchandise offered for sale.

cinema advertising: commercials that appear on a movie screen in theaters prior to the presentation of the feature film.

circ: shortened form of circular.

circular:
(1) regular or small sheets of printed paper to be sent in the mail or delivered by hand.

(2) an advertisement printed on one sheet of paper and distributed by third-class mail or by hand. Often contains technical and mechanical information that is important to the consumer. Shortened to circ. Cf. *flier.*

circular flow: a process that shows the exchange between households and firms in the interaction of the flow of real sources and commodities and money income and expenditures.

circulation:

(1) *advertising:* the number of copies of a publication that are distributed. Advertising rates for publications are traditionally based on circulation figures. Cf. *readership.*

(2) *broadcasting:* the number of homes regularly tuned to a specific station.

circulation rate base: circulation that a print media guarantees as a minimum. Should circulation fall below this on a regular basis, the publisher often makes a pro rata refund.

claim:

(1) *general:* a demand for payment, reimbursement, or compensation for damages or injury as identified in a contract or under law.

(2) *advertising:* a statement employed in advertising a product or service that points to a positive aspect of the item or service such as a benefit or value to be gained by its use.

claims-paid complaint: a customer complaint dealing with a bill, after the payment for the merchandise or service has been sent to the seller.

class-action suit: a lawsuit filed on behalf of many affected consumers.

class consciousness: the extent to which social status is desired and pursued by a person.

classification: in merchandising, an assortment of items, all of which are substitutable for one another to the customer.

classification data: information by which an audience, a location, or broadcast and print media, are to be organized into useful research data (e.g., by age, education).

classification merchandising: a system of record keeping that assists inventory control and results in categorization of merchandise.

classified advertising: advertising identified by product or service; usually appears in a particular section of the publication. Rates for classified advertising are determined by the size of the advertisement, either by word count or by line count. Cf. *display advertisement.* Synonymous with *undisplay advertising.* See *classified display advertising.*

classified display advertising: special sections in newspapers, sometimes called supplements, devoted to one product, service, or cause.

class magazine: a magazine designed to be bought by a special interest group, to those sharing a common interest. Class magazine advertising usually offers the advertiser a minimum of waste circulation.

class rate:

(1) *general:* an insurance rate applicable to risks that are so similar in character that it is unnecessary to go to the expense of differentiating among them as to varying factors of hazards.

(2) *distribution:* a special shipping rate for certain classes of commodities, expressed as a percentage of the base rate.

(3) *broadcasting:* a charge made for radio or television time according to the desirability of the time slot.

Clayton Antitrust Act of 1914: see *tie-in sales.*

clean bill of lading: used in international sales and marketing; a bill of lading accepted by the carrier for goods received in appropriate condition (no damages or missing items).

clean draft: a draft to which no documents have been attached.

clean report of findings: in international marketing, a document from a recognized inspection agency certifying that certain items were examined and found to be in order.

clear: in retailing, to reduce inventory (e.g., clear out merchandise).

clearance:

(1) *general:* an act of clearing.

(2) *retailing:* a reduction on the price of items; a special sale that is often used to clear inventory and/or off-season goods. Cf. *markdown.*

clear time: time periods reserved by a station for the messages of an advertiser; a check by a network on the availability of time slots with station affiliates.

clerking activities: retail store activities with direct customer contact.

client:

(1) *general:* a person, firm, or other organization that uses the professional services of other people.

(2) *advertising:* the customer of an advertising agency. The agency works for the client, who is frequently referred to as an *account,* although the term is not always synonymous. See *advertiser.*

client list: the list of clients belonging to a specific advertising agency.

client organization: a business firm that produces products and/or services and retains advertising agencies and other suppliers for special services.

Clio Award: in broadcasting commercials, an international prize for creative excellence; judged by a panel of advertising creative executives and specialists from countries around the globe.

close:

(1) *sales:* to secure the customer's written or spoken agreement to purchase the item or service being offered. See *buying signals.*

(2) *advertising:* that section of the copy containing the idea of interest to an advertiser. Synonymous with *urge line.*

closed assortment: an assortment where the structure of items needed by the consumer is present and is complete. Cf. *open assortment.*

closed display: items placed under glass, requiring a salesperson to open a case for the customer to see the item closely. Cf. *open display.*

closed door membership: the requirement by a retail store that customers must belong to a specific employment group, such as government employees. Usually discounts are provided.

closed sales territory: a geographically defined area used by market researchers, where the manufacturer allows only one middleperson to handle certain merchandise. See *exclusive distribution.*

closed stock: merchandise sold only in sets (e.g., glassware, china). Individual items from a set cannot be purchased, and there is no certainty that replacements will be available at a future time.

closeout: an offer by a manufacturer or retailer to clear away his or her inventory.

close rate: in assessing salespeople, the individual's number of successful closings divided by that salesperson's number of sales calls.

closing: see *close.*

closing clue: a verbal comment or body language movement that indicates the potential buyer is on the verge of placing an order.

closing date/closing hour:
(1) *advertising:* the last day on which advertisements can be accepted for publication in a magazine or other periodical. Copy must be in the publisher's hands if the advertisement is to be included in a specific issue. Synonymous with *forms close.*

(2) *broadcasting:* the deadline for all broadcast materials to be delivered to the station or network if the commercial is to be included in the broadcast schedule for a specific time period.

closure: see *close.*

clucking hens: new or unusual concerns for a store's senior management that demand time and attention.

cluster: a grouping of specialty stores located within a high-density populated area.

clustered demand: a demand pattern in which consumer needs and desires for a good or service category can be classified into two or more identifiable clusters (segments), each having distinct purchase criteria.

cluster marketing: featuring a number of related items in various advertisements as one unit that can be interchanged. The result is to position them to a specific target market.

cluster sample:
(1) a random sample using groups of people rather than individuals as the respondent unit. See *cluster sampling.*

(2) a sample used when no total listing of the statistical universe is available. Groups are established and then a sample of these groups is drawn to represent the population. See *sampling.*

cluster sampling: a means of evolving a probability sample by randomly choosing the elements in groups rather than by individuals. Synonymous with *single-stage sampling.* See *cluster sample; sampling.*

cluster selection: a means of choosing names from a list by assigning each name to a group with common characteristics and choosing only those clusters that can be predicted will buy.

clutter: excessive advertisements or commercials, which broadcasters and advertisers claim obstruct a customer in making a decision. At times, advertisers run clutter tests to measure the ability of their commercials to get the listener's or viewer's attention in this clutter situation.

clutter test: see *clutter.*

COD: see *cash on delivery; collection on delivery.*

code number: a designation for identifying the source from which sales and marketing materials evolve (e.g., used on cents-off coupons to determine where people obtained them).

code price: the price resulting when a trade discount is deducted from a list price.

coefficient of correlation: in marketing research, the statistical measure of the relationship between two variables, where one impacts the other. The correlation indicates both the magnitude and direction of that relationship.

coefficient of cross-elasticity: in marketing research, the arithmetic relationship between a percentage change in the price of an item and the actual percentage change in the sales of a substitute or competitive item.

COG: customer-owned goods; for example, suits left at a store for alterations after purchase. Synonymous with *customer's own merchandise (COM)*.

cognitive component (of an attitude): utilized by consumer researchers; a person's evaluation of the characteristics of an object.

cognitive dissonance:
(1) *general:* a mental state that occurs when there is a lack of consistency or balance among an individual's various cognitions after a decision has been made. Two cognitions are in a dissonant state if they disagree with each other (e.g., when a commercial indicates that a cigarette is mild, but the consumer finds, through experience, that it is strong and irritating).

(2) *merchandising:* the state of anxiety or uneasiness that follows a purchase decision and creates a need for reassurance that the decision was the best one. See *dissonance reduction*.

cognitive judgment: for the consumer, the result of his or her perceptions, or communications received from others.

coincidental telephone method: a procedure used by C. E. Hooper in the mid-1930s for ascertaining what radio programs and commercials people tuned in. Respondents were called on the telephone and asked whether they were listening to radio and, if so, to name the programs. Cf. *audimeter; diary method.* See *Hooperating; Trendex.*

cold call: contacting a potential customer to make a sale or arrange for an appointment without prior notice. It is used to obtain a meeting or to give a demonstration and is a form of prospecting to identify qualified prospects for an item or service. It is frequently conducted during a downtime period when the salesperson has some free time. Cf. *cold canvassing.*

cold canvassing: determining potential customers without assistance from others or from references (e.g., selecting every tenth name in the telephone directory within a given location and having a salesperson call on these persons). Cf. *canvass; cold call; territory screening.*

cold list: a list of people's names not used before in promoting a service or item.

cold mail promotion: a promotion sent by a mailer to prospects who presently are not listed customers.

collateral businesses: support business in the advertising industry, such as package design houses, sales promotion firms, premium shops, media buying services, marketing research organizations, printing companies, etc.

collateral materials: related materials used to enhance, support, or reinforce an advertising promotion (e.g., film strips, catalogs, brochures, annual reports); used to prepare materials for advertising campaigns and promotions, or as sales and informational materials about a firm and its products, or for special events that it sponsors.

collection:

(1) *general:* the presentation for payment of an obligation and the payment thereof.

(2) *retailing:* an organized gathering of related items.

collection agency: an agency chosen by a seller to attempt to collect on credit orders that have not been paid in response to the seller's own attempts. The fee can run as high as 30 percent, and therefore these services are used as a means of last resort.

collection on delivery (COD): synonymous with *cash on delivery.*

collective mark: considered in the marketing of goods; a trademark, service mark, or other symbol used by members of an association or group of organizations to indicate membership within their group.

collusion: a secret agreement to defraud.

colorable imitation: any mark or symbol resembling a registered mark that may confuse the customer; a form of deception.

column inch: a method of measuring print advertising space, which is sold based on the dimension of 1 inch × 1 inch. Should a column be 3 inches wide and an advertisement 4 inches long, the total column inches to be bought is 12. Rates for advertising are set by the number of column inches the advertisement occupies. See *standard advertising units.*

COM: customer's own merchandise. Synonymous with *customer-owned goods.* See *COG.*

combination compensation plan: a sales compensation plan that uses elements of both salary and commission methods. Such plans balance company control, flexibility, and employee incentives.

combination house: a merchant middleperson acting as the wholesaler in the industrial market in addition to the retail and institutional market.

combination offer: a type of consumer fraud involving the sale of an item at a low price tied to the purchase of a continuing service.

combination pricing: a pricing approach whereby aspects of cost-, demand-, and competition-based pricing methods are integrated.

combination rate: a special rate for advertising in two or more publications owned by a single organization. To take advantage of this rate, the advertisement must be identical for all publications in size, copy, and content, and each publication must be purchased at the same time or within one day.

combination sale: an item of merchandise that is combined with a premium at one price. It lowers the cost of promotion per dollar of revenue.

combination store: a superstore that emphasizes nonfood items and services.

combo promotion: a promotion that offers two or more items together.

command headline: a headline that encourages a reader to use or purchase a product or service.

commercial: the advertiser's message presented on any radio or television program. A commercial is produced on film or videotape, then duplicated with copies going to subscribing networks for future airing. Commercials are filmed or taped and copies are then distributed. Cf. *advertisement.* See *commercial time.*

commercial advertising: synonymous with *product reputation advertising.*

commercial audience: viewers or listeners to a specific radio or television commercial.

commercial break: the scheduled time break in radio or television programming allowing for the insertion of commercials.

commercial counterfeiting: the manufacture or sale of goods that defraud the purchaser by falsely implying that the products are produced by a reputable manufacturer.

commercial databases: computerized information on population characteristics, the business environment, economic forecasts, industry and companies' performance, specialized bibliographies, and other material.

commercial delivery:

(1) the full audience that has been "delivered" to a commercial, or received delivery of the commercial.

(2) the portion of an audience exposed to a particular commercial.

commercial exposure potential: the number of prospective recipients of a commercial, determined by comparing the number of television sets in the receiving area with the number of television sets that are tuned in to the commercial in a particular receiving area.

commercial integration charge: the cost to an advertiser by a broadcast medium to cover clerical costs for incorporating a commercial in its schedule.

commercialization: the stage a product is in when, following testing and changing as deemed necessary, it is to be brought to the market with a full promotional campaign, either grand or small, regional or national.

commercial minute: sixty seconds of broadcast time used for the airing of a commercial, or commercials.

commercial pool: a combined group of already prepared commercial tapes that the advertiser can choose for showing.

commercial protection: synonymous with *product protection.*

commercial set: in overseas merchandising, the four major documents covering a shipment—the invoice, the bill of lading, the certificate of insurance, and the bill of exchange or draft.

commercial time: the permitted time per hour of programming that can be used by a broadcasting medium for commercials. For example, during prime time (8 P.M.– 11 P.M.) a station can have no more than 9 minutes and 30 seconds of commercials in one hour. Advertisers can buy 60 seconds of commercial time and divide it into three 20 second spots, or purchase 30 seconds and break it into two 15-second spots. See *day parts.*

commissary: a small retail store that sells usually to the workers of the firm that owns it.

commission: the amount paid to an agent, which may be an individual, a broker, or agency, for consummating a transaction involving the sale or purchase of goods or services. Salespeople receive salaries based on straight commission (compensation solely based on commission income) or a combination compensation plan that offers a fixed base salary plus a commission or incentives. Most salespeople prefer the latter as it provides immediate income. See *agency commission*.

commissionable: an advertising agency's services to a client for which the agency receives money from another source (e.g., advertising space subject to a commission that is bought by an agency on behalf of a client).

commission agent: a functional middleperson who receives the shipment of goods, mainly perishables, to sell for a principal.

commission house: an agent who negotiates the sales of merchandise that he or she handles, with control over prices and terms of sale.

commission merchant: an agent who performs selling functions for manufacturers, normally on a one-time basis.

commission rebating: income earned by advertising agencies on the value of the orders they place with media owners, rather than being paid a fee by their clients.

commission with draw: a form of compensation for salespeople where payments are based on a percentage of sales and regular payments are made from an account set aside for the purpose.

committee purchasing: the decision to buy by a group of people within a company who are charged with the responsibility of study and recommending products.

commodity products: synonymous with *staple stock*.

commodity rate: in overseas marketing and sales, an allowable deviation from the class rate charged by shippers to customers.

commodity warehouse: see *warehouse, commodity*.

common carrier:
(1) used by international marketers to set consumer prices; a carrier that moves people or goods for a price and without partiality.

(2) a transportation company that transports products on a specified schedule and according to regulations and standards established by government regulatory agencies.

common market: affects on global marketing profits; a trade interaction among nations that maintains a common external tariff and no internal customs. The European Union is one of the most famous common markets.

communication channels:
(1) *general:* the paths that are used for delivery of messages.

(2) *marketing:* the means by which promotional communications are offered to the target market.

Community Trademark: of importance to the selling of merchandise in the European Union. In November 1980, legislation was set harmonizing national laws on trademarks and establishing the Community Trademark and a Community Trade Mark Office. It ensures that trademarks enjoy uniform protection under the laws of all member nations and regulates registration of trademarks directly affecting the movement of goods and services within the Union.

company-controlled price environment: an environment characterized by moderate competition, well-differentiated goods and services, and strong control over price by individual firms.

company-specific buying factors: company-based variables that lead to either autonomous (independent) or joint decision making by organizational consumers. These variables are a firm's basic orientation, size, and level of decision-making centralization.

company warehouse: see *warehouse, private.*

comparative advantage: a determinant in global marketing of goods; a country's or area's advantage in the manufacture of a particular item when its social cost of production for that item is less than the social cost experienced by other countries or areas for the same item. Cf. *competitive advantage.* See *social cost.*

comparative advertising: promotional material in which competitor's products are named. Synonymous with *comparison advertising.*

comparative marketing: in international marketing, methods for differentiating similarities and differences of how consumers throughout the world are induced to purchase items and services, and how demand is set.

comparative messages: statements that implicitly or explicitly contrast a firm's offerings with those of competitors.

comparison advertising: synonymous with *comparative advertising.*

comparison department: a unit within a retail operation responsible for comparing the store's quality, service, prices, etc., with competitors.

comparison shopper:
(1) an individual sent to competitors' outlets to determine goods carried and relative prices charged as part of information-gathering activity.

(2) an industrial purchasing executive's review of competitors' marketing strategies such as new products offered, competitors' pricing concepts, and promotional initiatives.

comparison shopping: see *comparison shopper.*

compatibility: the degree that a consumer perceives that a new item is consistent with his or her current requirements, self-image, and attitude.

compensating product: an input or product secured by a manufacturer in a domestic market to substitute for an imported input or product used to manufacture items for export.

compensation:
(1) *general:* payment for any services or items.

(2) *marketing:* an attempt to disguise an undesirable characteristic by exaggerating a desirable one.

compensation deal: a semibarter arrangement in which goods are bought partially in cash and with other goods; a common practice in merchandising worldwide.

compensation trading: in global marketing, when an exporter agrees to accept partial payment in items from the purchaser's nation in lieu of cash.

compensatory trade: any transaction that involves asset transfer as a condition of purchase.

competition:
(1) any rivalry.

(2) the situation in which a large number of manufacturers serve a large number of consumers, when no manufacturer can

demand or offer a quantity sufficiently large to affect the market price. There are three forms of marketing competition: (a) brand competition—competition by producers offering a similar item;, (b) generic competition—when items in totally separate categories perform the identical function, and (c) form competition—merchandise that performs the same function but is structured differently.

competition-based pricing: a pricing strategy approach whereby a firm uses competitors' prices rather than demand or cost considerations as its primary pricing guideposts. A firm can set prices below the market, at the market, or above the market.

competitive advantage: applied by international marketers, the position of superiority one company achieves over its competitors in the marketplace. A firm's competitive advantage can be based on its ability to provide superior output, or to have prices that are lower than a competitor's prices. It is often used in comparing the export of merchandise from another country. Cf. *comparative advantage.* See *unique selling proposition.*

competitive alliance: the cooperation between competitors for specific purposes; a practice in international manufacturing of goods.

competitive analysis: determining a firm's or a product's performance in comparison with its competitors, based on product sales, profit, price, quality, delivery, customer service, etc.

competitive bidding: synonymous with *bidding.*

competitive intelligence: data on a firm's competitors and marketing activities; used in developing new strategies. It involves a variety of research activities including studying of trade periodicals, obtaining information from a host of sources, and gathering data internally. Professor B. Gilad has been a leading advocate and pioneer of competitive intelligence.

competitive market: a price determined in the market by the bargaining of a number of buyers and sellers, each acting separately and without sufficient power to manipulate the market.

competitive parity: a budget allocation for advertising that matches the expenditures of competitors; based on the concept that a firm should defend against competition by spending at least as much (or as little) as its competitor spends on advertising. Synonymous with *defensive budgeting; defensive spending.* See *competitive parity technique.*

competitive parity technique: a method for setting an advertising budget wherein an advertiser determines how much money to spend on the basis of a competitor's spending. Since objectives differ, this method can be a poor predictor. See *competitive parity.*

competitive position: the place within the market that allows an item or service to compete on a level with other competitive items or services. At the time the item or service reaches a noticeable percentage share of the entire market, it is declared to be in a competitive position.

competitive price: the price determined in the market by the bargaining of a number of buyers and sellers, each acting separately and without sufficient power to manipulate the market.

competitive separation:

(1) *advertising:* usually, set in a contract, the space that is used for separating competitive advertisements from one another. See *exclusivity.*

(2) *broadcasting:* the time span, traditionally 10 minutes between competing commercials. See *back-to-back commercials; product protection.*

competitive stage: the advertising stage of a product at which its general usefulness is recognized, but its superiority over similar brands requires promotion for the product to stay competitive. Advertisements in this stage often emphasize the item's differences. Synonymous with *selective stage.* See *spiral stage.*

competitive strategy: a promotional approach in an advertising campaign that is designed to compete with other brands (e.g., discrediting the cereal of a rival manufacturer).

competitor:

(1) the seller or maker of an item or service that is sold in the same market as that of other producers.

(2) the provider of a service or item that fulfills a consumer need in a market where others offer items and services that may fulfill the same need.

competitor intelligence system: see *competitive intelligence.*

competitor orientation: a firm's plans in response to a competitor's activities. The company prepares a competitor response based on market share of a product. See *competitive intelligence; customer oriented.*

compiled list: names and addresses of people and organizations that represent a particular target market.

complaint management: the provision of quality customer service by requesting and quickly responding to customer complaints; involves securing information on how best to provide customer services and how to resolve existing customer problems. See *customer relations.*

complementary products: items that tend to round out a line of products (e.g., shoes and shoelaces). See *allied products; suggestive selling.*

complementation agreement: an agreement that impacts global merchandising and sales. An accord between a commercial entity and two or more governments to lower or eliminate duties among themselves on given items produced by the firm in one or more of the signatory states. The agreement induces a manufacturer to place a factory in one of the signatory nations to supply that nation and others with the output of the plant.

completed cancel: a consumer who fulfills his or her commitment to the seller prior to cancellation.

complete segmentation: a type of market that treats each potential consumer as an individual instead of as part of a mass group.

complexity:

(1) the measure of the relative difficulty that consumers experience in understanding a new item.

(2) the difficulty of an innovation as perceived by the public.

complex sales force: an organizational structure uniting three basic sales force types: product-structured, territory-structured, and market-structured sales forces.

component life-style: a living pattern whereby the attitudes and behavior of people depend on particular situations rather than an overall life-style philosophy.

component materials: semimanufactured industrial goods that undergo further changes in form. They are considered to be an expense rather than a capital item.

component testing: individual testing of various parts of the marketing program. Marketing testing looks at them in unison, but during the development process each item in the marketing mix may be put through separate testing. Copy testing is the most common form of component testing. See *copy testing.*

composite demand: the sum of demands for an item or service, beginning with any number of needs, all of which can be fulfilled by that particular item or service.

composition: the spread on a page of the visual characteristics of a print advertisement. See *layout.*

composition house: in the printing business, a firm that sets type, among other activities, for advertisers and advertising agencies.

comprehensive: a layout prepared to resemble a completed advertisement as nearly as possible. Once approved by the client, the layout becomes the basis for a final plate or print.

comprehensive layout: see *comprehensive.*

computerized checkout (electronic point of sale) system: a system in which a cashier manually rings up a sale or passes an item over or past an optical scanner; a computerized register then instantly records and displays a sale.

conative component (of an attitude): in consumer research, the intention or tendency to act that results from a person's evaluation of an object.

conative judgment: in marketing, a purchaser's decision to move on a certain belief or feeling, to use a product or service.

concealed damage: as it affects profits in marketing, damage to the contents of a package that is in good order externally.

concealed discount: where items, whether price fixed or not, are identified on the same purchase order at a common discount, that is subsequently shown on the invoice.

concentrated marketing: a form of marketing segmentation in which the marketer concentrates on a single segment of a large market. Cf. *niche marketing.*

concentric diversification: a firm's strategy for expansion by acquiring another firm with new product lines that are similar to theirs, in the hope that it will appeal to a different set of consumers. See *conglomerate diversification; horizontal diversification.*

concept: an idea or its presentation as used in an advertising campaign, advertisement, commercial, or other promotional program.

concept generation:
(1) the act by which new concepts, or ideas, are created.

(2) the second phase of the overall product innovation process, during which the concepts are created.

concept statement: a verbal and/or pictorial statement of a concept (for a product or for an advertisement) that is prepared for presentation to potential buyers or users to get their reaction prior to its being implemented. Product concepts are followed by prototypes, advertising concepts by one of several forms of semifinished production.

concept statement commercialized: used in distinguishing two types of product concept statements. A commercialized product concept statement is prepared in an advertising format, as a persuasive statement. A noncommercialized product concept statement is prepared in a neutral, nonpersuasive format.

concept testing: a marketing strategy whereby members of a psychological test panel conclude whether an idea is acceptable, as contrasted with market research that attempts to determine if an appropriate market exists. Cf. *market research.* See *advertising effectiveness.*

concession:

(1) *general:* any deviation from regular terms or previous conditions.

(2) *merchandising:* a right granted to a company to sell its product or services (e.g., to rent chairs at an outdoor party; to check coats and hats in a theater).

(3) *international marketing:* a tariff reduction, or other agreement to reduce import restrictions; usually accorded pursuant to negotiations in return for concessions by other parties.

conclusive stage: the stage of the research process in which the researchers develop a plan for collecting data, implementing the plan, and providing the resulting information to decision makers.

concurrence: the duplication of the structure stemming from the joining of marketing elements.

condition:

(1) *general:* a contractual clause, implied or expressed, that has the effect of investing or divesting with rights and duties for members of the contract.

(2) *advertising:* anticipating and preparing the marketplace for a forthcoming advertising campaign, advertisement, or other promotional presentation to the public.

conditional sale: see *conditional sales contract.*

conditional sales contract: a sales contract in which ownership of sold items remains with the seller until the goods are paid for in full or until other conditions are met.

conference report: synonymous with *call report.*

confined goods: merchandise sold by a producer or distributor to a limited number of stores so that each retailer can claim exclusive resale rights in his or her trading area.

confirmation:

(1) *merchandising:* a statement from a supplier that he or she will accept a buyer's purchase request.

(2) *advertising:* a written affirmation by a broadcaster to an advertising agency confirming spoken statements dealing with the availability of commercial time on a specific network or station.

confiscation: a fear of international marketers; the seizure of private property, without compensation, usually by a governmental agency.

conformance testing: a technical task of testing products to determine whether or not they meet the requirements defined in a standard.

confusion of items: the intermingling of the items of two or more different owners where, once combined, the items are difficult or even impossible to separate again.

conglomerate: often mentioned in advertising to suggest profitability and/or competitiveness; the result of a merging of organizations that produce different items and services to secure a large economic base, to acquire sounder management, and to gain greater potential profit.

conglomerate diversification: a firm's strategy for expansion where new acquisitions have no direct relationship to theirs. In retailing, the store then proceeds to set up this additional service. Cf. *concentric diversification.*

conglomerate market competition: sale of the identical item by different dealers and distributors; leads to multiplying channels of distribution.

conglomerchant: synonymous with *merchandising conglomerate.*

congruent innovation: one of a four-way classification of new items as to degrees of newness. It does not result in any shift to established consumption patterns. The other three are continuous, discontinuous, and dynamically continuous.

congruent production diversification: items or lines of items that are added to a company's offering based on management decisions. Synonymous with *production-oriented diversification.* Cf. *operational diversification.*

conjoint analysis: a method for presenting the framework of consumer preferences and predicting consumers' attitudes toward new stimuli. See *product design model.*

conmanship: the technique of persuading consumers to part with their purchasing power for something useless, or even for nothing. The opposite of salesmanship.

conscious parallel action: identical pricing behavior among competing organizations. It has been declared illegal by the courts in antitrust cases. See *price fixing.*

consign: in international marketing, the act or ordering, via a bill of lading, a carrier to deliver merchandise from a given point to a given destination.

consignee: the ultimate recipient of goods.

consignee marks: in international marketing, a symbol placed on packages for export, generally consisting of a square, triangle, diamond, circle, cross, etc., with designed letters and/or numbers for the purpose of identification.

consignment: in international marketing, the act of entrusting goods to a dealer for sale but retaining ownership of them until sold. The dealer pays only when and if the goods are sold. Merchandise can be consigned by manufacturers to wholesalers or by wholesalers to retailers. See *on consignment.*

consignment note: in international marketing, an instrument given when goods are dispatched, providing details of the item, the sender, and the individual to whom they are sent. The latter signs it on arrival, providing proof of delivery.

consignor: the originator of a shipment, a person who delivers goods to an agent.

consistency of a product mix: the relationship among product lines in terms of their sharing a common end-use, distribution outlet, consumer group(s), and price range.

conspicuous consumption: the purchase and use of items and services primarily for improving an individual's social prestige rather than for the satisfaction of material needs.

constant costs: the difference between the out-of-pocket, or variable costs, and the total costs; those costs that, within the limits of the range of output under study, are unaffected by increases or decreases in production.

constructed price: as it affects global profits on goods, a value for customs purposes that ignores the invoice price of the goods but is derived by computing the cost inputs of the item, to which are added the normal costs associated with preparing the goods for export.

consultative selling: a sales method that positions the seller as the customer's consultant; applies low-pressure sales hoping to fulfill the prospect's particular needs.

consumer: any person who uses or consumes goods and services. A consumer need not be the purchaser of an item or service (e.g., the consumer would be the child who eats the baby food purchased by the mother). Synonymous with *end-user*. See *ultimate consumer*.

consumer advertising: advertising pointed to the final user of a service or item in contrast to advertising directed at business or industry. The biggest users of consumer advertising are radio, television, newspapers, and magazines. Cf. *business-to-business advertising*.

consumer behavior: based on behavioral science research, manifestations of the decision processes and the search activities in purchasing and using merchandise and services. See *selective perception*.

consumer behavior research: a technique used to determine what satisfaction people want out of life, how they use products and services to achieve these satisfactions, how they perceive items and various brands, what forms of promotional activities will lead to successful marketing, and how to access the effects of these activities. See *marketing concept*.

Consumer Bill of Rights: see *consumerism*.

consumer convenience goods: low-priced, frequently bought consumer items.

consumer cooperative: a group of consumers who band together to gain buying power; user-owned retail outlets. Such organizations act for the benefit of their consumer owners.

Consumer Credit Protection Act of 1968: see *Truth in Lending Act of 1968*.

consumer deal: a price reduction to a consumer.

consumer demand: the characteristics and needs of final consumers, industrial consumers, wholesalers and retailers, government institutions, international markets, and nonprofit institutions.

consumer demographic profile: a composite description of a consumer group based on the most important demographics.

consumer demographics: objective and quantifiable population characteristics that are relatively easy to identify, collect, measure, and analyze.

consumer durables: see *consumer goods.*

consumer education: the formalized teaching efforts to provide consumers with the skills and knowledge to allocate their resources wisely in the marketplace.

consumer goods: items bought and used by the final consumer for personal or household purposes, such as automobiles, food, and clothing. Synonymous with *consumer products.*

consumerism: the organized demand that businesses increase their concern for the public in both manufacture and sale of merchandise. Consumerism grew in importance when President Kennedy signed the Consumer Bill of Rights legislation in 1962 stating that consumers have the right to be safe (from faulty merchandise), to be informed (of a product's negative attributes or inherent dangers), to choose (sustaining market competition absent of monopolies), and to be heard (to be able to make complaints and have legitimate grievances acted on). See *consumer protection legislation.*

consumerist: an individual or representative who takes a leading position to protect the interests and needs of the consumer. See *consumerism; Naderism.*

consumer jury: pretesting items or advertisements by seeking the reactions of potential buyers or users.

consumer list: a list of people, for future contact, who have inquired about or actually bought items or services.

consumer magazines: magazines directed to the public-at- large; used extensively in promoting merchandise and services.

consumer market:
(1) buyers who purchase for personal needs or family consumption.

(2) a market in which goods and services are actually used up. Cf. *organizational market.* Synonymous with *product market.*

consumer motivation: the driving force in a person that compels him or her to act in the marketplace.

consumer panel: a group of selected people who serve over a period of time as a sample group for marketing research studies.

Consumer Price Index (CPI): used by marketers and advertisers in planning their strategies; a measurement of the cost of living, determined by the Bureau of Labor Statistics; also indicates price trends of more than 400 different items and services. Synonymous with *Cost of Living Index.*

consumer products: synonymous with *consumer goods.*

Consumer Product Safety Act (CPSA) of 1972: legislation providing for control of the processing, manufacturing, and distribution of products that may cause unreasonable risk of personal injury.

consumer profile: a market research factor; a description of the personal, demographic, and psychological characteristics of a specific item or service user (includes age, sex, marital status, income, education, occupation, home location, previous buying patterns, credit rating).

consumer promotion: sales promotion methods offering prospects short-term incentives to stimulate product sales.

consumer protection legislation: a variety of federal, state, and local laws to protect the rights of consumers. See *antitrust acts; consumerism; Federal Trade Commission; product liability.*

consumer research: marketing research to predict the behavior of the consumer in the market; provides data about a consumer's needs, motivation, perceptions, and attitudes regarding advertising, reasons for purchasing a service or product, and what influences their choices. Consumer research is of value in determining the target market and setting strategy for advertising campaigns and other promotions. See *consumer survey.*

consumer sale disclosure statement: a form presented by a dealer giving essential details on financing charges relative to a purchase on an installment plan. This is required under the Consumer Credit Protection (Truth in Lending) Act.

consumer's cooperative: a voluntary association of consumers, organized to help fulfill members needs for goods and services. Synonymous with *credit union.*

consumer sovereignty: the belief that the consumer is supreme in the market.

consumer stimulants: promotions and incentives that purport to attract consumers and to stimulate interest and demand for a product or service.

consumer surplus: the difference, as perceived by a customer, between the price he or she pays for the item, and the value of the purchase.

consumer survey: a consumer research approach using a questionnaire to collect information from a sample of consumers, either by mail, telephone conversation, or personal interview. See *consumer research.*

consummatory purpose: as measured by consumer and market researchers, the goal of a message. It is fulfilled when it is consumed upon being received.

consumption: the utilization of goods and services for the satisfaction of human needs.

consumption patterns: the patterns of whether consumers use, or do not use, a product or service.

contact report: synonymous with *call report.*

container: in merchandising, a nonspecific term for a receptacle capable of closure.

content motivation theories: consumer buying theories that focus on the factors within the person that start, arouse, energize, or stop behavior.

contest: a sales promotion technique in which consumers are offered prizes for performing a task such as making up a slogan. Cf. *sweepstake.*

contiguity:
(1) *advertising:* commercial advertising time slots of equal cost value. See *contiguity rate.*
(2) *broadcasting:* two programs, one flowing into the other without any commercial interruption or announcement. Used mostly on radio.

contiguity rate:
(1) a special discount rate given by broadcasters to advertisers who sponsor contiguous program.
(2) a special discount rate given for contiguous commercial time slots. See *contiguity.*

contingency plan: that portion of a marketing plan that develops strategies for countering adverse developments that may occur during implementation.

contingency pricing: withholding of payment to a service organization for services performed until the consumer's satisfaction has been assured.

continuity in advertising: the extended utilization of advertising; in particular, repetition of theme, layout, or commercial format.

continuity program: synonymous with *box-top offer.*

continuity series: in direct marketing, a multipart product such as a set of books, that is sent one part at a time to the user.

continuity strategy: a media scheduling strategy in which advertisements are spread out over the entire period of the campaign. See *bonus plan.*

continuous improvement: frequent incremental improvements driven primarily by customer requirements and competitor actions; requires active organizational learning.

continuous innovation:
(1) a modification of an existing item instead of a new concept.

(2) one of a four-way classification of new products as to degrees of newness; requires alteration of a product but does not cause major disruption in set purchasing patterns. See *congruent innovation; discontinuous innovation; dynamically continuous innovation.*

contract account: a retailer's customer with whom there is agreement that periodic payments will be made on the basis of a fixed percentage of the amount owing as shown by a statement issued regularly.

contract carrier: used by marketers to determine added costs; a transportation firm that contracts with shippers to transport their goods. The price is negotiated between the carrier and the shipper. The contract carrier cannot accept shipments from the general public.

contract manufacturing:
(1) a joint venture where the foreign firm contracts with local manufacturers in the host nation to produce a product.

(2) a business arrangement where one manufacturer produces items for another manufacturer.

contract price: in overseas marketing, the sale price negotiated between a U.S. exporter of merchandise and the foreign buyer payable in the United States for the export from the United States of U.S. goods and services. This price may include, among other things, freight and marine insurance, but it excludes any charges payable for non-U.S. goods and services unless otherwise permitted, certain engineering services, import duties or levies of a similar nature, charges for local costs, and any other charges not legally payable in the United States.

contract purchasing: a form of purchasing defined in a contract for orders and deliveries, covering a specific time period, usually one year.

contractual channels: a channel system based on a contractual agreement between a producer and other members of the channel of distribution.

contractual vertical marketing system: a vertical marketing system in which channel members draw up a legal agreement that specifies the rights and responsibilities of each party.

contracyclical pricing: a pricing technique that runs counter to traditional economic policy. During periods of prosperity, the company increases output and lowers prices; during economic downturn, it lowers production and raises prices.

contribution margin technique: an approach to cost analysis that ignores non-traceable common costs.

control: in marketing, the monitoring and reviewing of overall and specific marketing performance.

controllable factors: decision elements internally directed by an organization and its marketers. Some of these factors are directed by top management; others are directed by marketers.

controllable marketing activities: those marketing activities over which a firm has control, such as the product itself, the product name, packaging, advertising, pricing, sales promotion, and method of distribution.

controlled brand: a brand of merchandise owned by a manufacturer that restricts its distribution to a small number of distributors.

controlled circulation: see *total paid circulation.*

controlled sale: a category of market testing techniques in which the ability of the firm to obtain distribution is not tested. Distribution is forced, for example, by giving the outlets free product.

control over use: a dimension of product use tests; the degree to which the product developers maintain control over how the user uses the new item.

convenience goods: products that the public wishes to purchase with a minimum of effort or time (toothpaste, sodas, paper, etc.). Cf. *bantam store; shopping goods.*

convenience sampling: a nonprobability sample in which respondents are selected to suit the convenience of the researchers. Synonymous with *opportunistic sampling.* See *nonprobability sampling; sampling.*

convenience store: a small retail outlet that carries a limited line of high-turnover convenience goods and usually operates for extended hours.

conventional channel: a channel of distribution loosely organized where members are traditionally autonomous.

conventional duty: a customs duty, or rate of duty, arising out of a treaty or other international agreement, as contrasted with an autonomous duty unilaterally imposed by a government absent of any international agreement.

convergent marketing: an efficient means of organizing the marketing activity within a company so that the same resources are employed to sell all the items made.

conversional marketing: activities dealing with negative demand to urge the market's reaction to the product up to a positive level adequate to absorb a reasonable quantity of the available supply.

conversion process: synonymous with *boomerang.*

conversion renewal percentage: the proportion of new magazine subscribers who have renewed their subscription; often sold for more than the original price.

cooling-off period: a period established by law that protects consumers by permitting them to reconsider a purchase, and if they so desire, to cancel any commitment. Three days is the typical time frame used.

co-op advertising: see *cooperative advertising.*

cooperative: an outlet owned and run by the final consumers for purposes of buying and selling items to the members.

cooperative advertising:

(1) *advertising:* advertising paid for jointly by the advertiser and its wholesalers or retailers. Sometimes shortened to co-op advertising.

(2) *retailing:* an arrangement between the manufacturer and retailer where the producer reimburses the retailer in part or in full for advertising costs. Synonymous with *manufacturer's cooperative advertising; vertical cooperative advertising.* See *cooperative mailing; fifty-fifty plan.*

cooperative exporters: used by international marketers, established international manufacturers who export other manufacturers' goods as well as their own.

cooperative mailing: where several messages from different advertisers are placed in the same mailing envelope. The goal of cooperative mailing is to lower the advertisers' individual mailing and production costs. Often shortened to co-op mailing. Synonymous with *group mailing.*

cooperative marketing: independent manufacturers, wholesalers, retailers, or any combination of them working collectively to buy and/or sell.

cooperative organization: a retail organization that consists of a set of independent retailers that combine their resources to maintain their own wholesaling operation.

co-op mailing: see *cooperative mailing.*

copy:

(1) all components to be included in a completed advertisement or direct-mailing piece.

(2) in print news media, the text in a newspaper or magazine article.

copy approach: the way the text of an advertisement opens. It may be informative, imaginative, or geared to human interest.

copy date: the date by which all elements of the advertisement have to be delivered to the publisher, contracting firm, etc.

copy platform: the primary, critical concept behind any advertising campaign, with instructions on how best to discharge the program.

copy research: the study of an advertising message; includes both the pretesting and posttesting of commercials and advertisements in print and broadcast. Pretesting examines the product claims, technical components, and target audience prior to an advertising campaign. Posttesting examines the effectiveness of the copy in communicating the advertising message and its intent, at the end of the advertising campaign.

copyright: an exclusive right, guaranteed by federal statute, to reproduce, publish, and sell the matter and form of literary, musical, or artistic works. Any attempt by another person or group to deprive the copyright holder of his or her property is cause for the latter to seek damages.

Copyright Act of 1976: federal legislation revising the copyright laws for the first time in 67 years. The Act extends the length of copyright protection to the duration of the creator's life plus 50 years. Previously, the protection ran 28 years from the date of publication and was renewable for another 28 years. The Act sets standards for fair use and reproduction of copyrighted material and a new system of compulsory licensing for cable television and jukeboxes. It also preempts state laws governing copyrighted materials that come within the scope of the federal act.

copy slant: the way in which a selling point is presented in an advertisement.

copy strategy: a brief statement that guides the preparation of advertising copy.

copy testing: the process of measuring the effectiveness of an advertising campaign. Its objective is to identify and eventually eliminate the negative components of an advertisement or an advertising campaign to obtain maximum effectiveness from the advertising. See *aided recall; component testing; hidden offer; inquiry test; keying an advertisement; split run.*

copy thrust: the message communicated by the written copy and the accompanying illustration, starting with the objectives of the promotion in an attempt to convince the consumer that the item is useful.

copywriter: the individual who writes the copy for advertisement. He or she may also play a primary role in the advertising campaign.

core benefit: see *core product.*

core product: the central benefit or purpose for which a consumer buys a product, which varies from purchaser to purchaser. The core product or core benefit may come either from the physical good or service performance, or it may come from the augmented dimensions of the product. See *augmented product.*

core services: the basic services that companies should provide to their customers to remain competitive.

corporate advertising: an advertising program that promotes a firm, instead of its products or services; often used in the image building of a company; used extensively by public corporations to increase their attractiveness to the public and to encourage investing in their company. Cf. *institutional advertising; prestige advertising.*

corporate culture: assessed by advertisers; an organization's set of values. It creates a distinct pattern that is reflected in all the organization's activities.

corporate licensing: the use of a company's name to enhance the saleability of a product.

corporate mission: used by advertisers in promoting the firm's goods; a statement of an organization's overall goals, usually broadly defined and difficult to measure objectively.

corporate responsibility research: market research created to assist firms to better understand the legal, political, or social environments in which they function, so as to better communicate their societal obligations to the general public.

corporate symbols: a firm's name (and/or divisional names), logo(s), and trade characters. They are significant parts of the overall company image.

corporate vertical marketing system: the control by a large organization of two or more levels of a marketing channel.

corrective advertising: Federal Trade Commission law requires that an advertiser found guilty of placing a deceptive advertisement devote space or time in future announcements with disclosure of the earlier deception.

correlation: in market research, a relationship or dependence reflecting the principle that two things or variables are so related that change in one is accompanied by a corresponding or parallel change in the other.

correlation coefficient: in market research, the quotient of the sum of the products of algebraic deviations of the corresponding numbers of two sets of data and the square root of the product of the sum of the squares of the deviations of each set.

cosponsoring:

(1) *general:* joining together in a mutual effort or activity.

(2) *advertising:* sharing by two or more advertisers of the cost of a single broadcast program.

cost:

(1) the value given up by an entity to receive goods or services.

(2) the value given up to obtain an item in the volume needed, shipped to the desired location. All expenses are costs, but not all costs are expenses.

cost analysis: a sales manager's measurement of the cost of sales activities; measures the levels of profitability of individual items and types of customers. Cf. *sales analysis.*

cost-based pricing: a pricing strategy approach whereby a firm determines prices by computing merchandise, service, and overhead costs and then adding an amount to cover the firm's profit goal. Demand is not analyzed.

cost complement: synonymous with *cost multiplier.*

cost efficiency: the cost of reaching members of the target audience for a specific item or service as contrasted with the cost of reaching the entire audience of the medium; expressed in cost per thousand. See *cost per thousand.*

cost multiplier: in retailing, the average relationship of the cost of merchandise to the actual retail value of the items handled in an accounting period. Synonymous with *cost complement; cost percent.*

cost of credit: an advertising variable; the cost, in addition to the cash price, for the opportunity of purchasing something with an obligation to pay in the future.

cost of goods sold: the purchase price of goods sold during a specified period, including transportation costs.

cost of living: the average of the retail prices of all goods and services required for a reasonable living standard.

Cost of Living Index: synonymous with *Consumer Price Index.*

cost percent: synonymous with *cost multiplier.*

cost per inquiry: the statistical determination of the promotion costs divided by the number of inquiries received. Cf. *cost per order.*

cost per order: a statistical determination of the costs incurred in selling merchandise divided by the number of orders that are received. Cf. *cost per inquiry.*

cost per sale: in direct mailing, the cost of making one sale as compared with the cost of mailing.

cost per thousand: in advertising, the expense in reaching one thousand potential customers with a particular advertisement or advertising campaign. See *cost efficiency; efficiency rating; selectivity index.*

cost plus pricing: the practice of adding a percentage of the costs of goods to the cost before the selling price is established.

cost tradeoff: the strategy of spending more on one aspect of marketing so as to lower the cost of another aspect even more.

count and recount: a method of determining the results of a sale—count the merchandise, run the sale, then recount the merchandise.

count certificate: a document confirming the count of merchandise at the time of shipment or delivery.

counteradvertising: advertising carried out by groups in the public interest to convince them not to purchase a product or service the group believes is harmful.

countercyclical advertising: planning the advertising campaign so that the majority of advertisements appear when sales do not normally occur, and little is run during normally large-volume times.

counterfeiting: the illegal use of a well-known manufacturer's brand name on copies of the firm's merchandise.

countermand: in sales, to cancel an order that has not yet been carried out.

countermarketing: activities that attempt to eliminate the demand for a product, especially by those who find fault with the item, or claim it to be unsafe.

counterpurchasing: placing an order with a manufacturer in one country with the expectation that merchandise of equal value and/or quantity will be sold in the opposite direction to the other nation.

countersegmentation: the lowering of the number of market segments targeted by a firm by eliminating items that have been serving narrow segments of the population.

countertrade:
(1) in global sales, the sale of goods or services that are paid for in whole or in part by the transfer of goods or services from a foreign country.

(2) in international sales, an export sale that is contingent on a reciprocal purchase or undertaking by the exporter.

(3) a practice whereby a supplier commits contractually, as a condition of sale, to reciprocate and undertake certain specified commercial initiatives that compensate and benefit the buyer.

coupling: the joining of efforts between the firm developing new products and other firms or persons; can be upstream (with vendors), downstream (with customers), or sideways (with competitors).

coupon:
(1) *general:* a certificate that entitles a consumer to a price reduction or a cash refund.

(2) *advertising:* a part of an advertisement that can be used for ordering items or redeeming premiums. See *cents-off coupon; couponing; direct-response advertising; premium.*

couponing: offering consumers a coupon that entitles them to a special, but temporary, price reduction on merchandise without changing the regular market price. It may be mailed or placed in a package of another item, or published in an advertisement. See *cross-couponing*.

coupon pad: promotional coupons attached to a card often hung on a wall or affixed to a counter.

coupon research: the use of coupons returned by consumers to analyze or compare the impact of promotions or advertisements in relation to where the coupons were distributed or published.

cover ad position: an advertisement placed on a cover of a periodical or magazine.

coverage:
(1) *general:* the appearance of a news story in print or broadcast news media.

(2) *advertising:* the number of homes or persons exposed to a specific advertising medium in a controlled location. See *reach*.

coverage map: a map showing the prime area of a medium's reach within a market.

covered under carnet: a strategy of marketers. Export items make temporary trips to overseas nations, then are reexported from them, and ultimately are reimported to their originating nation, under the authority of an international chamber of commerce carnet. See *carnet*.

cowcatcher: (slang) a brief announcement preceding a television or radio broadcast that features a product of the advertiser other than the ones associated with the program being shown or heard. Cf. *hitch-hike*.

CPI: see *Consumer Price Index*.

CPM: see *critical path method*.

CPSA: see *Consumer Product Safety Act*.

creaming a list:
(1) choosing from a list only key prospects, those who are most likely to purchase an item or service, based on a variety of selection criteria.

(2) making an offer that can't be turned down. It usually is made at a loss.

creative black book: a directory of people and firms that supply products and services for advertisers, marketers, and agencies. Advertisers in the book include photographers, producers, illustrators, etc. Cf. *Green Book*.

creative boutiques: advertising agencies that specialize in developing advertising and provide no marketing services.

creative demarketing: synonymous with *demarketing*.

creative director: the person who manages the creative department in an advertising agency. He or she is responsible for all creative aspects of advertising, advertising campaigns, and commercials, starting with ideas and ending with production.

creative selling: in sales, applying techniques and strategies that elicit consumer demand, by proving the benefits of an offering to those who have never purchased the merchandise from that salesperson before.

creative stimuli: a method of ideation whereby a person thinks of a problem or a product and then studies a set of words or phrases that research has shown to be stimulating. See *ideation*.

creative strategy: the outlining of an advertising or commercial message; traditionally discharged by members of the creative unit of the agency.

credit: sales or purchases that are accompanied by a promise to pay later.

credit bureau: an agency that holds central data files on consumers in a given trade area. These bureaus collect personal data, data on paying habits, and so on, and make impartial reports for credit grants. Some national credit bureaus have been accused of invading personal privacy. See *Fair Credit Reporting Act of 1971.*

credit buyer: synonymous with *charge buyer.*

credit cancellation: the cancellation of an unpaid credit order. Synonymous with *kill; kill bad pay.*

credit card: a card issued by an organization that entitles the bearer to credit at its establishments, restaurants, stores, etc.

credit card order: paying for merchandise by using a credit card.

credit order: an order received without any payment and that requires billing at a future time. Synonymous with *bill me order.* See *cash order; charge buyer.*

credit rating: the amount, type, and form of credit, if any, that a bank estimates can be extended to an applicant for credit.

credit suspension: the placement of names of people with unpaid credit accounts on an inactive status list so that they will not receive merchandise or services. At the same time, these people continue receiving bills.

credit union: a cooperative financial organization established within and listed to a specific group of people.

crescendo method: synonymous with *snowballing method.*

critical path method (CPM): in planning and scheduling a complex series of marketing and sales operations, the sequence of events that are most critical as to timing; the longest path of activities in a system. CPM is based on the network analog principle and was first used in 1957 by E. I. du Pont de Nemours & Co. to improve the planning, scheduling, and coordination of its new-plant construction effort.

cross-branding: brand promotion purporting to enhance a given item by utilizing the brand strength of one or more of its ingredients or constituents.

cross-classification matrix: a grid technique used to identify specific subdivisions in a market for purposes of segmentation.

cross-couponing: a coupon given with merchandise. It carries the price reduction offer of another item and may involve more than one seller. See *couponing.*

cross-elasticity: the impact on the demand for one product of price changes in a related product. For example, when the price of butter goes up, the price of margarine, sometimes used as a substitute, usually rises as well. See *elastic demand; elasticity.*

cross-elasticity of demand: see *cross-elasticity.*

cross-merchandising: placing displays of complementary items in positions facing each other, with the hope that customers when they see the displays will cross over from one product to another. Synonymous with *related-item display*.

cross-plug: in a continuing broadcast program of alternating sponsorship, a commercial broadcast during the current program promoting the alternating sponsor for the purpose of providing continuity of advertising for both sponsors.

cross-promote: to promote a firm's item to purchasers of another item of the same firm. See *tie-in advertisement; tie-in promotion*.

cross-promotion: synonymous with *tie-in promotion*.

cross-ruff advertisement: an advertisement or campaign involving cents-off deals, couponing, product sampling, and premiums, where several firms combine to link brands. Firms that participate in this program deal directly with each other and each continues to promote its own brands.

cross-selling: working as a salesperson in more than one department within a store, helping customers with a variety of purchases.

cross-subsidization: a marketing method in which a firm employs earnings in one foreign market to support its marketing activities in another foreign market.

cues: stimuli that are not powerful enough to arouse consumer action but are capable of providing direction to motivated behavior.

culture: in marketing, the way in which consumers behave in the marketplace.

cume: see *cumulative audience*.

cumulative audience: the number of unduplicated people contacts by a given schedule over a stated time frame. The higher the cumulative audience, the larger the audience. Often shortened to cume. Synonymous with *unduplicated audience*. See *cumulative reach; reach*.

cumulative cost curve: the shape of a line that depicts a firm's cumulative costs of developing and marketing a new product. It is plotted against the cumulation of time, so it runs from zero (start of project) to 100 percent of time (launch). The curve necessarily runs from lower left to upper right.

cumulative mark on: the difference between total delivered cost and total original retail value of merchandise handled within a stated time frame, inclusive of the accumulated inventory.

cumulative quantity discount: a type of rebate given to a store when the total price of all goods purchased is identified. The objective is to encourage the dealer to give the seller all his or her business in that line of trade.

cumulative reach: the same as cumulative audience but usually indicates the total number of households reached by a medium during a stated time period. See *cumulative audience*.

curiosity headline: a headline that encourages readers to read on into the advertisement because of heightened curiosity.

current account: in advertising, customer names taken from a list and ranked in order of past business and potential activity.

current assets: helps to determine an advertising agency's profitability; includes cash and those assets that are readily convertible into cash or are held for current use in operations, current claims against others, and amounts accruing to the carrier that are subject to current settlement. See *current liabilities.*

current issue: any printed material presently available; on the newsstand for sale.

current liabilities: amounts payable within a comparatively brief period, usually not exceeding one year from the date of the balance sheet. See *current assets.*

cushion: inventory added to a basic amount to provide for unexpected increases in demand, delays of delivery, a purchase in great quantity, etc. Cf. *cushioning.* See *safety stock.*

cushioning: the protection of an item from physical damage by placing about its outer surfaces materials that have been designed to absorb the impact of external forces. Cf. *cushion.* See *floatation.*

customary price: the established price of some items, not because of the seller's decision, but because of having prevailed on the market for so long that consumers habitually correlate that price to the item. Altering the package may be a significant way of changing this situation.

customer: an individual or organization that makes a purchase.

customer characteristics: distinctive, unique, typical features that help distinguish one consumer or group of consumers from others; becomes the basis for market segmentation.

customer database: a computer-based system housing information about customers' history of purchases and other buying patterns. It is used to encourage repeat sales and to test new merchandise.

customer departmentation: the grouping of jobs into subunits based on the customers to be served, a common practice in retail organizations.

customer franchise: a loyal item following by a group of consumers with repeat sales anticipated.

customer holdover: see *new-buyer holdover effect.*

customer market: purchasers of a firm's items in any or all of its markets—consumer, industrial, organizational.

customer market focus: the decision of a firm acknowledging that purchasers can accept or reject the firm's merchandise. See *marketing concept.*

customer orientation: see *customer oriented.*

customer oriented: describing the effort to comprehend the reasons, desires, and problems of the customer with the intent to use this information in fulfilling the customer's needs, at the same time increasing sales and profits. See *competitor orientation.*

customer-owned goods: see *COG.*

customer profile: the demographic breakdown of the consumers who purchase a brand; includes their purchasing behavior; provides salespeople with data on buyer traits and behavior patterns and becomes useful in choosing the best prospects for a given item or for preparing selling strategies. See *audience composition.*

customer relations: a salesperson's activities that attempt to ensure that consumers' needs are not neglected. Complaints are to be handled swiftly and courteously. See *customer service.*

customer satisfaction: the measure of the degree to which a customer's expectations of an item or service match the item or service's actual usefulness to that customer.

customer service: the department or special unit of an organization that responds to inquiries and consumer/customer complaints about their product or service; either by telephone or mail. Quality customer service usually leads to increased sales and customer attitudes. See *customer relations; query.*

customer's own merchandise: synonymous with *customer-owned goods.* See *COG.*

customized marketing: designing goods and services to fulfill each buyer's unique requirements (e.g., customized bookshelves, customized dishes).

custom marketing: marketing where the target consumers are totally segmented—each person is so unique from all others that he or she is treated as an individual.

custom marketing research firm: a firm retained by a client to conduct research, the results of which ultimately become the property, usually confidential and proprietary, of the client.

custom research firm: see *custom marketing research firm.*

customs: relevant to international marketers, taxes imposed by a government on the import or export of items.

custom selling: creative selling where at least a portion of an item or service is designed for a specific prospect.

customs harmonization: of relevance to global marketers; the continuing activity to standardize customs procedures and nomenclatures worldwide.

cutback:
(1) *general:* the curtailment of production or expenditures provided for in a budget that has been or is about to be adjusted.

(2) *manufacturing:* a reduction to a form level (e.g., in production).

(3) *advertising:* interrupting the chronological sequence of an event by a scene recalling an event from an earlier time. Synonymous with *flashback.*

cut-in: the substitution by a broadcast medium of a commercial for one station that is different from the commercial employed in the network.

cutlines: synonymous with *caption.*

CWO: see *cash with order.*

cycle: the unit of time identified in a contract, when the contract is for a longer time period. An advertiser might have a radio broadcast media purchase contract for a period of one year. Within that year's contract, there could be specified four 13-week periods of television programming. Each 13-week period would then be considered a cycle. Advertisers can change or cancel a contract at the end of a cycle.

cycle billing: matching of alphabetical breakdowns to specific days to assist in customer billing. Each breakdown is a cycle and occurs on the same day every month.

cyclical demand: see *cyclical forecast.*

cyclical forecast: changes in market demand that are primarily a result of general economic conditions.

daily: a newspaper that is published at least five times a week, Monday through Friday. Cf. *weekly.* See *daily rate.*

daily effective circulation: in outdoor advertising, the number of people who can be expected to observe a message; traditionally measured as 50 percent of all people passing the display in cars and trucks plus 25 percent of total mass-transit passengers.

daily rate: the cost of daily advertising space, usually used in dailies. See *daily.*

DAR: day-after recall; a posttest method for assessing advertising effectiveness. Information is obtained over the telephone by providing interviewees with the name of the item or brand and then asking them what information they can recall.

data:
(1) the representation of facts, concepts, or instructions in a formalized manner, suitable for communication.
(2) a collective mass of factual material used as basis for inference of conclusions. (The plural "data" is often incorrectly construed as singular. "Data" is the plural of "datum.")

data analysis: the coding, tabulation, and analysis of marketing research data.

data bank: in market research, a comprehensive collection of information on a principal subject and related areas.

database: a collection of information specific to an operation, business, or enterprise. In marketing situations, information on customers is retrievable for each application from a shared file that is not dependent on the applications programs for its structure. See *database marketing.*

database marketing: the utilization of computers to store data on consumers' characteristics and purchasing habits for use in future direct-marketing activities.

data capture: the act of collecting marketing and advertising data into a form that can be directly processed by a computer system. Some electronic funds-transfer systems are designed to capture transaction data at the precise time and place the transaction is consummated.

data reduction: the process of transforming large masses of marketing data into useful, condensed, or simplified intelligence.

data storage: the stage in a marketing information system involving the retention of all types of relevant company records (e.g., sales, costs, personnel performance), as well as the information collected through marketing research and continuous monitoring.

date for value determination: a critical factor in setting duties for merchandise shipped overseas; the date when imported goods were exported from their country of origin. The value of the merchandise in effect on that date is used in setting duties.

date line: in advertising, the payment-due line on an order blank or on a contract.

dating: a technique of extending credit beyond the time it was originally given; often used as an inducement to dealers to place orders far in advance of the coming retailing season.

datum: see *data.*

dawn raids: in sales, a means of dealing with price fixing; the right to raid firms for evidence of alleged price fixing.

day-after recall: see *DAR.*

day parts: the division of a broadcast medium's on-the-air time, usually into the following segments: morning, afternoon, early evening, night, and late night. Radio day parts are:

6:00 A.M.–10:00 A.M.	morning drive
10:00 A.M.–3:00 P.M.	daytime
3:00 P.M.–7:00 P.M.	afternoon drive
7:00 P.M.–12:00 A.M.	nighttime
midnight to 6:00 A.M.	all night.

Television day parts are:

7:00 A.M.–9:00 A.M. Monday–Friday—morning
9:00 A.M.–4:30 P.M. Monday–Friday—daytime
4:30 P.M.–7:30 P.M. Monday–Friday—early fringe
7:30 P.M.–8:00 P.M. Sunday–Saturday—access
8:00 P.M.–11:00 P.M. Monday–Saturday—prime time (7:00 P.M.–11:00 P.M.—Sunday)
11:00 P.M.–11:30 P.M. Monday–Friday—late news
11:30 P.M.–1:00 A.M. Monday–Friday—late fringe
1:00 A.M.–7:00 A.M. Sunday–Saturday—late night

See *afternoon drive; commercial time.*

days per outstanding: the ratio of accounts receivable to credit sales per day.

days purchases outstanding: a measure of how promptly a marketing firm pays its bills; calculated as accounts payable divided by purchases per day.

deadbeat:

(1) *general:* a person who tries to avoid paying for things.

(2) *retailing:* a customer who fails to pay his or her entire charge every billing period, thus incurring revolving credit charges. Often their names are ultimately purged from lists for future promotional items or services.

dead corner: the area in a retail store that is either empty or is used for nonretailing activities in order to affect the drawing power of the area for retailing purposes; it tends to stop the flow of shopper traffic between multiple shopping areas.

deadline: in advertising, the hour or day after which the advertising material will not be accepted to appear in a publication or specific broadcast time period.

dead stock: merchandise that cannot be sold.

deal:

(1) *general:* (slang) a large transaction involving a change in ownership.

(2) *marketing:* (slang) a sales promotion enabling a customer to save money on the purchase of a product or service, often with special discounts. By law, such arrangements must be offered on an equal basis to all dealers or retailers having business with a particular manufacturer. Synonymous with *trade deal.*

dealer:

(1) a retailer of goods.

(2) an individual or firm that divides quantity goods or services into smaller units for resale to customers.

dealer brand: a brand that is created and owned by an intermediary.

dealer imprint: a dealer's name, address, or other identification, put on material created by an advertiser.

dealer incentive: a point-of-purchase display incorporating as one of its parts a desirable unit for the dealer to bring home.

dealer listing: a list of local dealers appearing on a nationally presented advertisement in a local or regional magazine. The advertisement remains the same in all regional issues, but the dealer list changes by region. See *ad-slick.*

dealer loader: a retail point-of-purchase fixture provided by the manufacturer or supplier; usually placed next to a cash register or checkout counter to display items. Synonymous with *display loader.* See *buying loader; trade promotion.*

dealer's privilege: a card or similar display unit carrying an advertisement on one side that also provides for the retailer's message on the reverse side.

dealer tag: a mention of the local dealer at the conclusion of a nationally broadcast commercial.

dealer tie-in: a manufacturer's advertisement given at a countrywide rate with a list of local dealers to be included in the advertisement.

deal pack: an item of merchandise with an attached premium. Usually handlers (wholesalers or retailers) expect payment for handling these because regular items must be withdrawn during the promotional period.

debit transfer system: an arrangement in which the amount of a purchase is immediately charged against the buyer's account; delayed billing is not permitted without an interest charge.

debt: money, services, or materials owed to another person as the result of a previous agreement.

debt capital: funds borrowed to finance the operations of a business, such as an advertising firm.

debtee: a creditor.

debtor: one who owes money to another.

decay curve: the curve representing death of concepts during the development stage. It begins on the left with 100 percent of concepts and ends up on the right with the percentage actually marketed successfully; It usually declines rapidly. Synonymous with *mortality curve.*

decay rate: the number or proportion of customers lost within a time period, usually one year; shows the amount of weakening of the effects of earlier marketing activities. Indicates a need to continue marketing an item, even if presumed to be successful.

deceit: in business, a fraudulent representation that misleads a person who has the right to rely on such representation as the truth or is unable to detect the fraud. Cf. *false advertising; fraud.*

decentralization:
(1) placing the decision-making point at the lowest managerial level, involving delegation of decision-making authority.

(2) the redistribution of population and business from a city to its suburban areas.

decentralized sales organization: a firm whose sales management responsibility is delegated to lower levels within the hierarchy. Primary decisions are made, not at the highest levels, but with separate divisions, with sales management duties handled by the divisions' sales forces. Cf. *centralized sales organization.* ·

deceptive advertising: advertising that gives false claims or misleading information, in addition to creating a false impression. Should retailers, on a regular basis, advertise goods and services at low prices to lure people into their outlets and then fail to have the merchandise or services, they are guilty of deceptive advertising. Jurisdiction for regulating and enforcing laws in this area is with the Federal Trade Commission. See *consumer protection legislation.*

deceptive packaging: the utilizing of packages of differing sizes and shapes that seem to contain more of an item than they actually enclose; or the item may seem significantly bigger than it actually is. See *deceptive advertising; Fair Packaging and Labeling Act of 1966.*

deceptive practice: see *deceptive advertising; deceptive packaging; deceptive pricing.*

deceptive pricing: pricing methods that deceive or confuse consumers including misrepresentation of credit procedures. See *deceptive advertising.*

decider: in the exchange process, the person who chooses an alternative that will satisfy a want or need.

decision making: in marketing and advertising, the process of resolving differing options into one opinion or course of action so that, when supported by authority, the decision becomes a policy of the organization.

decision rule: the conditions determined following a marketing research activity that urges a particular course of action within a company.

decision tree: in marketing research, a description of the sequence of decision choices and the possible occurrence of chance events.

deck panels: in outdoor advertising, panels that are placed one above the other.

declared value: the value of merchandise stated by the owner when the goods are delivered to a carrier.

decline stage: the period in a product's life cycle between saturation and abandonment. Since sales are dropping, costs are carefully controlled to minimize added losses. Synonymous with *market termination stage.*

deep stock: frequently used merchandise kept in large quantities and in many sizes and colors.

defend-and-hold strategy: investment and marketing efforts designed to maintain sales and profit levels for a particular service or product.

defensive budgeting: synonymous with *competitive parity.*

defensive pricing: a firm's strategy of pricing its products so as to protect or defend well-known items or market share (e.g., introducing a new product at a higher price than other items of the firm so as not to upset their success).

defensive spending: synonymous with *competitive parity.*

deferred billing: the delayed invoicing of a credit order buyer at the request of the seller. It is traditionally used to promote a product by offering to send it without obligation to pay.

deferred discount: synonymous with *patronage discount.*

deferred payment sale:

(1) *retailing:* a purchase made with installment payments. See *layaway plan.*

(2) *sales:* a sale that is extended beyond a customary credit period.

degree of freedom (DOF): a concept describing a person's exemption or liberation from the control of some other person or power. Often, within a tightly controlled company where the president dominates, employees are allowed a minimal degree of freedom. It is used also to appeal, through advertisements, to people aspiring to become independent and possess greater control of their destiny.

delay card: a postcard that is sent to a customer advising of an expected delay in the delivery of ordered goods.

delayed broadcast: a repeat broadcast of a program, often used to compensate for time differentials between station locations of a network. It is used especially in rural communities where the different networks share the same local station at differing times.

delayed response impact: the lag that occurs between the time a marketing expenditure is made and the time the purchase induced thereby takes place.

delinquent: see *deadbeat.*

deliverability: the extent to which an organization is viewed as being capable of actually delivering to the customer and adequately servicing a particular new product concept. The measure is an attribute of the concept, much as manufacturability is. See *manufacturability.*

delivered at frontier: in global selling, the requirement that the seller supply items in conformance with the contract, at his or her own risk and expense. The seller must place the items at the disposal of the purchaser at the named place of delivery at the border at the specified time. The purchaser is responsible for complying with import formalities and duty payments.

delivered cost: the price at which goods are billed to a store, including transportation charges.

delivered duty exempt: in global selling, an obligation of the seller to pay the costs of the goods, insurance against loss, the freight charges to get them to the named port of destination, and any duties or surcharges or taxes levied on the items by the importing nation.

delivered price: the price to the purchaser's store, which also includes transportation costs.

delivery: the transfer of possession of an item from one person to another.

delivery date: in retailing and merchandising, the date by which a vendor must ship purchases to a store in order to comply with the agreed-on terms. Failure by the vendor to meet this deadline is considered reason for cancellation of the order.

Delphi technique: in market research, a forecasting approach whereby, at intervals, the organization polls experts who predict long-range technological and market changes that eventually will affect the organization. See *judgment forecasting.*

deluxe items: higher priced, unique goods maintained for sale to wealthier customers.

demand:

(1) *general:* a request to call for payment or for the carrying out of an obligation.

(2) *marketing:* the willingness and capability to purchase goods or services.

(3) *consumer behavior:* the composite desire for particular products and services as measured by how consumers choose to allocate their resources among different products and services in a given market.

demand-backward prices: synonymous with *market-minus prices.*

demand-based pricing: a pricing technique based on determining consumers' or distributors' attitudes toward the fair cost of goods and services. Ultimately, the prices are determined by market analysis that identifies consumer needs and the range of acceptable prices.

demand creation: synonymous with *sales promotion.*

demand curve:

(1) the graphic representation of the quantity of goods demanded in relation to price. On each point of the curve, the consumer is in equilibrium and the value of the item equals its price.

(2) the amounts of the goods or services buyers are prepared to purchase at different prices during a specified time period.

demand elasticity: synonymous with *elasticity of demand.*

demand expansibility: synonymous with *expansibility of demand.*

demand-oriented pricing: the determination of the price of an item by taking into account the nature and quality of market demand for the offering.

demand pattern: a pattern indicating the uniformity or diversity of consumer needs and desires for a particular category of goods and services.

demand price: the maximum price a purchaser is willing to pay for a stated quantity of a commodity or service.

demand-pulled innovation: innovation caused or at least stimulated by the needs, wants, or desires of customers.

demand sensitivity: the speed of movement for merchandise in a retail store. See *turnover.*

demand states: varying demands that are acknowledged by marketing planners to relate marketing mix elements to target market needs. The eight demand states are:

(a) *negative demand*—when most consumers dislike a product or service and avoid it.

(b) *no demand*—where consumers are casual and indifferent toward the item or service.

(c) *latent demand*—where consumers search for a product benefit not offered by items already available.

(d) *falling demand*—where trends lower the size of the market.

(e) *irregular demand*—where time factors, including season, time of day, etc. lead to fluctuations in product usage.

(f) *full demand*—when a firm has the full market share that it had sought.

(g) *overfull demand*—where market demand is in excess of the firm's ability to provide sufficient supplies of the service or good.

(h) *unwholesome demand*—where the demand for unhealthy products or services (e.g., cigarettes, alcohol) spawns organized efforts to lower market consumption.

Cf. *latent demand; overfull demand.* See *falling demand state; seasonality;*

supply and demand; unwholesome demand state.

demand stimulation: synonymous with *sales promotion.*

demarketing: term coined by Philip Kotler and Sidney J. Levy; the concept that part of marketing attempts to discourage customers, either individually or collectively, from desiring a good or service. Synonymous with *creative demarketing.*

demo: short for demonstration. See *sales demonstration.*

demographics:

(1) the statistical breakdown of the population within a given area.

(2) a market containing characteristics that can be used for making consumer predictions. See *demographic segmentation; market demography; vital statistics.*

demographic segmentation: the most popular segmentation method; a market segmentation approach that separates the market into groups based on age, sex, education, nationality, religion, etc. Cf. *psychographic market segmentation.*

demonstration: synonymous with *sales demonstration.*

demonstration advertising: advertising where the attributes of the item are displayed or communicated to consumers; usually the item's attributes are emphasized. Cf. *demonstration commercial.*

demonstration commercial: a broadcast commercial used by a producer, advertising agency, technical representative, etc., to demonstrate talent and to obtain new or repeat work. Cf. *demonstration advertising.*

de novo basis: commencing a new business as contrasted with acquiring an existing one.

density: in direct marketing, the proportion of target customers in a particular geographical location relative to the area's total population.

denying method: synonymous with *direct denial technique.*

departmentalization: the manner in which a store is structurally divided, for example, by function, territory, product, customer, or task.

departmentized specialty store: a specialty shop that has grown in size and now carries a variety of items that are accounted separately for profit knowledge and for general decision making by its executives.

department manager: an executive charged with the operation of a selling department of a store. Often this individual is the buyer, but he or she may also be involved with stock and sales.

department store: a retail organization that employs 25 or more people and sells merchandise in the following categories: home furnishings, apparel for men, women, and children; and home linens and dry goods. See *store; traditional department store.*

dependent variable: in market and consumer research, the variable in an experiment that the research tries to predict or explain, usually by altering the independent variables. By shifting independent variables, changes in attitudes can be determined. Only one independent variable at a time is altered so that its impact can be determined. Cf. *independ-*

ent variable. Synonymous with *response variable.* See *experiment; variable.*

deposit plan: synonymous with *layaway plan.*

depot store: a store carrying popular items that customers purchase because of the store's convenient location. In most cases, the customer is charged higher prices for the items than in supermarkets, discount stores, and other nondepot outlets.

depreciable value: in marketing goods and services; the cost of an asset minus the expected salvage value.

depreciation: charges against earnings to write off the cost, less salvage value, of an asset over its estimated useful life. It is a bookkeeping entry and does not represent any cash outlay, nor are any funds earmarked for the purpose. Synonymous with *capital consumption allowance.*

depth: the number of distinct items within a product line.

depth interview: a method, based primarily on the use of open-ended questions, to elicit from the person interviewed natural and lengthy statements about a predetermined subject. Depth interviews are critical in the assessment of consumer reaction to a product or service. See *motivational research.*

depth of assortment: the variations available within a product line, such as the variety of colors of a specific dress.

depth of exposure: the degree of penetration of the advertising message into the marketplace. The greater the frequency of repetition of the advertiser's message, the greater the depth of exposure. Usually, the consumer is more likely to buy an item or service when he or she has seen or heard the advertisement many times.

depth of market: the extent of business that can be done in a market without causing a price disturbance.

depth of product mix: the number of product items within each product line.

depth of space: advertising space dimensions, usually in reference to a printed column.

derived demand: the demand for an item that grows out of the wish to fulfill the demand for another item (e.g., when a demand for community tennis courts is filled, it leads to increased sales of supplies for the courts and tennis equipment). Cf. *suggestive selling.* See *whiplash impact.*

descriptive approach: synonymous with *institutional approach.*

descriptive billing: a billing system in which an account statement is not accompanied by copies of original invoices. Instead, the statement contains sufficient detail to permit the customer to identify the nature, date, and amount of each transaction processed during the statement period.

descriptive labeling:
(1) labeling that explains the important characteristics or benefits of a product.

(2) the labeling of merchandise by characteristic, but without considering grades or accepted standards. Cf. *grade labeling.*

descriptive model: an analytical model that attempts to explain or predict factors relating to a marketing issue or problem (e.g., used to explain the impact of advertising expenditures on sales).

descriptive research:
(1) *general:* research concerned with determining the nature of something.

(2) *marketing:* research that focuses on demographic information about markets and their composition.

descriptive studies: see *descriptive research.*

design: the full sequence of activities for a marketing research effort.

designated market area: as established by the A. C. Nielsen Company, a geographic area making up a specific television market. Areas do not overlap, and every county in the United States belongs to only one designated market area.

desire set: the benefits a consumer wishes or expects to receive from using an item. It is used by advertisers in planning and buying of media.

desk jobber: a merchant wholesaler who usually becomes a middleperson and rarely takes possession of merchandise. Instead, he or she sends items directly to the customer from the manufacturer. The desk jobber traditionally is responsible for billing the customer he or she services. See *truck jobber.*

detailer: a salesperson who places vendor displays and ensures that they are stocked with merchandise.

detail person:
(1) *sales:* a salesperson who visits a manufacturer's customers and is responsible for most of the service details that encourage future sales.

(2) *sales:* a salesperson whose major task is to increase business from existing and future customers by offering them current product information and other personal selling assistance. Synonymous with *missionary salesperson.*

determinant attribute: a product characteristic that helps consumers discriminate that product from others like it and that influences product preferences. See *brand awareness; differential advantages.*

determinant gap map: a two-dimensional map that uses two determinant attributes to plot all brands in a product category. The plotting is done by an experienced analyst, not by the consumers themselves.

determining behavioral variables: see *determining factors.*

determining dimensions: synonymous with *determining factors.*

determining factors:
(1) characteristics traditionally identified with a purchasing decision. It is used often in setting marketing strategies.

(2) a set of variables that determine whether or not a consumer is a member of a particular market segment. Synonymous with *determining dimensions.*

development expense: the cost of developing products, processes, or other commercial activities to make them functional.

diagnostic information: any information obtained from the evaluative steps of a product's development that goes beyond the current evaluation to give guidance to later steps. A product use test, for example, rates the product's usefulness but also gives suggestions on packaging, positioning, pricing, etc.

diary method: a technique used to determine brands purchased and the frequency of buying. The user makes arrangements with households to keep a continuous log of brands purchased day by day over a specified period; also used to follow consumers' product buying. Cf. *aided recall.* See *Videodex.*

difference threshold: the smallest change in the intensity of a stimulus that can be noticed.

differential: synonymous with *differential advantages.*

differential advantages: selling characteristics that provide an advantage over competitors. These include price, product features, location, method of delivery, advertising skills, packaging, and brand name. Cf. *brand awareness; competitive advantage.* Synonymous with *differential.*

differential oligopoly: an industry composed of a small number of sellers manufacturing products that are only slightly different. See *oligopoly.*

differentiated marketing: a form of market segmentation in which the marketer employs different products and/or different marketing programs to reach two or more market segments.

differentiation:
(1) *general:* the process by which subunits in an organization develop particular attributes in response to the requirements imposed by their subenvironments. The greater the differences among the subunits' attributes, the greater the differentiation.

(2) *marketing:* a marketing method used by the manufacturer to create close identity in a particular market. The manufacturer will introduce different varieties of the same basic item under the same name into a particular item category and thereby cover the range of items available in that category.

(3) *marketing:* the positioning of a brand to differentiate it from its competition and thereby create a unique image. Synonymous with *product differentiation; segmentation strategy.*

differentiation strategy: see *differentiation.*

diffused demand: a demand pattern in which consumer needs and desires for a good or service category are so diverse that clear clusters (segments) cannot be identified.

diffusion model: a method for forecasting the flow of an innovation through the population. It assists decision makers in setting the timing with which an innovation can spread through the target population. See *innovation diffusion.*

diffusion of innovation: see *innovation diffusion.*

diffusion process: the manner in which a new concept evolves in a product or service, going from idea to consumer usage. See *diffusion rate.*

diffusion rate: the speed at which the diffusion process takes place. See *diffusion process.*

dimensional analysis: a technique of attribute analysis, whereby new concepts are generated from an exhaustive listing of the dimensions of products in a given category.

dimensional marketing: in direct mailing, where the promotional package's contents have dimensions, consisting of more than printed papers. A costly marketing method, these packages are usually sent to a limited list of prospects who are chosen by the advertiser's salespeople.

diminishing marginal utility law: the concept that, in a specified period, the consumption of an item while tastes stay the same can lead to increasing marginal utilities per unit of the item consumed; however, a point will be reached when additional units of consumption of the item will lead to decreasing marginal utilities per unit of the item consumed.

diminishing relative values: used in consumer and marketing research, the concept that the value to a person of item A in terms of item B declines if there is a greater consumption of item A and less of item B, resulting in a condition under which the person is no better or worse off.

diminishing returns: a possible occurrence in a firm with high sales penetration if the firm attempts to attract nonconsumers because the costs of attracting additional consumers may outweigh the revenues. Cf. *point of indifference.*

diorama: in point-of-purchase advertising, a fancy display with scenery, that is usually lighted and three-dimensional.

direct accounts: a list of the firm's customers who are serviced by home-office salespeople or executives. These accounts are rarely assigned to regular sales personnel within a territory since they are perceived as the firm's major, large-buying clients. Synonymous with *house accounts; national accounts.*

direct-action advertising: a goal of an advertisement; to have the targeted audience react immediately, with little time to make a decision. Cf. *indirect-action advertising.*

direct advertising:
(1) print advertising sent by mail to prospects, salespeople, and dealers, in contrast to advertising presented by other media. Synonymous with *direct-mail advertising.*

(2) advertising that uses person-to-person communication instead of the mass media. Nearly 10 percent of all advertising is direct advertising, with a positive response rate hovering around 30 percent.

direct buying: bypassing of the middleperson; the process of buying directly from the manufacturer. See *direct channel.*

direct cancel: a subscriber's request to a publisher, to cancel his or her subscription.

direct channel: a channel of distribution free of a middleperson. The manufacturer sells directly to the consumer. Cf. *direct distribution; indirect channel.* See *direct buying.*

direct close: frequently employed after the seller receives positive buying signals from a prospect; a closing method of the salesperson, free of persuasive manipulations, that just asks the prospect for a favorable purchase decision.

direct competitor: a company running competitively with another, offering possible customers similar or identical items or services.

direct cost: the cost of any good or service that contributes to the production of an item or service (e.g., labor, material). Cf. *indirect costs.* Synonymous with *direct expense.*

direct costing: a technique for implementing the economic theory of marginal analysis to assist a firm in making short-term promotional and/or advertising decisions. See *marginal analysis.*

direct denial technique: a method in which the salesperson, to offset resistance to a product or service, presents reasons why the consumer is incorrect. Synonymous with *denying method.*

direct distribution: where the manufacturer sells directly to industrial consumers through his or her own salesperson and/or warehouses. Cf. *direct channel; indirect distribution.*

direct expense: synonymous with *direct cost.*

direct-mail advertising: synonymous with *direct advertising.*

direct-mail list: names and addresses of potential customers, purchased by or given without charge to an organization.

direct marketer: see *direct marketing.*

direct marketing:

(1) a more personal type of promotion than advertising, the process of selling to consumers, personal or industrial, free of a middleperson. The direct marketer chooses the people who will receive his or her promotion and is the direct recipient of the responses, if any. See *direct media; direct response agency; direct sales.*

(2) a procedure similar to retail mail-order presentations, but in addition, the advertisement is usually delivered by multiple media instead of only a local advertisement or direct mail piece.

(3) synonymous with *direct selling.*

direct material: all raw material that is an integral part of the finished good and can be conveniently assigned to specific physical units.

direct media: communication channels (e.g., direct mail, telephone) used in direct marketing to bring the promotion communication to the prospect, as contrasted with media that cannot be direct to a specific person (e.g., television or radio).

directory advertising: advertising that appears in printed directories (e.g., telephone books, city directories); usually less costly than other forms of advertising and calls attention to advertisers' merchandise or services at a time when the prospect is actively seeking and ready to purchase. Cf. *yellow pages advertising.*

direct ownership: a form of international marketing company in which a firm owns production, marketing, and other facilities in one or more foreign countries without any partners. The firm has full control over its international operations in those countries.

direct package: a bundle of letters tied together, all addressed to the same office.

direct premium: merchandise given without cost with the purchase at the time of the purchase. A form of premium giving.

direct promotion: the delivery of promotional communications directly to consumers without using communications media such as television or radio. Cf. *indirect promotion.*

direct response: see *direct response advertising.*

direct response advertising: similar to direct mail advertising, except that the message is not limited to delivery by a particular medium. Its impact is directly correlated with the volume of sales. See *direct response agency.*

direct response agency: a unit of an advertising agency, or an advertising agency that specializes in the creation of direct marketing promotions. See *direct response advertising.*

direct retailing: selling items to consumers without the involvement of middlepersons.

direct sales: sources of periodical or magazine subscriptions sold by a publisher without the use of a subscription agent. They utilize other approaches including direct mail advertising, insert cards, and space advertising. Synonymous with *direct-to-publisher sales.*

direct selling: synonymous with *direct marketing.*

direct selling house: a relatively new field where the firm creates its own items and sells them directly to the advertiser through its own sales force. See *specialty distributor.*

direct-to-publisher sales: synonymous with *direct sales.*

disaggregated market: a market where buyers are significantly different from each other and no aggregates can be formed. These markets are completely segmented.

discontinuous innovation: one of a four-way classification of new items as to degrees of uniqueness; involves the establishment of previously unknown merchandise and the formation of new usage patterns based on a concept or new behavior pattern. The other three classifications are congruent, continuous, dynamically continuous.

discotetic: descriptive of the chaos resulting from continuous shifts and changes within an organization that fail to achieve a primary objective or goal.

discount:

(1) *general:* a deduction from the list price in the form of cash or something else of value. It is often used as a strategy to counter competitors' initiatives.

(2) *sales:* the selling of an item or service at a price below the normal list price. Discounts are often given in reaction to competitive advertising; other discounts are given when customers pay for their services or products in cash instead of using credit cards. Cf. *rebate.* See *bulk discount; suggested retail price.*

discount house: a retail operation, usually a no-frills store, in which prices are lower than at other stores selling the same merchandise. Synonymous with *discount store.* See *below-the-market strategy.*

discount loading: in retailing, where all inventory and purchase figures are compared on a comparable basis by predetermining all invoice prices to reflect the assumed desirable cash discount percentage. Should a purchaser be unable to secure that size discount from a supplier, the item is costed in as though he or she has been successful. The higher cost base figure traditionally results in setting higher retail prices on the item.

discount store: synonymous with *discount house.*

discrepancy letter of credit: in international marketing; when documents presented do not conform to the letter of credit.

discrepancy of assortment: the difference between the extent of choice among goods that are usually interchangeable as expected by the purchaser and the choice that is available from a given source.

discrepancy of quantity: the difference between the quantity a seller should purchase at a specific time from the manufacturer and the quantity a purchaser chooses to purchase at one time from the seller.

discrepancy of variety: the difference between the number of distinct types of merchandise that the purchaser would like a given source to have available and the number actually in stock.

discretionary costs: fixed costs arising from periodic, usually yearly, appropriation decisions that directly reflect top-management policies, as with, for example, an advertising campaign.

discretionary fund: discretionary income enlarged by the amount of new credit extensions, which also may be deemed spendable as a result of consumer decisions relatively free of prior commitment or pressure of need.

discretionary income: the amount of disposable income that is left over after paying for essentials such as food, shelter, and clothing. Marketers of items compete with these essentials to obtain purchases. During a weak economy, people concentrate on necessities and often have less for advertised goods and services. Cf. *disposable income.*

discretionary spending power: money available to consumers after necessities have been purchased. Cf. *disposable income.*

discriminatory pricing: the sale of merchandise at different prices to different customers, thus giving one party an advantage over another. See *Robinson-Patman Act of 1936.*

diseconomies of scale: considered by market researchers, situations that occur when costs increase as a business grows in size. For all firms, there is a point at which, as the company becomes larger, costs also increase. Cf. *point of indifference.*

disequilibrium: a condition in which incentives to change exist; usually used in reference to markets in which either purchasers or producers, or both, have not yet adjusted prices and quantities to their satisfaction.

dispatcher: an agent responsible for efficiently routing and sending merchandise to its destined location.

display: a visual presentation of data or merchandise. Displays differ based on their placement and type (e.g., window displays, floor displays, point-of-purchase advertising displays).

display advertisement:

(1) an advertisement that uses attention-attracting features, such as illustrations, white spaces, or colors. Cf. *classified advertising.*

(2) freestanding advertisement created for exhibition in locations with heavy traffic, such as public buildings, railroad stations, department stores. Cf. *classified advertising.*

display advertiser: see *display advertisement.*

display allowance: see *retail display allowance.*

display card: a tear-off card containing an advertisement that is affixed to a store display.

display case:

(1) *merchandising:* a carrying case used by salespeople for displaying their merchandise, as with a door-to-door costume jewelry salesperson.

(2) *point-of-purchase advertising:* a display where the item is in a closed container of sturdy material. To examine the item, a prospective customer requests that the often-locked case be opened.

display loader: synonymous with *dealer loader.* See *trade promotion.*

disposable income: of particular interest to market- and consumer-behavior researchers, personal income minus income taxes and other taxes paid by an individual, the balance being available for consumption or savings. Cf. *discretionary income.* Synonymous with *personal disposable income.*

dissociative group: of importance to market analysts, a reference group to which a person does not choose to belong.

dissonance-reduction: a postpurchase behavior occurring when the customer becomes agitated in thinking that he or she has made the wrong purchase decision; often compensated by seeking new reinforcing information on the item or service, or ultimately by returning the item or service. Marketers, in anticipation of dissonance-reduction, suggest using thank-you letters to purchasers, forwarding additional information on the product. See *cognitive dissonance.*

distinctive competencies: used by advertisers to promote an organization; activities that a firm can perform better than other firms.

distress merchandise: goods that must be sold at reduced prices.

distribution:

(1) the separation of merchandise into different categories and group levels.

(2) the process of making sure that a product is available when and where it is desired. Different forms are:

(a) *intensive distribution*—the firm makes the item available in as many stores as possible.

(b) *exclusive distribution*—one store carries the item in a given market.

(c) *selective distribution*—the item is available in a select few stores in a market area. See *channel of distribution; physical distribution.*

distribution allowance: frequently used with new items, a price reduction from the manufacturer to a distributor, retailer, or wholesaler allowing for the cost of distributing products.

distribution center:

(1) a warehouse in which the emphasis is on processing and moving goods rather than on simple storage.

(2) a storage facility that takes orders and delivers products.

distribution cost analysis: when marketing an item in a particular location, the breaking down of all direct and indirect costs.

distribution intensity: the measure of the exposure a product receives at the wholesale or retail level. With more outlets, the distribution is more intense.

distribution intermediaries: wholesalers, retailers, and marketing specialists, such as transportation firms, that are acting in their roles as facilitators between manufacturers/service providers and their consumers.

distribution model: a statistical model used to assist management in choosing and assessing the values of various distribution channels; can also help in determining store and warehouse locations and logistics for inventory purposes.

distribution planning: the systematic decision making regarding the physical movement of goods and services from producer to consumer, as well as the related transfer of ownership (or rental) of them. It encompasses transportation, inventory management, and customer transactions.

distribution shipment: a truckload of small goods that are transported at a truckload rate to a specified destination.

distribution standards: customer service standards of performance.

distribution strategy: the conclusion that marketing items through a specific channel will achieve the most economic or cost-effective results. See *channel of distribution.*

distribution structure: the sum of all the distribution channels existing within a given industry.

distributor: synonymous with *wholesaler.*

distributor brand: a brand name that is owned by the retailer, wholesaler, or other distributor instead of the producer. A private-label item is sold as a distributor brand.

diversifiable:

(1) descriptive of a project-specific risk in marketing; such as that deriving from uncertainty over entry of competitors, strikes, or technological advances.

(2) the part of total risk in marketing that is unique to the firm or asset and is, therefore, the risk that can be eliminated by diversification. See *diversification.*

diversification: the manufacture or sale of unrelated products. Major diversification strategies include:
(a) *concentric diversification*—securing items with technical similarities to its existing product line.

(b) *horizontal diversification*—where the acquired items appeal to the firm's current customers but are not directly related to the present item line.

(c) *conglomerate diversification*—where the acquiring items are completely unrelated to the firm's product line and require reaching new market segments. Cf. *simplification.* See *concentric diversification; diversifiable; horizontal diversification.*

diversionary pricing: the pricing of some items very low to give the impression that all the store's prices are low. This is considered a deceptive practice when most of the merchandise is found to be priced higher than usual for such items.

diversion in transit: in the distribution process, a service of rail carriers that permits a shipper to reroute merchandise to a destination other than the original while the items are in transit.

divest-and-exit strategy: a strategy used when an item or service fails to sell well and its overall market growth rate is slowing. To avoid or minimize losses, the firm eliminates the product or service line by selling or discontinuing it. See *product life cycle.*

divest strategy: see *divest-and-exit strategy.*

dock warrant: a procedure that affects overseas sales and merchandising; items that are imported but are not required for immediate delivery may be deposited in a warehouse, owned either by the dock authority or by the public warehousepeople.

dodger: an advertising brochure brought from house to house.

DOF: see *degree of freedom.*

dog:

(1) (slang) an advertised item that has proved unprofitable and has a dismal potential.

(2) (slang) a small business unit that has a low relative market share and is in a low-growth market.

dollar merchandise plan: an estimate of anticipated sales, frequently over a six-month period, integrated with inventory estimates and purchases in harmony with sales and profit goals.

dollar value per order: the relative measure of the performance of a promotion or mailing list, determined by dividing the total gross revenue generated by the number of orders received.

domestic-based export agent: in international marketing; the independent middleperson used in indirect export, who negotiates foreign purchases for the domestic manufacturer and receives payment in the form of a commission. See *domestic-based export department.*

domestic-based export department: in direct exporting, the part of a domestic

company whose activities are directed toward selling merchandise overseas. A self-contained unit of the manufacturer, it does not make use of an independent international marketing middleperson. See *domestic-based export agent.*

domestic-based export merchant: an independent international marketing middleperson used in indirect export who purchases the manufacturer's items and sells it overseas. See *domestic-based export agent.*

domestic-exchange ratio: the relative costs of producing two goods domestically. The exchange ratio is the opportunity cost of one good in terms of the other. See *opportunity cost.*

domestic marketing: an organization's marketing efforts in its home country.

domestic-only orientation: a marketing approach that excludes all foreign sales, both imports and exports.

domestics: yard goods from which sheets, linens, towels, and so on, are cut. Today, the term is more commonly identified with finished products.

domestic value-added: the market price of a final item, less the cost of the imported inputs that were used in the production of the item. Cf. *value-added tax.*

domicile: a dwelling; a place of permanent residence. Cf. *legal residence.*

domination: the achievement of objectives by direct command; the utilization power or influence to impose one's will on others.

don't wants: (slang) COD packages refused by the customer.

donut: a prerecorded commercial with a blank time span in its center where a special advertising message is to be placed; produced by a production firm and used by repeat advertisers whose message is basically the same, but whose product differs from time to time (e.g., a retail store features a different item for sale every week although the theme of each sales promotion is the same).

door opener:

(1) *sales:* an inexpensive item that the salesperson gives as a premium (usually house-to-house), to get the customer to listen longer.

(2) *direct marketing:* any service or item offered free by mail or with a solicitation reprinted from a publication being sold, or consisting of materials related to the publication, that is used to increase response to a promotion.

door-to-door selling: selling of a product or service directly from the manufacturer by the manufacturer's employee to potential customers in their homes or offices. This process eliminates the middleperson, with the expectation of cutting costs. See *Green River ordinance; house-to-house selling.*

dormant account: an account that has had little or no activity for a lengthy period. Synonymous with *inactive account.*

double-decker: two outdoor advertising panels built one above the other; traditionally placed in high-volume traffic locations.

double-page spread (DPS): a costly presentation, used mostly with the introduction of a new product, in which an advertisement appears on two facing pages.

When featured in the center of the periodical or newspaper, it is referred to as a center spread. Synonymous with *center spread (2).* See *double truck.*

double search: the search by consumers for products they desire and the simultaneous search by manufacturers for customers. Each party searches for the other.

double spotting: placing of two broadcast commercials back to back with no program material intervening.

double spread:

(1) two pages facing each other in a publication and bought as a unit for a single advertisement.

(2) an advertisement occupying two facing pages in a publication.

double top: in marketing goods, a price that twice reaches a high point, only to fall back. The likelihood is that the price will continue to fall.

double truck: an advertisement on a double-page spread. See *double-page spread.*

doubling day: the moment in a direct-mail promotion life cycle when half the expected returns are received.

downscale: used by consumer and marketing researchers, a derogatory term for the low-income segment of the population; often, but not always, having less formal education than most. Cf. *upscale.*

downstream dumping: of concern to international marketers, the condition that occurs when foreign producers sell at below cost to a producer in its domestic market and the product is then further processed and shipped to another country.

DPS: see *double-page spread.*

dramatic strategy: a sales approach in the opening minutes of consumer contact in which the salesperson demonstrates how the product functions. Frequently, the item or service is shown in the context of a real-life highly emotional situation (e.g., replacing a defective tire on a wintery night). See *slice-of-life*.

draw: synonymous with *drawing account.*

drawing account: a regular allowance made available to salespeople employed on a straight commission basis. The commission earned is balanced against the drawing account at various intervals. Synonymous with *draw.*

drive: see *drive theory.*

drive stimulus: a sales promotion offered in the form of a deal to retailers, sales prospects, and consumers to stimulate sales for the duration of the campaign, when the item or service is being actively advertised.

drive theory:

(1) the psychological concept that attributes action to primary (biological) and secondary (learned) motives.

(2) a strong motivating tendency that arouses an organism toward a particular type of behavior. See *motive.*

drive time: in radio broadcasting, the local commercial placed within the time period of a nationally sponsored network program. Drive time is the equivalent of television's prime time, which also commands the highest audience figures and the most costly advertising rates. Cf. *prime time.* See *day parts.*

drop:

(1) *manufacturing:* to discontinue an item from production (verb).

(2) *direct marketing:* promotion that enters the direct mail system; frequently done for a specific holiday, event, or season (e.g., advertising fur coats in early fall). It enables prospective buyers to receive promotional information before the actual buying season for such items. Synonymous with *mail date* (noun).

drop date: see *drop.*

drop-in: a local television commercial that is shown during a network broadcast (e.g., a network film has drop-in commercials by retailers). Stations can sell a prescribed amount of time for drop-in commercials per hour of programming.

drop-out percent: a relative proportion of prospects who stop making purchases or stop renewing subscriptions of magazines each year.

drop shipment: in merchandising, items shipped directly from manufacturer to retailer. It usually involves large items, such as ovens and refrigerators, that are considered expensive to retain in inventory. Suppliers of drop shipments charge a premium to retailers, who, in turn, charge such costs to consumers. The wholesaler receives only the invoice and then bills the retailer. See *drop shipper.*

drop shipper: a wholesaler who performs most wholesaling activities except storage and handling. He or she sends requests to the manufacturer, who ships directly to the customer. The customer pays the drop shipper, who has already paid the bill to the manufacturer. See *desk jobber; drop shipment; jobber; shipment.*

drumming: a traditional American style of salesperson who calls on retailers of soft goods or meets them at buying centers.

dry goods: specifically, fabrics made from cotton, wool, rayon, silk, and other textiles; includes ready-to-wear clothing, bed linens, etc.

dry testing: promoting an item that is not yet available for delivery to the purchaser so as to test response to the item prior to production or delivery of the merchandise. Failure to continue production requires the maker to issue a refund.

dual adaptation: a technique in international marketing of offering an item for export that differs from the domestic merchandise and is promoted differently overseas.

dual billing and posting: posting a customer's purchases to ledger independently from the preparation of a bill for the customer.

dual channel market: a geographic location that receives at least two television stations.

dual distribution: the sale of a product through more than one distributive system.

dual drive: the strategic combination of technology and market as sources for product innovation. Innovations are based on at least one specific technical strength of the firm and at least one specific market opportunity. Cf. *market-driven economy; technology driven.*

dual marketing: see *dual merchandising.*

dual merchandising: the offering for sale by a particular company of items made by other firms as well as itself.

dual offer: an "either-or" promotional method; increases response because customers can select from two items, and because the offer enhances the perceived value of the items.

dual pricing: synonymous with *unit pricing (2).*

dummy: a model indicating the size, shape, and layout of a finished printed product. A dummy shows clients how the printed piece should look on completion and is traditionally made for client approval before developing the mechanical art.

dummy invoice: a statement prepared by a retailer as a temporary replacement for a vendor's invoice if the latter is not available when the goods are to be received, marked, and put in inventory.

dump bind: a container to hold items as they are dumped into it from the shipping case. Only the one item is displayed in it. See *jumble basket.*

dumping:
(1) the selling of goods abroad at prices below those that the exporter charges for comparable sales in his or her own country, often involving a subsidy.

(2) in the United States, selling imported items at prices less than the cost of manufacture.

(3) selling items to other countries below cost for purposes of eliminating surplus or to hurt foreign competition. See *rules of origin; unloading.*

dumping margin: in international marketing and sales, a margin determined once a product is declared to have been dumped. It represents the difference between the home market price and the price at which the items are sold abroad less incidental charges, such as export packaging peculiar to foreign sales. See *dumping.*

duopoly: an industry containing two businesses that sell the identical items. In a duopoly, both firms exercise control.

duopsony: a market situation in which only two buyers are seeking an item. Cf. *monopsony; oligopsony.*

duplicated audience: readers, viewers, listeners who are reached more than once by the same commercial or advertisement appearing in different media.

duplication: in advertising, reaching the same person or household by two or more media.

durability: the lasting quality of an item.

durable goods: see *durable merchandise.*

durable merchandise: synonymous with *capital goods; hard goods.*

Dutch auction: an auction sale in which the prices on items are continuously lowered until a bidder responds favorably and buys.

dutiable list: of importance to international marketers; a nation's tariff law naming those items that will be subject to duty and the applicable rate.

duty:
(1) an actual tax collected; impacts international sales volume.

(2) a tax imposed on the importation, exportation, or consumption of goods.

duty-free: descriptive of items that are not affected by any customs duty.

duty-free port: see *free-trade zone.*

dwelling units: places of residence where a person, family or group of unrelated people live (e.g., single-family homes, townhouses, apartments). Marketers and advertisers use this information since residents of these dwelling units tend to purchase items and services in common.

dyad: see *buyer-seller dyad.*

dynamically continuous innovation: one of a four-way classification of new items as to degrees of their newness, intended to fulfill new consumer needs, often brought about by changes in life style or fashion. The other three types are congruent, continuous, and discontinuous.

dynamic economy: an economy of growth and change.

dynamic models: in consumer research, models that identify the behavior of variables over a given period.

dynamic research: research that emphasizes the reaction of consumers to each other instead of how they react as individuals.

E: the European Union stamp placed on products indicating that the item(s) has met with the standards established by the European Union.

ear: the space adjacent to the masthead on either corner at the top of the front page of a newspaper. In only a few newspapers do ears carry advertising. The space is traditionally reserved for weather forecasts, newspaper logos, newspaper slogans, etc.

early acceptors: synonymous with *innovators.*

early adopters: consumers who buy a product early in its life cycle and influence other people to buy it. See *early majority; innovators.*

early followers: synonymous with *early majority.*

early fringe: in television broadcasting, the time period from 4:30 P.M. to 7:30 P.M. It precedes prime time and is on the early side, or fringe, of prime time. The cost of commercials in this slot is less than prime time, but still costly compared with other time periods. The hope is that television watchers will tune into programs prior to prime time programs.

early majority: early adopters in the innovation diffusion process. A new product or concept is considered after numerous early adopters have used it and found it fulfilling. Consequently, the time required between trial and adoption may be long. Synonymous with *early followers.* See *early adopters.*

earmuff problem: a condition that develops when a salesperson becomes so involved in monopolizing the interest that incoming communications from the prospective consumer are interfered with, thus destroying the value of listening.

earned rate: the amount an advertiser pays for media space or time actually used.

E Award: a prestigious award from the President of the United States to U.S. firms and individuals for excellence in the exporting of U.S. goods and services; at times used in an advertising campaign.

EBI: see *effective buying income.*

EC: see *European Community.*

eco-audit: impacts international marketing procedures; an eco-audit applies to a company's production method and sites anywhere in a trade or regional community.

Within the European Union, any company that submits its production facilities to an eco-audit by independent environmental monitors, covering areas such as energy efficiency, waste reduction, and accident prevention, would receive an environmental logo it could use for public relations purposes. Without an eco-audit system, there would be considerable risk that widely varying national standards would develop, leading to uneven environmental controls. Cf. *eco-label.* See *socioecological view of marketing.*

eco-label: impacts international marketing procedures; use of this European Union label helps consumers identify environmentally sound products and protects them from choosing the often misleading "green labels" that business are increasingly using to market their products in response to green consumerism.

Products will be examined and graded for their impact on the environment throughout their life span by national competent officials using criteria agreed at the EU level. Only products genuinely less damaging to the environment will receive the eco-label logo. The eco-label signals consumers that the product with the EU sticker will be less damaging to the environment than others without such a label. This label is a sign that the EU is willing to use market forces as well as the law to protect the environment and is intended to counter the plethora of dubious, unregulated advertisements of products claiming to be ecologically friendly.

The standards required for such labeling would be strict and based on an analysis of a product's impact throughout its life cycle—from the raw materials employed to produce it, through distribution, packaging, use and ultimately, disposal. Cf. *eco-audit.* See *socioecological view of marketing.*

economic: any action having to do with the evolution of goods and services that are purported to satisfy a human condition.

economic analysis: in marketing and advertising, the process of gathering and evaluating quantitative information about the costs and benefits of a project.

economic environment: the interaction of all the phasas of the economy through which a marketer conducts business.

economic forecasting: used by market researchers, the employing of behavioral relations (equations) linking many variables in the economy to obtain short-term projections of the future.

economic growth rate: used by advertisers to identify markets, the percentage rate at which total annual output grows; an increase in real per capita income.

economic indicators: government or commercial indexes reflecting economic activity and general business conditions. Marketers and advertisers analyze such measures when planning strategies and decisions and when projecting the demand for items and services.

economic lot technique: of interest to marketers and retailers; an approach that describes the quantity of an item that should be made or sold at one time to reduce the total costs involved.

economic man theory: in consumer behavior, where price is the primary motivating feature in consumer buying decisions.

economic needs: consumer needs that are related with making the best use of limited resources.

economic order quantity (EOQ) model:
(1) the optimum quantity of a product to order at a given time; used by marketers in setting strategies.

(2) an inventory decision-making approach used to create a formula for determining when to order supplies and in what quantity.

economic profit: the residual profit after explicit and implicit costs have been paid. Synonymous with *pure profit.*

economic shoppers: one of a four-way sociological classification of consumers who are interested primarily in price, quality, variety, and ease in forming conclusions. They are the largest group of the four, which also include apathetic shoppers, ethical shoppers, and personalizing shoppers. See *apathetic shoppers.*

economic system: a general concept of economics and marketing principles; the way in which society organizes its resources to produce goods and services that will satisfy its members' wants and needs.

economic value: a general concept of economics and marketing principles; the value given to an item as a function of its usefulness and its scarcity.

economies of scale:
(1) the savings that result when fixed costs are spread over more units of a product; applied in marketing strategies.

(2) the result of production functions showing that an equal percentage increase in all inputs leads output to increase by a large percentage. Cf. *economies of scope.*

economies of scope: of importance to marketers; the ability of a manufacturer to offer a wide product variety at the same time significantly limiting the costs for manufacturing and then distributing. Cf. *economies of scale.*

economy pack: in merchandising, packaging whose appeal derives from the savings when several items are included in one wrapping; a form of repackaging. "Two for the price of one" is an example of a *price pack.* When featured as two related items packaged together and priced at a reasonable rate (e.g., a toothbrush and toothpaste), it is a *banded pack.*

economy size: a large quantity of an item, sold in a single very large package to provide the customer with a lower per unit price.

ED: the abbreviation for a newspaper insertion order indicating that a particular advertisement be run every day. Cf. *EOD; EODTF.*

editing:
(1) *general:* to the preparation of an author's work for publication.

(2) *marketing:* in research data analysis, the step that precedes coding and involves checking collected data for errors, omissions, irrelevancies, etc.

editorial: synonymous with *editorial copy.*

editorial calendar: articles included in a periodical's upcoming publications. They are circulated to advertisers who use the calendars in planning their periodical media buys and publicity strategies. Closing dates are indicated on editorial calendars.

editorial copy: in a publication, reading material that is not advertising. It is prepared by the staff or contributing staff of the publication, whereas advertising copy is prepared by an advertiser or advertising agency. Synonymous with *editorial.*

editorial credit: identification of a specific retail operation as the source for a fashion item featured editorially (i.e., not in an advertisement) in a consumer magazine or newspaper.

editorial environment: the philosophical premise that is the basis for the editorial concept of a medium. Advertisers consider editorial environment in selecting an appropriate medium for promoting a product or service.

editorial matter: news, information, entertainment portions of a publication or broadcast, as distinguished from the portion given to advertising.

editorial mention: promotional copy about goods that is inserted without charge in a magazine because an editor believes it has value for readers. Editorial mentions are prepared by the seller and presented to publications with the hope that they will be accepted.

EDM: see *electronic direct marketing.*

effective buying income (EBI): the measure of purchasing power that is equivalent to after-tax income. It demonstrates actual consumer purchasing power. See *disposable income.*

effective circulation: the least number of persons composing the traffic passing by an outdoor advertising display who have a reasonable physical opportunity to see the poster, painted bulletin, or spectacular.

effective date:

(1) the starting date.

(2) the date on which an agreement or contract goes into effect (e.g., the beginning of an advertising campaign).

effective demand:

(1) the combination of the desire to buy and the ability to buy.

(2) the demand by a particular market to purchase, combined with the capacity to pay.

effective protection: in international marketing of goods, the belief that the real rate of protection afforded goods by a tariff depends not only on the nominal tariff rate on that good but also on the nominal tariff rates on all goods used as inputs in its production.

effective rate of protection: in global sales, the annual percentage of domestic prices of items attributed to tariffs that raise costs to consumers, in order to dissuade them from buying imported items.

efficiency rating: the measurement of efficiency of advertising money in terms of how many dollars are spent on media to reach how many consumers. See *cost per thousand.*

effort: a mailing in a series of promotional mailings with a common goal, such as renewing a subscription.

effort scale: a system for charting the amount of effort a buyer will expend to purchase a specified item.

ego-involved items: merchandise that consumers feel has an emotional or psychological stake.

800-number (eight-hundred number): a toll-free telephone number created for a company that pays for this service, to encourage consumers to order goods and services.

eighty-twenty principle: the concept that a business gets 80 percent of its activity from 20 percent of its product line, while spending 80 percent of its energy to get the remaining 20 percent of volume. This indicates a misdirected marketing effort.

elastic demand: used in setting marketing goals; demand that changes in relatively large volume as prices increase or decrease. When a small change in price results in a greater change in the quantity people buy, the demand for the items is said to be elastic. The demand for jewelry, furs, and second homes is considered to be elastic. See *cross-elasticity; elasticity; price elasticity.*

elasticity: used in setting marketing goals; the impact on the demand for an item created by changes in prices, promotion, or other factors affecting demand. See *cross-elasticity; elastic demand; negative elasticity.*

elasticity of demand: a theory relating quantities of merchandise sold to change in price. Usually, demand for merchandise varies inversely to price, with other factors remaining constant. Cf. *expansibility of demand.* See *expansionist price.* Synonymous with *demand elasticity.*

elasticity of expectations: a ratio of importance to marketers; the ratio of the future expected percentage change in price to the recent percentage change of the price.

elastic supply: supply that changes in relatively large volume with a minor change in price.

electronic catalog: a relatively new means of marketing; the electronic, preset presentation of goods to consumers on a television screen on a preset basis. Screens can be scattered throughout public buildings or shopping malls, or shown via a consumer's own television set. Electronic catalogs are now becoming interactive, thus permitting viewers to respond electronically; most, however, remain noninteractive, requiring the use of another means, such as the telephone, to place an order. Cf. *electronic retailing.* See *electronic direct marketing.*

electronic direct marketing (EDM): an interactive unit that unites the ideas of direct marketing with television, radio, and/ or the telephone. Its purpose is to secure a direct response on the part of potential customers. Cf. *electronic marketing.* See *electronic catalog.*

electronic marketing: utilizing electronically generated consumer purchase information in marketing and sales promotion activities; used in supermarkets and other stores where information is received by having customers use computer-readable cards, such as bar codes, that log data on their product purchases. Cf. *electronic direct marketing.* See *bar code; electronic retailing.*

electronic point-of-sale system: see *computerized checkout system.*

electronic retailing: utilizing electronically transmitted data to facilitate customer shopping without having to enter the grounds of the store. It is a form of direct marketing with telephones hooked directly to home computers, television screens, etc. The manufacturer usually bypasses the retailer and sells directly to

the consumer. Cf. *electronic catalog.* See *electronic marketing.*

electronic shopping: see *electronic marketing; electronic retailing.*

eligible exporter: in overseas marketing of goods; any of the following entities that sell products or services to a foreign buyer:
(a) a corporation, partnership, or other business entity organized and existing under U.S. or state law or under the law of the District of Columbia.
(b) an individual residing in the United States.
(c) a foreign corporation, partnership, individual, or other business entity that certifies to a participating commercial bank that it is doing business in the United States.

embellishment: a device for giving a larger surface area to an advertising display by fitting over the frame and extending its borders.

emergency items:
(1) goods that numerous consumers do not purchase until needed (e.g., tires for their car, plumbing repairs).

(2) goods that are needed to solve an immediate crisis.

emergency products: see *emergency items.*

emergency rate: the rate established to meet some immediate and pressing need, without due regard for the usual rate factors.

emotional appeal: a reference to advertising copy that is prepared to stimulate a person's emotions rather than a sense of the practical. Such copy arouses fear, love, hate, humor, etc. Cf. *fear appeal.*

emotional buying motives: subjective, irrational motivation that affects consumer purchasing.

empathy: the ability to perceive how potential customers feel and what their attitudes, needs, and expectations are.

emporium: a major place of trade; a large store; rarely used today.

empowering employees: giving workers broad latitude to satisfy customer requests. Companies with this policy encourage and reward employees for showing initiative and imagination.

emulative product: a new offering by a competitor of a similar product. See *adaptive product.*

enabling characteristics: elements of a company that indirectly have an impact on the success of the company's efforts to satisfy a target market at a profit. It includes financial resources, management experience, etc.

enclosure: material, such as an advertisement or promotional brochure, put in an envelope along with the primary reason for the mailing.

encode:
(1) to convert data by the use of a code or a coded character set in such a manner that reconversion to the original form is possible.

(2) to translate a message into words and signs that can be transmitted, received, and understood by the receiver; used by advertisers in their visual campaigns.

encoding: see *encode.*

end-aisle display: a point-of-purchase display of goods that is placed at the end of a row of shelving. It is found most frequently in discount stores and supermarkets, they attract the consumer's attention and increase sales of the featured item.

end display: a display with a considerable amount of goods set up at the end of a store aisle. It can be readily dismantled.

endless chain: a prospecting method where sellers solicit referrals from consumers and then obtain other names from the people to whom they were originally referred. In order, each individual contact is encouraged to offer additional names, thus evolving a chain of referrals, going on and on. Cf. *chain prospecting.* See *lead generation.*

endorsement advertising: a strategy of employing endorsers in advertisements so as to try and convince prospects of the increased credibility of the item or service. See *celebrity endorsement.*

end-product advertising: synonymous with *subordinate product advertising.*

end rate: the lowest rate at which a broadcast station will offer time.

end run: a competitive sales strategy of a company designed to avoid a direct collision with a market leader that is well known and established with consumers.

end sizes: the large and small sizes that set the range in the line carried by stores. Synonymous with *outsizes.*

end-use application segmentation: in industrial marketing, the subdivision of a market based on how the item is to be used by the buyer.

end-user: synonymous with *consumer.*

Engel's laws:
(1) an economic theory claiming that the lower a person's income is, the greater the

percentage of it that is spent for food; of value to marketers and advertisers.

(2) a set of statements concerning the proportional changes in expenditures that accompany increases in family income.

engineering design: a function of interest to marketers, in the product creation process where a good is configured. Specific form is decided. The activity is sometimes seen as a late step in the R&D process and sometimes as an early step in the manufacturing process. The design engineering department is therefore often independent of both.

engrossing: purchasing and holding away from the market large quantities of merchandise until the time arrives when it is believed they can be sold at a higher price.

enhancement: the introduction of a new item that tends to increase the sales rates of one or more other items in the firm's line. Opposite of cannibalizing the market.

en route: on the way.

ensemble display: in retailing, an interior display that shows all items suggested for simultaneous use. These articles are referred to as coordinates.

enterprise: any entity constituted or organized under applicable law, whether or not for profit, and whether privately owned or governmentally owned, including any corporation, trust, partnership, sole proprietorship, joint venture, or other association.

entireties doctrine: in marketing equipment parts overseas, the principle of customs law permitting components, in some situations, to be entered for duty purposes under the tariff item applicable to the finished item.

entrapment method: a method in marketing research where the goal of the study is not revealed to the participant.

entrepreneur: one who assumes the financial risk of the initiation, operation, and management of a given business or undertaking.

entrepreneuring: (slang) the taking of risk in the running of an organization and an advertising agency, usually a small business enterprise.

entry evaluation: the first evaluation done after a concept emerges. It may be performed by the person creating it, but usually involves others in the immediate vicinity. It is judgmental and experience based, not determined from new data or opinions.

envelope stuffer: direct-mail advertising placed in mailings of statements.

environment: a set of forces external to the organization that the marketer may be able to influence but cannot control.

environmental analysis: as part of the situational analysis portion of a marketing plan, assessing a firm's external environment for marketing planning and strategy purposes. See *macroenvironment.*

environmental forecasting: the projecting of future events by marketers and advertisers, in order to prepare strategy programs by adjusting existing strategies to the altering environment.

environmental scanning: a set of procedures for monitoring the organization's external environment; of particular importance to marketing specialists.

environmental selling: displaying items for sale in a setting that simulates a buyer's home.

EOD: the abbreviation for a newspaper insertion order indicating that a particular advertisement be run every other day. Cf. *ED; EODTF.*

EODTF: the abbreviation for a newspaper insertion order indicating that a particular advertisement be run every other day until forbidden. Cf. *ED; EOD.*

EOQ: see *economic order quantity model.*

EOWTF: a newspaper insertion order directing that an advertisement be run every other week until forbidden. Cf. *ED, EOD, EODTF.*

ephemeralization: Buckminister Fuller's concept for increasing the rate of obsolescence of products to increase the rate of recycling of their elements.

Equal Credit Opportunity Act: federal legislation prohibiting creditors from discriminating against credit applicants on the basis of sex or marital status. After March 1977, discrimination in credit on the basis of race, color, religion, national origin, age, and receipt of public assistance was prohibited. Compliance with the law comes under the jurisdiction of the Federal Trade Commission.

equal-store concept: a growing trend in retailing; a multistore retailing agreement where, in place of a flagship store and branch stores, all downtown and suburban outlets are given equal status. Synonymous with *sister-store concept.*

equation price: a price attained by the adjusting action of competition in any market in any time, or a unit of time, such that

the demand and supply become equal at that price.

equilibrium: in consumer and marketing research, any condition that, once reached, continues unless one of the variables is altered or the change of one variable is not offset by an equivalent change in another variable.

equilibrium price:
(1) *general:* the quantity that maximizes a firm's profitability.

(2) *manufacturing:* the quantity of goods determined in the market by the intersection of a supply and demand curve.

equilibrium quantity: the quantity of goods determined in the market by the intersection of a supply and demand curve.

erratic demand: a desire for goods and services that is unstable and unpredictable over a given time period. Cf. *seasonality.*

erratic fluctuations: short-term changes that are difficult to measure and predict because they tend to be unexpected; of critical importance to marketers and advertisers who seek ways of saving money.

escalator clause: in purchasing, a clause permitting adjustments of price or profit in a purchase contract under specified conditions.

esquisse: a reduced, rapidly sketched approximation of the layout of an advertisement, providing the artist with a basic idea of the advertisement's look and tone. Synonymous with *thumbnail.*

established trends: patterns of increased demand for particular items by color, style, price, etc., as shown by consumer preference reflected in either sales or consumer research.

establishment: a factory, store, or other place of business, under the ownership of one management, located usually in one geographic area, and producing related goods.

establish the differential: publicity and sales campaigns a company uses within its budgetary capacity to take advantage of a possible differential advantage. At times, the item makes a strong impact with considerable ease; the differential then becomes established without much effort.

estimating: computing the cost of an advertising media schedule based on rate cards. Such work is usually performed in a large advertising agency.

estimator: the person in a large advertising agency whose major responsibility is to calculate the cost of the advertising media schedules.

ethical advertising:

(1) advertising directed to doctors and medical practitioners.

(2) advertising that is determined to meet standards of fairness, honesty, and equitable content.

ethical pricing: consciously holding back from charging all that the traffic will bear; not overcharging customers.

ethical shoppers: in a four-way classification of consumers, those who feel obligated to support local and small retainers because they desire their availability and because it ensures viability to the community. See *apathetic shoppers; economic shoppers; personalizing shoppers.*

ethics: a system of moral principles and their application to particular problems of conduct.

ethnic buying habits: the ways a particular ethnic group conducts its buying activities. Market strategies are often targeted to fulfill needs of differing ethnic groups.

ethnicity: a marketing approach that emphasizes the satisfactions and fulfillment of needs in acquiring ethnic goods or services.

ethnic media: media directed toward a particular ethnic group and often broadcast or written in a language known to the group (e.g., Chinese radio station). Some items or services are best targeted through ethnic media.

ethnocentricity: one of a three-way classification of the policies of companies engaged in international marketing; dealing with the exploitation of a domestic manufacturing base in order that foreign business carried out is considered marginal and incrementally accomplished via the exportation of standard items. See *geocentricity; polycentricity.*

EU: see *European Union.*

Euro-Ad: see *Euro-Advertisement.*

Euro-Advertisement: advertising prepared for consumers in member states of the European Union. They are usually similar in concept, execution, and production standards, and differ only in language (9 languages of the present 12 nations) and purport to overcome differences in culture and traditions of the 360 million people in Western Europe. Often shortened to Euro-Ad.

Eurobrand: consumer items that carry the same brand name throughout the European Union thereby involving cross-cultural advertising that attracts prospective consumers in all 12 member nations of the Community.

Eurocard: a European credit card developed by the German banking system that is accepted in most western European nations for the purchase of goods and services.

Eurocheque: a credit card for purchasing goods and services in several western European countries.

European Common Market: synonymous with *European Community.*

European Community (EC): with a huge (365 million) consumer market, of great interest to marketers; by the mid-1980s, the European Economic Community had grown to 12 nations, the original 6 followed by Denmark, Ireland and the United Kingdom in 1973, and then Greece, Spain and Portugal.

Its aims are to break down trade barriers within a common market, and create a political union among the peoples of Europe. It has its own budget raised from its own resources (e.g., customs duties, agricultural levies, a proportion of value added tax) and offers loans, subsidies, or grants through a variety of financial instruments. Increasingly, since 1993, synonymous with *European Union.* Synonymous with *common market.* Cf. *European Union.*

European Journal of Marketing: a British journal, formerly the *British Journal of Marketing,* published every other month.

European Union (EU): effective November 1, 1993, with the passage and signing of the Maastricht Treaty, the new name for the old European Community with two additions: a common foreign and security policy, and cooperation between the 12 member governments in justice and police matters.

evaluation: a step in the adoption process; a consumer's estimate of the value, quality, and reaction to a product or service. See *adoption process.*

evaluation rights: in purchasing, the authority granted executives to evaluate performance and to reward or punish on the basis of these assessments.

evaluator: in the exchange process, an individual who provides feedback on a chosen product's ability to satisfy.

even-line pricing: a strategy to give the impression of high-end retailing by assigning whole number selling prices to goods.

even pricing: see *even-line pricing.*

events marketing: a marketing strategy where events are used as a sales promotion and/or public relations activity (e.g., sponsoring sporting events, film festivals, street concerts). See *sports marketing.*

evoked set: a specific group of brands to which a consumer limits the considerations of choice for purchase. See *span of recall.*

evolving product: a product that begins as a concept, or even just an opportunity, then goes through various stages, such as protocol, prototype, pilot plan product, and marketed product.

ex-: the point from which merchandise is shipped, not necessarily its point of origin. For example, a machine made in New York and exported through the port of Elizabeth, New Jersey, is said to have been shipped "ex-Elizabeth."

excess: synonymous with *scrap.*

excess demand curve: a graphic representation of the quantity of goods demanded less the quantity offered at each price. Cf. *excess supply curve.*

excess supply curve: a graphic representation of the quantity of goods offered less the quantity asked at each price. Cf. *excess demand curve.* See *supply curve.*

exchange:

(1) *general:* when two or more individuals, groups, or organizations give to each other something of value in order to receive something else of value. Each party to the exchange must want to exchange, must believe that what is received is more valuable than what is given up, and must be able to communicate with the other parties.

(2) *retailing:* the returning of an item to a store and the substitution of another item.

(3) *marketing:* when two or more parties trade item for item, or money for item, or item for money. An exchange is finalized when parties mutually agree to conditions of the sale, decide when and where it shall occur and, usually, prepare a contract governing the agreement. Cf. *barter; swap; transaction.*

exchange commercial: the last advertisement on a program when the time is used by the alternate series sponsor.

exchange efficiency: an aspect of marketing efficiency, the completion of the trading process at the lowest possible cost with existing information on markets and technology.

exchange flow: activities within an organization that connect manufacturers and consumers or industrial users; such connections, in turn, create demand and consummate exchanges of title.

exchange functions: the buying and selling activities in the market process resulting in the exchange of title to merchandise or services. Exchange is one of the basic marketing activities.

exchange permit: in international marketing of goods, a permit required by the importer's government that enables the importer to convert his or her own country's currency into foreign currency with which to pay a seller in another country.

exclusive:

(1) goods obtainable from a limited number of stores or dealers.

(2) sales of merchandise limited to a single retailer in a given location. See *exclusive outlet selling.*

exclusive agency selling: that form of selective selling whereby sales of an article or service or brand of an article to any one type of buyer are confined to one dealer or distributor in each area, usually on a contractual basis.

exclusive dealing: see *exclusive dealing contract.*

exclusive dealing contract:

(1) an agreement that a buyer will make all purchases of a specific item from only one seller and will refrain from carrying competing goods.

(2) a method of control over distribution in which the manufacturer forbids dealers to carry competitors' products.

exclusive distribution:

(1) a manufacturer's protection of a dealer against the location of other dealers in the same area, often giving the right to sell an item to the exclusion of other sellers.

(2) an approach to distribution in which the number of intermediaries is limited to one for each geographic territory. Cf. *intensive distribution; open distribution; selective distribution.* See *closed sales territory.*

exclusive merchandise: items not available in other retail outlets in a particular market. Synonymous with *exclusives.* See *exclusive outlet selling.*

exclusive outlet selling: one retailer or wholesaler in a location having exclusive control over the sale of an article or service, usually determined by contract. See *exclusive merchandise.*

exclusives: synonymous with *exclusive merchandise.*

exclusive selling: where a supplier or manufacturer agrees with a wholesaler or retailer not to sell to other wholesalers or retailers within the same market. It can be illegal if found to be in restraint of trade.

exclusivity:
(1) *general:* restricted status of a specific story that a public relations person offers to only one news medium.

(2) *advertising:* an arrangement between the medium and advertiser to have no competing items or services advertised in the same show or issue as the advertiser's items or services. It usually requires that the advertiser buy a large amount of space or time. See *competitive separation.*

execution: an approach in an advertisement to direct attention to and involve the public with the merchandise. The execution may be looked on as being more critical than the message, and some copywriters of advertisements apply this in their approach.

execution delay: a delayed response effect created by a market expenditure in the current time period for a presentation to be made to the market at some future time.

exempt commodity: merchandise shipped in interstate commerce to which published rates do not apply.

exogenous demand: a demand for goods determined by factors outside the present economy and including exports and government expenditures.

expansibility of demand:
(1) a concept that the use of salesmanship or advertising, or perhaps both, in the promotion of an item or service brings about an increase in the total demand for the item or service.

(2) the degree to which the demand curve for a product shifts to the right by some method or because of natural forces. This implies that the market accepted more product volume at the same price. Cf. *elasticity of demand.* Synonymous with *demand expansibility.*

expansionist price: similar to the penetration price, but also anticipates the cost savings projected as possible by increased scale of production. It assumes a high price and elasticity of demand. See *elasticity of demand.*

expectation: the benefits or satisfaction that the customer anticipates following the purchase of goods and services.

expectation impact: rising prices that increase the demand for merchandise as purchasers rush to secure the item before the price rises further. The opposite may also take place when buyers put off purchasing in a falling price situation.

expected effects matrix: used by marketresearchers; a matrix of two dimensions—damage and probability. It is used to classify negative events that might take place during the launch of a new item. A high score on both dimensions increases the need for action.

expected price: the level at which a customer expects an item or service to be priced.

expected product: a generic product plus a set of features that meet additional expectations of consumers.

expected profit concept: used by market researchers; a mathematical calculation applied to competitive bidding which states that as the bid price increases, the profit to a firm increases, but the probability of its winning the contract decreases. The long-run average expected profit (loss) at each bid amount equals a firm's profit (loss) times its probability of obtaining the contract at this bid amount.

expected return: the profit that is anticipated from a business venture.

expected value: a weighted average of all the conditional values of an act. Each conditional value is weighted by its probability.

expenditure multiplier: the amount resulting from an increase in sales because of the induced spending created thereby.

expense:
(1) the cost of resources used to create revenue.

(2) the amount shown on the income statement as a deduction from revenue. Should not be confused with cost. All expenses are costs, but not all costs are expenses.

experience curve:
(1) graphic representation of the effect of experience on the per-unit cost of producing a product.

(2) a phenomenon in which costs of production decrease arithmetically as experience increases geometrically; of concern to marketers in setting profit objectives.

experience items: merchandise that a consumer tries or samples prior to purchase to assess the claims made for the item. See *search goods.*

experiment:
(1) *general:* an investigation that involves two elements: manipulation of some variable (independent variable) and observation of the results (dependent variables). See *dependent variable; independent variable.*

(2) *in market research:* the activity of testing a hypothesis so that the results will be objectively measurable and can be differentiated from extraneous variables.

expert channel: statements offered by independent experts to target customers regarding specific items or services.

expert power: the capacity to influence based on some expertise or knowledge. It is a function of the judgment of those less powerful that the expert has ability exceeding their own; often utilized by advertisers.

expire: to arrive at the termination period of an agreement, contract, or other instrument; included in signed papers between advertising agencies and clients.

expire file: a list of expired customer records used primarily for promotional activities. Marketers use these files for a few years, and then the names and addresses are purged for they are no longer considered useful.

explicit costs: costs of a company that involve cash outlays to individuals, other businesses, or the government. Explicit costs include the purchase of resources, land, labor, and capital needed in a firm's production process and indirect business taxes.

exploration state: when developing new products; the first stage where ideas for such items are either searched out or internally generated by the company.

exploratory research: within marketing research; involves the collecting of preliminary information to suggest the nature of a marketing situation and to provide ideas and useful concepts.

exploratory stage: the stage of the research process in which the problem is defined, objectives are set, and possible solutions are explored.

exponential diffusion: see *exponential growth.*

exponential growth: following the introduction of a new product, the slow, initial growth of sales as the item becomes better known and accepted. It then slows down as the market becomes saturated and the purchase becomes a repeat or replacement decision.

export:
(1) to ship an item away from a country for sale to another country (verb).

(2) to send an item or service out of one sovereign domain to another for purposes of sale (verb).

(3) an item or service sent from one sovereign domain to another for purposes of sale (noun).

export agents: brokers and others in the domestic market who sell to or buy for foreign agents or customers.

export broker: a person or firm that brings together buyers and sellers for a fee but does not take part in actual sales transactions. See *export jobber.*

export credit:
(1) financing for a domestic supplier to generate goods and services that can be exported.

(2) deferred payment terms, loans, or other financial facilities, provided to overseas buyers/importers of goods and services; affects marketer's profitability.

export duty: a tax or tariff on a nation's exports; affects marketer's profitability.

Export Enhancement Program: a U.S. program of 1985, permitting exporters to sell and market American products to foreign customers at world market prices. The U.S. Agriculture Department subsidized the difference in the world price and the higher domestic price, which exporters have to pay for the product in the form of commodities.

export finance lease: in international marketing of goods, a lease the intent of which is to transfer the benefits and risks of ownership to the lessee, and title to the asset is expected to pass to the lessee at the end of the contract.

export incentives: applied by global marketers; a subsidy or tax rebate paid by a government to firms to encourage them to export goods and services.

export jobber: a nationally based intermediary, who purchases items domestically and resells them to foreign buyers, without ever taking physical possession of them.

export license: a government document that permits the licensee to engage in the export of designated goods to certain destinations. See *validated export license.*

export management company: used primarily by small firms in marketing and selling abroad; a private firm that serves as the export department for several manufacturers, soliciting and transacting export business on behalf of its clients in return for a commission, salary, or retainer plus commission. An export management company helps to establish an overseas market for the firm's products, usually on an exclusive basis and maintains close contact with its clients.

export quotas: synonymous with *quantitative restrictions.*

export restraint: a restriction by an exporting country of the quantity of exports to a specified importing country. Usually, this is a result of a request (formal or informal) of the importing country.

export: a general principle in global selling; an item produced in one country and sold to another.

export subsidies:
(1) payments made by a government to companies that export specific goods in order to encourage them to compete in foreign markets; affects marketing profitability.

(2) government benefits made available to domestic producers of goods contingent on their exporting those items for which the benefits received apply. These include support prices, tax incentives, etc. Cf. *export support effort.*

export support effort: of particular importance to overseas sales efforts; a program, usually maintained by governmental agencies, to assist domestic exporters, and usually located in the country where the import of goods will occur. Cf. *export subsidies.*

export tariff: a tax or duty on goods exported from a country.

export value: the price at which an overseas manufacturer offers for sale a given item for export to the United States in the usual wholesale quantities, less export discounts, packing, and costs of preparing the goods for export.

ex post facto: (Latin) in marketing research, the seeking of a cause after the observations were made.

exposure:
(1) *general:* the condition of being open to loss from a specific hazard, event, or contingency.

(2) *advertising:* how often and how well an advertisement is read in a print medium, especially a magazine. For example, if a tennis club advertisement is exposed to 1,000 tennis players, it has greater value than if it is exposed to 1 million nontennis players. See *media reach; reach.*

expressed warranty: see *express warranty.*

express warranty:
(1) a statement that specifies the exact conditions under which a manufacturer is responsible for a product's performance.

(2) a seller's position statement concerning the quality, benefit, or value to a consumer of his or her goods, intended to convince an individual to make a purchase. The consumer has the right to expect the

seller to back up these statements based on the seller's express warranty. Cf. *implied warranty.* See *warranty.*

extend: to prolong a contractual obligation beyond the originally stated date of maturity or termination, as with a magazine subscription.

extended consumer decision making: the expending of considerable effort on information search and evaluation of alternatives by a buyer before making a purchase. Expensive, complex items with which a person has had little or no experience require this form of decision making.

extended family: a nuclear family plus aunts, uncles, grandparents, and in-laws.

extended item: either a tangible or intangible element that follows merchandise or service, such as a warranty, service contract, ownership prestige.

extended terms:

(1) *general:* a contractual obligation that has been prolonged beyond the originally stated date of maturity or termination.

(2) *retailing:* an additional period in which a customer may pay for merchandise.

extensible market: a market with room for growth, either by securing more new customers, or by increasing per capita consumption.

extension: see *extend.*

extensive distribution: an approach to distribution that seeks the widest possible geographic coverage.

extensive market challenges: challenges for new expansion beyond the traditional marketing and advertising campaign. For example, creating a new product line to attract existing consumers.

extensive problem solving: in consumer behavior, the time and effort taken to comprehend people's needs and determine how best to satisfy them.

externalities: the external benefits or costs of activities for which no compensation is offered. Synonymous with *spillovers.* See *market failure.*

external stimuli: external forces that influence the attitudes or behavior of buyers in the market, such as trends, economic opportunities, etc.

extinction price: the price established to eliminate as much of the competition as possible, with variable costs used as the base. See *predatory pricing.*

extraction rate: the proportion by weight of a processed product to its raw material.

extra dating: the addition of days beyond the regular date for invoice payment. Extensions are usually for 30- or 60-day periods.

extraneous items: charges for gift wrapping, special mailing, and so on, that must be removed when auditing sales to arrive at true net sales totals.

extrapolation: the estimate of an unknown value beyond the range of a series of identifiable values (e.g., projecting the world's population in A.D. 2500). Advertisers extrapolate data from audience and copy-testing information to project trends when creating future advertising.

extrinsic cues: cues that can influence a consumer's perception of a product or service, as factors separate from the item or service itself.

eyeball control: the visual examination of inventory to determine whether there is sufficient stock on hand until requested by the wholesaler, retailer, or consumer. See *inventory control.*

eye camera: an instrument for measuring and observing eye movements of people reading advertising copy; used by researchers to determine which part of the copy attracts the greatest attention as well as how strong the holding power of the sales message is. See *advertising testing.*

fabricated parts: industrial goods used in manufacturing without further changes in form; they are considered to be an expense rather than a capital item. Synonymous with *semifinished items; semimanufactured items.* See *raw material.*

fabrication: the process of converting materials into units, parts, or items. See *fabricated parts.*

facilitating agency:
(1) an organization that services other institutions but does not take title to goods.

(2) an agency that aids in the performance of some marketing function but does not own the items and is not involved in buying or selling.

facilitating activities: typically, the marketing functions of standardization and grading, risk taking, financing, and market information.

facing:
(1) a shelf stock one unit wide that extends to the top and rear of a shelf in the display. It can be used for determining the space needed for packaged goods in a retail store.

(2) the direction of a poster face as determined by the traffic flow.

facing text matter: the position in a magazine in which an advertisement is opposite editorial materials.

facsimile broadcasting: transmission of words or pictures by electronic means. Often shortened to fax.

fact finding: investigating, collecting, and making known to a specified organization the facts regarding a specific situation.

factor:
(1) *general:* an individual who carries on business transactions for another.

(2) *merchandising:* an agent for the sale of goods who is authorized to sell and receive payment for the merchandise.

factorage: the commission collected by a factor.

factor analysis: used by market researchers; a statistical method for interpreting scores and correlations of scores from a number of tests. It searches for factors that can be multiplied to give all the correlation coefficients of a test with other tests. The most usual restriction is that the factors be as few as possible to yield all the correlations.

factoring: selling accounts before their due date, usually at a discount; used by some advertising agencies.

factors: ingredients needed for the production of any good or service. The primary factors are land, labor, capital, and enterprise.

factor's lien: a factor's right to retain the merchandise consigned to him or her as reimbursement for all advances previously made to the consignor.

factory outlet: historically, a manufacturer-owned store located at the factory where merchandise is sold at greatly reduced prices. Today, it also includes the selling of top-graded merchandise, often of more than one manufacturer. Synonymous with *outlet store.*

factory outlet mall: a shopping center that focuses on offering quality, name-brand items at lower than usual prices.

factory pack: synonymous with *banded pack.*

factory position warehouse: a facility for storing merchandise, usually close to the manufacturer.

fact sheet: an informational document included in a package of sales material, providing data on the firm manufacturing the item, the item itself, etc.

factual approach: a copy approach that emphasizes technical information about merchandise or a service to indicate the logic of the benefits for which the market should purchase the merchandise or service. Synonymous with *reason-why approach.*

fad item:

(1) a short-lived fashion, usually limited to a small portion of the population.

(2) a demand pattern for merchandise or services that rapidly achieves considerable popularity but loses it just as quickly. Such goods or services have extremely short product life cycles as they rarely satisfy major consumer needs.

failure rate: the percentage of a firm's marketed new products that fail to achieve the objectives set for them. It should only be used on products that go to the full intended market target, not a trial or roll-out subset.

Fair Credit Billing Act: an amendment to the federal Truth in Lending Act that protects charge account customers against billing errors by permitting credit card customers to use the same legal defenses against banks or other third-party credit card companies that they previously could use against merchants. See *Truth in Lending Act of 1968.*

Fair Credit Reporting Act of 1971: federal legislation giving the user of credit, the buyer of insurance, or the job applicant the right to learn the contents of his or her file at any credit bureau. See *credit bureau.*

Fair Debt Collection Practices Act of 1978: federal legislation prohibiting the use of abusive, deceptive, and unfair debt collection practices.

fair market value: applied in establishing market strategies; the value an imported item would command, under similar circumstances of sale, were the goods sold in the country of origin.

Fair Packaging and Labeling Act of 1966: federal legislation requiring manufacturers of many consumer items to state clearly the net quantity of contents on the principal display panel of a package. That Act is of importance to manufacturers since they are required to meet all government labeling requirements prior to introducing a new product. Synonymous with *Truth in Packaging Act.*

fair trade: see *fair-trade acts.*

fair-trade acts: laws passed by various states by which retailers are obliged to maintain specified prices on select goods. In recent years, fair trade pricing has been withdrawn by a great number of retailers and manufacturers. The Consumer Goods Pricing Act of 1975 is federal legislation that prohibits the use of resale price maintenance laws in interstate commerce, resulting in the near elimination of fair trade arrangements. Cf. *unfair practices acts.* See *Miller-Tydings Resale Price Maintenance Act of 1937.*

fair-trade price: the retail price fixed by the manufacturer of a branded item, below which the retailer is prohibited by law from making sales. Increasingly, states are removing this form of pricing. Cf. *list price.* See *price control; resale price maintenance; retail price maintenance.*

fairy money: (slang) in advertising, a coupon used by a consumer, thereby reducing the cost of the item for the consumer, with the difference paid by the manufacturer.

falling demand state: a market situation where goods or services lose demand because of increasing social or environmental factors. Faced with this issue, marketers often attempt to restimulate sales by targeting different people, adding new promotional strategies, etc. See *demand states.*

false advertising: advertising that is misleading in a material respect, including not only false representation of the benefits or results of using the advertised commodity or its contents but also failure to reveal any potentially damaging consequences that are likely to follow from its use. Cf. *deceit.*

faltering demand: that time in a product life cycle when demand for the item or service begins to decline.

family brand: a brand that appears on two or more products of a company (e.g., Hershey Company using the Hershey name for both candy bars and cocoa; Lipton Corporation using its name for both soups and teas). Synonymous with *family packaging; umbrella brand.* See *brand awareness.*

family life cycle: the identified consumer marketing stages:

(a) *bachelor*—young, single person.

(b) *newly married couples*—young married couple with no children.

(c) *full nest I*—married people where the youngest child is under age 6.

(d) *full nest II*—married people where the youngest child is over age 6.

(e) *full nest III*—older married couples with dependent children.

(f) *empty nest I*—older married couples with no children at home and the head of the household still earns income at work.

(g) *empty nest II*—older married couples with no children at home and the head of the household is retired.

(h) *solitary survivors*—older people living alone, either retired or still working.

family of orientation: as used by market researchers, the family into which a person is born.

family of procreation: as used by market researchers, the family that a person establishes through marriage.

family packaging: synonymous with *family brand.*

fantasy commercial: a media commercial using special effects or caricatures to form a framework of fantasy about an item, such as elves who make bread, or the Jolly Green Giant on a can of peas. Fantasy commercials stress the fantasy rather than the message or the actual item or service.

farm out: to subcontract; a practice of advertising agencies.

fashion: the style that is popular within a major part of the market at any given time period.

fashion coordination: in retailing, continuous monitoring of fashion trends to assure that store merchandise is in keeping with updated style, quality, and appeal.

fashion cycle: a variation of the product life cycle reflecting the sales history of the prevailing style of consumer items such as clothing, car design, etc. It has the following cycles:
(a) *distinctiveness*—when the fashion is first sought.

(b) *emulation*—where followers seek it out.

(c) *economic stage*—when the style enters the mass market.

fast evening persons report: from the A. C. Nielsen Company, a document giving audience estimates and composition information for network evening television programming. See *day parts.*

fat budget items: merchandise approved by buyers in the hope that the goods will substantially increase sales potential.

fax: see *facsimile broadcasting.*

FCC: see *Federal Communications Commission.*

fear appeal: advertising purporting to develop anxiety within the consumer based on fear that can be overcome by purchasing a particular item or service, as often done with mouthwashes and deodorants. Another example is selling fire insurance by depicting a burned-out house. See *emotional appeal.*

feature:
(1) *marketing:* a characteristic of a product or service (noun).

(2) *sales:* a component of an item or service that yields a benefit (noun).

(3) *sales:* a product given special sales promotion (noun).

(4) *advertising:* to advertise a brand at a reduced price (verb).

(5) *retailing:* to give an item a dominant display and space (verb).

features/benefits approach: in sales, the assumption that a product's characteristics mean little to the consumer unless he or she can be convinced that it will provide a benefit. It results in the salesperson seeking a way to incorporate this message into the sales presentation.

Federal Cigarette Labeling and Advertising Act of 1967: federal legislation intended to protect consumers from the hazards of cigarette smoking; requires that cigarette packaging and advertising bear appropriate and specific health warnings.

Federal Communications Commission (FCC): a federal agency established in 1934 to regulate interstate and foreign commerce in communications by both wire and radio activity. Its jurisdiction now includes radio, television, wire, cable, microwave, and satellite. The FCC consults with other government agencies on matters involving radio communications and with state regulatory commissions on telegraph and telephone matters; it also reviews applications for construction permits and relevant licenses. Responsible advertisers are in compliance with FCC regulations.

Federal Equal Credit Opportunity Act of 1977: federal legislation prohibiting discrimination, when responding to credit requests, on the basis of race, color, religion, national origin, sex, marital status, or age; because all or part of a person's income derives from any public assistance program; or because a person has exercised in good faith any right under the Truth in Lending Law. It gives married persons the right to have credit information included in credit reports in the name of both the wife and the husband if both use or are responsible for the account. This right was created, in part, to ensure that credit histories will be available to women who are later divorced or widowed.

Federal Hazardous Substances Labeling Act of 1960: federal law establishing a list of hazardous household substances subject to stringent labeling standards. As a result, the words "danger," "warning," and "caution" now appear more often in labeling.

Federal Trade Commission (FTC): a federal agency established in 1914 to enforce antitrust laws by seeking voluntary compliance or civil remedies. The enabling legislation, which also declared unfair methods of competition illegal, was amended by the Wheeler-Lea Act of 1930. The FTC is empowered to investigate interstate and foreign commerce as well as to take legal action to enforce the laws that fall under its jurisdiction. In the advertising industry, the FTC attempts to prevent fraudulent or deceptive advertising and unfair trade practices. See *consumer protection legislation; grade labeling.*

fee: a remuneration for services.

fee basis: an agreement with an advertising agency in which the agency accepts a fixed fee for providing specific services. See *agency commission; fifteen and two (15 and 2).*

feed: to transmit a program to stations, particularly those included in the network whose key station originates the broadcast.

feedback:

(1) market data collected in the field from surveys, polls, and/or interviews.

(2) information that tells an organization's managers about the performance of each marketing program. See *advertising testing.*

fee system: a compensation method for the involved advertising agency. Under this approach, the agency estimates the total cost of its services for the entire year, and projects its hourly costs for creative media and other services. The firm will add another 25 percent to cover overhead costs and to realize a profit. Materials and other expenses incurred from employing outside vendors are to be billed at cost.

field: in marketing, the geographic location where goods or services are sold. Consumer research is carried out, via interviews with people, by sending interviewers into the field. See *field testing.*

field-intensity map: a geographic map prepared by a radio or television station to plot the location of those areas in which the station can be heard.

field person: an employee, sometimes a salesperson, who travels in a certain territory, developing new agencies and servicing agencies that already represent the company.

field salesperson: a salesperson who travels about visiting prospects and customers in their office, factory, or residence.

field testing: describes product use testing. *Field* separates this type of testing from in-house, laboratory-type testing. See *field.*

field warehousing: a method for receiving collateral pledged in business loans. The warehouseperson usually leases part of the borrower's facility and appoints a custodian to care for the items.

FIFO (first-in-first-out): relating to inventory valuations; the balance sheet figures for inventory should be qualified accordingly. That means the cost shown for the first shipment of an item is used for valuations. This could inflate or deflate profits.

:15: the symbol for a 15-second radio or television commercial, as shown on the program script.

fifteen and two (15 and 2): the usual discount to advertising agencies permitted by most media, whereby 15 percent of the gross bill is the commission retained by the agency and 2 percent of the net bill is a cash discount given to the advertiser. See *advertising agency; fee basis; net rate.*

fifty-fifty plan: in cooperative advertising, where 50 percent of the advertising costs are paid by the manufacturer and the other 50 percent by the retailer. See *cooperative advertising.*

fighting brand: the brand presented to the consumer that is intended to engage in price competition without harming the prices of its regular products. It may be a one-run offer and rarely finds a permanent place in the firm's lines.

file proof: a copy of an advertisement found in a publication for record purposes instead of for corrections.

file segment:
(1) *general:* a group of records in a file.
(2) *marketing:* the extraction of customer records from a file to establish a promotion test segment that is representative of the entire file.

filler: a short item of less than 500 words, found in the print media to fill in spaces between editorial material or advertisements.

fill-ins: merchandise secured during a period of demand to replace those already sold to avoid lost sales of merchandise that is moving well. See *running.*

final consumer: synonymous with *ultimate consumer.*

final consumer's decision process: the procedure by which consumers collect and analyze information and make choices among alternative goods, services, organizations, people, places, and ideas. It consists of six basic stages: stimulus, problem awareness, information search, evaluation of alternatives, purchase, and postpurchase behavior. Demographics, social factors, and psychological factors affect this process.

final sales: the total of net sales to consumers, governments, and foreigners. Final sales exclude sales made to producers, except sales of durable plant and machinery.

financial advertising: advertising directed to the world of investing and finance. The Security and Exchange Commission enforces strict legal rules in regard to this form of advertising. Much of financial advertising deals with promoting and building the image of financial institutions, such as banks, insurance firms, investment houses.

financial distress: difficulty experienced by an advertising or marketing firm in meeting contractual obligations to its creditors.

financial documents: bills of exchange, promissory notes, checks, payment receipts, or other similar instruments used for obtaining the payment of money.

financial position: the status of a company, including advertising agencies, indicated by combining the assets and liabilities listed on a balance sheet.

financial statement: any statement made by an individual, a proprietorship, a partnership, a corporation, an organization, or an association regarding the financial status of the legal entity.

financing: a marketing activity that includes the management of money and credit needed to obtain the goods and services desired by consumers. It excludes manufacturing activities.

finder's fee:
(1) *general:* a payment to an individual for bringing together a buyer and seller. The finder serves as an intermediary until the deal is concluded. The fee is based on either a percentage of the profit or the value of the deal, but it may also be a flat rate paid.

(2) *advertising:* the fee paid by an advertising agency to a person or firm responsible for bringing a large account into the agency.

fine: a consumer-protection legal concept in which a monetary penalty is levied on a firm for deceptive promotion.

finished art: advertising artwork that is completed and camera-ready.

finished goods: completed products awaiting sale.

finished-goods inventory: all items a manufacturer has made for sale to customers. Cf. *work-in-process inventory.*

fire sale: goods sold at reduced prices because they have been damaged or water-soiled in a fire.

firm:
(1) describing the full acceptance of an obligation to perform, deliver, or purchase (e.g., a firm bid, a firm offer).

(2) any business, corporation, proprietorship, or partnership.

(3) an unincorporated business or a partnership. Unlike a corporation, a firm is not recognized as a separate person apart from its managers; it is not an entity.

firm bidding: a policy of requesting bids for merchandise in which prospective vendors are informed that original bids are to be final, that changes cannot be accepted under any circumstances.

firm market: a condition of stable prices.

firm order: a definite order that cannot be canceled. It may be written or oral. See *firm order date.*

firm order date: the time after which an order for advertising space or time is no longer cancellable. Following the firm order date, found in the original contract, the advertising will run, no matter what the appeal.

firm price: an obligation to the maker of a stated price that must be met if accepted within a specified time period.

first-in-first-out: see *FIFO.*

first-time buyer: a customer who purchased an item or service from a seller for the first time. They are considered sound future prospects and are often recipients of promotional materials.

first-to-market: the first product that creates a new product category or a substantial subdivision of one. It distinguishes the pioneering product from those that follow.

fiscal period: often chosen by advertising agencies when billing clients; a 12-month accounting period for which business activities are reported.

fiscal policy: a planned course of action on budgetary issues.

fix: to set the cost of an item or service.

fixed assets: permanent assets required for the normal conduct of a business, which usually are not converted into cash during the period after they were declared fixed (e.g., furniture, land, buildings).

fixed charges: business expenses that are not related to the level of operations.

fixed cost: a cost for a fixed period and range of activity that does not change in total but becomes progressively smaller per unit as the volume increases. Cf. *variable cost.* Synonymous with *period cost.*

fixed-cost contribution: the portion of a selling price that is left over after variable costs have been accounted for.

fixed factors of production: those productive resources that a company cannot alter in the short run (e.g., basic plant facilities).

fixed location/position:

(1) *advertising:* space in a periodical carrying an advertisement by the same advertiser in two or more consecutive issues.

(2) *broadcasting:* the time period on television or radio for which an advertiser's commercial has been held for future playing. Cf. *preferred position.*

fixed-order period model: a method for determining the number of items to be ordered at fixed time intervals up to a predetermined maximum level.

fixed-order quantity model: a method for determining the standard number of items to be ordered when the inventory reaches a predetermined level.

fixed position: in broadcasting, the commercial delivered at a given time agreed to in advance.

fixed routing: calling on customers on a regular basis. Cf. *irregular routing.*

flag:

(1) *general:* a character that signals the occurrence of some condition, such as the end of a word.

(2) *advertising:* in outdoor advertising, a strip of poster paper hanging loose.

flagging an account: temporarily suspending activity on an account until it is brought up to date or for other relevant reasons.

flagship station: the main station of a broadcasting network.

flagship store: a downtown or home office store where executive, merchandising, and sales personnel are located. To qualify, the store must have one or more branches. See *main store.*

Flammable Fabrics Act of 1953: federal legislation banning the sale of certain items of clothes and household furnishings that present an "unreasonable risk of death, personal injury or significant property damage" due to fire.

flanker brand: see *flanker product.*

flanker product:

(1) a new product similar to an already existing companion product, with the same brand name.

(2) a new product introduced into a product category by a firm that already markets an existing brand in that category. The flanker can be of a different shape or size, but basically is the same product.

flanking: see *flanker product.*

flashback: synonymous with *cutback (3).*

flash sales report: an unaudited report of a previous day's sales.

flat: with no interest.

flat rate:

(1) *general:* a uniformly charged rate for each unit of goods and services, irrespec-

tive of quantity, frequency of purchase, and so on.

(2) *advertising:* a standard rate for advertising space or time, with no discounts given for volume or repeat times.

(3) *direct marketing:* the fixed cost for a list rental regardless of the number of names remaining after a purge is performed. Cf. *variable pricing.*

flexform: the use of a nontraditional form for presenting an advertisement in a medium; shaped in any manner.

flexible charge account: synonymous with *all-purpose revolving account.*

flexible price policy: synonymous with *variable pricing.*

flexible pricing: a pricing strategy based on the study by the manufacturer of all market forces, as contrasted with a rigid adherence to a set ratio of profit to sales. Synonymous with *variable pricing.*

flier:

(1) *general:* a handout used to promote an idea, product, or person (e.g., a political candidate).

(2) *advertising:* an advertising medium that is traditionally a single, standard-size page print on one or two sides with an advertising message; also used in direct-mail advertising and as handbill given out by retailers. Although relatively inexpensive, fliers have a high throwaway rate. Cf. *circular; handbill.* Synonymous with *flyer.*

flight:

(1) *advertising:* the length of the advertising period; usually a set number of weeks, followed by a period of inactivity, which is often reactivated. Each

activity period is called a flight. See *flight saturation.*

(2) *broadcasting:* the length of time an advertiser runs spots in a broadcast medium when the total period is less than 52 weeks, as in a winter flight, or November flight.

flighting strategy: a media scheduling strategy in which there is heavy advertising during some parts of the campaign and no advertising in between.

flight saturation:

(1) maximum concentration of spot advertising in a relatively short period.

(2) a heavy concentration of advertising during a flight, when the medium has become saturated with an advertising message and therefore additional advertising not only will have no positive impact but may have a negative effect on the marketplace. See *flight; saturation; spot advertising.*

float:

(1) *general:* the amount of funds in the process of collection.

(2) *retailing:* variations in the placement of a label on a form.

(3) *advertising:* placing of a space advertisement in an area larger than needed to accommodate the dimensions of the advertisement.

(4) *advertising:* funds given to an advertising agency by an advertiser that may be invested or otherwise used, prior to its delivery to the media owners for which it is targeted.

floatation (flotation): a method of interior packaging to protect a packed item from shock and vibration by wrapping it in a cushioning substance thick enough that the wrapped shape of the item conforms to the dimensions of the container.

floor limit: the largest amount for which a merchant may accept noncash payment (check or credit card) without obtaining an authorization. A zero floor limit calls for authorization for every transaction, and this is becoming more feasible as the time and cost of obtaining authorization decline. See *negative authorization.*

floor plan financing: short-term financing of big-ticket items, where the retailer borrows funds and pays the vendor for the goods at time of receipt. The lending institution that has loaned the money retains title to the items as collateral and is repaid by the retailer once the merchandise is sold.

floor price: in the marketing of goods and services; the minimum price. Normally, it cannot be further reduced, due to economic, political, or trade reasons.

floor pyramid: in retailing, a point-of-purchase advertising display where products for sale are piled in the shape of a step pyramid, usually within arm's reach.

floor stand: a rack, frame, or mounting used by retailers for goods in a point-of-purchase advertising display.

floor stock: items accessible to customers within the store. Cf. *shelf stock.* See *back-up merchandise.*

floorwalker: a person who moves about a store through various selling departments and assists customers in ways not handled by sales personnel.

flop: (slang) an failed effort, such as an unsuccessful advertising program or a broadcast that has disappointed its audience.

flow chart: see *flow process chart.*

flow process chart: utilized by consumer and marketing researchers; a graphic approach used for the classification and analysis of organizational activities in terms of the various individual operations, transfers, inspection points, and storages, so as to make these activities as feasible, economical, and efficient as possible.

fluctuating demand: in industrial marketing, the haphazard demand for goods and services; usually less stable than demand for consumer goods and services.

fluff: in broadcasting, a minor error while on the airwaves.

flyer: synonymous with *flier.*

flying squad: seasoned salespeople able to move freely, as needed, to work throughout a store's system; employees who go from branch to branch.

FOB: free (freight) on board. Identifying the point from which a store is to pay transportation on incoming shipments. When the terms are FOB shipping point, the store must pay all charges from the vendor's shipping point. When the terms are FOB store, the vendor must pay all charges up to the store's receiving dock. See *FOB pricing.*

FOB pricing: a geographic pricing policy in which buyers pay transportation costs from the point at which they take title to the product. See *FOB.*

focus: a subject, concept, or issue that is the center of attention; of value to advertisers in setting strategies.

focused market unit: a market-oriented division that services potential customers regardless of their location.

focus group: a form of personal interview in which a group of 8 to 12 people are brought together, usually in a studio where they can be properly monitored and often videotaped for future study, to offer their views on an issue, idea, or product.

focus of sale: a benefit or claim about an item or service that is emphasized in the advertising and toward which a prospect is directed by the advertising agency.

folder: a large, direct-mail advertisement, folded more than once, forming a leaflet. It is usually a self-mailer. Synonymous with *leaflet.*

following, next to reading matter: an order for placement of advertisements in a periodical; indicates a position that is either totally flanked by reading matter or located at the top of the page and alongside reading matter.

follow-up: a step in a marketing strategy after the implementation of an advertising campaign or promotion or the introduction of a new item, to evaluate the results.

follow-up letter: a letter that is never-mass mailed; a sales communication sent to someone who has made an inquiry inviting the prospect to make a purchase; generally reserved for expensive merchandise.

Food and Drug Administration: a U.S. agency established in 1930 by federal legislation (now part of the Department of Health and Human Services) to develop standards and conduct research with respect to reliability and safety of drugs. It evaluates new drug applications and claims for drugs, conducts clinical studies on the safety of drugs, operates an adverse drug reaction reporting program, maintains a nationwide network of poison control centers, and advises the Justice Department on the results of its research. See *Food, Drug, and Cosmetic Act of 1938.*

food broker: a person who introduces buyers and sellers of foods and related general-merchandise items to one another and brings them together to complete a sale.

Food, Drug, and Cosmetic Act of 1938: federal legislation that strengthened food labeling requirements and extended strict requirements to advertising and labeling of cosmetics. The Act requires that drug advertising and labels include "all material facts" about a drug. See *Food and Drug Administration.*

forced relationships: in marketing research, a concept generation technique that stimulates creativity by bringing two or more separate things together. The items are unrelated, and the mere combining of them shows new and unexpected patterns.

forced saving: the situation that occurs when consumers are prevented from spending a portion of their income on consumption.

forcing style: of importance to consumer analysts; the tendency to use coercive and reward power to dominate another person by suppressing differences and requiring the adoption of one's own position.

forecasting: of critical importance to market researchers for goal setting; projecting events of the future utilizing current data. See *predictive research; sales forecast.* Synonymous with *projection.*

forecasting model: a model for predicting the sale of goods or services, market share levels, and other related variables.

foreign: in advertising, a newspaper advertisement placed by an advertiser located outside the area in which the paper is usually sold.

foreign national pricing: local pricing in another nation.

foreign sales agent (FSA): an individual or firm that services the foreign representative of a domestic supplier and seeks sales abroad for the supplier.

foreign-trade zone (FTZ): synonymous with *free-trade zone.*

forestall:

(1) to dominate the supply by purchasing up items on the way to the market, thus allowing the merchant to obtain a higher price.

(2) to anticipate resistance from the prospect, thereby permitting a reply in the presentation dealing with the buyer's concern.

forfeiting: the purchase, without recourse, of receivables from the export sales of items.

forfeiture: the automatic loss of cash, property, or rights, as punishment for failure to comply with legal provisions and as compensation for the resulting losses or damages.

forgetting rate: the rate at which memory of an advertisement is lost from one advertising period to another without prolonged reinforcement. The forgetting rate plays a large role in developing advertising strategies. Ideally, an effective strategy contains minimal or no forgetting.

form: in marketing, the physical state of goods, as with liquid or solid gas.

formal balance: advertisements having all the elements in it of equal optical weight at all point vertically pairs on opposite sides of a line drawn from top to bottom through the center of the advertisement. Synonymous with *symmetrical balance.*

form analysis: the method and practice of examining and analyzing organizational forms, charts, documents, and other records to discover the most appropriate way of facilitating procedures.

format:

(1) *general:* an arrangement of data.

(2) *broadcasting:* the style or content of material used by a radio or television program, such as musical, talk show, etc. Synonymous with *personality.*

former purchaser: a customer who has not bought additional goods within a specified time period, traditionally one year. In general, they represent future potential sales in that they have shown an ability to buy merchandise.

forms close: synonymous with *closing date.*

formula pricing: a pricing technique in which the final price is set using a formula.

form utility: the characteristic of merchandise that makes it possible to fulfill a consumer's needs when processing is altered to put it into a more useful form. See *utility.*

fortuitous scan: a class of concept-generating techniques not based on the problem find/solve route. The techniques are many, usually logical, and tend to make variations in products currently on the market.

forward buying: committing bought items to provide for needs during a time period longer than is needed for immediate gratification.

forward integration: a marketing system where the producer owns or controls the distribution channels through which his or her goods pass as it approaches prospects. See *integration.*

forward invention: the development of new goods for overseas markets.

forward market segmentation: the identification of segments of a population using race, age, education, psychological characteristics, etc.

forward order: a commitment to accept merchandise to be delivered at a later time.

forward stock: stock that is brought into the selling department. Cf. *shelf stock.* See *inventory.*

foul-weather pricing: selling an item without profit, at times not even covering costs of production and advertising; used to keep a firm in operation during recession.

fourchette: in international sales of farm items, the higher and lower price levels between which member nations must operate their agricultural prices. It was first introduced for cereals.

four Os: primary characteristics of a market. They are objects—what was purchased; objectives—why the item or service was purchased; organization—who was the buyer; and operations—how the buyer operated. Cf. *four Ps.*

four Ps: primary characteristics of a marketing mix. They are product—the right one for the target market; place—all considerations and institutions involved in getting the correct item to the target market; promotion—communication to the target market about the merchandise; and price—determination of the price that will best attract buyers so as to make a profit. Cf. *four Os.* See *marketing mix.*

fourth cover: synonymous with *back cover.*

fractional page advertisement: a print advertisement that occupies only a part of the page (⅛, ¼, or ½), as distinguished from a full-page advertisement.

fragmentation: the identification and then division of the total market into units with common characteristics, interests, and needs. Cf. *segmentation.*

frame of reference: a sociological-psychological interpretation of how a person perceives his or her external environment. A significant portion of consumer behavior is based on an individual's frame of reference.

franchise:

(1) a privilege granted to a dealer for distribution of a manufacturer's product.

(2) a legal contractual relationship between a supplier and one or more independent retailers. The franchisee gains an established brand name and operating assistance, while the franchisor gains financial remuneration as well as some control over how the business is run.

(3) specific territory or outlet involved in such a right. See *refusal to sell.*

franchised dealer: a retail dealer who, under terms of a franchise agreement carries a supplier's products.

franchisee: see *franchise.*

franchiser: see *franchisor.*

franchise extension: a new product that capitalizes on a firm's market strength. A franchise is a strength of relationship with customers and may be based on a brand, a sales-force relationship, a favorable trade relationship, etc. The new item is often not unique but sells based on the favorable franchise.

franchise store: an independently owned store that sells branded items produced by a franchise holder. The store pays the franchisor a percentage of sales for the use of the name.

franchise wholesaling: a full-service merchant wholesaling format whereby an independent retailer affiliates with an existing wholesaler to use a standardized storefront design, business format, name, and purchase system.

franchising: see *franchise.*

franchisor: an individual or company that licenses others to sell its products or services. See *franchise.*

fraud: intentional misrepresentation of the truth to deceive another person. Aspects of fraud include the false representation of fact, made with the intent that the deceived person act thereon; knowledge that the statement would deceive; and knowledge that the person deceived acted, leading to his or her injury. See *bad faith; deceit; voidable contract.*

free and open market: a market in which the supply and demand are freely expressed in terms of price as contrasted with a controlled market, in which supply, demand, and price may all be regulated.

free association: used by some creators of advertising; the first thought entering a person's mind when presented with a given word. It is used in advertising research to determine a person's awareness of and attitude toward a given item, service, concept, or firm. Synonymous with *word association.*

free carrier: similar to free on board, except that the seller fulfills his or her obligations when the merchandise is delivered into the custody of the carrier at the named point. Cf. *FOB.*

free examination offer: synonymous with *trial offer.*

free goods: items that are so abundant that it is not profitable to attempt to charge for them (e.g., sunlight).

free goods offer: merchandise received at no cost by a buyer who purchases some other unit of goods. Cf. *giveaway.*

freelance: an independent person, including one who does advertising, and receives assignments from a firm, but is not its employee.

freelancer: see *freelance.*

freely offered: the concept that merchandise will be offered in the normal course of trade to all buying on essentially the same basis.

free on board: see *FOB.*

free on rail: the price of goods that includes the cost of moving them to a railhead for shipment and loading into a railroad car.

free on truck: the price of goods that includes the cost of moving them to a truck for shipment and loading onto a truck.

free samples: the easiest way to get a prospect to try an item. It is expensive and usually used with high-volume merchandise; a popular sales promotional method for new product introductions.

freestanding stuffer: synonymous with *newspaper stuffer.*

free trade: a preferred ideology of marketers; trade among countries in the absence of policy restrictions that may interfere with its flow. Cf. *managed trade.*

free-trade agreement (FTA): of importance to marketers; a means for lowering tariffs of exported merchandise; a comprehensive agreement design to remove barriers to substantially expand all trade through eliminating tariffs and quotas, enhancing market access, improving standards for treatment of investors, etc.

FTAs cover virtually every aspect of trade between signatories. They purport to remove all significant barriers to trade in goods and services. Under free-trade agreements, firms will be able to make decisions based on their market advantage, rather than on arbitrary tariff and nontariff barriers. See *free-trade zone.*

free-trade zone: of importance to global marketers; a port designated by the government of a country for duty-free entry of any nonprohibited goods. Merchandise may be stored, displayed, used for manufacturing, and so on, within the zone and reexported without duties being paid. Duties are imposed on the merchandise (or items manufactured from the merchandise) only when the goods pass from the zone into an area of the country subject to the customs authority. Synonymous with *foreign-trade zone.*

free trial offer: synonymous with *trial offer.*

freight: all merchandise, goods, products, or commodities shipped by rail, air, road, or water, other than baggage, express mail, or regular mail.

freight absorption:
(1) charges paid by the seller rather than the customer for freight outward.

(2) a geographic pricing policy in which the seller charges the same freight rate as the competitor located nearest to the buyer. See *mill net return.*

freight allowed: an agreement whereby a store pays the transportation charges on incoming goods but is permitted to charge back all or part of that cost to the vendor. Synonymous with *postage stamp pricing.*

freight equalization: see *unsystematic freight equalization.*

freight forwarder:
(1) a transportation company that pools many small shipments to take advantage of lower rates, passing some of the savings on to the shippers.

(2) an organization that consolidates the less-than-carload or less-than-truckload shipments of manufacturers into carload or truckload shipments. Synonymous with *make-bulk center; package consolidating agency; packing house.*

freight inward: freight paid on shipments received.

freight on board: see *FOB.*

freight outward: freight paid by a seller on outgoing customer shipments. See *freight absorption.*

freight paid to: freight charges based on the seller forwarding the goods at his or her own expense to the agreed destination and taking responsibility for all risks of the goods until they are delivered to the first carrier.

frequency:
(1) *general:* the number of cases in a class or other subdivision of a group.

(2) *advertising:* the number of times an advertisement is delivered within a set time period.

(3) *advertising:* the average number of times that the average prospect will be exposed to a specific advertisement in a specified period. See *reach.*

frequency discount: a reduction in advertising rates based on the number of insertions or broadcasts used in a given time period.

frequency distribution: used by market researchers; the categorization of statistical information according to size or magnitude, with the number of items (frequency) applicable to each interval.

friend-of-a-friend promotion: a promotional method that offers established customers incentives (e.g., a free gift) for referring to the seller names of people who might be interested in securing the product or service. Cf. *member-get-member promotion.*

fringe area: in broadcasting, the outer listening or viewing area. Within miles close to the fringe area, reception is lost or becomes static.

fringe market: that segment of a firm's customers who are outside the firm's core market and who frequent the firm on an occasional basis.

fringe time: time slots when there are relatively few people in the audience to receive an advertisement. See *prime time.* Synonymous with *transition time.*

front: in retailing, the selling area of the store.

front end: in retailing, where store buyers pay for their merchandise.

front load: a scheduling of the bulk of an advertising budget for a given time period in the early days or weeks of an advertising campaign.

FSA: see *foreign sales agent.*

FTA: see *free-trade agreement.*

FTC: see *Federal Trade Commission.*

FTC rule: see *30-day delayed delivery rule.*

FTZ (foreign-trade zone): synonymous with *free-trade zone.*

fulfillment: processes for receiving, servicing, and tracking orders sold via direct marketing. They include subscriptions, book club orders, catalog items, fund raising. Fulfillment systems are designed to fill orders rapidly, maintain customer files, sent invoices and record payments, react to customer complaints and other inquiries, and to produce purchase and payment information to be used in future marketing programs. See *customer service.*

fulfillment system: see *fulfillment.*

full-cost approach: used by advertising agencies in setting pricing policies; an approach to cost analysis that takes both direct and common costs into consideration. Cf. *full-cost pricing.*

full-cost pricing: the practice that includes all appropriate manufacturing costs in determining inventory. Cf. *full-cost approach.*

full demand: the desire and ability of buyers to purchase all the items that are being manufactured.

full disclosure: the provision of total information to consumers regarding merchandise and services. It is found on labels of products and in advertisements.

full-function wholesaler: see *full-service wholesaler.*

full line: goods in all styles, sizes, colors, etc. that a customer can reasonably expect to find in a store.

full-line discount store: a department store with lower prices, a broad merchandise assortment, a lower-rent location, more emphasis on self-service, brand-name merchandise, wide aisles, shopping carts, and more merchandise displayed on the selling floor. Synonymous with *promotional department store.*

full-line forcing: urging the customer to purchase the least desirable item of a seller's line in order to secure the more desirable goods. See *cherry picking.*

full mark: a 100 percent markup in goods.

full position: in a newspaper page, the space occupied by an advertisement so placed that it appears at the top of the column with editorial matter along one side or placed so that editorial matter appears directly above it and along one side.

full run: a request for advertising to be inserted in all editions of a newspaper that are put out on any one day. To advertise on a full run is to advertise in all editions of a newspaper, even those of different regional editions. See *full showing.*

full sale: a class of market testing techniques where the marketing is complete and in the mode that would be used to launch. There are no limitations on distribution, advertising, etc., unless planned in launch. See *launch.*

full screen: a screening stage where all preliminary work is finished, a scoring model is usually used, and a favorable assessment is followed by a preliminary business analysis that releases the concept to development.

full-service agency: an advertising agency that will handle all the client's advertising needs, such as developing, production, and placement of an advertisement. Such agencies offer total service in both advertising and nonadvertising activities, from preparation and placement, to dealing in production and preparation of annual reports, exhibits at trade shows, and useful sales training materials. See *advertising agency*.

full-service wholesaler: a wholesaling middleperson who takes title to goods that are resold, and frequently takes physical possession of the items. Such people often operate warehouses, extend credit, and assist customers with accounting and marketing data. Cf. *limited-service wholesaler*. Synonymous with *service wholesaler*.

full showing:

(1) a 100 percent (full) display of outdoor advertising.

(2) the purchase of all the outdoor advertising positions in a particular area for an advertising display for a specific time period, usually 30 days. It suggests that 100 percent of the population in a community pass by the advertising at least once on any day.

functional costing: classifying costs by allocating them to the various functions performed (warehousing, delivery, billing, etc).

functional discount: a deduction taken to effect different prices for different customers (e.g., retailers get 40 percent off the list price, wholesalers 40 to 50 percent off) Cf. *price discrimination.* Synonymous with *trade discount.*

functional manager: a manager who is responsible for a specialized area of operations, such as marketing.

functional matrix: an organization option in which the matrix leans toward the functions. Participants have dual reporting relationships, but the functional reporting is intended to dominate thinking and action.

functional middleperson: an independent business that assists in the passing of title to merchandise without taking title to the items in the process. Synonymous with *agent; middleperson.*

functional obsolescence: considered in preparing an advertising campaign; obsolescence created by structural defects that reduce a property's value and/or market ability. Cf. *planned obsolescence; product development.* See *weakest link theory.*

functional satisfaction: the satisfaction received from the tangible or functional features of a product.

functional spin-off: in an established market channel relationship, the agreement of each member to fulfill specific activities based on expected cost structures.

functional standards: standards that provide needed selections from the range of options in the use of international standards, and do so in a harmonized way.

functions of exchange: the marketing functions of buyer and seller.

functions of physical supply: the marketing function of distribution, transportation, and warehousing.

Fur Products Labeling Act of 1951: federal legislation protecting the public against false labeling and advertising of furs.

further processing method: synonymous with *superdeductive method.*

future shock: considered in advertising efforts, especially targeted for senior citizens; coined by Alvin Toffler to describe people's problems in dealing with rapid changes in society, including fads in lifestyles.

GAFF (GAFFO): abbreviations for a store category including the *g*eneral merchandise, *a*pparel and accessories, and *f*urniture and home *f*urnishings and appliances stores.

GAFFO: see *GAFF.*

gain opportunity: the difference between a company's goal in a market and its actual sales.

galvanometer: one of numerous measuring instruments used to determine advertising effectiveness. Perspiration on the palm can be measured as an emotional reaction to advertisements.

game plan: any strategy designed to achieve organizational goals.

game theory: used by advertisers; a mathematical process used for choosing an optimum strategy when faced by an opponent who has a strategy of his or her own.

Gamma test: a product use test wherein the developers measure the extent to which the item meets the needs of the target customers, solves the problem(s) targeted during the development, and leaves the customer satisfied. Cf. *Alpha test; Beta test.*

gap analysis: a category of techniques based on the idea that if one can position all of a market's products onto a two-dimensional chart, they will not be spread around. Instead they will clump in some places and be void in others. Any void (gap) thus offers an opportunity for a new product. The charting uses x- and y-axes and plots against such attributes as price, strength, speed, and ease of use.

gatefold: a magazine or periodical page of extended size that is folded over and reinserted. Gatefolds are expensive and are primarily used for introducing new products.

gathering: the collation of promotional package components prior to inserting into an outer envelope.

gender analysis: separating names on a mailing list into male and female categories; especially useful to marketers when promoting products and services meant for one sex more than another, such as shaving cream, cosmetics.

general acceptors: synonymous with *late majority.*

general advertising: national or nonlocal newspaper advertising.

general export license: any of various U.S. export licenses covering export commodities for which validated export licenses are not required. No formal application or written authorization is needed to ship exports under this license.

general line distributor: an industrial distributor called a general line wholesaler. Synonymous with *general line house.* See *general line wholesaler.*

general line house: synonymous with *general line distributor.*

general line retailer: a retailer who carries a wide range of products.

general line wholesaler:

(1) a merchant wholesaler who carries merchandise in a host of unrelated lines.

(2) a full-service wholesaler who carries a wide variety of product lines.

general merchandise retailer: see *general line retailer.*

general merchandise store: a retail operation with a wide variety of items.

general merchandise wholesaler: see *general line wholesaler.*

general rate: synonymous with *one-time rate.*

general sales manager: the sales executive responsible for complete coordination of the firm or division's sales force. Although he or she will not traditionally set policy, developing strategies and methods to fulfill the firm's marketing plan is a major responsibility along with supervisory involvement.

general sales tax: a tax on most items, collected at the time of purchase. In many states, purchases of food and medicine are excluded from this tax.

general store: a small retailing operation, not departmentalized, often found in rural areas, where a wide variety of items can be bought, including food, clothing, and supplies.

generic advertising: synonymous with *primary advertising.*

generic appeal: advertising appeal on behalf of a product category where no mention is made of a particular brand name (e.g., advertising that encourages the use of plastics). Its primary purpose is to make the public aware of the product category.

generic brand: an unadvertised, plain-label grocery item that often sells for 30 to 40 percent less than advertised brands. Packaging tends to be sparse, with only the generic product name and required governmental labeling information given. See *branding; generic product.*

generic competitor: an organization that competes with others to satisfy consumers' wants or needs within a general category of products or services.

generic market: a market where vendors offer substitute items that are different perceptually and physically.

generic name: a brand name that has become associated with a product category rather than with a particular brand.

generic product:

(1) an item sold under a common name rather than a brand name.

(2) not the product itself, but a concept that incorporates the hopes the purchaser has for the item.

(3) a set of tangible or intangible attributes that are assembled into an identifiable form. See *generic brand.*

geocentricity: one of the three-way categories of the policies of firms active in international marketing; focuses on the techniques of understanding the economic, cultural, and legal conditions among nations that are included in the global target, and the means by which they can be managed. See *ethnocentricity; polycentricity; regiocentrism.*

geographic demographics: the basic identifiable characteristics of towns, cities, states, regions, and countries.

geographic hole: the absence of a global corporation from an important regional area of the world. Such an absence is harmful to the globalization of the firm's market offerings.

geographic pricing: a system for outlining the responsibility for transportation charges. The basic forms of geographic pricing are free on board (FOB), mill pricing, uniform delivered pricing, zone pricing, and base-point pricing.

geographic segmentation: where the target market is divided by world regions, population density, city size, etc. By doing this, a firm takes into account the varying consumer preferences in different locations.

geographic skew: where the advertiser, resulting from inadequate knowledge of the market, significantly overspends in one area and underspends in another.

getting by: a frugal consumer life-style that people usually pursue because of their economic circumstances.

giant insert: synonymous with *newspaper stuffer.*

Giffen good: see *inferior goods.*

gift close: a salesperson's closing method, in which the prospect is offered an incentive to buy the item or service immediately. Usually a service (e.g., shipping the same day) is the "gift" rendered, not a hard item as suggested by the term. Cf. *gift with purchase offer.* See *close.*

gift with purchase offer: an advertising incentive program that provides a premium with the buying of a service or good; frequently used in direct-response promotions as with direct-mail advertising. Cf. *gift close.*

gimmick:
(1) *general:* any clever idea or device.

(2) *advertising:* an attention-getting device used to promote an item or service; can be clever wording in the copy, a different type of display, or any other unusual form of promotion for an item or service. Cf. *giveaway.* See *hook.*

giveaway:
(1) a premium available without charge. Cf. *free goods offer.*

(2) the award of prizes to studio contestants, radio listeners, or television viewers. Cf. *gimmick.*

global approach: synonymous with *standardized approach.*

global firm: a firm that markets a standardized item worldwide and permits only minimum adaptations to local conditions and tastes from one country to another. Its marketing, and advertising strategies are global with little differentiation among nations or areas as to product.

globalization: the tendency for markets to expand across national boundaries, leading to increasing competition among firms from different nations and a growing dependence on diverse multinational and multicultural customer bases.

global marketing:
(1) the goal of a multinational firm to achieve long-run, large-scale production efficiencies by producing standardized products of sound value and long-term reliability in every segment of the market.

(2) the marketing of a standardized product worldwide with little allowance for, or acceptance of, regional or local differences. Cf. *international advertising*. See *Euro-ad; Eurobrand*.

global quotas: explicit limits set by one country on the value or quantity of merchandise that may be imported or exported through its borders during a given period on a global basis.

glut: to oversupply.

goal: an objective or something specific to be achieved.

godown: in the Far East, a commercial storage warehouse. See *warehouse, commodity*.

going-rate pricing: applying the average price level charged by the industry to determine the price charged by the firm. Synonymous with imitative pricing.

golden circle: a group of brands in a particular product field, all of which are equally acceptable to consumers.

gondola: in retailing, a merchandise display stand; a bank of freestanding shelves open on all sides.

good: see *goods*.

Good Housekeeping Seal: a seal of approval of a product that meets the standards of *Good Housekeeping* magazine. The magazine, to protect consumers, will license an advertiser's use of the seal but will set limits on the ways it is used. Since the public recognizes and trusts this seal, it provides a seemingly independent endorsement of a product's safety and quality, leading to the belief that using the seal in advertising will enhance sales of the product.

goods:
(1) the result of industrial work, equaling the gross national product for one year.

(2) any movable personal property, excluding livestock and excluding intangible property such as leases. Cf. *merchandise; product*.

goods in free circulation: merchandise not subject to customs restrictions.

goods marketing: marketing that entails the sale of physical products.

goods on approval: items obtained when a potential buyer requests and receives from a seller the right to examine the products for a stated time period before deciding whether to purchase them.

goods-services continuum: visualizing the distribution between objectives and services. The continuum is shown graphically as a spectrum with pure goods at one extreme (e.g., a bottle of hair conditioner), and a pure service at the other extreme (e.g., a haircut). The continuum shifts gradually from the tangible to the intangible.

good 'til canceled order (GTC): an order to buy or sell that remains in effect until it is either executed or canceled. Synonymous with *open order*.

good will: the intangible possession that enables a business to continue to earn a profit in excess of the normal or basic rate of profit earned by other businesses of similar type.

gouge: (slang) to acquire an excessive profit by either overcharging or defrauding.

government-controlled price environment: characterized by prices being set or strongly influenced by some level of government.

government market:
(1) that portion of the industrial market within the public sector, including all levels of government.

(2) a set of federal, state, country, or local agencies that buy goods and services for use in meeting social needs.

government procurement policies and practices: the means and mechanisms through which official government agencies purchase goods and services.

grade label:
(1) the product's label indicating its quality.

(2) a label that identifies the quality of a product by a letter, number, or word.

grade labeling: as authorized by government agencies, the labeling of certain consumer items as specified by standards (e.g., the grading of meat). See *Federal Trade Commission; Food and Drug Administration; standardization.* Cf. *descriptive labeling.*

grading:
(1) the classification of major commodities into well-defined grades.

(2) the standardization of quality differences of staple commodities for purposes

of identification during trading periods. When combined with standardization, it is one of the marketing functions.

graduation: as applied in international marketing of goods and services; the presumption that individual developing countries are capable of assuming greater responsibilities and obligations in the international community, within GATT, for example, as their economies advance through industrialization, export development, and rising living standards.

grand strategy: the long-term set of goals and the means for achieving them used for setting tactics over a given time period.

graphic design: the creation of the visual element of a printed communication, such as an advertisement or product packaging.

graphics: all visual elements of communication affiliated with the presentation of an item or service to the market. It includes art, color effects, photographs, copy, etc.

grass-roots method: a sales forecasting method that relies on input from salespeople in the field.

gravure: the printing process that transfers an image to paper by means of the ink retained in plate depressions.

gray market:
(1) sources of supply from which scarce items are bought for quick delivery at a premium well above the usual market price.

(2) commodities that are either mimics or counterfeits of genuine items.

gray trade: international marketing of goods between nations that do not officially recognize one another, often by transshipment through third-country ports.

Green Book: an international directory, published by the American Marketing Association's New York chapter. It lists marketing research firms and research service providers. Cf. *creative black book.*

green label: a label awarded to consumer products considered friendly to the environment in the hope that the initiative will increase the pressure on industry to develop products with reduced pollution levels.

green marketing: promoting items that are biodegradable (that will rapidly disintegrate when exposed to the air) in an attempt to protect the environment.

Green River ordinance: a municipal law regulating house-to-house selling, unless the resident has invited the salesperson. See *door-to-door selling.*

greige goods: unfinished fabric as it comes from the loom before bleaching, dyeing, printing, or the application of particular finishes.

grid card: a station's rate card in which the commercial times are priced separately, spot by spot. See *day parts.*

gross: in merchandising, 12 dozen.

gross amount:

(1) *general:* the total before deductions. The gross amount minus deductions equals the net amount. See *gross profit.*

(2) *advertising:* the total amount owed by the advertiser to an advertising medium for advertising time and space bought prior to the deduction of the advertising agency's commission. See *gross audience; gross billing; gross night hour; gross rating point.*

(3) *direct mail:* responses from a promotion, including prepaid order and credit orders.

gross audience: the total number of people or households in a listening, viewing, or reading audience without concern for the duplication of audience members (e.g., a person is counted twice should he or she appear in the audience of two of the television programs in the broadcast schedule being counted). See *gross rating point.*

gross billing:

(1) *advertising:* the cost of advertising with a communications medium, including the advertising agency commission.

(2) *broadcasting:* the cost of a one-time insertion in a communications medium.

gross circulation: the maximum amount of people who walk past an outdoor advertising display and have a good chance of viewing the message; determined for a particular display over a given period of time, usually 30 days.

gross domestic product (GDP):

(1) the total goods and services produced in a nation over a given time period, usually a year. Cf. *gross national product.*

(2) the market value of a country's output attributable to factors of production located in the country's territory.

gross margin:

(1) *sales:* the amount, determined by subtracting the cost of goods sold from net sales, that covers operating and financial expenses and provides net income. Synonymous with *gross profit.*

(2) *retailing:* the dollar difference between net sales and the net cost of goods

sold during a stated time frame. Gross margin percentage is calculated by dividing net sales into this figure.

gross national product (GNP): the total retail market value of all items and services produced in a country during a specified period, usually one year. Distribution is presented in terms of consumer and government purchases, gross private national and foreign investments, and exports. Cf. *gross domestic product.*

gross night hour: in television, a one-time cost to sponsor one hour of prime-time programming.

gross processing margin: the difference between the cost of existing raw materials and the sales revenue from the finished items.

gross profit: synonymous with *gross margin.*

gross rating point (GRP):
(1) *broadcasting:* the number of advertisements required in a medium to achieve the desired percentage of exposure of the message to the consumer.

(2) *advertising:* in outdoor advertising, the number of panels used for delivering in one day the desired percentage of exposure opportunities.

gross response: see *gross amount.*

gross sales: total sales over a specified period, before the customer returns and allowances have been deducted.

gross savings: the sum of capital consumption (depreciation) and personal and corporate savings.

gross state product: the total monetary value of all final goods and services produced and marketed in a state during one year.

gross weight: the full weight of a shipment, including goods and packaging. See *tare.*

groupage: a service that consolidates small shipments into containers for movement.

group discounting:
(1) *broadcasting:* a special discount for the use of a group of broadcasting stations simultaneously.

(2) *merchandising:* a special discount for the purchase of large quantities of an item or service (e.g., group discounts on air fares).

group mailing: synonymous with *cooperative mailing.*

group norms: standards of behavior established by a group that describe the acceptable behavior of members.

group plan: synonymous with *party selling.*

group purchase plan: a selling where the retailer offers purchase incentives to a group. An identity card is frequently distributed to users.

group rate: synonymous with *blanket rate.*

group selling: the presentation for sale of goods or services to two or more people simultaneously.

grow-and-penetrate strategy: active marketing efforts designed to increase the size and sales of a firm.

growth-share matrix: a display matrix showing market growth on the vertical axis and relative market share on the horizontal axis, used in analyzing the cash flow and marketing requirements of a firm's products. Cf. *harvesting strategy.*

growth stage: the second phase in a product's life cycle, characterized by a rise in sales and profit and the appearance of competitors in the market. See *product life cycle.*

growth strategy: the strategy used by a firm that wants to expand its product's market share at the expense of a short-term profit, either by targeting users of a competitor's item to get them to switch, or by targeting people who have never used the item before.

GRP: see *gross rating point.*

GTC: see *good 'til canceled order.*

guarantee: a written statement assuring that something is of stated quantity, quality, content, or benefit, or that it will perform as advertised for a stated period. In some cases, all or part of the purchaser's money will be refunded if the item fails to meet the terms of a guarantee. Cf. *warranty.* See *guaranty; product reliability.*

guaranteed draw: a means of compensating salespeople by permitting them a draw that is not repayable if the commissions earned in a stated time period are less than the draw.

guarantor: see *guaranty.*

guaranty: a contract, agreement, or undertaking involving three parties. The first party (the guarantor) agrees to see that the performance of a second party (the guarantee) is fulfilled according to the terms of the contract, agreement, or undertaking. The third party is the creditor, or the party to benefit by the performance.

guaranty against price decline: synonymous with *price guaranty.*

guerrilla warfare: a marketing warfare technique used by small firms that are trying to compete with large firms. A tightly bounded or well-defined small market is chosen to defend, and the remaining portion is let go to the larger firm. Two additional concepts are:

(a) guerrillas do not accept the marketing or organizational practices of brand leaders, no matter how successful the former become.

(b) guerrilla firms respond firmly and quickly to market changes by exiting the market when situations call for it.

gutter position: the position of an advertisement that adjoins the inside margin or gutter of a newspaper, magazine, or other publication. Many advertisers think that a message placed in such a position is adversely affected because of decreased readership.

HABA: see *health and beauty aids.*

habitual purchasing: a person's repeated buying of an item or service, done out of habit as contrasted with brand loyalty, especially when the consumer concludes there is little difference between products or services. It is a marketer's dream to have repeat sales with habitual purchasers. See *brand loyalty.*

haggling: synonymous with *higgling.*

half-page double spread: a magazine advertisement placed on either the bottom half or the upper half of two facing pages. Usually, this layout is as expensive as a full-page advertisement, but it is selected by advertisers over a full-page when the copy more readily lends itself to this format, which allows a continuous flow of material. See *horizontal half-page.*

halo effect:

(1) a bias whereby one favorable characteristic influences an overall judgment of an individual. Ratings of consumers are sometimes inaccurate because of the frequency with which a single or general impression tends to permeate the rater's application of evaluation criteria.

(2) a subjective evaluation by consumers when analyzing consumer attitudes and their relationship to the market structure, especially when dealing with advertising or brand evaluation. This effect makes it difficult to assess brands based on strengths and weaknesses. At times, when a brand name has a positive reputation, the halo effect provides a brand advantage, especially when the manufacturer introduces a new product.

handbill: a form of direct advertising, usually a single sheet or a small pamphlet, distributed by hand. Handbills are frequently placed on a counter in the store or entranceway for customers to pick up while shopping. They are also distributed by hand for placement on car windows. Handbills provide an inexpensive form of advertising and are easy to produce. Synonymous with *throwaways.* See *flier.*

handling allowance:

(1) a special price or discount given by the manufacturer to a wholesaler, distributor, or retailer when a manufacturer's goods demand special handling.

(2) an incentive given to the retailer for handling a particular promotional program that demands extra effort on the retailer's part.

hand-to-mouth purchasing: purchasing that satisfies needs of the moment only, neglecting long-range requirements of the individual or entity.

hard copy:

(1) a record that can be read by the human eye. It has the advantage of being accessible to everyone, anywhere.

(2) information printed on paper in contrast to being electronically shown, usually on a computer screen.

hard goods: cf. *soft goods.* Synonymous with *capital goods.*

hard offer: a promotion, especially in direct marketing, that requests payment at the time an order is placed, but includes an option to review the merchandise first and then pay or return the items as desired by the customer. No matter what the offer, the right of the purchaser to return unwanted items for a refund or prior to payment will be honored by most marketers.

hard sell: a dynamic, determined, and insistent approach to sales; the seller attempts to control the sales situation by creating a level of tension. Cf. *soft sell.* Synonymous with *high-pressure selling.*

hardship point: in sales, the territory of a prospective customer who lives in a difficult area to reach or in a part of the community that is isolated.

harmony: the impact of an advertisement on a desired product image in terms of the goals of the message.

harvesting strategy: a response to an anticipated deterioration of the market; also, a method for maximizing a product's short-term cash flow when a firm is deciding whether or not to withdraw the product from the market. The strategy requires lowering the investment in the product to cut costs and improve cash flow that, if and when created, is used for other needs of the organization. Cf. *growth-share matrix.*

harvest strategy: see *harvesting strategy.*

Hawthorne effect:

(1) *general:* the tendency of people who are being observed to react differently than they would otherwise; an outgrowth of the Hawthorne studies undertaken at the Hawthorne Plant of Western Electric, in Chicago, between 1924 and 1933. These investigations showed the importance of the social system of an organization and became the foundation of human relations theory.

(2) *consumer research:* a factor taken into consideration, by disguising or concealing the true purpose or reason of the research, so as not to affect the interviewee's true feelings or attitudes. See *bias.*

Hazardous Substances Labeling Act of 1960: see *Federal Hazardous Substances Labeling Act of 1960.*

HBA: see *health and beauty aids.*

header: a sign or marking at the top of a display, merchandiser, or exhibit.

headline: the beginning statement in a print advertisement, in which the advertiser anticipates what will attract the reader's attention. Its goal is to encourage the reading of the copy. In print advertising, it is considered to be a critical element as it maneuvers the reader into the advertisement. Consequently, to be effective, it should stimulate interest and curiosity from the reader.

head of household: of target importance to market researchers, the individual who is responsible for managing the household and is the major source of financial support; may be married or unmarried, male or female.

head of stock: in a large retail store, a major sales key clerk or other specialist responsible for maintaining front stocks and for advising the buyer of shortfalls and other related problems.

head-on position: an outdoor advertising location that faces the flow of traffic, rather than being placed on an angle or parallel to the traffic.

health and beauty aids (HABA) (HBA): a product category that includes:

(a) over-the-counter medicines and remedies.

(b) personal care products (e.g., toothpastes, mouthwashes).

(c) hair-care products (e.g., shampoos, setting lotions).

(d) body-care products (e.g., body lotion, skin moisturizers).

(e) cosmetic products (e.g., perfume, face makeups).

healthcare marketing: public service marketing carried out for hospitals, clinics, medical associations, etc., to promote the health benefits of a product or service.

heartland: synonymous with *primary market area.*

heavy buyers: people in the market for an item who account for more than half the total volume of sales of the merchandise. They represent less than half the number of users of the item. Synonymous with *heavy-half users; heavy users.*

heavy-half users: synonymous with *heavy buyers.*

heavy market: a declining market created when buying exceeds the demand for orders.

heavy-up: in advertising, to increase the use of a medium by an existing long-time user. Should an advertiser's item be actively used at a given time over another, the advertiser often chooses to heavy-up the advertising for that time period, as with promoting the sale of Christmas ornaments in early December.

heavy users: synonymous with *heavy buyers.*

hedging clause: a caution to customers attached to circulars, brochures, advertisements, and so on; a protective statement of warning for customers that customarily reads: "The information furnished herein has been obtained from sources believed to be reliable, but its accuracy is not guaranteed."

hedonic items: consumer products whose attractiveness is that they offer the user considerable pleasure.

heterogeneous shopping items: merchandise perceived by the customer as different in quality and suitability.

heuristic: a concept used by advertisers; any method used to assist a person in discovering or learning something for himself or herself.

hidden offer: a special offer buried in the copy of an advertisement as a test of readership. Synonymous with *blind offer; buried offer.* See *copy testing.*

hidden persuader: a term popularized by Vance Packard in 1957 in connection with the motivational and manipulative techniques used by advertising agencies in their campaign programs. See *motivational research; subliminal advertising.*

hidden service sector: the delivery, installation, maintenance, training, repair, and other services provided by firms that emphasize goods sales.

hierarchy of effects models: models of advertising communications that conceptualize communications as proceeding through a succession of stages from awareness to purchase.

hierarchy of needs: see *motivational needs; primary needs.*

hi-fi: (slang) a color advertisement preprinted on one side of a continuous roll of smooth coated paper, so that the advertisement looks like a wallpaper pattern; it is then fed into a newspaper's printing press.

higgling: the procedure whereby, when the buyer offers a low price and the seller asks a high price, a third price is arrived at through bargaining to satisfy both parties. Synonymous with *haggling.*

high-end: the most expensive items in a classification.

high involvement: an advertising medium demanding involvement on the part of the buyer. For example, print media are high involvement because people must actively participate by reading to obtain information. Cf. *low-involvement merchandise.*

high-pressure selling: synonymous with *hard sell.*

high spot: in outdoor advertising, the location of significantly heavy traffic at which a showing is feasible.

hire purchase: purchasing by installment payment where title does not pass to the buyer until final payment is made.

hi-spotting: synonymous with *cherry-picking*.

historical design: in marketing research, a design using information recorded from the past. The design can be statistical or more descriptive, as in a report.

hitchhike: an end-of-program commercial, within the sponsor's time featuring a sponsor's product not shown in the program's other commercials. See *cow-catcher.*

hitlist: a salesperson's list of prospective customers he or she plans to pursue; includes both weak and strong prospects, with the stronger ones receiving the greatest attention. See *prospecting.*

hoarding:
(1) collecting for the sake of accumulating.

(2) a planned effort by persons to accumulate items beyond normal need (e.g., purchasing dozens of cartons of socks in anticipation of a price hike).

holding fee: an additional payment given to talent in a commercial; gives the advertiser the right to hold the commercial after its initial airing and use it again without having to renegotiate any payment.

holding power: the ability of a product, program, or entity to retain an audience over time.

holdover audience: in broadcasting, an audience that remains to watch at least the commencement of a succeeding program over the same network or station.

hold strategy: a firm's decision to retain a product's existing market share, with a continuance of levels of production and promotion needed to do so.

holism: a tool of marketing; the concept according to which economic knowledge can be gained from totals or aggregates rather than from the action of individuals.

home audit: the determination of consumer patterns in a product field by recruiting a sample of homes that will represent the larger target market.

home country orientation: a marketing approach where the firm gives domestic business the highest priority, making little or no effort to build up global markets.

homogeneous demand: a demand pattern in which consumers have relatively uniform needs and desires for a good or service category.

homogenization: the mixing together of response data from consumers; a situation in which variations in response by advertising campaign components cannot be identified because those components were poorly key coded.

hook:
(1) *advertising:* items in copy that attract the reader's, viewer's, or listener's attention.

(2) *retailing:* a free offer given along with the purchase of a product.

(3) *broadcasting:* a giveaway offer (e.g., a free tape to the next 15 callers).

Hooperating (Hooper rating): the percentage of individuals who are listening to radio stations, ascertained by using the telephone coincidental method of data gathering. These data are supplied by

C. E. Hooper, Inc. See *coincidental tele-phone method; share of audience.* Cf. *Nielsen rating.*

horizontal audit: the study of the overall marketing performance of a firm, with particular emphasis on the interrelationship of variables and their relative importance.

horizontal buying:
(1) an advertising schedule using periodicals and magazines with varying audience appeals for the widest coverage of people.

(2) any use of many units of the same medium.

horizontal conflict: conflict that occurs between channel members at the same level of the distribution channel.

horizontal cooperative advertising: advertising in which marketers at the same level in the distribution system advertise jointly.

horizontal diversification: the use of unrelated products that are added to existing line items, to enhance total sales. New items are technologically different from existing product lines and have a different manufacturing process. See *concentric diversification; diversification.*

horizontal half-page: space, usually in periodicals, offered for advertisements; either the upper or lower half of a page.

horizontal industrial market: the broad market for industrial items, which includes a number of industries.

horizontal integration: a strategy for a firm's expansion where the organization attempts to increase sales and profitability by expanding within its own industry

(e.g., by acquiring a competitor that markets the same item).

horizontal market:
(1) a market made up of a broad spectrum of industries.

(2) the condition of a market where the manufacturer's item is sold to buyers in several industries. Cf. *vertical market.*

horizontal price fixing:
(1) an agreement on price among competitors at similar levels of distribution.

(2) a form of price fixing in which marketers at the same level of the distribution system get together and decide the price at which all of them will sell the product.

horizontal publication: a trade periodical directed to businesspeople in general as contrasted with a specific industry or professions. Cf. *vertical publication.*

horizontal sales company: a sales force company employing both company and external salespeople who are assigned sales responsibility on a geographic basis, form of merchandise, type of customer, or specific selling activity.

horizontal saturation: synonymous with *saturation.*

hot items: (slang) any goods that show quick salability.

house: an internal product or possession, controlled by customers or owners, or a house advertising agency owned by an advertiser. See *house agency.*

house accounts: synonymous with *direct accounts.*

house agency: an advertising agency that has only one client. Not very popular today. Synonymous with *house shop.*

household: a person or group of persons occupying a housing unit, whether related or unrelated.

household life cycle: a cycle that incorporates the life stages of both family and nonfamily households.

household saving: household disposable income less existing household consumption.

house list: a mailing list of existing customers and those who are not yet customers, but have made inquiries about the product or service.

house shop: synonymous with *house agency.*

house-to-house salesperson: a sales representative who visits homes in an attempt to make direct sales; made with or without an appointment. See *door-to-door selling.*

house-to-house sampling: the distribution of a product sample to homes in a market location as a way of introducing people to the merchandise; a promotional strategy to stimulate word-of-mouth advertising.

house-to-house selling: synonymous with *door-to-door selling.*

housewife time: that portion of the day, between 10:00 A.M. and 3:00 P.M., when most viewers and listeners are women. With women returning to the workplace in great numbers, their percentage during this time period is declining, but still they represent the largest number. See *day parts.*

huckster: a peddler or petty retailer who will attempt to sell anything for a profit.

huckstering: see *huckster.*

human interest approach: synonymous with *imaginative approach.*

humorous sell: an advertising message that jokes about the merchandise being sold.

hurdle rate: any criterion or test figure that a new product must meet or exceed as it goes through development.

hybrid technology: a technique for industrializing services that combines both hard and soft technologies, such as computer-based truck routing and specialized low-priced repair facilities.

hype:
(1) *advertising:* (slang) an activity that attempts to encourage consumer interest and sales (e.g., advertising).

(2) *broadcasting:* special promotional activities in programming presented by a network to attract a significant audience and to generate a higher audience rating for a specific time period. Synonymous with *hypo.*

hypermarche: a large operation, combining the features of a supermarket and a discount house. Synonymous with *hypermarket.*

hypermarket: synonymous with *hypermarche.*

hypo: synonymous with *hype.*

hypothecated deposit: the aggregation of periodic payments on an installment contract received by a reporting institution in a state in which, under law, such payments are not immediately used to reduce the unpaid balance of the installment note, but are accumulated until the sum of the payments equals the entire amount of principal and interest on the contract, at which time the loan in considered paid in full.

hypothesis:
(1) used by market researchers; a tentative statement of an apparent relationship among facts that can be observed and therefore measured.
(2) used by market researchers; a theory imagined or assumed to account for what is not understood; a model for testing.

iceberg principle: the concept that 10 percent of required data are apparent and the other 90 percent are not seen. Used in sales predictions to indicate that gross numbers can hide the bulk of the critical data that would be determined on closer examination.

ID: a broadcast station's call letters and location.

idea advertising: advertising whose objective is to communicate a position or platform on a public concern.

idea generation: the development of concepts to be used for promoting new products and their promotional campaigns. See *synectics.*

ideal marketing exposure: the degree of exposure an item receives in its potential market so as to meet customers' needs without exceeding them.

ideal other: the concept of how a person wishes others to perceive him or her; impacts on buying behavior and advertising promotions. Cf. *ideal self-image.*

ideal points: the combination of attributes that consumers would like products to possess.

ideal self-image: the way an individual would like to be. Cf. *ideal other.* See *self-image.*

ideation: the process of finding either new ways to capitalize on the available resource or potential solutions to the problems. Stages include problem identification, problem solving, scanning, and pooling of new concepts. See *creative stimuli.*

identity disclosure: the issue of whether to release to the user the name of the firm making the product being tested.

illegal: behavior that is contrary to the basic principles of law. An illegal act is forbidden by law, whereas an unlawful act, though not forbidden by law, is not given the protection of law.

illegal merchandise: the unlawful sale of items (e.g., stolen goods).

illth: consumer items that are harmful to people who consume them and to the general welfare.

illustration: the visual element in an advertisement; helpful in making copy believable. To maximize its effectiveness as a communication tool, the illustration should complement and reinforce the advertisement's other elements of copy and headline.

illustrator: in advertising, the artist who creates, by hand, and develops pictures to be used in an advertisement. Cameras, computers, and other mechanical devices are not used by the illustrator.

image:

(1) *general:* what people believe to be true about something.

(2) *marketing:* a buyer's mental picture of himself or herself; how an individual sees a product.

(3) *merchandising:* the feelings of customers toward a store.

image advertising: synonymous with *institutional advertising.*

image builder pricing: in retailing, where one item within the line is offered at a significantly higher price than the other line products so as to upgrade their image in the consumer's perception.

image building: a marketing relations approach to advancing, upgrading, or generally improving the customer's attitude toward an item, service, organization, or person.

image liner: see *pop-in.*

image sell: an advertising message that focuses on creating and sending a specific image for an item or service being advertised.

imaginative approach: a copy approach that concentrates on ways to enrich life by using the product or service. Synonymous with *human interest approach.*

imaginative segmenter: a segmenter that attempts to offer an improved marketing mix to fulfill the requirements of a target market that has already been identified by an innovative segmenter. Merchandise developed this way often resemble or at time copy the innovator's item. Cf. *innovative segmenter.* See *segmenter.*

imbricative marketing: a marketing strategy whose implementation demands an understanding of the company's capabilities, the true needs of the market, the determination of that market, an awareness of the total system within which the firm functions, and the commitment to fulfilling in an orderly way all aspects of the company's marketing activities.

imitative innovation: a strategy of copying the creativity of others but modifying each copy enough to give it originality and market value.

imitative pricing: synonymous with *going-rate pricing.*

immediate objectives: objectives that the organization can accomplish now without obtaining more resources or doing additional research.

impact: the way in which an advertisement or a medium affects the audience receiving it. See *impact advertising; motivational research.*

impact advertising: a strategy of placing advertising messages in the media where they are expected to have the greatest impact, where more consumers are exposed to it, recall it, and are motivated to purchase the advertised item or service. Some advertisements are best in one medium instead of another.

imperfect competition: circumstances under which prices are usually altered by one or more competitors. This occurs because of unusual conditions in the market or advantages secured by some buyers or sellers. Cf. *perfect competition; pure competition.*

implementation:

(1) the planning and/or putting of an idea, schedule, method, or proposal into actual practice.

(2) the actual execution of a strategic plan.

implicit costs: costs originating within the business that are the responsibility of the owner (e.g., time, money).

implied warranty: a legal promise that a product will serve the purpose for which it is intended, whether stated by the manufacturer or not. Cf. *express warranty.* See *warranty.*

import:
(1) to receive goods and services from abroad (verb).

(2) an imported item (noun).

(3) to bring goods and services from abroad (verb).

importance of a purchase: the degree of decision making, level of perceived risk, and amount of money to be spent or invested. The level of importance of a purchase affects the time and effort a consumer will spend shopping for a product as well as the amount of money allocated.

import quota: a protective ruling establishing limits on the quantity of a particular product that can be imported. See *quantitative restrictions.*

import quota auctioning: the allocation of the right to import a good with an import quota by auctioning the quota, in whole or part, to future importers.

import restrictions: a scheme for reducing or controlling imports through a variety of measures including import deposits, licenses, or quotas.

imports: see *import (2).*

import surcharge: a charge on imports over and above regular tariffs or customs fees.

impost: a tax, usually an import duty.

impressions:
(1) *advertising:* the total number of exposures to a specific advertisement in a specified period.

(2) *broadcasting:* the reaction to a single exposure from a broadcast commercial in a specified period.

imprint: the identification printed on a container during the process of manufacture. It may give the brand, container capacity, material quality, freight classification, and similar data.

impulse buying: purchasing by the customer without any prior planning; usually determined by a rapid appeal of the item or service; a spontaneous purchase made in response to an unexpected urge or external stimulus. Synonymous with *impulse purchasing.* See *impulse merchandising; planned impulse buying.*

impulse merchandising: items susceptible to spontaneous rather than purposeful purchasing. These goods benefit from display in store locations that have a considerable flow of customers; they are a specific category of convenience goods and tend to be low-cost items (e.g., candies, candles). See *impulse buying.*

impulse products: convenience items that the consumer does not plan to buy on a specific trip to a store.

impulse purchasing: synonymous with *impulse buying.*

imputed cost: a cost that is not specified but is implied to exist by the policies of the organization (e.g., interest that would have been earned on cash spent to purchase inventories).

inactive: a customer who has not bought something over a set time period, usually 12 months.

inactive account: synonymous with *dormant account.*

in-ad coupon: a coupon placed along with an advertisement; used mostly by stores to get people into a specific outlet. This coupon can only be used in the store sponsoring the advertisement.

in bond: items shipped by a producer several months before a store's usual selling season. The items are held in bond in the store's warehouse until the selling season.

inbound telemarketing: in direct-marketing, where the sales representative handles incoming telephone calls from customers who place orders, make inquiries, or voice complaints. Traditionally, an 800-number is used in inbound telemarketing systems. Cf. *outbound telemarketing.*

incentive: a motivational force that stimulates people to greater activity or increased efficiency. Customer sales promotions often involve incentives such as coupons, rebates, and discounts.

incentive agency: a company providing a variety of incentive products, usually representing a number of manufacturers. Serving as middlepeople, they often assist in preparing promotional materials.

incentive plan: a reward scheme that attempts to tie pay directly to job performance (e.g., a piece rate, a sales commission).

incentive rate: a salary increment given after the completion of a specified, usually probationary, period.

inchoate: newly begun or incomplete.

income: money or its equivalent that is earned or accrued, arising from the sale of goods or services.

income distribution: used by market researchers; the way in which personal income is dispensed throughout the various socioeconomic levels in a nation.

income effect: used by market researchers; the change in the quantity of an item demanded because a person's purchasing power has been altered.

income elasticity of demand: variables that remain constant; the percentage change in quantity demanded that can be expected to follow from a percentage change in a person's income. Cf. *price elasticity.*

income segmentation: the division of markets or customers on the basis of their earnings.

income statement: the profit and loss statement of a given concern for a particular time period.

increasing-cost industry: an industry that experiences increases in resource prices or in manufacturing costs as it expands when new firms enter it.

incremental costs: costs that increase or decrease as the direct result of a specific decision.

incrementalism: a decision-making approach whereby executives begin with a current situation, consider a limited number of changes in that situation based on a small number of alternatives, and test those changes by instituting them one at a time.

incremental pricing agreement: the pricing arrangement between a buyer and seller utilizing a schedule of price that shifts with the cumulative increment purchased. Cf. *blanket pricing agreement.*

incremental revenue: the increase or decrease in revenue that results from a subtraction or addition of a unit of sales or from the advance or decline in price.

incremental spending: the budget allocation permitting more or less spending on media for advertising in direct proportion to sales.

incremental technique: a promotional budget method in which a company bases its new budget on previous expenditures. A percentage is either added to or subtracted from this year's budget to determine next year's.

incumbent agency:

(1) an advertising agency under contract with a specified client.

(2) the current tenured advertising agency for an advertiser's goods or services.

indebtedness: a debt that is owed; any form of liability.

indent: the request from a purchaser to an importer to import specific items at a stated price. The importer has a given time period in which to accept or refuse the offer.

independent: in retailing, a store that does not belong to an association of companies or chains.

independent distributors: individuals and firms that buy from producers and other intermediaries and sell to other resellers and to end users.

independent media: communication vehicles, such as newspapers and television, not controlled by a firm; yet, they influence the government's, consumers' and public's perceptions of that firm's products and overall image.

independent network: any broadcast system that is not affiliated with the three major networks, ABC, CBS, or NBC. Presently, with the increase in cable stations, the term has lost its critical status and influence. Cf. *independent station.*

independent retailer: a retailer that owns a single outlet that is not affiliated with any other retail outlet.

independent station: a broadcast station not owned or controlled by or affiliated with a network. Cf. *independent network.*

independent store: a retail operation that is controlled by individual ownership or management, not by outside management.

independent variable:

(1) *general:* a factor that is not dependent for change on other factors. Synonymous with *predictor variable.* See *experiment; variable.*

(2) *advertising:* an element that is subject to random change, in order to test the results. For example, an audience response is dependent on the stimulus provided and advertising copy can be considered the independent variable when it is time to chart results. Cf. *dependent variable.*

index: a symbol or number used to identify a particular quantity in an array of similar quantities. Synonymous with *index number.*

index number: synonymous with *index.*

index of sales activity: a relative measure of a store's sales record within a given market.

indicia: imprinted designations used on mail pieces to denote payment of postage.

indifference barrier: a reference to purchases that are made from habit to save time and effort, without regard to advertising. Advertising purports to neutralize this barrier with new products and approaches.

indirect-action advertising: the creation a positive attitude toward an item or service via long-range planning of frequent exposure over a time period, so that at a given moment when the potential consumer is ready, the impact already made will encourage a positive decision to buy. Cf. *direct-action advertising*. Synonymous with *indirect advertising*.

indirect advertising: synonymous with *indirect-action advertising*.

indirect channel: a channel of distribution using numerous middlepeople. The opposite of direct channel. Cf. *semidirect channel*. See *indirect distribution*.

indirect competition: the effect created by potential consumers for a product who satisfy their needs by purchasing a different item or do not make a purchase at all, instead of securing the item or service from another company.

indirect costs: important to marketers and advertisers in measuring profits; costs not usually identifiable with or incurred as the result of the manufacture of goods or services but applicable to a productive activity generally. Included are costs from manufacturing operations (wages,

maintenance, overhead, etc.). Cf. *direct cost*.

indirect damage: a consequential loss.

indirect distribution: the use of middlepeople to sell a product. Traditionally, manufacturers prefer indirect distribution when they have limited financing, few lines, require assistance at the customer level, and prefer not to be involved in distribution matters. Cf. *direct distribution*. See *direct channel; indirect channel*.

indirect exposure: a consumer purchase of a good or service resulting from the influence of another person who has been exposed to an advertisement.

indirect material costs: the costs of materials that are included as manufacturing overhead and are assigned to products on some reasonable allocation basis.

indirect production: producing an item needed for the manufacture of major goods or services (e.g., producing a machine designed specifically to manufacture a given consumer product).

indirect promotion: sales promotion that is impersonal, as contrasted with personal selling. Advertising, packaging, etc., are examples. It purports to make a service or item known to the market and to present it in the most favorable light. Cf. *direct promotion*.

indirect retail outlet: a retailer that purchases items via a wholesaler.

individual brand: a name applied to one product only (e.g., Crest, Tide). Cf. *family brand*.

individual change stimuli: forces that determine a part of the activities of a purchasing unit in the market following changes in the characteristics of the purchasing unit, such as age, educational level, and income.

individual characteristics: a person's unique interests, values, attitudes, and needs.

induced consumption: additional consumer buying caused by new capital formation.

induced investment: new capital formation caused by an upturn in consumer buying.

industrial advertising: advertising goods or services for use in the manufacture or distribution of other goods and services. Advertised items include raw materials, components, or equipment required in the making and distribution of goods and services.

industrial buying behavior: patterns and purchasing procedures of groups in the organizational market. These actions differ from those of the consumer; characterized by highly professional, detail-oriented purchasing activities. Items bought are usually large-scale acquisitions of raw materials or office supplies and equipment.

industrial classification: analysis and synthesis of the factors pertinent to a business into a logical and systematic hierarchy, in which like things are combined in terms of their similarity and then are categorized according to their essential differences.

industrial coding: assigning identifying symbols to the permanent characteristics of items classified singly or in logical groupings, to ensure that characteristics contain the same identification.

industrial concentration: a factor reflecting the extent to which a large proportion of an industry's sales are produced by a few companies.

industrial consumer: a user of industrial goods or services.

industrial distributor:

(1) a full-service wholesaler representing industrial manufacturers and selling to industrial buyers.

(2) an independently owned operation that buys, stocks, and sells industrial products.

industrial goods: merchandise purchased for commercial reasons, instead of for personal or domestic needs.

industrial market: a producer market that consists of firms that engage in the manufacture of goods. See *industrial buying behavior.*

industrial marketing:

(1) the marketing of industrial goods and services.

(2) the process of anticipating, discovering, and designing product and service specifications that will satisfy the requirements of industrial customers. See *industrial marketing research.*

industrial marketing research: the systematic gathering, recording, and analyzing of data for use in solving problems related to the marketing of industrial goods and services. See *industrial marketing.*

industrial products: see *industrial goods.*

industrial purchasing: buying of goods and services at the business or institutional level.

industrial services: maintenance, repair, and business advisory services.

industrial standardization: the orderly and systematic formulation, acceptance, usage, and revision of the given requirements to attain a goal.

industrial store: synonymous with *commissary.*

industrial supplies: convenience goods that are necessary for the daily operation of a firm.

industrial user: an individual or company that purchases goods or services for commercial rather than personal or domestic reasons.

industry:

(1) trade, business, production, or manufacture.

(2) as determined by the Standard Industrial Classification (SIC) of the U.S. Bureau of the Census, any commercial activity identified by this listing.

inelastic demand: the condition that exists when a price increase leads to a higher total sales revenue, or a price decrease leads to a lower sales revenue. A perfectly inelastic demand occurs when the demand for an item does not change with changes in price. Cf. *price out of the market.* See *price elasticity.*

inelasticity: see *inelastic demand.*

inelastic supply: a condition in which the quantity of an item produced does not alter, or changes minimally, with a price change.

inept set: in consumer behavior, those particular brands that a potential customer refuses to consider when seeking an item within the product category. Cf. *inert set.*

inertia: any form of resistance to change; often considered a human and natural characteristic.

inert set: in consumer behavior, those particular brands that a potential customer remains indifferent toward when seeking an item within the product category. Cf. *inept set.*

inferential statistics: a statistical technique in marketing research of projecting the results of a sample to a larger group of people.

inferior goods: any item for which demand decreases as income increases.

inflation: of concern in setting market strategies; an increase in the price level, creating a decrease in the purchasing power of the monetary unit.

inflationary bias: the tendency toward a persistent upward trend in the price level.

inflationary spiral: affects marketing strategy; a pattern occurring in the time of rising prices: Employees demand higher wages, which in turn increases costs, leading sellers and producers then to demand still higher prices.

influencer:

(1) any person who, though not directly involved in a purchase, affects the buying decision of another person.

(2) in the exchange process, an individual who provides information about how a want or need may be satisfied.

infomercial: a program-length television commercial that is created to appear as a regular television show, thus making it difficult for the viewer to differentiate between a paid-for commercial and noncommercial programming.

informal balance: an advertisement layout that appears to appeal to a person's sense of balance but is off-balance or uneven. Synonymous with *asymmetrical balance.*

informal buying group: synonymous with *pooled purchasing.*

informal economy: these businesses often pay no taxes, have no licenses, offer no social security benefits to workers, and sometimes deal in smuggled goods; represented by companies that are involved in legal activities but are not registered with the government because of excessive red tape, which in some countries takes up to one year.

informal groups: natural (unorganized) groups of people in a work situation, or market.

informal organization: a rather complicated and nebulous network of communication and interaction patterns of groups, or cliques within the formal organizational structure. Such a phenomenon usually arises spontaneously in order:

(a) to augment, interpret, speed up, or change the formal communication system (or the lack of it).

(b) to regulate the flow, extent, manner, and enforcement of formal authority.

(c) to humanize the formal organization by trying to maintain a feeling of individuality among the members, while providing some security, unity, integrity, and feelings of belonging.

(d) to meet related psychological and social needs to such an extent as to give the impression of being the organization.

informal selling: a type of market test in which one or a few salespeople call on intended market users and make full presentations. There is actual request for the order. However, product has not been released to the full sales force.

information search:

(1) *consumer buying:* the securing of information about an item or different brands prior to making a purchasing decision, often by asking people, reading articles about the item or service, etc.

(2) *industrial buying:* the acquisition by purchasing agents of information on vendors or suppliers when wishing to fulfill a given item or service wanted.

informative institutional advertising: synonymous with *institutional advertising.*

informative label:

(1) a message or affix to merchandise providing data about the item.

(2) a label that advises consumers about the care, use, or preparation of a product.

informative product advertising: advertising in its earliest stage. See *pioneering stage.*

infrastructure: used in international marketing; the basic structure of a nation's economy, including transportation, communications, and other public services on which the economic activity relies.

infringement:

(1) *manufacturing:* production of a machine that yields the same results by the same action as a patented machine. This is a patent infringement.

(2) *merchandising:* the reproduction of a registered trademark and its use on merchandise to mislead the public into believing that the items bearing the reproduced trademark are the product of the true owner of the trademark. This is a trademark infringement.

inheritance audience: the segment of a broadcast audience that stays tuned to a succeeding program. The percentage of a program's audience that is inherited may be a clue to the show's strength.

inherited audience: synonymous with *holdover audience.*

in-home: media seen, heard, or read in one's home. Cf. *out-of-home.* See *alternative media.*

in-home retailing: retail sales that occur within the purchaser's house.

in-house advertising agencies: advertising agencies that are owned and controlled by client organizations.

initial margin: the amount a buyer is requested to deposit with a broker before commencing trading.

initial mark-on: the difference between the retail value of goods and the delivered costs when they are first priced and placed on display. See *mark-on.*

initial mark-up: see *initial mark-on.*

initial purchase:

(1) the first-time purchase of an item or service by a consumer.

(2) the first-time purchase of a media vehicle for purposes of advertising.

initiator: in the exchange process, the person who first recognizes an unsatisfied want or need.

innate needs: synonymous with *primary needs.*

inner-directed: used by market researchers; a consumer's purchase based on the satisfaction of an inner need that is consistent with his or her own values, such as being self-sufficient. Cf. *outer-directed.* See *VALS.*

innocent purchaser: an individual who, in good faith, does not expect any hidden property defects to appear when he or she has purchased something.

innovation: a concept or approach in the production cycle, frequently involving the use of inventions in a practical task. The innovation theory suggests that waves of innovation are followed by lulls, which mean depression. See *adopter categories; innovativeness.*

innovation diffusion: the concept that anything introduced into the market as new is quickly purchased for use by a group of people. See *diffusion model.*

innovation-dominated strategy: a focus of key managers on the creation and/or implementation of new technologies, products, or services.

innovative combiner: a marketing organization that applies the combined target market approach to identify a new combination of submarkets.

innovative efficiency: an aspect of the concept of marketing efficiency; the availability of items or services desired by and supplied to the market by activities that together with the offerings are the most appropriate for purchase under the existing knowledge of markets and technology. Such efficiency usually demands constant choice making among given alternatives.

innovative maturity: a stage at the end of the product life cycle where the item is either altered to extend its lifespan or rejuvenated by identifying new or differing uses for the item.

innovativeness:

(1) when applied to the seller, the degree to which the firm has the capability of, and follows the practice of, being innovative.

(2) when applied to a buyer, the extent to which that person or firm is willing to accept the risks of early purchase of an innovation. See *innovation*.

innovative segmenter: a segmenter who finds new submarkets, identifies unsatisfied needs of consumers, and evolves a marketing mix to fulfill sales to new customers. Cf. *imaginative segmenter; segmenter*.

innovators: people who are among the first to try or adopt an idea, service, or product. Synonymous with *early acceptors*. See *innovation*.

inoculation strategy: used in a comparative advertising campaign to create customer resistance to competitive merchandise or to resist the attractiveness of competitive advertising. A commercial that uses a portion of its length attacking the value of its competitor is an example.

INP: information-need-product; a traditional method of selling in which the sales presentation is made step by step.

in-pack: a direct premium found in a product package. With a high redemption rate, traditionally it offers the next purchase of the named item at a lowered price. Cf. *on-pack; with-pack premium*. Synonymous with *package enclosure*.

input-output strategy: a means for measuring and predicting fluctuations in supply and demand within the industrial market; based on the correlation between industries where the output of one is purchased by the other industries within the marketplace.

inquiry: information requested about a particular item or service, either solicited or unsolicited. Inquiries can represent valuable sales leads since consumers have already indicated some interest in the item or service. Inquiries are frequently followed up by salespeople with telephone calls or letters. Cf. *inquiry and follow-up*. See *query*.

inquiry and follow-up: a promotional method involving the offer of information about a product or service, followed by pressure to purchase the item or service. To increases sales, follow-up of such inquiries is important. Cf. *inquiry*. See *inquiry conversion*.

inquiry conversion: the conversion of an inquirer to a customer. See *inquiry and follow-up*.

inquiry test: a technique for testing advertisements by noting the number of inquiries from listeners, viewers, or publication readers. See *copy testing*.

insatiability concept: the concept that people are never fully satisfied and seek out new products and services. This leads to increased consumer sales and a further demand for more services and items to satisfy future needs.

inseparability of services: the inability of many services to be separated from the service provider. Customer contact is often considered an integral part of the service experience.

insert:

(1) a special advertising page found within a newspaper or magazine.

(2) promotional material found within a mailing, such as merchandise coupons. Inserts are sold as advertising with the design and production handled by an advertiser. See *insertion.*

insertion: the advertisement itself. See *insert.*

insertion order: written instructions for an advertisement to be placed in a particular issue of a publication at a stated rate. See *insertion.*

insertion schedule: the schedule of insertions in the media for a specific advertising campaign.

inside back cover: in magazine advertising, a preferred place for advertisements. Cf. *inside front cover.* Synonymous with *third cover.*

inside front cover: in magazine advertising, a preferred place for advertisements. Cf. *inside back cover.* Synonymous with *second cover.*

inside-outside approach: a strategy approach whereby managers look first at the organization and then at the environment.

inside salesperson: a salesperson, usually involved in industrial and wholesaling, who takes calls from customers within an office. Cf. *field salesperson.*

inspection purchasing: buying an item only after each item has been thoroughly studied for imperfections; found primarily in industrial consumption, especially with nonstandardized goods.

inspirational strategy: the use of imitation, intuition, feelings, or creativity.

installations: nonportable industrial capital goods used in the production process that involve a high degree of consumer decision making, are very expensive, last for many years, and do not change form. Synonymous with *process machinery.*

installed base: the volume of products of a specific product category and of a given brand currently in use in a market area.

installment buying: acquiring goods or services with no down payment or a small down payment, to be followed by payments at regular intervals.

installment credit: a form of consumer credit involving regular payments, permitting the seller to reacquire the purchased item if the buyer fails to meet the payment schedule.

instantaneous audience rating: the size of a radio or television audience as measured during any specific instant or point in time expressed as a percentage of a specific base, such as total number of individuals or households able to receive the broadcast under study.

instantaneous reference recording: a recording of a radio program made at the time of its broadcast by the radio station for delivery to the program's sponsor, who may use it for reference purposes.

institutional advertising: an attempt to sell the image of a firm—its quality, services, role in community activities, merchandise—rather than specific items. Goodwill and position are foremost in the development of institutional advertising. Synonymous with *image advertising; informative institutional advertising.* Cf. *corporate advertising.*

institutional approach: a way of examining marketing by considering the middlepeople and facilitating agencies that discharge the marketing functions. Synonymous with *descriptive approach.*

institutional decisions: decisions that involve long-term planning and policy formulation aimed at assuring the organization's survival as a productive part of the economy and the society.

institutional market: a set of not-for-profit organizations that buy goods and services for use in achieving a particular goal or mission.

in stock: status of merchandise on hand, available for shipment or sale.

in-store demonstration: a presentation by a salesperson of an item's features and capabilities to increase store sales.

instrumental performance: the performance of the physical product per se.

instrumental purpose: the intent to induce action at some future time; becomes critical in changing attitudes before any potential consumer can be convinced of the need to buy.

instrumented store: a retail outlet designed and organized based on computer analysis of the setting's efficiency, layout, shelfspace, inventory control, ordering, etc.

intangibility of services: the inability of many services to be displayed, transported, stored, packaged, or inspected before buying.

intangible rewards: synonymous with *psychic income.*

integrated commercial: a broadcast commercial that appears or is heard as part of the program's entertainment.

integrated marketing: the handling of a firm's marketing efforts by one organization, usually a large advertising agency, that can provide appropriate services. It evolved as a popular strategic approach when the spread of advertisements caused advertisers to become disenchanted with media advertising's decreased effectiveness.

integrated marketing communications: a concept of marketing communications planning that recognizes the added value of a comprehensive plan that evaluates the strategic roles of a variety of communications disciplines—advertising, public relations, personal selling, and sales promotion—and combines these disciplines to provide clarity, consistency, and maximum communication impact.

integration: the centralization of authority in the hands of a top administrator or executive. There are three forms of integration:
(a) *backward integration*—the firm acquiring supplier to evolve greater control over materials procurement.

(b) *forward integration*—the firm securing retailers or wholesalers.

(c) *horizontal integration*—the firm taking over one or more of its competitors, as long as it doesn't violate federal or state regulations. See *backward integration; forward integration.*

integrative market opportunity: the potential within the marketplace for new expansion, based on new production and differing levels of distribution.

intellectual property: an intangible creation that is possessed; examples include patents, trademarks, copyrights, computer software, industrial designs, and trade secrets. Knowledge of this subject is critical if marketers and advertisers are to avoid violations. See *intellectual property rights (IPRs)*.

intellectual property rights (IPRs): critical in international marketing and sales; accords that attempt to provide adequate and effective protection for intellectual property rights. Needs of intellectual property include:

(a) to create a trademark applicable throughout a regional trading area.

(b) to ensure that registered trademarks enjoy the same protection under the legal system of all trading countries.

(c) to specify the fees payable to a trademark office and its methods of payment. See *intellectual property*.

intensity:

(1) the extent to which an advertiser's message is shown.

(2) the number of posters found in a showing.

intensive distribution:

(1) placement of an item in all available outlets. Its shortcoming is that retailers have little commitment for promoting the item as their competitors will also be offering the merchandise.

(2) an approach to distribution that seeks the largest possible number of outlets in a given territory. Cf. *exclusive distribution; open distribution; selective distribution*.

interaction: in sales, the impact or relationship that exists between a salesperson and his or her potential customer.

interactive television: a relatively new concept in television that provides opportunities for consumers to shop, along with other activities. Merchandise is displayed before the consumer and can be ordered by pressing keys on a special keyboard or on a touch-tone telephone dial that is connected directly to the seller.

interest: following the awareness stage in the adoption process, the consumer's curiosity in pursuing the value of a product or service. See *activities, interests, opinions*.

interface: the point where difference functions in a firm come together during the product innovation process. Usually applies to pairings of the major players: technical (R&D), operations (especially manufacturing), and marketing.

intermedia comparison: comparisons of media classes based on their potential for inclusion in an advertising schedule. Cf. *intramedia comparison*.

intermediaries: see *intermediary*.

intermediary: synonymous with *middleperson*.

intermediate customer: a buyer who is not a consumer.

intermediate market: a set of wholesalers and retailers that buy goods from others and resell them.

intermediate sort: the assemblage of any large inventory of items from a host of sources; the items are then separated into smaller units for resale.

intermittent process: any process designed to produce a variety of items.

internal economies scale: utilized by advertising executives; factors that bring about increases or decreases to an organization's long-run average costs or scale of operations resulting from size adjustments with the company as a product unit.

They occur primarily because of physical economies or diseconomies. See *diseconomies of scale.*

internal forecast: a forecast relating to a firm's output and its internal operations.

internal inventory transfer: the shifting of semifinished goods through the plant's manufacturing process.

internal reports system: that portion of a marketing information system providing up-to-date data on sales, costs, inventory levels, accounts receivable and payable, etc.

international advertising: with increased activity in global markets, a form of advertising carried out overseas. Differences in culture, language, tradition, government regulations, and consumer requirements suggest a different approach to advertising, as contrasted with advertising in the United States, both nationally and locally. Often, but incorrectly, used synonymously with global advertising. Global advertising is worldwide, whereas international advertising suggests advertising in a foreign market, which could be restricted to one nation.

international division: a division in the organization that is at the same level as the domestic division in the firm and is responsible for all nondomestic country activities.

international forwarding agent: see *freight forwarder.*

international freight forwarder: see *freight forwarder.*

international marketing:
(1) operations within the home nation, to produce merchandise and services for export, for marketing overseas.

(2) activities in foreign nations that manufacture merchandise for sale in those nations. Some overseas operations are wholly-owned subsidiaries of the parent firm, while others may be joint or licensed ventures or contract manufacturing operations.

International Organization for Standardization: see *ISO.*

international product life cycle: a product life cycle theory that aids in the explanation of trade flows and investment on the basis of a product's position in the following four stages:
(a) exports of an industrialized country.

(b) beginning of foreign production.

(c) foreign competition in export markets.

(d) import competition in the nation where the product was introduced originally.

international trade: foreign trade measured by merchandise exports and imports of a country for a stated period, often one year.

interpretation: a step in the process of how a consumer gains awareness of advertising or a particular service or item; involves understanding of how advertising messages are received and comprehended by people.

interselling: assigning sales personnel so that each is able to work in two or more related departments rather than being limited to one. See *cross-selling.*

intertype competition: competing for business using differing methods of distribution.

interurbia:
(1) the urban-suburban sprawl.

(2) a continuous population center composed of many communities with significant populations (e.g., the entire coast of California).

interview: a conversation designed to yield information for purposes of research or assistance in attitudes, marketing, etc.

interview bias: see *interviewer bias.*

interviewer: the person who conducts an interview.

interviewer bias: the influence resulting from the presence of personal prejudice in the individual conducting the interview. See *bias; halo effect.*

intrabrand competition: competition, usually among resellers or between resellers and the direct sales force, for sales of same-brand products.

intramedia comparison: comparisons of media vehicles within a media class, in terms of their potential for inclusion in an advertising schedule. Cf. *intermedia comparison.*

in transit: items that have left the consignor's location and are en route to the destination.

intrapersonal variables: utilized by market researchers; psychological determinants that influence a person's awareness, values, beliefs, and ideas.

intrapreneurship: an approach to new-product development in which a small team of employees is set apart from the rest of the organization and freed from ordinary bureaucratic requirements long enough to develop a particular product.

intrastore transfer: the purchase of goods from one selling department for use by another selling department.

intrinsic cues: reasons for a buyer's feelings toward a product or service, as physical characteristics of the item itself. Cf. *extrinsic cues.*

intrinsic value: the market value of the material in an item.

introduction stage of the product life cycle: the period during which only one or two firms have entered the market, and competition is limited. Initial customers are innovators.

introductory offer: an offer, such as a free gift, premium, or discount given to prospects of a new product, or a reintroduced item that has been altered or improved on.

introductory price dealing: the temporary lowering of prices during the introduction phase of an item with the intent of raising them at the end of that period.

introductory stage of product life cycle: the first stage of the product life cycle. The new product is introduced to the market, sales are slow, promotion is usually heavy, costs are accumulated, and expectation is focused on determining when and if the product will soon enter the second (growth) stage of the cycle.

introductory technique: see *introductory price dealing.*

intrusiveness: the point at which an advertisement ceases to have a positive effect and becomes an irritant to consumers, thereby having a negative impact. It often leads to a complete reevaluation of the campaign.

invention: a new device, process, etc., that has been created; can be in either physical or conceptual form. Preexisting knowledge is combined in a new way to yield something that did not heretofore exist. It should not be confused with a product innovation, which is an invention that has been converted by further management and process development into a marketable product.

inventive creativity: the creativity required for product innovation. It combines artistic creativity and engineering creativity, either of which alone can be very strong but not productive of new product ideas.

inventory: the name given to an asset of a business. Inventories are of two general types, direct and indirect:

(a) direct inventory in an industrial concern consists of raw materials, work in process, and finished goods. Direct inventories represent various stages of fabrication; in commercial and retail businesses, they are inventories purchased for resale.

(b) indirect inventories, in general, are all supplies used to carry on the business and not purchased for resale. Indirect inventories are usually considered deferred assets. See *forward stock; perpetual inventory.*

inventory carrying costs: costs for conducting business related directly to the merchandise found in inventory, along with warehouse and insurance costs.

inventory change: the amount of increase or decrease in business inventories during a specified period.

inventory control: the control of merchandise on hand by accounting and physical methods. See *eyeball control; periodic stock control.*

inventory cutoff: the determination of which inventory items to include in the year-end inventory balance.

inventory management: a method for providing a continuous flow of goods and matching the quantity of goods in inventory with sales demand.

inventory model: a type of production control model that answers two questions relating to inventory management: "How much?" and "When?" An inventory model tells the manager when goods should be reordered and what quantity should be purchased.

inventory policy: the relationship desired between the quantity of stock on order and the quantity available, and the rate of usage.

inventory profit: the profit accrued on merchandise held in inventory during a period when the value of the items increased.

inventory risk: the financial risk of carrying items in inventory based on the likelihood of decreased value or reduced demand.

inventory shortage: inventory reduced by theft, internal or external fraud, waste, sabotage, or careless operation. Synonymous with *inventory shrinkage.* See *pilferage; shrinkage.*

inventory shrinkage: synonymous with *inventory shortage.*

inventory turnover: the number of times, on the average, that inventory is replaced during a period. It is calculated by dividing cost of goods sold by average inventory.

inverse demand pattern: the situation that exists when price and volume vary at the same time and more is sold at a higher price than at a lower one.

invisible supply: uncounted stocks in the hands of middlepeople, manufacturers, and consumers. Cf. *visible supply.*

invoice: an instrument prepared by a seller of goods or services and rendered to the buyer. The instrument usually lists all items making up the bill for the convenience of the buyer; to prevent disagreements, the amount is stated on the instrument.

involvement: the importance made by a consumer to the purchase of a specific service or item; varies based on the degree of relevant the item or service has to the purchaser (e.g., a high-involvement item has a significant degree of emotional importance to the consumer).

involvement device: synonymous with *action device.*

IPRs: see *intellectual property rights.*

irregular demand: fluctuations in demand for a product or service not attributed to seasonal changes or in the nation's economy. Marketers faced with an irregular demand state frequently attempt to alter the pattern of demand by establishing special promotions and incentives to increase demand during slow periods. See *demand states; seasonal demand.*

irregular routing: a sales call pattern in which the sales representative determines the frequency of calls to be made. Cf. *fixed routing.*

irregulars: items having defects that may affect appearance but not wear.

island display: merchandise shown in a store's aisle or open space. Items are readily accessible from all sides and the display is often freestanding.

island position: the placement of newspaper advertising copy that is surrounded by editorial matter or page margin. An island position is enviable, in that no other advertising message is nearby to compete for consumer attention. See *commercial protection; competitive separation.*

ISO: the Geneva-based International Organization for Standardization; sets worldwide technical standards in areas dealing with international commerce. See *ISO 9000.*

ISO 9000: critical for those marketing and selling overseas; a series of five international industrial standards for quality assurance. ISO 9000 aids a trading firm in devising quality standards for each core process in almost every department. Development of a system that complies with the external standards leads to registration or certification and uniform standards that are acceptable universally. The five standards cover the following areas: (a) *ISO 9000*—an overview and introduction to the other standards in the series, including definitions of terms and concepts related to quality used in the other standards.

(b) *ISO 9001*—comprehensive general standard for quality assurance in design, development, manufacturing, installation, and servicing of products.

(c) *ISO 9002*—less comprehensive standard focusing specifically on manufacturing and installation of products.

(d) *ISO 9003*—the least comprehensive standard covering final inspection and testing of completed products.

(e) *ISO 9004*—guidelines for managing a quality control system.

isolated location: a store located alone within a residential area; usually a convenience store.

issue:

(1) a hard copy.

(2) one of a series of regularly published materials, such as newspapers, magazines, newsletters.

issue definition: a statement of the topic to be investigated via market research. It directs the research process toward collecting and analyzing appropriate information for the purpose of decision making.

item: singular for good or merchandise.

itemized response: a unique response whereby one person hearing another person's new product idea is to (a) give a full statement of support by citing several advantages to the idea and (b) express any problems or concerns in positive (what's the best way to solve this) form.

item merchandising: the attempt to take advantage of sales opportunities presented by merchandise that is in the greatest demand by customers. Lost revenue is created when such demand cannot be filled because stock is not available.

item price removal: a practice whereby prices are marked only on store shelves or aisle signs and not on individual items.

items of trade: merchandise or service that a country buys or sells in the world markets. Items include commodities, credit, and services.

iteration: the process of repeating a sequence of logical steps for purposes of improving or refining.

jam auction: (slang) a store that sells inexpensive jewelry, souvenirs, and the like. Synonymous with *jam pitch.*

jam pitch: synonymous with *jam auction.*

jebble: synonymous with *bluefingers.*

jingle: a musical commercial; usually part of a television or radio commercial.

JIT purchasing: see *just-in-time purchasing.*

JND: see *just noticeable difference.*

job: in merchandising, to purchase or sell merchandise in quantity, not in selected categories.

jobber: a middleperson who handles merchandise in odd or job lots. Some jobbers take possession of the title to the goods, which they resell to another jobber, to a retailer, or directly to the consumer. Others have a buying agreement with the manufacturer to drop-ship the merchandise on orders obtained by the jobber. Cf. *wholesaler.* Synonymous with *reseller.* See *drop shipper; limited-service wholesaler; premium jobber; rack jobber; truck jobber.*

job lot: in merchandising, a miscellaneous grouping of items of various styles, sizes, colors, and so on, bought at a reduced price by a store or an individual middleperson.

job price protection: the guarantee of quoted prices on sufficient material to complete a specific task in which the purchase is engaged.

job ticket: a tag affixed to an order that provides details about the pertinent data about work to be done as well as the information about the person or firm for whom the job is being done. For advertising agencies, the job ticket gives the date, name of agency, name of client, and printing instructions to be carried out.

joint cost:

(1) a cost that is common to all the segments in question and that can be assigned to the segments only by arbitrary allocation.

(2) the costs of two or more items that must be manufactured together.

joint decision making: the process whereby two or more consumers have input into purchases.

joint demand:

(1) demand for two or more items that are usually used together because of necessity or consumer preference; used primarily with industrial goods.

(2) demand for two products that are complementary.

joint production costs: the costs of two or more produced goods that are made by a single process and are not identifiable as individual products up to a certain stage of production, known as the *split-off point*.

joint promotion: a sale sponsored by a group of companies.

joint venture: a commercial undertaking by two or more people, differing from a partnership in that it relates to the disposition of a single lot of goods or the termination of a specific project. Cf. *partnership*. Synonymous with *strategic alliance*.

judgment forecasting: utilizing judgment in forecasting sales of both present and future merchandise. Methods used are the aggregate of individual sales representative forecasts, expert consensus, and the Delphi method. See *Delphi technique*.

judgment sampling: used by consumer and market researchers; nonprobability sampling in which researchers select respondents on the basis of criteria designed to result in a group that is representative of the population being surveyed. See *nonprobability sampling; sampling*.

jumble basket: a merchandiser's mixed display of a number of different items. See *dump bind; jumble display*.

jumble display: a collection of items tossed together in a container or on a table counter. It is an open display that is primarily used in retail operations; customers can rummage through it to find different items. See *jumble basket*.

junior department store: a retail operation smaller than a traditional department store that carries a wide variety of merchandise. Often large appliances, such as washing machines and television sets, are not sold in such stores.

junior page: a space designation for periodical and magazine advertisements, where the space is the standard size of a page in small material. Synonymous with *junior unit*.

junior spread: synonymous with *pony spread*.

junior unit: synonymous with *junior page*.

junk mail: promotional mail containing unsolicited material. See *direct-mail advertising.*

jury of executive opinion: a forecasting approach utilizing the opinions of senior executives as to their estimate of the market potential and sales. Following that, they attempt to reach a consensus.

jury of expert opinion: see *jury of executive opinion.*

just-in-time inventory system: see *just-in-time purchasing.*

just-in-time (JIT) purchasing: an approach to inventory management in which products are bought in small quantities to reduce inventory carrying costs and obtain delivery just in time for use.

just noticeable difference (JND): the small difference in an item that is apparent to consumers when the item's characteristics are modified, either to face competition or to save money. See *Weber's Law.*

KBI: see *key buying influence.*

KD: knocked down; applies to sales or shipment of equipment to be assembled by the receiver. Cf. *knocked-down price.*

keep-out price: synonymous with *preemptive price.*

Kefauver-Harris Drug Amendment to the Food and Drug Act of 1962: federal legislation requiring the manufacturer to test both the safety and effectiveness of drug items before marketing them to the public. Also, the generic name of the item must appear on the label of the product. See *Food and Drug Administration.*

key: one or more numerals or letters or combination of these usually inserted as part of an advertiser's address appearing in an advertisement for the purpose of identifying the source of the inquiries or orders received in response to the sales message.

key account:
(1) *general:* a crucial, important, or primary account. Synonymous with *major account.*
(2) *advertising:* any client who spends a considerable sum of money on advertising with a particular advertising agency.

key account marketing: synonymous with *national account marketing.*

key buying influence (KBI): the person in an organization who is the central figure in making buying decisions of specific merchandise or services. See *multiple purchasing influence.*

key code: either numeric or alphanumeric codes; a graphic designation found in an advertisement or print communication that is used in tracking responses to that communication.

keyed advertising: see *keying an advertisement.*

key industry: an industry that, because of a unique characteristic, holds major importance in the country's economy (e.g., steel, automobile).

keying an advertisement: placing a code or letter in a coupon or in the advertiser's address so that the specific advertisement producing an inquiry can be noted. See *copy testing.*

key items:

(1) those in greatest consumer acceptance.

(2) merchandise that determines the acceptance of a line of products.

keynote idea: the central or single concept in an advertisement that will be the most important for the potential buyer. Often, it becomes the continuing theme for a promotional campaign.

key resource: a vendor whose former activities with a specific retailer have been outstanding and from whom the retailer has consistently purchased a significant portion of its merchandise.

key station: the station that originates the principal program of a broadcast network.

keystone markup: synonymous with *keystoning.*

keystoning: the doubling of the maker's prices to determine retail prices. Synonymous with *keystone markup.*

kickback:

(1) *general:* an illegal rebate given secretly by a seller for granting an order or contract (e.g., a payoff).

(2) *advertising:* an unethical practice where an advertising agency secretly offers to split the media commission with an advertiser or a person representing the advertiser so as to receive the advertiser's business.

kicker: in advertising, the subheadline in the writing of copy that appears above the headline for the copy.

kill: synonymous with *cancel; credit cancellation.*

kill bad pay: synonymous with *credit cancellation.*

Kimball tags: prepunched tags affixed to goods, containing the size and style data utilized in speeding inventory control. See *marking.*

kiosk: originated in European cities, a freestanding display used to provide merchandise information. They are located on streets, in shopping malls, and in stores.

knocked down: see *KD.*

knocked-down price: in retailing, a seller's asking price that has been lowered for purposes of making the sale. Cf. *knocked down; upset price.*

knocker: (slang) a door-to-door salesperson.

knockoff:

(1) (slang) to cease working for a break, for lunch period, or at the end of a working day (verb).

(2) (slang) the imitation of a design of clothing or of a textile item, usually done so to sell at a lower price than the original (noun).

know-how licensing: in international sales and marketing; an agreement through which one firm possessing technical information covered by patents authorizes another to use it to produce goods or services. Such agreements are procompetitive in that they facilitate the transfer of technology and boost innovation, but in particular circumstances, they may inhibit competition within the trading nations by imposing territorial restrictions.

knowledge stage: the beginning stage of an innovation decision process; commences when a customer receives physical or social stimuli that give exposure and attention to the innovation's existence and a comprehension of how it functions or operates.

known loss: a loss discovered before or at the time of delivery of a shipment.

kurtosis: a measure of the concentration or

label:

(1) *general:* an identification record.

(2) *advertising:* the portion of an item that provides information about the item to the buyers. A tag that may be attached to the item, or inserted with the package.

(3) *advertising:* the classification of people according to a type, such as single parent, housewife, divorced.

(4) *merchandising:* the brand name of a clothing manufacturer, retailer, fashion house, or recording company.

(5) *direct-mail:* the small piece of paper or sticker on which a mailing address appears.

(6) see *labeling; performance label.*

label copy: advertising copy written primarily for the labels of goods.

labeling: all labels and other written, printed, or graphic matter appearing on any article or any of its containers or wrappers. See *label.*

label panel: synonymous with *label set.*

label set: records, categorized by name and address, that are printed in label form and separated from the total list before printing. Every record within the label set is given a code to identify it as a member of that particular set. Synonymous with *label panel; label split.*

label split: synonymous with *label set.*

laggards:

(1) consumers who are strongly oriented toward the past and very suspicious of new concepts; they are the last to adopt a new product. They follow the late majority in the innovation diffusion process, and usually have the lowest economic and social status. See *nonadopters.*

(2) the fifth, and last, group of users to adopt an innovation.

lagged effects: synonymous with *carry-over effects.*

lag indicators: used by market researchers; a series of economic indicators that often follow changes in the economic cycle.

laissez-faire: a doctrine that governments refrain from any form of trade regulation, leaving productivity and wealth distribution purely to market forces and individual industry.

Lanham Act of 1947: officially the Lanham Trade-Mark Act; federal legislation governing trademarks and other symbols for identifying goods sold in interstate commerce. As amended, it allows a manufacturer to protect his or her brand or trademark in the United States by having it recorded on a government register in the U.S. Patent Office, and provides for the legal right to register any distinctive mark. See *trademark.*

large-scale production: synonymous with *mass production.*

last-in, first-out: see *LIFO.*

lasting distinctiveness: see *distinctive competencies.*

late fringe: in broadcasting, the 11:00 P.M. to 1:00 A.M. segment designated by the television media for purposes of selling commercial time, which is usually charged at a significantly lower rate than prime time. See *day parts.*

late majority:

(1) consumers who are committed to familiar ways of doing things and skeptical of new ideas. They follow the early majority in the innovation diffusion process, are below average in economic and social status, and usually have minimal use of mass media and sales force.

(2) the fourth group of users to adopt an innovation. Synonymous with *general acceptors.*

latent defect:

(1) a defect in goods that is not visible to the naked eye.

(2) a deficiency in merchandise offered for shipment not discernible by careful inspection.

latent demand: a market situation in which a major segment of that particular market exhibits a preference for an item that is not being offered. The marketer's goal in dealing with a latent demand state is to measure the potential market's size and manufacture a product that will meet demand in the best possible fashion. Cf. *demand states.*

lateral search: a category of fortuitous scan ideation techniques that are partly miscellaneous but tend to force the ideator to stretch mentally out of normal channels. They are forcing techniques, based on the ideas that ideation can take place only when the mind assumes unique positions of viewing people or happenings. See *ideation.*

launch: signifying the marketing of a new product; can be either in a full-scale form of market testing or in the final marketing stage. See *beachhead; launch control.*

launch control: the process by which a management plans for and supervises the introduction of a new product; the product's progress is monitored against preestablished norms, variances are detected, and corrections are made to achieve the original goals set for the product.

launch cycle: the subphases of the innovation stage of a traditional product life cycle. The big step of innovation is broken into preparation (for marketing), announcement, beachhead, and early growth.

law of demand: the effect that is felt when the quantity demanded in a time period is negatively related to price; based on the assumption that the average potential customer is aware of alternative goods, has limited purchasing power, and a determination to maximize the utility accruing to him or her. See *bandwagon impact; Veblen effect.*

law of increasing costs: the concept that the average total unit cost in a production process increases as the volume of a firm increases. Cf. *proportional law.*

lawyer: (slang) a friend who advises another in a store whether or not to purchase an item, frequently resulting in the customer's not buying the item.

layaway plan: a method of deferring payments whereby goods are retained by the store until the customer has completed payments for them. Synonymous with *deposit plan.* See *deferred payment sale.*

layout:

(1) *general:* the sequence of printed matter, such as the pages of a brochure or booklet.

(2) *advertising:* the plan or makeup of an advertisement. The job readied to typesetting showing the arrangement of the copy elements and style of print; usually required before the production of an advertisement can begin because it serves as a guide to those concerned with approving and executing the printed advertisement. See *composition.*

L/C: see *letter of credit.*

lead: in sales, the name and address of a potential customer, either an individual or organization. See *referral leads.*

leader: in marketing, a dealer offer conditioned by a unit volume-purchase.

leader pricing: a method of setting prices for specific merchandise at levels so low that they yield minimal or no profit. Its purpose is to increase consumer traffic and to give the impression that the establishment offers items at low prices. See *loss leader.*

lead generation: a salesperson's identification of the best possible prospects (leads) that he or she can approach using sales calls or personal visits, by either asking known customers for names of others believed to be candidates; joining associations; speaking before professional or community groups, etc. See *endless chain.*

lead-in:

(1) *sales:* that part of the interaction that permits a sales representative to move toward a summing up or to close with a customer.

(2) *broadcasting:* a program immediately preceding another program on the same station. The lead-in program leads the audience to an advertiser's program on the same station. Cf. *lead-out.*

(3) *advertising:* the opening words in the copy text of the advertisement; used to lead the reader to the next text.

lead indicators: applied by market researchers; a series of economic indicators that often precede changes in the economic cycle.

lead-out: in broadcasting, a program directly after another program on the same station that leads the audience out of the advertiser's program on the same station. Cf. *lead-in.*

leads: see *lead.*

lead time: in purchasing and marketing, synonymous with *order cycle.*

lead user: those people or firms who most need the innovation being worked on and who will most likely participate in the innovation process. The idea itself often originates with a lead user and may even appear in prototype form in the lead user's firm.

leaf: a single section of paper constituting two pages of a book or other publication, one page being formed by either side of the paper.

leaflet: synonymous with *folder.*

learning curve: a graphic representation of the measured changes at successive units of practice.

learning curve pricing: a pricing technique where the manufacturer lowers the price of an item as production increases and becomes more cost-efficient.

learning requirements: various types of learning that new products often require from their purchasers. Without that learning, the purchase, trial use, or satisfaction will be threatened.

leaseback: a seller who remains in possession as a tenant after completing the sale and delivering the deed.

leased department: a department in a retail store, usually a department, discount, or specialty store, that is rented to an outside party.

leave-behind: synonymous with *leave piece*.

leave piece: printed information that the salesperson uses and leaves with a prospect. This piece usually has the name and telephone number of the salesperson so the prospect, on making a decision, will contact the salesperson and no one else. Synonymous with *leave-behind*.

leftover matter: copy that has been set in type but not used in the printing of an issue of a periodical or magazine.

legal lexicography: see *nationally advertised brand*.

legal residence: where a person lives; used by marketers and advertisers in sending materials by mail, etc. The law does not require anyone to spend a majority of his or her time in a certain place for it to be categorized as a legal residence; however, federal law recognizes only one legal residence for an individual. Cf. *domicile*.

legal weight: used in international marketing and sales; the weight of the goods and interior packing but not the container.

legitimization: with new merchandise, where early users serve as examples for future consumers who may be somewhat more conservative.

letter gadget: a three-dimensional article attached to or enclosed with direct-mail literature and used as a means of attracting attention and stimulating interest in the sales message.

letter of credit (L/C): an instrument or document issued on behalf of a buyer by a bank on another bank or banks or on itself. It gives the buyer the prestige and the financial backing of the issuing bank. The acceptance by the bank of drafts drawn under the letter of credit satisfies the seller and the seller's bank in the handling of the transaction. The buyer and the accepting bank also have an agreement as to payment for the drafts as they are presented.

letter of indemnity: a document issued by a merchandise shipper to a steamship company as an inducement for the carrier to issue a clean bill of lading, where it might not otherwise do so. It serves as a form of guarantee whereby the shipper agrees to settle a claim against the line by a holder of the bill of lading arising from the issuance of a clean bill.

level expenditure technique: a means of developing a media advertising schedule where each segment of a campaign is treated equally.

leveling: a cognitive process in which the information retained becomes shorter and more concise.

leveraged creativity: working a lesser creativity off the major creativity of others. A strategy of pioneering whereby the innovations are technically new and unique but considerably less significant than the original.

leveraged marketing: the process by which companies making industrial items diversify into high-profit consumer goods by shifting production to the needs of consumers; may be accomplished with minimal extra cost.

leveraging: the advantage (or disadvantage) obtained from using borrowed money to finance a business when the net interest rate of the borrowed funds is less (more) than the company's earnings rate.

levies: varying duties applied to imports from another nation.

liability:
(1) *general:* an obligation an individual has by virtue of law (e.g., a debt, a responsibility).
(2) *advertising:* an amount owed by advertisers for space or purchased time.

liberal return policy: the practice of a store to accept goods returned for refund or exchange with a minimum of difficulty to the customer.

licensing: a business arrangement in which the manufacturer of a product (or a firm with proprietary rights over technology or trademarks) grants permission to a group or an individual to manufacture that product in return for specified royalties or other payments.

licensing agreement: of importance to international marketers; the contracts between the exporter (a licensor) and an importer (a licensee) to make available to an importer some property of the exporter for a charge.

lien: a legal claim on goods for the satisfaction of some debt or duty. See *seller's lien; vendor's lien.*

life: in advertising, the length of time during which response may be felt from an insertion of an advertisement in a publication. When a message calling for an inquiry or an order is placed in a newspaper or magazine or other medium, requests are received soon after the appearance of the advertisement and continue for some time.

life cycle hypothesis: a theory of the saving decision stating that consumers save to be able to maintain a stable level of consumption in the future. See *marginal propensity to consume; marginal propensity to invest; marginal propensity to save.*

life cycle of product: the pattern of sales for an item as competition and new products evolve, bringing the item to its maturity, then decline, and eventual disappearance. The cycle time varies and is influenced by numerous variables as each product progresses through the stages of its life cycle. See *saturation.*

life cycle purchasing: where marketers promote consumer items to deemphasize acquisition cost as the major variable, and focus instead on four factors—acquisition, operating costs, servicing costs, and disposal.

life-style (lifestyle): the way in which a person lives and spends time and money. It is a function of the social and psychological factors that have been internalized by that person, as well as his or her demographic background.

life-style segmentation: dividing a market into subunits based on the way the members of each group choose to live, their activities, interests, and opinions.

LIFO (last-in, first-out): in valuation of inventories, the system whereby the price shown on the last incoming shipment of a particular item is the one used for current valuations and cost. Cf. *next-in, first-out.*

lift: material used in an advertisement that is taken from one advertisement and used in another, thus giving continuity, such as in a television soap opera.

limen: see *subliminal advertising.*

limited assortment store: a convenience store carrying up to 1,000 food items, usually private labels or packer labels. Usually the customer does his or her own packing of purchased items.

limited consumer decision making: takes place when a person uses every step in the final consumer purchase process but does not spend a great deal of time on any of them. The person has previously bought a particular good or service but makes some fresh decisions when that good or service comes under current purchase consideration.

limited distribution: synonymous with *selective distribution.*

limited-function wholesaler: synonymous with *limited service wholesaler.*

limited line stores: smaller retail operations that carry most goods in a narrow line of items (e.g., a women's apparel shop that carries casual and formal ladies' garments, sportswear, and lingerie, but not baby clothes).

limited line strategy: the choice of a company to concentrate on only a small number of variations of an item. See *broad-line strategy.*

limited-line wholesalers: synonymous with *specialty-merchandise wholesalers.*

limited marketing: a type of market testing that follows test marketing and precedes full-scale availability. Commitment has been made to full-scale marketing, but the marketing is tentative and based on limited geographic areas, specific firms, or specific applications.

limited order: an order in which the customer has set restrictions with respect to price.

limited service advertising agency: an advertising agency that specializes in a specific advertising function, such as having only copywriting services or art design services. Cf. *full-service agency.* See *advertising agency.*

limited service wholesaler: a wholesale middleperson who takes title to merchandise he or she resells but provides few services in an effort to lower costs. Synonymous with *limited-function wholesaler.* See *jobber.*

limited time station: a broadcast station that is assigned a channel or frequency for broadcasting during a particular time period. At all other times, the channel or frequency is then shared by other stations, as found in numerous local television stations.

line:

(1) *merchandising:* the silhouette and description of any apparel style.

(2) *retailing:* items carried by a merchant. Cf. *product line.*

(3) *advertising:* a unit of space measure equal to $1/14$ of a column-inch.

linear programming: a means for indicating how materials should be combined to produce the highest profits, given a set of materials with specified characteristics and a set of prices for the finished product.

linear system: a marketing system adjunct to a plant. Should the merchandise not be correct for a market, it piles up at the factory.

line consistency: the lines of items closely related to each other as determined by usage and production requirements, or that are distributed through the same channel.

line extension:

(1) a new variety of a basic product.

(2) adding of another variety of an item to an already established brand line of goods. Cf. *brand extension.*

line haul: the movement of cargo between cities and towns, as distinguished from pickup and delivery activities.

line of business: the general goods/service category, functions, geographic coverage, type of ownership, and specific business of a firm.

line rate: the cost of advertising in a printed medium based on a per-line basis.

line structure: the extension of a line of item by a manufacturer beyond the range currently produced.

linking phrase: in sales, the words that connect a feature with a benefit in a smooth, logical fashion. See *objection.*

liquid assets: assets that are easily converted into cash.

liquidity: the solvency of a business, with special reference to the speed with which assets can be converted into cash without loss.

list:

(1) *general:* an ordered set of items.

(2) *direct mail advertising:* the completed assembly of the names and addresses of people to whom an advertiser chooses to send his or her message. Synonymous with *mailing list.*

list broker: a commission agent who rents direct-mail lists to advertisers. A list broker also advises clients on which lists to rent and often evaluates list performance. See *list supplier.*

listening area: the territory surrounding a radio or television station in which are to be found set-owning families who can hear the station satisfactorily or those families who actually listen to the station.

list house: an organization specializing in the sale of lists of names and addresses of individuals and firms of various business classifications used for circularization by direct-mail advertisers.

list manager: the person or organization responsible for marketing a list to list buyers. This manager places advertisements regarding lists in trade bulletins.

list marketing: see *list manager.*

list price:

(1) *general:* the price of an item, subject to sale and cash discounts; any quoted price in excess of that obtained in the actual sale. Synonymous with *base price.* See *phony list price.*

(2) *retailing:* the retail price suggested or fixed by the manufacturer rather than the retailer. Cf. *fair-trade price.* See *unchanging list price.*

list supplier: the company that provides direct-mail advertisers with names and addresses of groups of people segmented by some common characteristic. See *list broker.*

list trade: the major activity of direct marketing, the business of selling and purchasing lists.

list user: people who rent or use, frequently on a one-time basis, a list for promotional purposes.

live: in broadcasting, not prerecorded; said to be happening in "real time." See *live time.*

live goods: displayed items for sale that are in great demand.

live time: in broadcasting, time set aside for a live broadcast. See *live.*

loader: a dealer offer tied to a single, volume purchase. A form of dealer premium.

load factor: the average number of passengers per automotive vehicles passing any outdoor advertising display.

loading:
(1) the amount added to an installment agreement to cover selling and administrative overhead, interest, risk, and so on.

(2) the addition of overhead to prime cost.

local advertising: advertising paid for by the retailer at a local rate. Often the advertisement suggests that the customer purchase the item "here." See *retail advertising.*

local brand: a brand found in a limited geographic territory.

local broadcast: a program sent out by a local advertiser over a station within a community.

local channel station: a radio station operating by license of the Federal Communications Commission with a power of 250 watts or less with a coverage area that is limited because of interference from other stations in the vicinity.

local costs: expenses incurred for goods or services purchased from suppliers in the buyer's country. The goods or services purchased must be needed to execute the exporter's contract or to complete the project of which the exporter's contract is a part.

local market: the area where the first steps are taken in assembling items from a number of farmers. Synonymous with *primary market.*

local media: newspapers; magazines and periodicals; radio, television, and cable stations established to service the communication needs of a particular community or urban area. Local advertisers are usually given a special discount rate to advertise in local media. See *local rate.*

local plan: the media choice determined by an advertiser's limitation of sale of his or her products in one town and its immediate trading area.

local program: a broadcast program that originates from a local broadcast station, as contrasted with a network program.

local rate:
(1) the advertising rate applied to regular advertisers in a newspaper as contrasted with transient rate. Cf. *one-time rate; single rate.* Synonymous with *retail rate.* See *local media.*

(2) the transportation rate when a shipment is handled totally over the lines of a single carrier.

local wholesaler: a wholesaler who operates within a small circle from his or her operation, usually less than 100 miles. Cf. *sectional wholesaler.*

location habit: the buyer's idea as to the type of marketing establishment he should use as a source of supply for certain goods.

logical appeal: an advertising strategy that purports to appeal to a consumer's sense of logic in promoting a product or service.

logistics: the science of planning, organizing, and arranging the most feasible combination of resources, areas, personnel and time needed to carry out established objectives, policies, and procedures.

logistics manager: synonymous with *physical distribution manager.*

logo (type): two or more letters, often making a short word, that represents the name or signature of an advertiser (e.g., NBC).

lollipop display: in outdoor advertising, a large round advertisement mounted onto a pole.

long-range plan:
(1) *general:* a plan in which the organization's managers set goals for a period of more than one year.

(2) *advertising:* a systematic procedure for directing and controlling future activities of an advertising agency for periods longer than a year. It predicts the future and establishes a strategy of action and expected results.

long-run: an extensive time period that permits a firm to develop its capability to manufacture.

long-run planning capacity: the rate of activity needed to meet average sales demand over a period long enough to include seasonal and cyclical fluctuations.

long-term sales: sales of goods and services on terms of five years or more.

looking-glass self: used by consumer psychologists; the way a person thinks he or she is perceived by other people.

loose market: synonymous with *buyer's market.*

loss leader: a retail merchandising strategy of advertising an item at a price below cost, to attract customers to the store in the expectation that they will purchase other items at full profit margins. See *leader pricing; merchandising leader; price lining.*

low-baller: (slang) an executive who has underestimated his or her expected financial situation.

low-ball price: the promotion, usually by telephone, of a product to lure the customer into the store, where the salesperson is unwilling to sell the customer the item at the previously announced price and attempts to pressure the customer to purchase a more expensive item.

lower-involvement model: advertising media needing little or no active participation by consumers to receive the advertising message, such as radio and television.

low-involvement merchandise: items that are bought routinely by the consumer without much thought, search, or purchase time. These people are usually indifferent to particular brands since there is minimal personal consequence to the purchase decision, nor does it relate to major objectives or values of the consumer. Cf. *high involvement.*

low-margin retailing: discount selling or mass merchandising.

low-pressure selling: a strategy used by a relatively new salesperson where the potential buyer is led to make the purchase by skillful questioning and apparent hesitation and reluctance on the part of the salesperson. It purports to give the customer the impression that throughout the conversation he or she has been in full control of the situation.

loyalty: see *brand loyalty*.

luxuries: comforts and beauties of life that are in excess of what is needed for a normal standard of living. See *optional consumption*.

macroeconomics: the study of statistics (e.g., total consumption, total employment) of the economy as a whole, rather than as single economic units. Cf. *microeconomics*. Synonymous with *aggregate economics*.

macroenvironment: all external market forces that determine a firm's ability to sell its products and services. These include:

(a) *economic environment*—economic forces that affect consumer's ability and preparedness to buy items or services.

(b) *demographic environment*—the examination of the population of target purchasers, with attention to their geographic dispersion, income levels, and distribution.

(c) *socio-cultural environment*—those sociological variables that influence consumers' attitudes and behavior and that, consequently, affect demand patterns.

(d) *political-legal environment*—monetary and fiscal factors (e.g., taxes, environmental legislation, federal laws) affecting advertising.

(e) *technological environment*—new technologies that influence the market by altering the ways people use items and services (e.g., the introduction of VCRs, microwaves).

(f) *competitive environment*—the process of evaluating competitors and the characteristics of their product and service offerings. Cf. *microenvironment*. See *environmental analysis*.

macromarketing:
(1) the study of the economic exchange process of a total economy. Cf. *micromarketing*.

(2) the bringing about of exchanges between individuals and/or groups so as to provide satisfaction of a society's wants and needs.

macrosales model: a way of illustrating the sales process by permitting sales to be presented in terms of a single variable consisting of units or dollars, and then examining this in relation to other pertinent variables. Cf. *microanalytic sales model*.

macrosegmentation:
(1) primarily used in industrial marketing; the determination of market potential by studying broad segmentation variables, such as data from the U.S. Bureau of the Census.

(2) a process in which an industrial market is divided into segments based on types of buying organizations.

MADA (money, authority, desire, access): in marketing strategy, an acronym for a method of predicting sales and measuring market potential. MADA attributes are assigned to differing populations to quantify consumers who have the money to buy a product, the power to make the buying decision, the interest in making a purchase, and the actual ability to obtain it.

Madison Avenue: a grouping of communications and advertising enterprises found along Madison Avenue in New York City. Today, many advertising firms have moved to different addresses within the city, and other major companies have moved out of New York City. The phrase, however, is still used to refer to the advertising industry and its agencies.

magazine: a print publication, usually issued regularly, devoted to a specific category of editorial matter. The majority of the revenue generated comes from the sale of advertising space rather than from the sale of the magazine. Synonymous with *periodical.*

magazine coupons: cents-off coupons printed within a magazine.

magazine group: several magazines published by one publisher that appeal to differing interest groups, such as the magazines of Time, Inc., which publishes *Time, Life, People, Money, Fortune,* and *Sports Illustrated.*

magazine impact technique: a means of recall testing to determine the communications effectiveness of periodical advertisements. With this method, respondents are asked to read the magazine and afterward describe the advertisements they recall from that issue.

magazine plan: a media strategy for placing advertisements solely in magazines within the target audience's area. For example, to reach people in the southwestern United States, advertisers would primarily place advertisements in magazines that have a circulation in the Southwest.

Magnuson-Moss Improvements Act of 1975: federal legislation designed to broaden the powers of the Federal Trade Commission with respect to misleading packaging and advertising of toys. Fines can result when violations are determined. Cf. *Magnuson-Moss Warranty Act of 1975.*

Magnuson-Moss Warranty Act of 1975: federal legislation requiring that all consumer items distributed in interstate commerce and sold with a written warranty must have the warranty designated as "full" or "limited," as the only permitted designations. To be known as a "full warranty," it must promise to remedy any defect or malfunction within a given and reasonable time period, by refund or free repair or replacement with an equivalent or very similar product. The consumer need not do anything more than give notice of the defect or malfunction. Cf. *Magnuson-Moss Improvements Act of 1975.*

mail-ballot map: a form of coverage map prepared for a radio or television station showing the location of those areas in which set owners listen to the station with a specified degree of regularity.

mail date: synonymous with *drop.*

mailer: a business that uses the mail primarily as the source of contact with purchasers. See *direct marketing.*

mail-in: synonymous with *mail-in premium.*

mailing list: synonymous with *list (2)*.

mail-in premium: a gift given as a special promotion by a manufacturer in exchange for appropriate representation of purchase of his or her goods, which is mailed to the manufacturer. Synonymous with *mail-in*.

mail interview: a survey technique in which questionnaires are mailed to potential respondents.

mail key: see *key code*.

mail-order: direct marketing activities that use the mail as their primary means for promoting and delivering goods and services, and to communicate with customers. Mail-order is different from other forms of direct marketing in that the purchaser and seller do not have any direct contract with each other. See *mail-order advertising*.

mail-order advertising: advertising designed to yield orders directly from prospects by mail. Media of any form can be used to deliver the advertising message. Its primary characteristics are that there is no interaction between the consumer and the advertiser and that, except for telephones, the mail is the only means of interaction between the two parties.

mail-order house: a commercial organization that receives its orders and makes its sales by mail. Some retail stores conduct a mail-order business, usually through departments set up for that purpose, but this does not make them mail-order houses.

mail-order retailer: a reseller who enters and fulfills customer orders through the mail.

mail-order wholesaler: an individual who sells by mail and usually advertises goods and services in a catalog. See *catalog*.

mail-survey map: a geographic map prepared by a radio or television station for the purpose of plotting the location of those areas in which the station may claim a listening audience.

main store: synonymous with *parent store*.

maintained mark-on: the difference between the cost for delivering goods and the price at which they are sold.

maintenance marketing: the monitoring of the market for shifts in customer demand.

major account: a customer of the firm whose business is critical and therefore requires special treatment and attention. Usually, such accounts are dealt with by senior personnel. Synonymous with *key account*.

major account marketing: synonymous with *national account marketing*.

major appliances: electrical housewares that are large in size and price, such as refrigerators, freezers, television sets.

major innovation: an item that has never been sold by any other organization.

majority fallacy: the belief that the trust of a promotion is pitched to the majority of the market. See *segmentation*.

major media: the principal advertising media—newspapers, television, posters, radio and movies.

make bulk: in international marketing, the process of placing together large shipments from multiple or smaller shipments to take advantage of large-volume discounts from carriers.

make-bulk center: synonymous with *freight forwarder*.

make good:

(1) *general:* to discharge an obligation or debt.

(2) *advertising:* to repeat a message without additional charge or to refund space or time charges as compensation for an error or omission of an advertisement. Usually, this credit is in the form of a rerun of the advertisement, subject to negotiation between the advertiser and the medium.

(3) *broadcasting:* an offer in the form of an extra run of a commercial when the medium did not deliver the anticipated audience volume or composition promised for a previously contracted commercial. It also is given when transmission is poor because of a problem at the broadcasting firm, or the commercial is run at a time not originally accepted by both parties.

make-or-buy decision: a firm's decision whether to produce an item or purchase it elsewhere.

maker:

(1) a manufacturer, processor, or producer of merchandise or products.

(2) an individual, firm, or other legal entity that signs a note, check, or other negotiable form as a responsible party.

makers and shakers: (slang) those who are in power.

make the cash: to decide whether the funds on hand, following receipts and payments, balance with the record of sales and payments of obligations.

make-up: the appearance of a page of the newspaper.

make-up restriction: a limitation imposed by a publication on the size and layout of an advertisement, to assure that the publication will not end up with an unusually shaped space on its pages, which tends to be unsuitable for editorial copy as well as being unsalable as advertising space.

mala fides: see *bad faith.*

malfeasance: a wrongdoing; a criminal act. Cf. *misfeasance.*

mall:

(1) a shopping center of a few or numerous blocks closed off to car traffic.

(2) a public promenade or concourse open only to pedestrian traffic. Synonymous with *shopping mall; shopping plaza.*

mall intercept interview: an interview conducted by a researcher in a shopping mall. The interviewer randomly chooses people walking around the mall, thus introducing a potential bias through his or her choices.

managed obsolescence: synonymous with *planned obsolescence.*

managed trade:

(1) of concern to international marketers; where goods entering borders are primarily determined by the political and economic weight of more dominant economic nations, with others left very much on the margins.

(2) any international commercial transactions that are impacted by nonmarket factors such as nontrade measures and quantitative restrictions. Cf. *free trade.*

management:

(1) *general:* the individual or group of individuals responsible for studying, analyzing, formulating decisions, and initiating appropriate actions for the benefit of an organization.

(2) *advertising:* the functions of planning, coordinating, and directing the activities of an advertising agency.

management by crisis: a leadership style that attempts to deal with shortcomings and failures by waiting until things get so bad that people will accept drastic measures. It is usually destructive and fails to attain stated organizational goals of marketing and advertising agencies.

management by exception: the practice by an advertising executive of focusing attention primarily on significant deviations from expected results. See *variance (3).*

management by objectives: see *MBO.*

management consulting: the service performed, for a fee, by independent and objective professionals, or by an organization, to assist managers in analyzing management problems, to recommend practical solutions and, at times, to help in the implementation of the recommendations.

management functions: the basic activities required of advertising and marketing managers in the performance of their jobs. The major management functions are planning and decision making, organizing for effective performance, leading and motivating, and controlling performance.

management information system (MIS): a specific data-processing system designed to furnish management and supervisory personnel with current information in real time. In the communication process, data are recorded and processed for operational purposes. The problems are isolated for referral to upper management for higher-level decision making, and information is fed back to top management to reflect the progress in achieving major objectives. Cf. *marketing information system.*

management of demand: a method of management that includes stimulation, facilitation, and regulation tasks.

management science: used by market researchers; the formulation of mathematical and statistical models applied to decision making and the practical application of these models through the use of digital computers.

managerial marketing: marketing carried out in large firms; involves planning, setting goals, developing strategies to achieve goals, etc.

Manchester Man: synonymous with *bagman.*

mandatory copy: copy that appears in an advertisement or on a product's label because it is required by law (e.g., "Warning: the Surgeon General has determined that cigarette smoking is dangerous to your health").

manifest: a statement itemizing the contents, value, point of origin, destination, and so on, of cargo that is shipped.

manit: one man-minute of production.

manpower planning: used by consumer researchers; a forecast of the future manpower requirements of an organization and the establishment of a plan to meet these needs.

manufacturability: the extent to which a new product concept or prototype is figured to be capable of effective and efficient manufacturing by available resources; also used during the design process, particularly when using computer-aided design. See *deliverability.*

manufacture: to produce, make, or fabricate something, by hand or using equipment.

manufacturer's agent: an agent (wholesale or middleperson) who takes neither title to nor possession of the merchandise he or she sells. The agent represents several noncompeting producers of goods that are purchased by one type of trade (e.g., a manufacturer's agent in women's apparel might sell dresses, blouses, belts, coats, stockings, etc., for different manufacturers). Synonymous with *manufacturer's representative.*

manufacturer's brand:

(1) items licensed for sale by other firms outside the manufacturer's product category. For example, a clothing manufacturer may license its name to a firm for use on jewelry. See *brand.*

(2) a brand name owned by the item's maker (e.g., Hershey's Kisses). The primary goal of having such a brand is to attact people loyal to the manufacturer's name. Synonymous with *national brand.*

manufacturer's cooperative advertising: synonymous with *cooperative advertising.*

manufacturer/service provider wholesaling: the policy of a producer's undertaking all wholesaling functions itself. These may be carried out through sales offices and/or branch offices.

manufacturer's representative: synonymous with *manufacturer's agent; sales representative.*

manufacturer's sales branch: an operation owned and controlled by a manufacturer, separate from his or her factories, where his or her salespeople may work and which contains stocks for deliveries to customers. Cf. *manufacturer's sales office.*

manufacturer's sales office: synonymous with *manufacturer's sales branch;* except no stock is housed within the office.

manufacturers'/service providers' agent: an agent who works for several manufacturers/service providers and carries noncompetitive, complementary products in exclusive territories. A manufacturer/service provider may employ many agents, each with a unique product-territorial mix.

manufacturer's/service provider's branch office: a form of manufacturer/service provider wholesaling. It includes facilities for warehousing goods as well as for selling them.

manufacturer's/service provider's sales office: a form of manufacturer/service provider wholesaling. It is located at a company's production facilities or a site close to the market and no inventory is carried there.

manufacturing: converting raw materials into a completed product by a mechanical, electrical, or chemical (i.e., not manual) process. See *production.*

manufacturing costs: costs incurred in the manufacturing process to bring a product to completion, including direct-materials, direct-labor, and manufacturing overhead costs.

manufacturing-driven firm: a company that gives major emphasis on manufacturing requirements in lieu of marketing considerations. Special attention is given to smooth production scheduling, low costs of production, and high volume. Cf. *marketing-driven firm.*

manufacturing inventory: a general term covering all items of inventory for a manufacturing entity. Items included are usually raw materials, work in process, and completed goods.

manufacturing order: instructions for directing production.

manufacturing overhead: all expenses arising from manufacturing activities except those of labor and materials.

margin:

(1) the difference between the market value of collateral pledged to secure a loan and the face value of the loan itself. See *gross margin; markup.*

(2) the difference between the cost of sold items and the total net sales income.

marginal analysis: analysis of economic information by examining the results of the value added when one variable is increased by a single unit of another variable. See *direct costing.*

marginal borrower: a borrower who will reject an opportunity to borrow if the interest charge is increased.

marginal buyer: a buyer who will refuse to buy if the price is increased.

marginal cost: the increase in the total cost of production that results from manufacturing one more unit of output.

marginal cost pricing: the rule enforced by competitive markets that price should be equal to the cost of producing the final (marginal) unit.

marginal customer: a purchaser judged by the seller to be at the edge between providing a profit large enough to be continued as a customer by the seller and a profit so small that he or she may be dropped as a customer.

marginal producer: a producer who is just able to meet his or her costs of production, with little actual profit.

marginal product: the additional product derived by increasing a given factor of production by one further unit.

marginal profits: the increase in total profits obtained by producing an additional unit of output.

marginal propensity to consume (MPC): the percentage of increases in income spent for consumption purposes. See *life cycle hypothesis.*

marginal propensity to invest (MPI): the percentage of increases in sales spent on investment items. Cf. *liquidity; quantity demanded.* See *accelerator principle; life cycle hypothesis.*

marginal propensity to save (MPS): the percentage of increases in income that individuals save. See *life cycle hypothesis; multiplier principle.*

marginal rate of factor substitution: the number of units of one factor of manufacturing needed to replace a unit of another factor of manufacturing to maintain the same level of output.

marginal return: the amount of sales of goods generated by an increment in the cost of advertising.

marginal revenue: the added revenue a business receives from the sale of one additional unit. In the short run, under conditions of competition, this is the same as the market price.

marginal seller: a seller who refuses to sell if the price is lowered. See *upset price.*

marginal utility: the increase in satisfaction the consumer receives from adding or consuming one more unit of an item.

marginal worker: a worker the value of whose production equals his or her actual wage.

margin of preference: the difference between the duty that would be paid under a system of preferences and the duty payable on a most-favored-nation basis.

margin of profit: operating income divided by sales. Income taxes are usually excluded, and depreciation is usually included in the operating expenses.

margin of safety:
(1) *general:* the balance of income left after payment of fixed charges.
(2) *sales:* the amount by which sales exceeds the break-even point, thus providing a cushion against a drop in sales or other unforeseeable forces. See *break-even point.*

mark: see *trademark.*

markdown: a reduction of an originally established selling price; popular with domestic goods sold in overseas markets where incomes tend to be lower, where wholesalers require a large piece of the revenue, and/or where surplus items are discarded. Cf. *clearance; markup.*

markdown cancellation: the increase in the retail price of an item that has been reduced. The increase can be up to the retail price at which the item was originally placed for sale, but not higher. See *retail method of inventory.*

market:
(1) *general:* people who possess the ability and desire to purchase, or prospects for a product or service. Cf. *marketplace.*

(2) *marketing:* a geographic area that includes a significant number of potential customers.

(3) *marketing:* an estimated or realized demand for an item or service.

marketable: that which can be sold.

market access:
(1) the degree of difficulty of admittance to an overseas market by an exporting nation.
(2) the ability of a domestic industry to penetrate a related market in a foreign country. The extent to which the foreign market is accessible generally depends on the existence and extent of trade barriers.

market aggregation: synonymous with *undifferentiated marketing.*

market analysis: an aspect of market research involving the measurement of the extent of a market and determination of its characteristics. See *Delphi technique.*

market anticipation: determination of how consumers will react in the marketplace at a given time.

market appeal: the attractiveness of a market based on its size or annual rate of growth. This appeal is influenced by economic and technological forces, to competitive variables and to environmental considerations.

market atomization: a marketing strategy that treats each consumer as a unique market segment.

market attractiveness: see *market appeal.*

market audit: a method for studying the marketing activities and structure of a business designed primarily to identify areas that require improvements to boost profits.

market basket pricing: setting prices so that the sale of one item encourages a buyer to purchase other items. Specials and tie-in sales are often used.

market breakdown technique: a forecasting technique that breaks down the sales forecast for a large unit into forecasts for smaller units.

market buildup technique: a forecasting method where data from a number of market segments is collected, analyzed separately, and then added together to yield a picture of the marketing environment for the purpose of sales forecasting.

market-by-market allocation: synonymous with *area-by-area allocation.*

market-by-market buy: a technique of buying commercial time on broadcast stations, where the time is purchased in one market at a time, as contrasted to a network purchase, where the time is purchased all at once on all the stations that are affiliated with the network throughout the nation or region. See *network buy.*

market channel: the path of the direct or indirect transfer of ownership to a product as it goes from a manufacturer to industrial or retail customers.

marketcide: self-inflicted and avoidable harm to an organization caused by a lack of attention to and poor implementation of marketing concepts and principles.

market cleavage: synonymous with *segmentation.*

market concentration:
(1) a form of market segmentation where the firm's efforts are concentrated on one segment of the potential population.

(2) that portion of an item's sales volume determined by a small number of large firms, expressed in dollars, units sold, etc.

market-controlled price environment: a situation characterized by a high level of competition, similar goods and services, and little control over price by individual companies.

market coverage: the measure of the degree of market exposure achieved. It is the total product sales of all the producer's retail customers expressed as a percentage of all retail sales for the product group or classification. The strategies used in determining what types of item to offer to which parts of a market include:
(a) *single market strategy*—where the firm concentrates on one segment of the market.

(b) *production specialization strategy*—where the firm chooses to manufacture one item for all segments of the market.

(c) *market specialization strategy*—where the firm develops all items for a particular market segment.

(d) *selective specialization*—where the firm develops different merchandise for different market niches.

(e) *full coverage*—where the firm makes different items for each individual customer (a rare approach).

market delineation: determining who will be the customers and prospects for a product and identifying their particular characteristics. See *market segmentation.*

market demand: the total amount of an item that is wanted at a specified price at a specific time. Market demand is measured by:

(a) *product levels*—determined by product type, form, sales (national, industry-wide, etc).

(b) *space levels*—determined by territory (regional, national, global).

(c) *time levels*—determined by whether the demand is for a short, medium or long-term period. See *overall market capability; potential demand.*

market demography: the application of demographic data to a particular market. See *demographics.*

market development: an approach that involves a firm's development of new markets for its merchandise or services, or the creation of alternate uses for the same items with the goal of increasing sales.

market disruption: difficulties in a domestic market as a result of a sudden increase in imports into that market.

market-driven economy: an economic system in which supply, demand, and price determine what products will be produced and who will receive those products. See *dual drive.*

market-driven firm: see *marketing-driven firm.*

marketer: those involved in the activity of attempting to sell something to someone.

market factor: a variable within the environment that can determine the call for a product or service.

market failure: a condition under which markets do not allocate resources efficiently, usually because of ignorance or externalities. See *externalities.*

market fit: the likelihood that a new item will be purchased by the same people who buy a firm's other goods. Cf. *test marketing.*

market growth rate: the yearly increase or decrease of a market, either presently or in the future; usually expressed as a percentage.

marketing: activities that accelerate the movement of goods or services from the manufacturer to the consumer, including everything connected with advertising, distribution, merchandising, product planning, promotion, publicity, research and development, sales, transportation, and warehousing of goods or services. Cf. *merchandising.* See *brand marketing; cause-related marketing; comparative marketing; concentrated marketing; convergent marketing; conversional marketing; custom marketing; database marketing; dimensional marketing; electronic direct marketing; electronic marketing; events marketing; global marketing; healthcare marketing; imbricative marketing; key account marketing; leveraged marketing; limited marketing; major account marketing; managerial marketing; mass marketing; metamarketing; mismarketing; multinational marketing; national account marketing; Pan-European marketing; pilot marketing; political marketing; pooled marketing; preemptive marketing; premarketing; retail marketing; service marketing; social marketing; societal marketing; sports marketing; stimulation marketing; symbiotic marketing; target marketing; telemarketing; undifferentiated marketing; value marketing.*

marketing audit: a careful study of the marketing system within a company to determine the value of the system's parts and how well the parts are performing their given tasks. To be successful, these audits should be comprehensive (should examine all critical components of the marketing program), and systematic (should include appropriate diagnostic steps that deal with the marketing environment, resources, and existing marketing initiatives).

marketing boards: agencies established to monopolize the sale of specified products, especially agricultural commodities. Marketing boards are similar to labor unions in that they organize large numbers of small producers to negotiate with a small number of purchasers.

marketing budget: a financial plan, based on projected sales of merchandise or services, that is used for allocating funds to cover marketing costs over a time period.

marketing channel: synonymous with *channel of distribution.*

marketing communications mix: efforts to communicate product information to existing and future customers.

marketing company era: recognition of the central role of marketing. The marketing department becomes the equal of others in the company. Company efforts are well-integrated and frequently reevaluated.

marketing concept:

(1) a strategy or idea for marketing products or services.

(2) a business philosophy consisting of the notions that marketing strategy should be developed based on customer needs and desires and that all marketing functions should be structured within the firm, with one person having overall responsibility.

Synonymous with *marketing philosophy.* See *consumer behavior research; marketing management; market research.*

marketing control chart: a chart that combines trend analysis with the performance standards set by the organization.

marketing cost analysis: examination of the costs incurred from the time items are produced to final delivery and payment, with a view toward providing useful quantitative financial data for the marketing firm.

marketing decision support system: a coordinated collection of data, models, analytic tools, and computing power by which an organization gathers information from the environment and turns it into a basis for action.

marketing department era: a stage during which the marketing department participated in company decisions but remained in a subordinate or conflicting position to the production, engineering, and sales departments.

marketing director: the individual who is responsible for overseeing all marketing activities.

marketing-dominated strategy: a focus of key managers on managing the consumer.

marketing-driven firm: a company that places its major effort in satisfying customers, such as shifting production schedules to accommodate customers' requirements, even if it incurs a loss to the manufacturer. Cf. *manufacturing-driven firm.*

marketing dynamics: usually within the control of management, shifts in the marketing mix determined by changes in the external environment.

marketing environment: contains controllable factors, uncontrollable factors, the organization's level of success or failure in reaching its objectives, feedback, and adaptation.

marketing ethics: the values and moral principles that should govern the marketer's behavior in the marketplace.

marketing function: an activity such as buying, selling, shipping, warehousing, grading and standardization, financing, assuming responsibility for taking the risk, and data accumulation.

marketing information: a marketing function characterized by the accumulation and dissemination of intelligence concerning market developments and other market information. See *marketing research.*

marketing information system (MIS): the entire system employed by a firm to gather, analyze, store, and disseminate relevant marketing information to the persons who require these data. Cf. *management information system.* See *marketing intelligence.*

marketing institutions: manufacturers and producers, wholesalers, retailers, transporting firms, advertising agencies, etc.

marketing intelligence: the part of the marketing information system that includes the procedures a company routinely uses to keep abreast of developments in the external environment. See *marketing information system.*

marketing management: the planning, directing, and controlling of the total marketing operation, including formulation of marketing goals, policies, programs, and strategy. It often embraces product development, the organization and staffing needed to discharge plans, supervision of marketing operations, and monitoring of performance. See *product manager.*

marketing-manager system: a product management organizational format under which a company executive is directly responsible for overseeing a wide range of marketing functions and for coordinating with other departments that perform marketing-related activities.

marketingmanship: the measure of skill in marketing a product or service.

marketing mix:

(1) the concept of Neil Borden that market strategy is based on the product, price, promotion, and channels in an integrated marketing program.

(2) the combination of activities involving product, price, place, and promotion that a firm undertakes to satisfy consumers in a given market. See *four O's; four P's.*

marketing myopia: a shortsighted, narrow approach to the marketplace. For example, a firm may fail to emphasize the assets or services inherent in an item's design, but instead will emphasize only the product's physical attributes.

marketing objectives: goals that are more customer oriented than the overall goals set by top management.

marketing opportunity analysis: a study of the marketing environment to determine what shifts may occur and to determine when problems might develop.

Important in setting strategies in dealing with competitors.

marketing organization: the organization of the marketing function by either: (a) *functional units*—where individual marketing functions are headed by managers.

(b) *product management units*—where distinctive items are assigned to product managers who oversee the activities of functional specialists.

(c) *marketing management units*—where major accounts are assigned to marketing managers who supervise the activities of functional specialists.

(d) *division units*—where a diversified firm has division marketing departments led by managers who report to a central corporate marketing department.

marketing performers: manufacturers and service providers, wholesalers, retailers, marketing specialists, and organizational and final consumers.

marketing philosophy: synonymous with *marketing concept.*

marketing plan: a carefully designed outline providing the firm's self-image, its objectives, all marketing programs to fulfill goals, and the means for assessing the effectiveness of such efforts. The term also encompasses responsibilities for discharging the plan, the strategies involved in the suggested development of the items, the definition of its target market(s), and the types of media and sales promotions to be incorporated. Synonymous with *action program; marketing strategy.*

marketing program: the coordination of the features of the marketing mix for a firm as a whole in reaching an objective.

marketing relativism: in international marketing, where decisions are based on experiences in selling people of differing backgrounds, traditions, and cultures. Synonymous with *principle of marketing relativism.*

marketing research:

(1) a systematic, objective approach to the development and provision of information for decision making regarding a specific marketing problem. The results provide facts required to make marketing decisions and will determine the extent and location of the market for a product or service.

(2) the process of gathering, recording, and analyzing information pertaining to the marketing of goods and services. Cf. *market research.*

marketing risks: possible losses of the marketer, including waste, obsolescence, damage, physical deterioration, stealing of items, credit, discontinuity of supply, shifts in demand affecting pricing, and Acts of God. See *risk.*

marketing strategy: synonymous with *marketing plan.*

market leader: the firm that controls the market share of products or services.

market-mapping inquiry: a study for identifying consumer attitudes, product comparisons, or marketing evaluations, where results can be charted on a graph to show a correspondence among variables.

market minimum: the rate of sales for an item or service that would be accomplished without any demand-stimulating costs such as promotional campaigns or advertisements.

market-minus prices: in retailing, the policy of trying to price similar items for less than that of the competition. Synonymous with *demand-backward prices*. See *at-the-market prices; market-plus pricing; variable pricing*.

market news: information regarding the condition of the marketplace.

market niche: usually a strategy of small firms; a narrow market segment that a firm targets because the segment lacks competitors yet offers a sizable sales potential. Cf. *niche marketing*.

market order: an order to buy or sell something at the price prevailing when the order reaches the market.

market-oriented production: production of a product or products in a foreign country that uses that product.

market outline: a summary of the relative place of a type of brand or item in the total market. Cf. *market structure analysis*. See *positioning*.

market penetration:
(1) the degree to which a product captures a percentage of the total market for that item. This includes the absence of competition for the item.

(2) a marketing strategy of the manufacturer to increase his or her sales within an existing market through using more aggressive marketing methods, such as greater concentration of commercial advertising or special promotional methods. See *penetration strategies*.

market period: the period from when an item is made until the moment it has been purchased.

marketplace: a general term identifying business and trade activities. Cf. *market*.

market planning: the process of identifying a firm's potential customers and their needs; affects the entire promotional campaign. See *planning*.

market-plus pricing: the price at which an item is exchanged in the market from day to day. Synonymous with *above-the-market strategy*.

market-position analysis: synonymous with *attribute mapping*.

market-positioned warehouse: a storage facility where merchandise is kept that is owned by the manufacturer, distributor, or retailer and is used to consolidate shipments and position items near their ultimate destinations.

market positioning: synonymous with *positioning*.

market potential: the maximum sales potential for all sellers of a product or service over a fixed period. See *sales potential*.

market power: the ability of a purchaser or seller to control price and quantity of an item.

market presence: in advertising, recognition in the marketplace; a product's reputation or identity with competitors or consumers.

market price:
(1) the price established in the market where buyers and sellers meet to buy and sell similar products.

(2) a price determined by factors of supply and demand rather than by management decisions.

market profile:
(1) a description of the characteristics of a market or market component.

(2) data about potential customers or an analysis by individual background (sex, age, etc.) of people who make up the market for a particular item or service. Cf. *market structure analysis*. See *market segmentation; market target*.

market rate: the interest rate charged a firm to borrow funds.

market ratio: the strength of one item or service to command another in exchange for itself in the open market.

market representative: the executive of a firm's buying office who gives his or her time and effort to a particular grouping of goods and makes data about it available to buyers of owned or operated stores.

market research: the part of marketing research that deals with the pattern of a market, measuring the extent and nature of the market and identifying its characteristics. Market research precedes marketing research. Cf. *concept testing; marketing research*. See *product planning*.

market review: synonymous with *situational analysis*.

market segment: a subdivision of the population, the people sharing similar characteristics. The firm often develops different marketing programs for each segment of its target market. Cf. *market segmentation*.

market segmentation: the separation of the market for an item into categories of location, personality, or other characteristics for each division; evolves as a result of the observations that all potential users of goods or services are different and that the same general appeal will not appeal to all prospects. Once the market has been segmented by a firm, it then engages in one of the following marketing strategies: differentiated marketing, undifferentiated marketing, or concentrated marketing. Cf. *market segment*. See *market profile; market target; segment; segmentation; subculture; whole market approach; zoning price*.

market share:

(1) a firm's percentage of its industry's total sales.

(2) the total number of units of a product (or their dollar value) expressed as a percentage of the total number of units sold by all competitors in a given market. Synonymous with *brand share; share of the market*.

market share analysis: a forecasting technique in which it is assumed that the firm's market share will remain constant and sales forecasts for the firm are based on forecasts for the industry.

market share goal: a benchmark representing that portion of a market a firm wishes to capture.

market size: the total demand for a given item or service in terms of the volume and/or value of that demand.

market skimming: an introductory pricing strategy of charging a high price to recover investment quickly.

market strategy: a marketing approach designed to enable a product to fulfill the objectives set for it by management. See *strategy*.

market stretching: a competitive strategy involving narrow segmentation where competitors aim on a wide basis; or the simplification that occurs where a market has been unduly fragmented.

market structure analysis: the study of competitive product offerings and buyer product preferences that account for the design features of items and the item preference characteristics of purchaser/consumer segments. Cf. *market outline.*

market-structured sales force: a sales force structure where sellers specialize in particular market segments and individual sales forces are created for different industries or for major customers within those industries. Cf. *product-structured sales force.* See *sales force.*

market target: the people or groups for whom an item and its program or marketing are intended. A strategy and a meaningful approach to fulfilling a stated goal must be established with respect to a market target. Cf. *target audience.* See *market profile; positioning.*

market temper: a consumer's attitude toward his or her future.

market termination stage: synonymous with *decline stage.*

market testing: a marketing method where the new item or service, once introduced is tested to predict its success in the marketplace. It also permits the firm to adjust production schedules. See *product testing; test marketing.*

market value: the prevailing price at which a product can be expected to sell within a given market.

marking: placing the correct tag on new goods, usually containing price, size, and style data. See *Kimball tags.*

marking duties: a special duty, in addition to ordinary duties, imposed on merchandise not properly marked so as to indicate to the ultimate purchaser the country of origin.

mark-on: the difference between the billed-cost price and the original retail price of an item. See *initial mark-on.*

Markov chain: used by market analysts; a probabilistic model of events in which the probability of an event is dependent only on the event that precedes it. Cf. *Monte Carlo method.*

marks of origin: in oversales sales, the physical markings on a product that indicate where the article was produced. Most countries have customs rules requiring marks of origin.

markup:
(1) an increase in the value of assets that reflects an improvement in their market value.
(2) an increase, in dollars or percentage, between cost and selling price. See *variable markup policy.*

markup cancellation: in retailing, decreases in further markups that will not lower the sales price of goods below the original retail. Important in retail accounting. See *retail method of inventory.*

mass appeal: nondirect marketing method purporting to appeal to all possible users of an item or service; best used when the item or service crosses all demographic and psychographic boundaries.

mass communication: the delivery of quantities of identical messages at the same time by communication firms or media.

mass display: in retailing, a large additional display of merchandise already on the shelf, positioned in a separate prominent place where the majority of store traffic will walk past it.

massed promotion: communication concentrated in peak periods (e.g., Christmas season).

mass magazine: a magazine (e.g., *Reader's Digest*) that is not designed or targets for a particular readership, but instead has an editorial structure of a general nature and appeals to a diversified readership.

mass marketing: the approach used to sell large volumes of items to everyone. This usually requires distribution in discount stores and supermarkets.

mass medium: an advertising medium used and accepted by a significant portion of the population.

mass merchandiser: an outlet with a discount image and following; it requires the handling of at least three merchandise lines within a floor space of 10,000 or greater square feet.

mass production: the utilization of mechanization to produce a large quantity of standardized items. Synonymous with *large-scale production.*

mass promotion: sales promotion activities concentrated at a specific time, such as the summer season.

master contract: synonymous with *blanket contract.*

master schedule: a schedule in production control that applies only to a completed product and its major elements.

matched sample: a sample group for test purposes that is the same as another group in terms of demographics, size, and psychographics. Matched samples are primarily employed to reinforce results, or test variations of an item or communications.

material budget: a forecast of how much material will be necessary to achieve a result.

material cost: the cost of an item that is a direct result of the cost of raw material and does not include indirect expenses such as wages and overhead.

material management: the material-handling functions as they relate to the physical distribution chain.

materials controller: an individual responsible for the physical movement of materials and goods. Synonymous with *stockroom supervisor; tool-crib supervisor.*

materials handling: the physical movement of materials and products within a work facility.

materials requisition form: a document used to request raw materials from the storeroom.

matrix:

(1) a device for problem solving by placing data in rows and columns for statistical analysis; used by market researchers in interpreting information.

(2) an enclosure that gives form to what lies within it.

mature economy: a national economy with a declining rate of population growth and a decrease in the proportion of national income utilized for new capital investment, accompanied by a relative increase of national income used in purchasing consumer goods.

maturity date: the date on which a financial obligation becomes due for payment and/or the date an obligation or contract expires.

maturity stage: the beginning of the demise of a product. The product's life cycle conclusion is measured by the leveling off of demand, a decline in profit, and increasing competition. Small and financially insecure institutions tend to drop out of the market in the maturity stage.

maximax criterion: a basis for decision making within an advertising agency whereby a manager determines the greatest payoff for each possible strategy and then chooses the one that is most favorable, thus maximizing the potential gain. Cf. *maximin criterion.*

maximil rate: the cost of a line of newspaper space that reaches 1 million circulation, based on the highest possible rate chargeable to an advertiser by the publisher.

maximin criterion: a basis for decision making with an advertising agency whereby a manager determines the most negative payoff for each possible strategy and then chooses the one that is most favorable, thus maximizing the minimum gain. Cf. *maximax criterion.*

maximizing: decision-making behavior in which an advertising agency manager selects the best alternative from all possible alternatives.

maximum depth requirement: the maximum height or depth a print advertisement must be to claim a fractional column rate, instead of being charged for a full-column rate.

maximum distribution: the number, usually given as a percentage, of outlets that have stocked the item at any time since an earlier retail audit.

MBO (management by objectives): a process whereby superiors and those who report to them jointly establish marketing and/or advertising objectives over a specified time frame, meeting periodically to evaluate their progress in meeting these goals.

McGuire Act: see *Miller-Tydings Resale Price Maintenance Act of 1937.*

mean:

(1) any statistical measure of central tendency. Cf. *median; mode.*

(2) the sum of all the numbers in a set of scores divided by the number of scores. The mean is a sound representation of quantitative data (e.g., the mean number of items bought per catalog order); used in statistical work by market and consumer researchers.

measure of value: a function of money that gives the standard for identifying the results of production, using the monetary unit as the common denominator.

measures of central tendency: see *average; mean; median; mode.*

mechanical recorder technique: a way of measuring broadcast audience size by program, using equipment attached to the set with the owner's permission. It automatically records when the set is placed on, to which station, and for how long.

media (singular—medium):

(1) *general:* the means used by transmitters of messages to deliver them to the intended receivers in a communication system.

(2) *advertising:* newspapers, radio, television, magazines, billboards, direct mail, and other such institutions that are used to carry advertisements. The four categories

of media are print media, broadcast media, out-of-home media, and direct-mail media. See *advertising media; alternative media.*

media analysis: the study and evaluation of various media approaches for promoting items and services to a wide or specific audience. Cf. *audience study.* See *zero-based media planning.*

media buy: buying of time and space in an advertising medium.

media buyer: the person working in an advertising agency who places orders for advertising space or advertising time. Cf. *space buyer; time buyer.*

media buying service: an organization that buys print space or broadcast time for a sponsor. See *rating.*

media class: the largest subunit of advertising media (e.g., national magazines, radio, television).

media coverage: synonymous with *reach.*

media director: an advertising agency executive who is responsible for choosing the media to be employed and scheduling the appearance of promotional material in such media.

media flighting: used with limited funds or for seasonal services or items; scheduling advertising for a stated time period, followed by a period free of advertising, then completed with another sequence of advertising.

media mix: the combining of various media in any promotional or advertising program. See *media support.*

median: a statistical average indicating central tendency, identified by a midpoint. Half the items being averaged must fall below the midpoint and half above. Cf. *mean; mode.*

media option: a single purchasable unit of advertising space or advertising time; determines the size, color, and place of a print advertisement or commercial. Usually given in a media plan. See *media plan.*

media owners: those firms having the right to sell advertising space or advertising time; usually, newspapers, magazines, radio and television stations. Somewhat of a misnomer in that they do not actually own the advertising media, but only the selling rights.

media placement: the generation of print and broadcast publicity.

media plan: the dimensions of the media selected in an advertising plan, giving goals, strategy, funds available, and time schedule. See *media option; media planning.*

media planning: inclusive of the advertising strategy; answers these questions: Who should be reached? Where are they located? What is the nature of the message? When should the advertising be scheduled? See *across-the-board.*

media reach: the size of an audience reached by an advertisement or commercial with a specific medium. It can also be determined by interviewing people (e.g., to gauge the reach of a particular magazine, asking people what magazines they have read within the past month). See *exposure.*

media representative: the salesperson retained by a publication or broadcast station who is responsible for selling advertising.

media schedule: the choosing of the media to be used and the timing of media options composing an advertising campaign.

media selection strategy: an approach for selecting the appropriate advertising media, usually, by determining which media will effectively reach the target audience and establishing a schedule to fulfill the advertising objectives.

media support: advertising media in its totality that is used to back up a promotion. See *media mix.*

media weight:

(1) the total audience delivery.

(2) the volume of audience delivery by an advertising promotion based on the number of advertisements and commercials, inserts, time dimensions, and budget.

medium: singular form of media. See *media.*

megaselling: selling orders of large quantities, or for significant sums of money. Synonymous with *big-ticket selling.*

"me" generation: a consumer lifestyle that stresses being good to oneself.

member-get-member promotion: a sales promotion method used in getting new customers by providing an incentive to current customers who then make referrals. As contrasted with friend-of-a-friend promotion, this form of promotion only provides incentives to people who are existing customers. Cf. *friend-of-a-friend promotion.*

membership group: a reference unit to which a person belongs and is an active participant, such as clubs, unions, religious organizations.

membership warehouse club: a retailing format in which final consumers and businesses pay small yearly dues for the right to shop in a huge, austere warehouse. Consumers buy merchandise at deep discounts.

memorandum sale: the sale in a retail operation of consigned goods whose title rests with the vendor for a stated period. At the end of the period, unsold items are eligible for return to the vendor, and the sold or held goods are billed to the merchant. Cf. *on consignment.*

mercantile agency: an organization that supplies its subscribers with credit data on individuals and firms. In addition, some mercantile agencies gather statistical information and serve as collection depositories of past-due accounts.

mercantile credit: the deferring of payment between a buyer and the seller, both of whom are merchant middlepeople.

mercantile customer: any merchant middleperson.

merchandise:

(1) *general:* purchased articles of business held for sale (noun).

(2) *sales:* to plan or promote the sale of goods (verb). Cf. *goods.*

merchandise budget: in retailing, a plan in dollars of identified efforts involving merchandise for a given time period; includes sales projections, inventories, markdowns, discounts, expenses, returns, and controllable net profits. It is used for assessing current practices as well as for projecting future activities.

merchandise charge: extraneous costs (including shipping, insurance, demurrage, etc.) added to the cost of goods prior to mark-on.

merchandise control: the collection and analysis of data on purchases and sales items, either by unit or by dollars.

merchandise inventory: products held by an entity for resale to customers.

merchandise manager: an executive who is responsible for supervising the purchasing, selling, and inventory control activities in a store.

merchandise mart: a building, usually large, that contains manufacturers' showrooms where retailers can examine the goods and place orders. Cf. *resident buyer; sales office.*

merchandiser: a display unit that holds items to be sold on the floor of the store.

merchandise resource: the source of supply from which salable and reliable goods are purchased on a recurring basis with few complications, if any, over an extended time period. See *resource.*

merchandise transfer: the transfer of goods from one accounting unit of a store to another. Merchandise can be transferred from department to department, from one branch store to another branch, or from home office to branch store.

merchandising:
(1) *retailing:* all activities connected with buying and selling of merchandise, including displays, promotions, pricing, and buying. See *loss leader.*
(2) *manufacturing:* the activities required in the attempt to make a product interesting to buyers (packaging, promotion, pricing arrangements, etc.). Cf. *marketing.*

merchandising allowance: the lowering of the wholesale price as an incentive to middlepeople and to wholesalers by compensating the retailer for expenditures made to promote the merchandise.

merchandising conglomerate: a corporation of a number of diversified retailing organizations under a single management. Their stores may be of various types. Synonymous with *conglomerchant.*

merchandising group: several members of a cooperative chain that join forces under a common name to facilitate their advertising and promotion.

merchandising leader: a store that promotes several items at attractive prices to entice customers into the store. See *loss leader.*

merchandising service: merchandising assistance provided by one of the communications media for the placing of copy, advertising, commercials, layouts, etc. Traditionally, this type of service is provided without charge to advertisers.

merchandising the advertising: selling the advertising and sales promotion program to channel intermediaries to generate their enthusiasm and gain their support.

merchant: an individual who takes title to goods by buying them for the purpose of resale.

merchantism: the responsibility of the merchant to his or her customers; deals with appropriate customer service, emphasizing merchandise awareness and knowledge of the goods.

merchant middleperson: an intermediary who takes title to the products he or she distributes.

merchant wholesaler: a middleperson who receives title to merchandise purchases for resale to firms that plan to resell the goods or process them in some fashion for resale. See *wholesaler.*

merge-purge: the combining of two or more mailing lists, to identify duplications and eliminate unwanted names.

merger: the combining of two or more entities through the direct acquisition by one of the net assets of the other. A merger differs from a consolidation in that no new entity is created by a merger, whereas in consolidation a new organization comes into being and acquires the net assets of all the combining units.

merit goods: items for which the government determines or heavily influences levels of consumption according to the argument that individuals are not qualified to make the choices (e.g., education, automobile safety equipment).

message:
(1) an idea that is to be conveyed from a source to a receiver.

(2) any communication between persons. See *advertising message; message development.*

message channel: a vehicle for delivering a message.

message development: determining what is to be said in the advertisement. Objectives are first established. See *source; unique selling proposition.*

message feedback: the response of a message receiver to the message.

message impact: the effect of the message contained within an advertisement on the target audience's perception of it and their reaction to it, especially as it leads to further buying of the item advertised.

message permanence: the number of exposures one advertisement generates (repetition) and how long it remains available to the audience.

metamarketing: the study of marketing by focusing all social, ethical, scientific, technical, and business experience on marketing, thereby setting a full range of experience with the human being.

methods study: the analysis of the flow of work, particularly the utilization of materials to permit more efficient use of manpower.

metroarea: see *metromarket.*

metromarket: the area, usually the inner city and its suburbs, from which a retail store draws most of its customers.

metro rating: households with television within a metromarket that is tuned into a specific program or station.

microanalytic sales model: identifying the sales process by having all sales be the item of the number of purchasers within the market, the percentage who purchase from the company, and the average rate of buying. Cf. *macrosales model; microbehavioral sales model; microcomponent sales model.*

microbehavioral sales model: identifying the sales process by having awareness of the individual customer's knowledge, attitudes, actions toward products, and environmental variables affecting him or her so that the probability of a purchase can be determined. Cf. *macrosales model; microanalytic sales model; microcomponent sales model.*

microcomponent sales model: identification of the sale process by displaying sales as composed of additive components, each subject to separate analysis. These variables can be sales by item, customer, or salesperson, etc. Cf. *macrosales model; microanalytic sales model; microbehavioral sales model.*

microeconomics: the examination of the economic behavior of individual units in the economy, such as households or corporations. Cf. *macroeconomics.*

microenvironment: internal factors within the organization that influence the firm's marketing efforts, such as adequacy of capital, talent, absenteeism, etc. Cf. *macroenvironment.*

microlevel approach: a method used to respond to changes of small magnitude, such as for individuals or groups.

micromarketing:
(1) the study of the economic exchange process of individual firms. Cf. *macromarketing.*

(2) strategic management of human and organizational exchange relationships so as to provide socially responsible want and need satisfaction throughout the world while achieving the marketer's objectives.

microsegmentation:
(1) a process in which industrial market segments are subdivided on the basis of characteristics of the buying center and individual participants.

(2) in industrial marketing, the determination of the market potential for items or services by collecting data about the characteristics of potential customers, usually through the personal experience of salespeople.

middleman: see *middleperson.*

middle management:
(1) management personnel who report directly to top management.

(2) the level of management responsible for carrying out the directives of top (senior) management.

middle-of-month dating (MOM): an invoicing system that uses the 15th and the last day of the month as cutoff dates. All invoices dated before the 15th are considered dated the 15th; on and after the 15th, when the credit period begins, invoices are dated with the last day of the month. Discount and due dates are counted as from one of the two cutoff dates.

middle-of-month terms: see *middle-of-month dating.*

middleperson: formerly middleman (rarely middlewoman); an individual who buys merchandise with the expectation of reselling it for profit. At times, a middleperson may arrange for such transactions without actually having possession of the goods. Synonymous with *intermediary.*

milestones of life: the stages of the life cycle that an individual passes through.

milking:
(1) *general:* (slang) management's attempt to squeeze the last remaining profits from a firm without leaving sufficient reserves for improvements or for a downturn period.

(2) *marketing:* (slang) a short-range strategy to get the largest possible profit from a product in the shortest amount of time, regardless of the product's long-range projections for sales. It is used most often when budgets are minimal

and funds are in demand, so that profits from one item can be used to evolve other company items that could have an even greater profitability. Cf. *abandonment stage.*

Miller-Tydings Resale Price Maintenance Act of 1937: federal legislation enabling manufacturers to take advantage of state fair trade laws without being prosecuted for violation of the federal antitrust laws. See *fair-trade acts.*

milling in transit: synonymous with *transit privileges.*

mill net return: the amount the plant receives for an item sold on a delivered price basis after the actual freight cost to the factory is subtracted from the price. See *freight absorption.*

mill supply house:

(1) a general-merchandise wholesaler that operates in an industrial setting.

(2) the industrial equivalent of a general line, full-service merchant wholesaler, often focusing on supplying one industry.

minimarket test: a controlled-sale market testing in outlets that are a small, nonrepresentative sampling of the market. Product is usually placed into the outlets (not sold), and promotion is much less than planned ultimately. Primarily tests just the willingness to spend some money for a product trial.

minimax regret criterion: the directive to choose that alternative offering the lowest chance of loss or failure.

minimum depth requirement: a newspaper tradition that advertisements be in proportion, usually an inch in depth for every column in width. For example,

should an advertisement be three columns wide, it must also be three inches high.

minimum markup laws: synonymous with *unfair practices acts.*

miniwarehouse mall: a type of shopping center in which a large warehouse offers space to a variety of sellers, including both retailers and wholesalers.

minor innovation: a product that was not previously sold by the company but has been marketed by some other company.

mirror principle: a marketing approach suggesting that customers will respond in the same fashion as they are treated. Cf. *mirror response technique.*

mirror response technique: a sales technique of responding to a customer's objections to a product or service by repeating what the prospect is understood to have said. The goal is to have the customer reconsider the statement. Synonymous with *repeating technique.*

MIS:

(1) see *management information system.*

(2) see *marketing information system.*

misdirected marketing effort: see *eighty-twenty principle.*

misfeasance:

(1) illegal or improper exercise of a legal responsibility.

(2) failure to properly perform a lawful act, or performance of an action without proper notice to those involved. Cf. *malfeasance.*

misleading silence: a deceptive advertising practice in which the advertising fails to mention or identify a potentially negative aspect of an advertised service or product. The Federal Trade Commission may determine that the incomplete disclosure can confuse or misrepresent the item or service to the public and will issue a letter of concern to the maker or the product or creator of the service.

mismarketing: a failed or curtailed marketing program, usually resulting from poor decision making and inappropriate information.

misredemption: the incidence of error and fraud in offering for redemption to the manufacturer coupons given to or secured by retailers as the result of a couponing effort.

misrepresentation: the practice of giving a positive statement or claiming an alleged fact about a product or service that is not true, thus leading to a false conclusion.

missionary sales: the activities of a manufacturer's representative who works closely with various firms and middlepeople to increase the product sales. See *detail person.*

missionary salesperson: synonymous with *detail person.*

mission statement: a part of corporate or division strategy; the essential character of the business that is a necessary input to new product strategy.

mix:

(1) *retailing:* the combination of merchandise in a retail package or the complete variety of inventory of a retailer, wholesaler, or distributor.

(2) *merchandising:* the combination of goods, including various sizes of the same item, for a specific brand in a particular store.

(3) *broadcasting:* the combining of programs in a contract, for a series.

(4) see *audience composition; product mix; promotional mix.*

mixed approach: an international marketing strategy that combines standardized and nonstandardized efforts to enable companies to maximize production efficiencies, maintain a consistent image, exercise some home-office control, and yet be sensitive and responsive to local needs.

mixed brand method: a strategy where a manufacturer produces a number of similar items under differing brand names, or where the retailer or middleperson sells items under differing brand names, or where a retailer or middleperson sells items under a dealer or generic name as well as under the manufacturer's name.

mixed costs: costs that include both fixed and variable elements within a relevant range of activity. Synonymous with *semivariable costs.*

mobile franchise: a conventional franchise except that the franchisee dispenses the merchandise from a vehicle that is taken from place to place.

mode: used by consumer and marketing researchers; a statistical measure of common tendency or average that identifies the value of the variable giving the greatest height on a graph of the frequency distribution. Cf. *mean; median.*

model: a theory used to analyze various forms of behavior. The closer the model is to the real world, the more useful it is for analysis.

model bank: the component of a marketing information system that contains mathematical marketing models that show relationships among various marketing activities, environmental forces, and desired outcomes.

model stock: the ideal sales situation of having the right goods at the right time in the right quantities at the right price. Cf. *basic stock.* See *assortment plan.*

mode of reaction: the manner in which product testees give their reaction to a product use test. Options include like/dislike, preference, and descriptive, diagnostic information.

modification:
(1) any adjustment of an existing product's style, color, or model.

(2) any product improvement; or a brand change.

modified break-even analysis: a form of demand-based pricing that combines traditional break-even analysis with an evaluation of demand at various levels of price. It reveals the price-quantity mix that maximizes profits.

modified rebuy: in industrial purchasing, where adjustments are made in the price or specification of the item to be ordered, thereby making the process more complicated than a straight rebuy. Cf. *straight rebuy.* See *new-task purchasing.*

modular service agency: synonymous with *a la carte agency.*

MOM: see *middle-of-month dating.*

mom and pop outlet: an affectionate term for a small store, generally operated by members of a family with limited capital. See *bluefingers.*

monadic test: a product use testing format where only the new item is tested.

money, authority, desire, access: see *MADA.*

money illusion: the perception that an increase in all prices and incomes by the same proportion produces an increase in consumption, although real incomes remain the same.

money income: the amount of money received for work performed.

money pinch: see *pinch.*

money supply: the total sum of currency circulating in a country.

monger: a trader or seller, often used in a derogatory fashion.

monitoring results: comparing the actual performance of a firm, business unit, or product against planned performance for a specified period.

monitor role: an informational role in which a marketer continually scans the environment to collect information pertinent to the campaign or unit he or she manages.

monopolistic competition: a form of competition in which the product of each competitor in a particular field differs from other competitors' products in some way so that an exact duplicate cannot be obtained from another source. Most competition in the United States is monopolistic competition.

monopoly:
(1) the ownership of the source of a commodity or domination of its distribution.

(2) the exclusive dominance of the supply and price of a commodity or product acquired by a franchise or government patent. Cf. *oligopoly.* See *perfect monopoly.*

monopsonist: a purchaser working in a market where there are no other buyers.

monopsony: a market situation in which there is only one buyer for an item. Cf. *duopsony; oligopsony.*

monostasy: the fundamental drive in people that creates the desire to be independent from others.

montage format: in print and television media, advertising that juxtaposes a number of pictures or images to create overall impression in the mind of the viewer.

Monte Carlo method: used by market analysts; statistical sampling techniques that obtain a probabilistic approximation to the solution of a mathematical or physical problem. Cf. *Markhov chain.*

mood advertising method: advertising without any explicit claim about an item or service; the claim is suggested by the mood, such as fun, sex, youth, set around the item or service.

morale: the extent to which an employee's or customer's needs are met and the extent to which the person perceives that satisfaction as stemming from his or her total job and life situation.

morning drive: the radio broadcast time period from 6:00 A.M. to 10:00 A.M., from Monday thru Friday. This time period plus the afternoon drive period (3:00 P.M. to 7:00 P.M.) represents the largest listening radio audience. See *day parts.*

morphological research: a form of marketing research that focuses on how decisions are made.

mortality curve: synonymous with *decay curve.*

motivation: an important component of consumer buying; a stimulus that differentially energizes certain responses within a person. See *rational buying motives; self-concept theory; trio of needs.*

motivational needs: psychological forces that affect thinking and behavior (e.g., needs for self-actualization, belonging, feelings of security). A theory developed by A. Maslow details an individual's motivational needs. Cf. *motivator-hygiene theory.*

motivational research: a technique developed by E. Dichter, purporting to correlate behavior, needs, emotions, and desires with consumer activity. The information collected is useful to advertisers and advertising agencies in planning new items, planning advertising campaigns and, in general, preparing new strategies. See *consumer behavior research; hidden persuader; impact.*

motivation research: see *motivational research.*

motivator-hygiene theory: F. Herzberg's theory that identifies conditions operating primarily to dissatisfy people when they are not present (e.g., hygiene factors—salary, job security) and job conditions that lead to a high level of satisfaction when they are present (e.g., achievement, growth). Failure to meet the latter conditions is not highly dissatisfying. Cf. *motivational needs.*

motive: a need or want that is activated by a particular stimulus and initiates behavior toward some goal. See *drive theory.*

moving average: a perpetual inventory cost-flow assumption whereby the cost of goods sold and the ending inventory are determined to be a weighted-average cost of all merchandise on hand after each purchase.

MPC: see *marginal propensity to consume.*

MPI: see *marginal propensity to invest.*

MPS: see *marginal propensity to save; multiplier principle.*

MRO: maintenance, repair, and operation of supply items; consumable supplies used in the production of goods and services.

MS: see *multidimensional scaling.*

multiattribute segmentation: market segmentation based on two or more demographic factors (e.g., a firm can segment the market based on people's age and sex).

multibrand strategy: a product strategy based on the expectation that a firm markets two brands in the same market will, with all else constant, hold a greater brand share than one brand will obtain on its own, and with the right circumstances, three brands can also achieve greater share than two, etc.

multichannel marketing system: the supplier's technique of making use of two or more channels to reach consumers with his or her items. It can create friction between the supplier and a middleperson when interchannel competition to sell the same item intensifies. When the channels are used for different goods, there are rarely problems.

multidimensional scaling (MS): in marketing research, the geometric presentation of the perceptions and attitudes of respondents. The data are then analyzed to assist decision makers in solving marketing concerns (e.g., determining how a group of people perceive a particular

product). See *perceptual mapping; positioning; product design model.*

multimedia:

(1) *general:* a partnership of technology (the telephone, television, and computer) and commerce, with advances in each driving the others forward.

(2) *advertising:* advertising promotion using two or more media; usually one serves as the primary medium and is reinforced with the secondary medium. For example, a television commercial may support a newspaper insert. The majority of more costly advertising campaigns include several media.

multinational marketing: the setting of resources and goals of an organization on a global market basis. It involves the crossing of national borders, not only physically but also in terms of financial transaction, capital investments overseas, licensing, royalty payments, etc.

multipack: a container holding two or more separately packaged items.

multiple brand entries: several brand names used by a manufacturer on essentially the same product to open up new market segments. See *adaptive product.*

multiple buying influence: any purchase decision shared by several people, usually at differing levels of management.

multiple packaging: the inclusion of more than one item in a single container (e.g., the six-pack approach to beverage packaging).

multiple pricing: a price reduction offered if more than one unit is purchased. Cf. *multistage pricing.*

multiple purchasing influence: in industrial marketing, the requirement that a number of people approve the purchase of an important item. See *key buying influence.*

multiple regression analysis: used by market researchers; a technique for studying the relationship between independent and dependent variables with the derivation of a regression equation that is used to predict the latter from the former.

multiple retailers: see *chain store.*

multiple sales: the result of selection by customers of multiple rather than single items to purchase.

multiple source purchasing: purchasing from more than one supplier the goods considered to be particularly important to the company.

multiple unit packaging: combining a variety of units of an item into one wrapping or container with the expectation that the purchaser will take the number as a unit item. Example, beer six-packs.

multiple-unit pricing: pricing goods by "so many for a price," (e.g., 5 for $1.00). Cf. *unit pricing.*

multiplier principle: the reciprocal of the marginal propensity to save. The multiplier is a figure that relates the changes in investment and spending to alterations in aggregate income.

multistage pricing: a planning method that sets a broad price policy by integrating a series of individual pricing decisions into a coherent price framework for the company. A number of steps are taken in sequence commencing with the selection of a target market and finishing with the formulation of a specific price. Cf. *multiple pricing.*

multistep flow of communication: the communication theory that suggests opinion leaders not only influence but also are influenced by others.

multiunit advertising: the practice of including two or more company products in a single advertisement to reduce media costs.

multivariable segmentation: market segmentation that uses more than one factor (e.g., age, sex) to differentiate the population.

Murphy's law: the theory that if something can go wrong, eventually it will.

musical advertising approach: in broadcast advertising, using music to communicate the product message.

mystery technique: a method of salespeople in the first few minutes of customer contact. A dangling statement is used to attract the prospect's attention.

N: used by market and consumer researchers; the number of instances, of whatever sort, in the total population being studied.

n: used by market and consumer researchers; the total number of cases or observations in a subgroup of a population being studied.

NAD: see *National Advertising Division.*

Naderism: at times, used as synonymous with *consumerism.* Named for consumer advocate Ralph Nader. See *consumerist.*

NAFTA: see *North American Free Trade Agreement.*

nailed down: goods advertised at an extremely low price but which the store makes every effort not to sell. See *bait advertising.*

NAM: see *National Association of Manufacturers.*

name advertising: see *retentive stage.*

name slug: an advertiser's signature or logo (type).

NARB: see *National Advertising Review Board.*

narrowcasting: a technique for reaching small yet highly defined market segments with specialized broadcast programming (e.g., producing a program on ballet that appears on a public television station only).

narrow market: a condition that exists when the demand for a product or service is so limited that small alterations in supply or demand will create major fluctuations in its price. See *broad market.*

national account marketing: a marketing approach where the company's biggest and most important customers are provided with special recognition for the volume and profitability of sales they provide. Synonymous with *key account marketing; major account marketing.*

national accounts: synonymous with *direct accounts.*

national advertising:
(1) the advertising of a manufacturer or wholesaler, whose goods or services are sold nationally, as contrasted with that of a retailer or local advertiser.

(2) advertisements that appear in national media, print or broadcast. See *nationally advertised brand; promotional advertising.*

National Advertising Division (NAD): a unit of the Council of Better Business Bureaus which is the investigative arm of the advertising industry's self-policing organization, the National Advertising Review Board. NAD decisions can be appealed to NARB. See *National Advertising Review Board.*

National Advertising Review Board (NARB): the advertising industry's self-policing organization, created by the Council of Better Business Bureaus and three trade groups in 1971. NARB reviews national advertising for deceptive practices and hears appeals brought against the NAD. See *National Advertising Division.*

National Association of Manufacturers (NAM): a major organization of employers, founded in 1895 and structured with departments of trade, law, industrial relations, and publicity.

national brand: synonymous with *manufacturer's brand.*

national competition: the ability of a nation's producers to compete successfully in the world markets and with imports in their own domestic markets.

national income: of major use by market analysts; the total of the incomes received by all the people in a country over a stated period. It is equal to the gross national product minus depreciation minus sales taxes and other small items.

nationally advertised brand: the basis for legal lexicography; a New Jersey case before the State's Alcoholic Beverage Commission where Seagrams attempted to disenfranchise liquor distributors based on the statute permitting this action if the liquor or wine sold was not appropriately a "nationally advertised brand." Applying definitions from English dictionaries going back to the 17th century to the present, J. M. Rosenberg helped to convince the Commission that Seagrams had improperly disenfranchised the distributors since their products were indeed national advertised brands. See *national advertising; word-of-mouth advertising.*

national plan: a geographic plan for using media where the intent is to reach the largest number of different customers over the entire nation at the lowest cost per thousand.

national rate: synonymous with *one-time rate.*

national rating: for a television or radio network system or program broadcast over the United States, the percentage of radio or television households or individuals estimated to be in the audience as measured over a specific period of time.

national treatment: important in international marketing of goods; a form of friendship where laws governing the marketing of domestic items in nations that have signed treaties are extended to items designated as "foreign" or "imported." The United States accords national treatment in virtually every sector and believes that it should be granted unconditionally.

national wealth: the combined monetary value of all the material economic products owned by all the people in a country.

national wholesaler: a wholesaler whose activities can reach most or the entire nation. Cf. *sectional wholesaler.*

natural account: an accounting category that reflects how money is actually spent.

natural brands: synonymous with *producer-controlled brands.*

natural business year: a 12-month period, usually selected to end when inventory or business activity is at a low point.

natural expenses: a firm's expense items categorized according to the quality of its cost rather than the reasons for which it was first incurred; a form of cost analysis.

natural fold: folding a direct advertisement so that the continuity of the message is emphasized as the piece is unfolded.

natural monopoly:

(1) a monopoly that results from natural conditions (e.g., a crop that demands special climate is subject to monopolization by a grower in the area having that climate).

(2) among industries that experience economies of scale, the situation in which cost per unit is lowest when there is only one company in the industry.

natural products: see *natural resources.*

natural resources: all materials furnished by nature (minerals, timber, water, etc.).

natural trading area: the geographic boundaries containing customers that use a particular store or company. In most studies, customers become fewer as the distance increases from the store or company.

near-pack premium: discounted merchandise or gifts that are too large to include inside or to affix to the item being promoted. Such premiums are placed near the product display so as to visually and physically connect the item and the premium.

neck hanger: the tag placed around a bottle's neck that becomes a coupon, a means of communicating information, or a special product offer.

need: something that is necessary for a person's physical or psychological well-being.

need awareness: the degree to which customers become aware of their needs and are prepared to talk about them with others.

need directed: descriptive of a customer's purchase based on the need for sustenance and survival. See *VALS.*

need hierarchy model: see *motivational needs.*

needle trades: apparel-producing industries.

need-satisfaction approach: a higher-level selling method based on the principle that each customer has different characteristics and wants. The sales presentation is adapted to each individual customer.

negative appeal: advertising copy concept describing the negative conditions of life without the advertised item or service; appeals to consumers' anxiety about not using the item or service by emphasizing the loss they would experience by not buying the merchandise or service. Cf. *positive appeal.*

negative authorization: credit approval where a list is maintained of delinquent payments. Should a customer's name not appear on the list, his or her request for credit is then approved. See *floor limit.*

negative demand: the situation created if a major segment of a market dislikes an item so much that it takes appropriate action to avoid the item.

negative elasticity: the concept that demand moves in the same direction as price. See *elasticity.*

negative group: any reference unit whose life style or action patterns an individual attempts to avoid. Synonymous with *negative reference group.*

negative option selling: where the consumer informs the salesperson by a given date not to forward the items that he or she does not want. Used extensively by book clubs and record clubs. Cf. *positive option selling.*

negative reference group: synonymous with *negative group.*

negligence: a source of product liability, more common decades ago. If negligence occurs in the design or manufacture of a product, the manufacturer is liable for the injuries that result.

negotiable: anything that can be sold or transferred to another for money or as payment of an obligation.

negotiable instrument: as stated in the Uniform Negotiable Instruments Act: "An instrument, to be negotiable, must conform to the following requirements:
(a) it must be in writing and signed by the maker or drawer;

(b) it must contain an unconditional promise or order to pay a certain sum in money;

(c) it must be payable on demand, or at a fixed or determinable future time;

(d) it must be payable to order or to bearer;

(e) where the instrument is addressed to a drawee, he or she must be named or otherwise indicated therein with reasonable certainty."

negotiated contract: a contract to buy goods or service where the buyer and seller negotiate specific terms for agreement; often used when there is only one supplier and therefore no competition in the market.

negotiated price: the result obtained by a purchaser who desires something different from what is available or is powerful enough to force the seller to accept prices lower than those usually charged. See *upset price.*

negotiation: the act by which a negotiable instrument is placed in circulation by being physically passed from the original holder to another person.

neighborhood cluster: the centralization of several stores surrounded by a residential community. Most are convenience stores, and the majority of customers are from the area.

neighborhood showing: a group of posters used in outdoor advertising, the purchase of which is confined to a particular shopping district in which the advertiser's product is available.

nested: packaged one within another.

net:

(1) short for broadcast network.

(2) net amount, that which remains after certain designated deductions have been made from the gross amount.

net advertising circulation: a measurement of the number of people exposed to outdoor advertising, based on two considerations:

(a) the effective circulation—the least number of persons composing the traffic passing by an outdoor advertising display who have a reasonable physical opportunity to see the display.

(b) space position value—the efficiency with which a poster panel dominates the traffic to which it is exposed.

net amount: see *net.*

net back: the sale of an item less out-of-pocket expenses to move it from the factory to its point of sale. Such costs include freight expenses, agents' commissions, etc.

net cash flow: the net cash consumed or produced in a period by an activity or product during a unit of time, including all revenue and expenses except noncash items such as depreciation.

net circulation: the number of people viewing a billboard, display, or other outdoor form of advertising during a stated time period.

net controlled circulation: the number of copies of a publication that have been printed and distributed, whether paid for or not, to members of a specific industry, business, trade, or profession, equivalent to the total edition printed minus office and complimentary copies, samples, exchanges, unclassified copies, and copies delivered to advertisers, agencies, and prospective advertisers. Cf. *net paid circulation.*

net cost: the true cost of an item; determined by subtracting all income or financial gain from the gross cost.

net credit period: according to its terms of sale, the maximum time that a company takes to pay its bill. For example, 1/20, n/60 provides a net credit period of 60 days; following the twentieth day no discount can be taken and the bill is payable net.

net effective distribution: the measure of the intensity of the distribution accomplished.

net export of goods and services: of major importance to international marketers; the excess of exports of goods and services (domestic output sold abroad and production abroad credited to U.S.-owned resources) over imports (U.S. purchases of foreign output, domestic production credit to foreign-owned resources, and net private cash remittances to creditors abroad).

net income: the remains from earnings and profits after all costs, expenses, and allowances for depreciation and probable loss have been deducted.

net loss: see *net profit.*

net national product:
(1) the gross national product minus capital consumption (depreciation).
(2) the market value of net output of goods and services produced by the nation's economy.

net paid circulation: the number of copies of a publication that have been paid for by the purchasers, not for resale, under the following conditions:
(a) if the sale is a single-copy sale, it shall be paid for at not less than 50 percent of the basic single-copy price.
(b) on a term order for a year, the subscription must be paid for at not less than 50 percent of the basic annual price.

(c) a term subscription for one year or more paid in accordance with this rule may be included.

(d) a term subscription for less than one year may not be included after its expiration unless the amount actually paid equals at least 50 percent of the full basic annual subscription price and not simply 50 percent of a pro rata of the basic annual subscription price. Cf. *net controlled circulation.*

net price: the price after deductions, allowances, and discounts have been made.

net profit: the excess of all revenues over all costs and expenses incurred to obtain the income in a given enterprise during a given period of time. If the total expenses exceed the income, such amount is known as net loss. Synonymous with *net revenue.*

net purchases: the invoice cost of merchandise purchased plus the transportation charges for the items, minus the sum of returns, allowances, and cash discounts taken.

net rate: an advertising medium's published rate, less the agency commission. See *fifteen and two.*

net rating point (NRP): one percent of the cumulative audience for a given broadcast commercial or program. These points are totaled to arrive at a program's rating.

net realizable value: the selling price of an item less reasonable selling costs.

net revenue: synonymous with *net profit.*

net sales: gross sales, minus returns and allowances, over a stated period. See *sales.*

net terms: conditions called for the billed amount of an invoice to be paid in full, with no cash discounts permitted.

network:

(1) *general:* the diagram of the sequence of activities that must be performed to complete a project.

(2) *broadcasting:* a group of broadcasting stations affiliated by contract and interconnected for instant broadcast of the same program. There are national networks, regional networks, cable networks, and tailor-made networks.

network buy: the buying of commercial time directly from the network, in order that all affiliated stations with the network are purchased at the same time. Most advertisers who choose to advertise nationally purchase commercial time this way. See *market-by-market buy.*

networking:

(1) *general:* see *network.*

(2) *broadcasting:* radio or television station and programs banded together for network broadcasting.

network option time: those hours that a station affiliated with a network system has contractually agreed to permit the network to sell, along with time over other affiliates, to a national sponsor.

network rating: the percentage of television or radio households or individuals among those in a specified area estimated to be listening to a network's broadcast over a specified time.

net worth:

(1) the owner's equity in a business, represented by the excess of the total assets over the total amounts owed to outside creditors at a given time.

(2) referring to an individual, the figure determined by deducting the amount of all personal liabilities for the total value of personal assets.

neutral approach: in sales, the strategy of using minimum effort, although constant, to maintain a share of the market.

never-outs: items that should never run out of stock during a season because of continuous demand.

new-business man: an advertising agency executive whose job is to contact advertisers and prospective advertisers and persuade them to employ the services of the agency he or she represents.

new-buyer holdover effect: synonymous with *customer holdover effect,* with the difference that no further marketing expenditures are made.

new product:

(1) any item perceived by prospective customers as being significantly different from other available items.

(2) for manufacturers and retailers, an item never before produced, either by being completely unique or significantly different from earlier products.

new-product development (NPD): the process of bringing an idea or concept forward from its earliest development stages to a final commercialization of a product or service. See *new-product planning process.*

new-product failure: a new product that does not meet the objectives of its developers. Depending on what those objectives are, a profitable new product can be a failure, and an unprofitable new product can be a success.

new-product planning process: a process involving idea generation, screening, analysis and evaluation, product development and production, branding, test marketing and positioning, and full-scale marketing and production. See *new-product development.* Cf. *brainstorming.*

new products management: the overall management of a new product project or a total product innovation program.

new products manager: a product manager with a new products assignment; may direct a single project team, or several teams, or an entire product innovation program. It is nonfunctional, or general management in perspective, regardless of the department it is housed in.

new-product strategy: a strategy that guides the product innovation program. It is unique to new products and is a spin-off from overall corporate or division strategy.

newspaper stuffer: advertising copy inserted loosely in a newspaper supplement section; may be only one sheet of paper, or a booklet of numerous pages. Synonymous with *freestanding stuffer; giant insert; Sheridan stuffer; stuffer.*

news technique: a sales approach used within the first few minutes of communication with a prospect. The salesperson pulls news items for discussion (e.g., a neighborhood fire is mentioned to promote the sale of fire extinguishers).

new-task purchasing: in industrial purchasing, procurement of a new item or service by the purchasing agent. New task involves particular attention to detail, and in most cases, decisions are made by more than one person. See *modified rebuy; straight rebuy.*

new unsought item: the offering of items based on new concepts and uses that the consumer is unaware of; requires promotion to inform the customer of their potential. Cf. *regularly unsought items; unsought goods.*

next-in, first-out (NIFO): purporting to reflect the replacement cost of inventories in terms of existing financial statements that have been practicable in the past. Cf. *LIFO.*

NGT: see *nominal group technique.*

Nice Agreement: synonymous with *Nice Agreement Concerning the International Classification of Goods and Services for the Purposes of the Registration of Marks.*

Nice Agreement Concerning the International Classification of Goods and Services for the Purposes of the Registration of Marks: of importance to international sales of intellectual properties; a 1977 multilateral treaty signed by countries providing protection of intellectual properties. The Treaty is administered by the World Intellectual Property Organization. Synonymous with *Nice Agreement.*

niche marketing: a marketing approach, usually undertaken by small firms or by divisions of larger companies, in which a manufacturer or supplier defines a narrow market segment that he or she feels best equipped to compete in. Often, items or services are especially created or made for a niche market. Cf. *concentrated marketing.* See *market niche.*

Nielsen Drug (Food) Index: developed by A. C. Nielsen, statements on the market change of products, by type and brand, issued through panels of experts from drugstores and other stores.

Nielsen Market Sectional Reports: reports distributed by the A. C. Nielsen Company offering market research and/

or broadcast analysis, broken down by geographic area; by product's sales, market share, and competition. Most popularly called on for advertising within a geographic area rather than for national programs.

Nielsen rating: the percentage of households tuned to a stated radio or television program, as reported by the A. C. Nielsen Company. A device called an audimeter is installed out of sight in each sample household and is electronically connected to each television set in the home. The audimeter produces a minute-by-minute photographic record identifying the times the sets are turned on and off and the stations tuned in. Cf. *Hooperating.* See *audimeter.*

Nielsen station index (NSI): an audience measurement service of A. C. Nielsen Company providing information concerning the size of local television viewing audiences in approximately 225 markets; purchased by subscription.

Nielsen television index (NTI): a syndicated national network television audience measurement of the A. C. Nielsen Company providing audience estimates for commercially sponsored network programs in the country; utilizes 1,200 audimeters, located in private homes and 2,400 viewing diaries of people in television households; purchased by subscription.

NIFO: see *next-in, first-out.*

nixie mail: letters or packages not easily deliverable because of incorrect, ineligible, or insufficient address.

no demand: synonymous with *absence of demand.*

no frills product: see *generic product.*

noise: interference in a communication channel that may distort a signal or interfere with openness, thus rendering the message difficult or impossible to interpret.

nominal:
(1) signifying that values are expressed in current money prices.

(2) signifying the probable level of a market, but not based on actual transactions.

nominal group technique (NGT): used to set marketing and advertising goals; a forecasting strategy in which 7 to 10 experts gather to exchange their ideas and projections.

nonadopters: consumers who try an item but fail to become regular users. Cf. *laggards.*

noncommercial advertising: advertising placed by not-for-profit organizations, such as governmental agencies, charitable institutions, and religious groups, to create enthusiasm and support for causes they sponsor or support. See *institutional advertising; promotional advertising.*

noncumulative quantity discount:
(1) a price reduction based on the size of the individual order placed.

(2) a quantity discount offered on each sale to a particular buyer.

nondegradable pollutants: impurities (e.g., glass, plastics, certain industrial wastes) that do not disintegrate or dissolve naturally.

nondisguised survey: in marketing research, a means for gathering data in which respondents are told the true purpose of the inquiry.

nondumping certificate: often used by global marketers; a seller's certificate indicating that the item described are being sold at a price no lower than that applicable to like sales in the country of origin.

nondurable goods: synonymous with *soft goods.*

nongoods service: where no tangible item is offered for sale or rental (e.g., medical services).

nonliquid assets: valuable property (e.g., real estate, jewelry) that can be difficult to turn into immediate cash.

nonmanufacturing expenses: expenditures that are not closely associated with the manufacture of products, including selling and administrative expenses.

nonmarket production: production that occurs outside the market (e.g., production regulated by custom or law rather than by prices). This is a common phenomenon in less-developed nations.

nonpareil: see *surrogate positioning.*

nonperformance: the failure of a contracting party to provide goods or services according to an agreement.

nonpersonal retailing: purchases made without entering a store. Customers do this using a catalog, mail-order house, or vending machine.

nonpreemptible time: broadcast media time sold with the expectation that the program to be inserted in that time period will not be pulled or removed in favor of another program. Usually, an extra charge per time unit is called for. See *preempt.*

nonprice competition: markets in which a seller maneuvers for influence on the basis of promotion, marketing strategy, or special aspects of the items to be sold. Most larger organizations avoid price competition by emphasizing nonprice marketing forces. Cf. *price competition.* See *pricing.*

nonprobability sampling: choosing a sample for research where judgment of the researcher enters the selection process. The three types of sample are the convenience sample, the judgment sample, and the quota sample. This approach has shortcomings: It may be biased and can lead to false conclusions or misinterpretations of data. See *convenience sampling; judgment sampling; quota sampling.*

nonproduct: an item or service that a seller prepares for a specific segment of the market only to discover that the segment does not really exist. Should the item or service be offered, it almost always fails.

nonprofit marketing: the application of marketing concepts and activities to nonprofit organizations.

nonsampling error: any deviation from correct data arising in marketing research because of a variety of poor judgments or statistical treatments.

nonstandardized approach: an international marketing strategy that assumes each country or region is different and requires a distinct marketing plan.

nonstore retailing: activities of vending, mail-order, and house-to-house sellers.

nentariff barrier (NTB): of importance to international marketers; any law, regulation, or requirement that prevents or impedes the importation of goods without good cause. The most direct of these

barriers are import licensing requirements and quotas. Other examples are
subsidies that distort trade and injure
competing firms, and requirements that
specify a certain level of domestic content in a product being manufactured or
sold. Some legal and regulatory protec-
tions for consumers or the environment
can operate as nontariff barriers. Cf.
nontariff measures.

nontariff measures (NTM): of importance to international marketers; an action by a government that differs from
NTB only in that it may eventually have
restrictive implications on goods traded
in the world market. Though the restrictive effect cannot always be proven, an
NTM is perceived as having such a result. Cf. *nontariff barriers.*

nontraceable costs:
(1) costs that are not directly identified
with the responsibility center to which
they are assigned.

(2) common costs that are assigned to
functional areas on an arbitrary basis.

nonvariable price policy: synonymous
with *one-price policy.*

nonverbal communication:
(1) *general:* the sharing of ideas without
the use of words.

(2) *general:* the act of imparting or in-
terchanging thoughts, attitudes, or information without words.

(3) *marketing research:* used as a factor
determining consumer attitudes and beliefs pertaining to a product or service.

nonzero sum situation: a competitive situation in which not only the winning group
benefits but the other group also wins or
its position remains unchanged.

norm:
(1) a point of reference; a standard used
for comparison.

(2) a rule that tells the members of a
particular cultural group what behavior
is correct in certain situations.

normal good: an item whose consumption changes directly with money income when prices remain constant (e.g.,
consumer goods). Synonymous with *superior goods.*

normal price: the price to which the market price tends to return following fluctuations up or down. When the purchase
price does not reflect all consideration
given by the buyer to the seller, the value
of the goods will be adjusted for customs
purposes.

normal sale: a transaction that pleases
both the buyer and the seller of an item
and in which no unforeseen or abnormal
situations surface.

normative forecasting: a forecasting technique that begins with the identification
of some future objectives and works back
to the present, identifying problem areas
that will have to be surmounted along
the way.

norms: see *norm.*

**North American Free Trade Agreement
(NAFTA):**   effective January 1, 1994, a
trade accord that can create challenges
and opportunities for overseas marketing
of U.S. sales and promotion of goods
and services. NAFTA is the name given
to economic links formed by the United
States, Canada, and Mexico.

Supplemental or side agreements on environmental cooperation and labor cooperation were signed in September 1993.

Congress debated the NAFTA in Fall 1993 where approval by a simple majority of both houses was needed for passage. On November 17, 1993, the House of Representatives, followed by the Senate on November 20th, 1993, voted approval to the trade pact. The accord went into effect on January 1, 1994.

no sale final: an organizational policy that a sale is not final until the customer is totally pleased with the purchase made.

nose-to-nose selling: synonymous with *belly-to-belly selling.*

notation credit: a credit specifying that any person purchasing or paying draft drawn or demands for payment made under it must note the amount of the draft or demand on the letter or advice of credit.

note: an instrument, such as a promissory note, that is the recognized legal evidence of a debt. A note is signed by the marker, called the borrower, promising to pay a certain sum of money on a specified date at a certain place of business, to a certain business, individual, or bank, called the lender.

not-for-profit: describing the activities of an organization established with the sole goal of providing services for society rather than for the purpose of making a profit.

noting delay: a delay response effect resulting from a time lag between the completion of the execution delay and the reception of the specific stimulus by the market. In a sales message, the noting delay is zero.

novelty: see *advertising specialty.*

NPD: see *new product development.*

NRP: see *net rating point.*

NSI: see *Nielsen station index.*

NTB: see *nontariff barrier.*

NTI: see *Nielsen television index.*

NTM: see *nontariff measures.*

nuclear family:

(1) a husband and wife and their children.

(2) a unit composed traditionally of at least two adults, with or without children. Recently, the demand that the adults be of the opposite sex has been dropped.

nudum pactum:

(1) an empty promise.

(2) a statement for which no consideration has been given.

null: applied by consumer and marketing researchers; referring to an absence of information, as contrasted with zero or blank for the presence of no information.

null hypothesis: the logical contradictory of the hypothesis that one seeks to test. If the null hypothesis is proved false, its contradictory is thereby proved true. Essentially, the null hypothesis is that there is no difference greater than could be expected by chance.

nullification of agreement: the setting aside of the terms of an agreement.

number of stock turnover: stock turnover as determined by dividing average inventory at retail to net sales for a year.

nut:

(1) *general:* (slang) uneliminable operating costs. Synonymous with *variable costs.*

(2) *broadcasting:* (slang) the complete dollar amount reflecting the advertiser's

entire sponsorship of either a television or radio broadcast (e.g., a $1 million advertising expenditure for a program sponsorship).

nutritional labeling:
(1) a form of labeling in which consumers are informed of the amounts of protein, fat, carbohydrates, and calories in a processed food product.
(2) showing on packaged foods the nutritional value of an item, especially the U.S.-recommended daily allowances supplied by a particular quantity of the item, and the specific ingredients contained.

objection: in sales, the reason provided by a prospect for rejecting a salesperson's offer for a product or service. See *linking phase.*

objective-and-task technique: a promotional budget method in which a firm outlines its promotional goals, determines the activities needed to satisfy those goals, and then establishes the appropriate budget.

objectives: the goals or specific aims of a business.

objective value: the price an item can command in terms of other items in the market.

objectivity: the quality of a perception or observation that is free of bias.

obligation: the legal responsibility and duty of a debtor (the obligor) to pay a debt

when due, and the legal right of the creditor (the obligee) to enforce payment in the event of default.

obligee: a creditor or promisee.

obligor: a debtor or promisor.

observational technique:
(1) a research method that entails observing consumer behavior.
(2) a research method in which a researcher observes people's behavior and records what is seen but avoids direct interaction.

obsolescence: the state of being out of date and therefore of little use to society. See *functional obsolescence; planned obsolescence; postponed obsolescence; product obsolescence.*

obsolete material: inventory items that have little or no possibility of being used in the near future. Such items often have undergone structural design changes or are products that have been discarded for new ones.

occasion: in broadcasting, synonymous with *spot.*

occupant list: the list of addresses for the sending of direct mail advertising. The word "occupant" is used instead of a person's name.

occupational mobility: the extent to which individuals in a particular occupation move into work other than that for which they were specially trained.

oddball pricing: the selling of an assortment or a group of related products at the same price, which does not relate to cost, desired markup or margin, or customary price of any of the separate products.

odd-ending pricing: synonymous with *odd pricing.*

odd-even pricing: a means of pricing purporting to make the cost of an item or service psychologically attractive to prospects without markedly lessening the desired profit margin.

odd-number pricing: synonymous with *odd pricing.*

odd pricing:
(1) a form of psychological pricing in which the price is an odd number or a number just below a round number.

(2) pricing at odd amounts (e.g., at 99 cents instead of at a dollar). Cf. *persuasive pricing.* Synonymous with *odd-ending pricing; odd-number pricing; off-even pricing; psychological pricing.*

OEMs: see *Original Equipment Manufacturers.*

off-brand: a brand that is not considered acceptable to a consumer.

off-card: a special rate to the advertiser for advertising space or time; does not show on the medium's rate card.

offensive warfare: the marketing warfare strategy for firms not in the lead in a product market; demands attacking the market leader, basing movements on the following principles:
(a) after examining the strength of the leader, focusing an attack on lessening the leader's market share.

(b) finding a weakness in the leader's dominance and attacking at that point.

(c) launching the attack on as narrow a front as is possible, by going after one of the leader's items at a time.

offer:
(1) to present for acceptance or refusal (verb).

(2) a contractual agreement made by a seller pending acceptance by a purchaser (noun).

offer list: of importance to global marketers; the list of items, usually prepared in conjunction with multilateral trade negotiations, on which a country is prepared to negotiate trade liberalization; may also identify merchandise that will be exempted from discussion.

offer test: a promotion test that assesses responses to differing prices and/or terms of quantities. For example, usually the price of $9.95 results in greater purchases than $10.00. Cf. *package test.*

off-even pricing: synonymous with *odd pricing.*

off factor: a chain discount brought to a single percent. This is the complement of the on-factor. Cf. *on-factor.*

official value: used by global marketers; the value for duty purposes officially assigned by a country to certain imported items. It is usually compared with the invoice value, and ad valorem duties are levied on the higher value.

off peak: see *prime time.*

off-price store: a discount store that buys manufacturer's overruns and end-of-season goods at below-wholesale prices and resells them at prices significantly lower than the regular department store price.

offset: in printing, a lithographic printing process in which an image is transferred to a rubber roller, which in turn places the impression on the paper.

ogive: used by market researchers; a distribution curve characterized by cumulative frequencies.

oligopoly:

(1) a competitive situation in which a few firms account for a large percentage of the industry's sales and in which there are substantial barriers to entry.

(2) an industry in which a small number of producers sell identical products. Cf. *monopoly; differential oligopoly; perfect monopoly.*

oligopoly price: a price that develops when the market has numerous buyers and few sellers, thus giving the sellers the greatest power.

oligopsony: control by a number of buyers who attempt to influence the demand for a specific item. Cf. *duopsony; monopsony.*

oligopsony price: a price that develops when the market has few buyers and numerous sellers, thus giving the buyers the greatest power.

OMAs: see *orderly marketing agreements.*

omnibus cooperative advertisement: for wholesaler agreements, a full-page advertisement from a retailer over his or her own name. The retailer bills each manufacturer a pro rata share of the cost of the entire advertisement based on an earlier cooperative advertisement agreement with the manufacturers.

on account:

(1) a payment made toward the settlement of an account.

(2) a purchase or sale made on open account.

on-air method: a technique applying audience feedback for evaluating the talent, format, and quality of a broadcast program or commercial that is being considered for a later broadcast. Real broadcast material is used for testing factors such as audience recall, attitude shifting, etc.

on-approval offer: a proposition that permits a consumer to see, feel, taste, use, or otherwise experience a product without first paying for it and without being placed under the obligation to buy. Usually, such an offer has a time limit, at the expiration of which the consumer is expected to return the product or to pay for it.

on consignment: items turned over by an owner (the consignor) to someone else (the consignee) with the expectation that the items (the consignment) will be sold by the consignee. If all the items are not sold, the owner is entitled to the return of the items. Cf. *memorandum sale; purchase allowance.* See *consignment.*

one-cent sale: a sales offer where two products are sold with each other for the price of one of the items, plus one additional penny. Often used to introduce a new product. The general practice of manufacturers is to indicate in advertisements that the offer is restricted to a specific market area and is good for a limited time.

one hundred percent location: the location within a given shopping area that is the best possible place for a specific type of store.

one hundred showing: a standard showing of outdoor posters. The number of panels in the poster in a 100 showing varies with market size.

one-level channel: a marketing channel where only one intermediary appears, usually the retailer, between the manufacturer and the consumer.

one-more-yes close: a salesperson's closing method based on the concept that people are creatures of habit and tend to say "yes." Consequently, the seller raises questions about the prospect's feelings toward the merchandise, with the final question suggestive of a positive reply from the prospect.

one-price policy:

(1) a situation in which the price of goods is firm and cannot be negotiated.

(2) a pricing policy in which the marketer assigns a price to the product and sells it at that price to all customers who purchase the same quantity of the product under the same conditions. Cf. *single-price policy*. Synonymous with *nonvariable price policy*.

one-sheet poster: a printed sheet of advertising matter pasted on a display panel on subway platforms as a form of transit advertising.

one-shot promotion: a one-time promotion that involves items that cannot be re-ordered at a later time. At times, a supplier can be persuaded to provide items manufactured especially for a specific event.

one-side messages: messages in which only the benefits of a good, service, or idea are mentioned by a firm.

one-time purchaser: a customer found on a list who has made only one purchase since an initial order.

one-time rate: the advertiser's rate paid when not enough space or time is purchased to earn volume discounts. Synony-

mous with *general rate; national rate*. See *rate differential*.

on-factor: the difference between 100 percent and the single discount representing a chain discount. For example, a chain discount of 40 percent and 10 percent equals a single discount of 46 percent. The on-factor is 100 percent less 46 percent or 54 percent. Cf. *local rate; off-factor; single rate*.

on order: goods paid for but not yet received.

on pack: a package with a display card used by hanging on hooks, to which an item has been attached without using any cover. Cf. *in-pack; with-pack premium*.

on-spec: see *on-speculation*.

on-speculation: advertising, or another work effort, that is carried out for a client without a contract or order; often shortened to on-spec. The client pays for the service only if the work is used. Working on-spec is done by advertising agencies seeking to enhance their reputation.

open account:

(1) credit extended that is not supported by a note, or other formal written evidence of indebtedness (e.g., shipments of merchandise for which a buyer is billed later).

(2) an arrangement between the seller and purchaser where the purchaser receives no written confirmation of a purchase.

open advertisement (open ad): a want advertisement identifying both the position and the name of the potential employer and his or her address. Cf. *blind advertisement*.

open assortment: an assortment where the consumer does not have at hand all the items usually needed. Cf. *closed assortment.*

open bid: the offer to perform a service or provide merchandise to a buyer with an adequate public communication in order that all interested bidders are aware of the price submitted.

open charge account: see *charge account.*

open circuit system: a marketing system providing for feedback from all the influences that affect the firm. Data are often taken into account rapidly so that action can be taken quickly.

open code dating: synonymous with *open date labeling.*

open credit: credit that is allowed without immediate proof of a customer's credit-worthiness.

open credit account: a credit arrangement in which a buyer receives a monthly bill for goods and services bought during the preceding month. The account must be paid in full each month.

open date labeling: clearly printed, the date marked on merchandise with limited shelf life, usually an item that can spoil, identifying the last date that the item can safely be sold to the public without danger of deterioration or spoilage. Synonymous with *open code dating.*

open dating: see *open date labeling.*

open display: products placed where they can be handled and studied by prospects. Cf. *closed display.*

open distribution: the distribution of the same merchandise by a given area or region, by differing dealers. The dealers carry competitive lines and there are no barriers regarding the number of items a deal sells, offers, or delivers to a retailer. Cf. *exclusive distribution; intensive distribution; selective distribution.*

open-end commercial:

(1) *broadcasting:* a commercial designed to accommodate a dealer tag at its conclusion.

(2) *advertising:* the ending to a network program or commercial that is left blank for local advertising.

open-end contract: an agreement whereby a supplier contracts to meet the buyer's requirements for a specific item during a stated period, whatever those requirements may be. The agreement is open-end because all the terms are left indefinite.

open-ended: pertaining to a process or system that can be cut back.

open-end pricing: the release of a purchase order without an agreement as to the fixed price. It happens where the price is set by the free market, and the supply is more critical to the company than a fixed price.

open-end program: any broadcast program that permits the inclusion of local commercials.

opening: the first showing of a new season's line of items by a manufacturer or an entire industry.

opening price point: the lowest price line of a particular item, such as the least costly of several brands of toothpaste.

open interest: the number of outstanding contracts in the market or in a particular class or series.

open market: a condition of trading that is not limited to any particular area or persons.

open order:

(1) an order made without price or delivery stipulation.

(2) an order shipped to a market representative without specifying the vendor.

open pricing: marking merchandise with shelf-life expiration dates clearly shown in acceptable symbols. See *open date labeling*.

open rate:

(1) an advertising rate subject to discounts for volume or frequency. See *base rate*.

(2) a rate for space established by some newspapers and magazines that is subject to discounts based on quantity of space purchased or frequency of insertions authorized during a year.

open stock: replacement items or additions of goods carried in quantity and retained in a warehouse for several years.

open the kimono: (slang) to reveal to prospective customers company plans regarding future products, to impress on the buyer that the firm is ahead of its competitors in developing new or superior items.

open-to-buy (OTB): the quantity of goods that a store can receive in stock over a stated time without exceeding its planned inventory levels.

open trade: any transaction that has not yet been closed.

operant conditioning: a motivation approach that focuses on the relationship between stimulus, response, and reward.

operating budget: a quantitative expression of a plan of action that shows how a firm, including an advertising agency, will acquire and use its resources over a specified period.

operating cycle: the general pattern of business activity whereby cash and other resources are converted to inventory and operational assets and eventually into a product or service that can be sold and for which cash and other resources are received.

operating expenses:

(1) any expenses incurred in the normal operation of a business. See *margin of profit*.

(2) expenses of furnishing transportation services, including the expense of maintenance and depreciation of the plant used in the service.

operating income: income to a marketing and/or advertising business produced by its earning assets and by fees for services rendered.

operating losses: losses incurred in the normal (i.e., nonnegligent) operation of a marketing and/or advertising business.

operating profit ratio: the ratio of a firm's operating profit to its net sales.

operating statement: a statement for a store's management, providing net sales, costs, expenses, and the net operating profit or loss for a fixed period.

operating supplies: materials consumed during the manufacture process that do not appear in the final consumer or industrial product.

operational buying motives: consumer motives based on how the item being considered for purchase works or performs.

operational diversification: the extension of a company's offerings based on some degree of gain in the market, such as the lowering of cost through economies of scale, or the increasing of the customer family. See *congruent production diversification.*

operations budgeting: the setting of immediate goals for sales, production, expenses, costs, and the availability of cash.

opinion: used by consumer and marketing analysts; a feeling leading to the formation of an attitude that is less subject to change or shift and is more likely to influence behavior. See *activities, interests, opinions.*

opinion leader: a member of an organization who, because of ability, power, access to information, or prestige, can influence the attitudes, opinions, or behavior of those around him or her. See *reference group.*

opinion research: market research to determine prospects' thoughts and beliefs toward a given object or situation.

opinion strategy: a method of salespeople who display the item under consideration to the prospect and invite opinions. The prospect is directly involved in the conversation.

OPM:

(1) operations per minute.

(2) other people's money.

opportunistic sampling: synonymous with *convenience sampling.*

opportunity: an unsatisfied want or need that arises from a change in the organization's environment.

opportunity cost: a maximum alternative profit that could have been obtained if the productive good, service, or capacity had been applied to some other use. See *domestic-exchange ratio.*

opportunity cost of capital: the expected rate of return from employing funds effectively in the company.

optimum capacity: the quantity of output that permits the minimum cost per unit to be incurred.

optional consumption: the buying of items and services not required for daily fulfillment and well-being. See *luxuries.*

optional product pricing: a pricing method for items offered to the public with several options (e.g., refrigerators with numerous options). Decisions have to be made as to the options that are and are not included in the base price, or that represent additional costs to the consumer.

orange goods: in merchandising, consumer goods, such as clothing, that will eventually have to be replaced as they wear out, at a rate, or at the consumer's discretion. Cf. *brown goods; red goods; yellow goods.*

orbital structure: any marketing operative or organization that is not fixed in space (e.g., a truck jobber, a traveling salesperson).

order: a request to deliver, sell, receive, or purchase goods or services.

order card: a self-addressed postcard, postal card, business reply card, or similar form without self-addressing mailed to or otherwise delivered to prospects by an advertiser for their convenience in mailing an order for goods or services, an inquiry for information, or any other response to the sales message usually accompanying the card.

order cycle: the activity pattern of the vendor. It is divided into four parts:

(a) *order transmittal*—what happens and how long it will take to get the order to the vendor from the moment of initiation.

(b) *order processing*—what the vendor does and how long it takes from the time of receipt of the order to notification of the proper warehouse to get the order prepared for shipping.

(c) *order picking*—what occurs at the warehouse and how long it takes to prepare the order for pickup and to place the shipment into the hands of the chosen carrier.

(d) *order delivery*—what occurs and how long it takes during the process of pickup and final delivery to the customer. Synonymous with *lead time*.

order delivery: see *order cycle.*

order entry: approaches used in entering customer orders into an order processing system, to provide an efficient and accurate means to ensure that customers receive their merchandise quickly and as ordered.

order-filling cost: a marketing cost incurred in storing, packing, shipping, billing, credit and collection, and other similar aspects of selling merchandise.

order form: a form for requesting goods or services from a wholesaler, manufacturer, or direct-mail retailer; often included in such direct-marketing materials as catalogs.

order-generating costs: revenue-producing costs, such as advertising and personal selling.

order getter: a salesperson who uses highly developed approaches to deal with prospects in a creative fashion.

order-getting cost: a marketing cost incurred in an effort to attain a desired sales volume and mix.

ordering cost: a major cost component that is considered in inventory controls decisions. Each time the firm orders items for inventory, it must formally contact the supplier, which usually involves some clerical and administrative work. Labor is also used in placing the order and putting the items in inventory. The clerical, administrative, and labor costs make up the ordering cost element in inventory control models.

orderly marketing agreements (OMAs): bilateral agreements limiting imports from one country to another; generally undertaken to avoid imposition of unilateral import restrictions.

order margin: the total cost of items sold, including product, selling, and delivery expenses but not including promotional costs, subtracted from the total sales revenue generated, and divided by the number of units sold. A promotion budget should not exceed the order margin and must be small enough that a profit margin remains.

order picking: see *order cycle.*

order processing: see *order cycle.*

order processing costs: expenses associated with recording and handling orders, such as order entry, computer-information handling, and merchandise handling.

orders: requests made for the delivery of goods or services.

order size: the appropriate amount of merchandise, parts, and other items to purchase at one time. It depends on the availability of quantity discounts, the resources of the firm, the inventory turnover rate, the costs of processing each order, and the costs of maintaining goods in inventory.

order taker: a salesperson whose function is primarily to receive calls and who accepts orders for items and services.

order transmittal: see *order cycle*.

ordinal scale: used by market researchers; a level of measurement that describes a variable in terms of a rank order.

ordinary course of trade: a principle that places the dutiable value of merchandise at the price at which it would normally sell if customary channels of distribution were observed.

ordinary interest: interest that is calculated based on 360 days to the year.

ordinary terms: as found in invoices, a cash discount that is deducted if the bill is paid within the discount period. If not, the full payment is due at the end of the cycle shown. The cash discount and the net credit periods are both counted from the date of the invoice, which is traditionally the date of shipment.

organizational buying objectives: includes the availability of items, reliability of sellers, consistency of quality, delivery, price, and customer service.

organizational climate: a set of properties of the work environment perceived by consumers and assumed to be a major factor in influencing their behavior.

organizational consumer: includes manufacturers, wholesalers, distributors, retailers and government units, and not-for-profit organizations. Usually these institutions use the items they receive to make other products, or to maintain their operations, or to be offered for resale.

organizational consumer expectations: the perceived potential of alternative suppliers and brands to satisfy a number of explicit and implicit objectives.

organizational consumer's decision process: a process consisting of expectations, the buying procedure, conflict resolution, and situational factors.

organizational learning: the process whereby individuals within an organization learn as a group and apply that learning to their work. Traditionally, it has been thought to vary with amount of experience (as measured for example by number of units produced), but increasingly, it is seen as an independent variable that can be managed as a source of competitive advantage.

organizational market: the market segment made up of people and firms that buy merchandise and services for reasons other than for individual consumption, such as goods to be used in the manufacturing of other goods. Its purchasers engage in large-volume, highly professional, and detail-oriented purchasing efforts. Cf. *consumer market*.

organizational mission: a firm's long-term commitment to a type of business and a place in the market. It can be expressed in terms of the customer group(s) served, the goods and services offered, the functions performed, and/or the technologies utilized.

organizational structure: a set of relationships among individuals with different responsibilities.

organization marketing: the methods used by not-for-profit institutions to sell their goals and/or receive contributions.

organizing function: the managerial activity involved in creating a formal structure of tasks and authority.

original equipment manufacturers (OEMs):

(1) *general:* an organization that purchases industrial goods to incorporate into other products.

(2) *international:* used in reference to the right to appeal. In 1990, the European Union's Court of Justice ruled that OEMs may have the right to appeal from regulations of the Commission and Council imposing antidumping duties. Previously, this had been limited to complaining parties, producers/exporters, and related importers.

original order: the first order received from a specific customer; it is important to maintain records of sources of original orders so that first-time purchasers can be concentrated on the best sources.

original retail: in the retail accounting method, the sales price of items which is a total of the cost plus the original mark-on.

original source: see *original order.*

OS&D: see *over, short, and damaged.*

OTB: see *open-to-buy.*

other directed: descriptive of individuals who are easily influenced by others.

others self-image: our mental picture of ourselves as we believe others see us.

outbid: to offer a higher price for an item than that offered by other bidders.

outbound telemarketing: a direct-marketing approach of seeking out customers and prospects using the telephone; involves sales representatives calling individuals to both generate and qualify leads. Cf. *inbound telemarketing.* See *telemarketing.*

outdoor advertising: an advertising medium where the message is not delivered to an audience as it will be with media that enter the home. Instead, the units are at carefully situated locations where they are seen by an audience on the move. Communications from this medium are usually brief and easily read as the reader has only a few seconds to see the advertisement. Outdoor advertising is a splendid reminder medium and is frequently used in an advertising program to supplement other media. See *approach phase; billboard.*

outdoor buyers: media purchasers who specialize in outdoor advertising purchases.

outer-directed: a consumer purchase based on how the consumer perceives others see him or her and his or her actions. Such purchase behavior is affected by the person's wish to conform to peer group pressures.

outer envelope: the envelope, in direct-mail, that includes the package's promotional materials.

outgo: any expense or other cost in the running of a business.

outgoing: a posted or painted bulletin that displays the advertiser's message to traffic passing through a central part of a shopping or urban area.

outlay: any expenditure.

outlays costs: the actual cash outflows directly associated with the production and transfer of goods or services.

outlet store: synonymous with *factory outlet.*

out-of-home: advertising media viewed outside the household, which are not available in the home, such as displays on shopping carts, advertising in subways. Cf. *in-home.*

out-of-home media: advertising viewed or listened to by people outside of their residence; includes billboards, transit advertising, outdoor displays, and skywriting. See *alternative media.*

out-of-pocket expense: a cost incurred by an individual, often when on a business trip. The item or service is paid for in cash or by check or charge account, and the employee expects reimbursement from the company.

out-of-stock: goods that are not in the store when requested by a customer. See *periodic stock control.*

out-of-stock cost: estimated profits that are never realized because inventory is insufficient to fulfill the demands of customers. Customers and sales are lost through a stock-out.

outpack: any premium attached to the outside of a package. Cf. *outsert.*

outpost display: items placed with signs at well-crossed points within a store away from the traditional selling department of the merchandise.

output:
(1) the quantity yielded in any operation.

(2) the average dollar gross domestic product produced in a stated period.

outsert: separate printed material attached to the outside of a package. Cf. *outpack.* Synonymous with *zip advertisement.*

outshopper: an individual who travels outside his or her usual community or local area to obtain products or services. *See* outshopping.

outshopping:
(1) the number of shopping trips made outside a buyer's usual community or local area over a given time period.

(2) the proportion of dollars spent away from the buyer's usual community or local area. See *outshopper.*

outside dimensions: the outer measurements of a container, a package, or any of its parts.

outside-in: determining from consumers or industrial readers what media they follow so as to determine what form of media should be used as a preferred match.

outsizes: synonymous with *end sizes.*

outstanding: any unpaid or uncollected debt.

outward processing: synonymous with *production sharing.*

over, short, and damaged (OS&D): used in international marketing; the discrepancy between the amount and/or condition of cargo on hand and that shown on the bill. Cf. *clean bill of lading.* See *short merchandise.*

overall expenses technique: a method for determining the cost of goods sold by dividing the seller's total expense over time by the number of products sold during that time frame. It prevents the seller from failing to include relevant expenses in the calculation and is a helpful measure of the change in expense realized relative to a change in the number of sold units.

overall market capability: the quantity of an item or service that is absorbed in the general market without allowing for price or market considerations. For example, the overall market capability for television sets includes everyone who owns a television and everyone who would like to own a television but hasn't purchased one to date. Cf. *potential demand; potential market saturation.*

overall objectives: the broad, measurable goals set by top management.

overbought:

(1) reflecting an opinion about price levels of an item that has had a sharp rise or of the market as a whole after a period of vigorous buying, which some argue has left prices too high.

(2) when some element in the planning process has not evolved as anticipated, leading to a zero open-to-buy.

(3) where the store finds that it is overstocked with merchandise in excess of its demand.

overcapitalize:

(1) to provide an excessive amount of capital to a business.

(2) to place too high a value on the nominal capital of a company.

overcarriage: in international merchandising, the transportation of goods, beyond the initially intended destination, usually resulting from the goods being refused at the destination.

overcoverage: in marketing research, a nonsampling error that occurs when some of the units in the sample are repeated on the lists given to separate interviewers, thus creating a bias.

overdue: a payment that has not been made at the time it was due.

overextension: credit received or extended beyond the debtor's ability to pay.

overfull demand: where demand for an item or service exceeds the capacity of suppliers to supply or manufacture it. In this situation, firms often engage in demarketing, which is marketing to less demand on a temporary or permanent basis, either by increasing the price of the item or service, or by decreasing service or promotional efforts. See *demand states.*

overhead: costs of materials and services not directly adding to or readily identifiable with the product or service of the entity. Synonymous with *burden.*

overheating: excessive price or money activity that some economists believe will lead to inflation.

overkill: an expensive promotional effort that yields diminishing returns because it repels rather than attracts prospect interest.

overlay:

(1) a unified theme that unites all the elements in an advertising campaign.

(2) a transparent flap over artwork to allow writing of instructions or corrections or to indicate color breaks.

overnights: the tentative report of household ratings and audience share of network program time slots in the top 25 markets in the nation; estimated audience figures that are gathered the day following the program's appearance.

over (or short): the difference between established sales statements and the actual audited figure. This discrepancy is often a result of errors in making change or missing sales checks.

overproduction: producing more than can be sold at any price or at a profitable price. See *Say's law.*

overproduction theory: the idea that an excessive expansion of productive capacity occurs whenever demand increases. Cf. *underconsumption theory.*

overrun:

(1) excess production.

(2) the number of pieces of printed advertising in excess of the specified quantity. A 10 percent overrun is usually acceptable at pro rata cost. Overruns are produced to permit distribution of copies to prospective buyers or advertisers, as well as to readers who may request back issues. Cf. *underrun.*

overseas marketing research: the systematic gathering, recording, and analyzing of data to assist in minimizing uncertainty and aid in the decision-making process in overseas markets. It tends to be more costly than domestic marketing research, as it is broader in scope.

overseas sales branch: a branch or subsidiary of an exporting company that is in a foreign country, thereby permitting the exporter greater exposure and control in the foreign market. It also minimizes the dependence on a domestic-based export department with other personnel.

oversold: the situation of a manufacturer who has become obligated to deliver more than he or she is able to supply within the stated period.

overstock: synonymous with *remainder.*

overstored conditions: the situation of retail operations that are opened longer

than the need for extended hours suggest. This policy leads to an extra expense and overinvestment.

owe: to be obliged to pay something to someone for something received. An indebtedness results.

own brand: an item bearing the name or brand of the store selling the item rather than the name of the producer.

owned-goods service: a service that provides a customer with a service that had previously been used (e.g., plant maintenance).

owner-operator: a regular driver who owns equipment and is a subcontractor to a carrier on a long-term basis.

ownership: possession of a legal title with the rights to enjoy the benefits derived from any assets accompanying or accruing from such title.

ownership utility: the value or satisfaction added to a product or service when it is in the possession of the correct person at the proper moment. Synonymous with *possession utility.*

P: each of the Ps of the marketing mix: product, price, promotion, and place.

pack:

(1) to add to the total cost of merchandise charges for items not included or inflated charges.

(2) to give an undeserved discount without lowering the actual price.

package:

(1) *merchandising:* any container or wrapping in which goods are placed for shipping or carrying.

(2) *broadcasting:* a combined assortment of time units, sold as a single offering at a set price.

(3) *broadcasting:* a program, purchased as a unit for a lump sum, including all components ready for the addition of commercials.

package consolidating agency: synonymous with *freight forwarder.*

package design: the planning and deciding on the form and structure of a product's package.

packaged goods: consumer items packaged by producers and sold through retail stores (e.g. food, tobacco, beauty aids, household cleaners). Firms usually promote packaged items heavily with mass media advertising.

package enclosure: synonymous with *in-pack.*

package engineering: a discipline of scientific and engineering principles applied to solving problems of functional design, formation, filling, closing, and/or preparation for shipment of containers, regardless of the product enclosed.

package goods: items within a container designed for display and handled by the retailer (e.g., detergents, paper goods, cereals).

package insert:

(1) printed material packaged with the item to explain its operation.

(2) advertising material placed in a package; usually identifies a firm's different products.

(3) synonymous with *package stuffer.*

package plan: spots that broadcast stations or networks offer to broadcast advertisers at a special price. Synonymous with *total audience plan.*

package program: in broadcasting, a program complete with all elements, except commercials, that is sold as one unit.

package show: a radio or television program created, cast, and rehearsed by an independent producer, a network, or a station for sponsorship by an advertiser.

package stuffer: synonymous with *package insert.*

package test: in direct mailing, a small-scale survey to set response rates and, thereby, determine which package elements to place in the full mailing. Direct mailers, by applying an independent variable, alter only one factor in a test package because otherwise it would be difficult to conclude which change affected the higher response. Cf. *offer test.*

packaging:

(1) the preparation of merchandise for shipping and marketing.

(2) all activities that are related to designing and producing the container or wrapper for a product.

packaging functions: the factors of containment and protection, usage, communication, segmentation, channel cooperation, and new-product planning.

packaging wants: the variables addressed in the attempt to impart the subconscious feeling that an item will satisfy basic psychological wants other than the obvious needs for which it was produced.

packing house: synonymous with *freight forwarder.*

packing list: a list showing the number and kinds of items being shipped, as well as other information needed for transportation purposes.

packing slip: the form used for listing items to be shipped and for identifying the recipient of the shipment. The slip goes with the shipment and, on arrival at its destination, is used to confirm that the shipment is sound and complete.

packing wants: see *packaging wants.*

page traffic: the measure of the number of readers of a newspaper or periodical who look at a particular page or a particular advertisement.

paid circulation: the total number of copies of a magazine or other periodical sold through subscription or by single-copy sales in stores or newsstands.

painted display: in outdoor advertising, a display with a hand-painted advertising communication.

painted wall: see *painted display.*

painting the bus: (slang) altering the appearance of a presentation, proposal, or idea without changing any of the basics. See *window dressing.*

paired-comparison: a mode of product use testing where the new product is paired with (usually) the category leader for direct comparisons.

pallet: a portable platform for retaining material while in storage or shipment.

panel:
(1) *marketing:* a group of people used for obtaining information on perceptions, attitudes, etc., toward a product, service or organization. Synonymous with *test panel.*

(2) *advertising:* that portion of an outdoor sign which has a message or advertisement painted or pasted onto it.

(3) *advertising:* a printed unit that comprises the entire advertisement on an outdoor sign.

panel research: see *panel (1).*

Pan-European marketing: standardizing products and/or marketing communications to be used in European Community nations. This form of marketing requires changing merchandise and promotional strategies to deal with different languages and cultures. See *Euro-Advertisement; Eurobrand; standardization.*

pantry check: the physical examination of items possessed by respondents.

paperboard: board made of matted or felted fibrous material that is more than 0.012 inches (12 points) thick.

parallel exporting: impacting the profits of international marketers; a situation where, in addition to the official route by which the goods are exported by the exclusive distributor from a given territory, there is also a second parallel route, by which another trader in the territory exports the goods, which he or she has obtained from a third party outside the territory. The parallel exporter is a source of competition for the exclusive distributor. Cf. *parallel importing.*

parallel importing: impacting the profits of international marketers; the importing of goods by an independent operator that is not part of the manufacturer's channel of distribution. The parallel importer may compete with the authorized importer or with a subsidiary of the foreign manufacturer that produces the item in the local market. Cf. *parallel exporting.*

parameter:
(1) in marketing and consumer research; a quantity to which arbitrary values may be assigned.
(2) a variable that is given a constant value for a specific purpose or process.
(3) a definable characteristic of an item, device, or system.

parasalesperson: usually a sales trainee who rarely completes the closing with a customer, but is assisted for this task by a more experienced salesperson.

parasite store: a store depending on traffic flow originating from events external to those generated by the store itself, which is usually negligible compared with the total traffic flow.

parcel shipment: a small package restricted as to value, generally samples of goods or advertising matter.

parentage: see *surrogate positioning.*

parent store: a controlling organization that owns or manages store properties. Synonymous with *main store.* See *flagship store.*

Pareto's law: of interest to marketing analysts, the theory of Vilfredo Pareto, an Italian sociologist and economist, that income tends to become distributed in the same proportion among consumers throughout the world, regardless of differing forms of taxation.

pari delicto: fault or blame that is equally shared.

Parkinson's laws: as developed by C. Northcote Parkinson, concepts stating that (a) work invariably expands to fill the time available for its completion, and (b) expenditures climb to reach income. Although they are called "laws" no legislative decisions are involved.

partial equilibrium analysis: an inquiry that looks at only one market of an economy under the assumption that solutions in other markets will not be altered by a change in the market examined.

partial monopoly: a situation that exists where there are so few sellers of an item or service that each may alter the price and market. Cf. *perfect (pure) monopoly.*

partial payment: a payment that is not equal to the full amount owed and is not intended to constitute the full payment.

participating announcement: an advertising message broadcast as one of many such announcements for several sponsors during a participating program heard over a radio or television station. Cf. *participating program.*

participating program: the broadcast program sponsored by more than one advertiser. Cf. *participating announcement.*

particular average: damage or loss less than the total value; partial loss.

partnership: a contractual relationship between two or more people in a joint enterprise who agree to share, not necessarily equally, in the profits and losses of the organization. Cf. *joint venture.*

parts: unit components of a product that are complete without additional processing but are useful only when incorporated into the product. See *raw material.*

party plan selling: synonymous with *party selling.*

party selling: door-to-door selling where a hostess invites friends to a gathering so that a salesperson can demonstrate items. Usually, the hostess receives a gift for her participation. Synonymous with *group plan; party plan selling.*

pass: one cycle of processing a body of data.

pass-along circulation: the cycle of a periodical or magazine without having been purchased by the reader. For example, readers find the issue in a doctor's office, in a public library, etc. A magazine's total circulation includes both paid and nonpaid circulation, and pass-along circulation. Such readers are referred to as secondary readers. Cf. *primary circulation.*

pass-along deal: an arrangement to induce the retailer to lower the price of merchandise, thus increasing the volume and perhaps share of the market for the manufacturer.

passive philosophy: a philosophy of competitive behavior where the company participates in only minimal competitive tactics to remain in the market. Cf. *aggressive philosophy.*

patent:
(1) a government grant to an inventor to protect the results of an invention.
(2) the legal right of exclusive use and licensing granted by a government to the person who invents something. An invention is patentable if it is a useful, novel, and nonobvious process, machine, manufacture, or composition of matter. See *patent applied for.*

patent applied for: a statement declaring form showing the actual application by an inventor for a U.S. patent has been filed. If the inventor is dead, the administrator of the estate must apply for the patent. The application must contain a written description of the invention, a drawing, an oath of inventorship, and a government filing fee. See *patent pending.*

patent pending: after filing for a patent, the Patent Office's statement that a search is being conducted in the United States and other countries to determine whether the invention is in fact new and patentable under the law. Should the patent be rejected, an appeal is permitted in the Patent Office and, if necessary, in the federal courts. See *patent applied for.*

patronage discount: a discount permitted on the basis of the amount of business carried out with a company. Synonymous with *deferred discount; quantity discount; volume discount.*

patronage dividend and rebate: wholesaler vouchers given to retailers to be used as incentive builders by wholesalers to generate increased retailer sales and goodwill. The patronage dividend occurs when the wholesaler offers the retailer a pro rata share of earnings from one or many of the wholesaler's goods. A patronage rebate occurs when the wholesaler refunds part of the retailer's original payment for merchandise. In both cases, payment is issued to retailers in the form of a merchandise credit voucher or a bank check.

patronage institutional advertising: advertising intending to convince an audience to use the sponsors as the source of supply for reasons other than the obvious merits of the offering. Cf. *public relations institutional advertising.*

patronage motives: the reasons that customers shop in a particular retail outlet.

patronize:
(1) to frequent a store.
(2) to be a regular customer.

payback:
(1) *general:* the return on investment equal to the original marketing expenditures; represents the minimum amount of

dollar sales that must be generated to off-set the cost of an advertising campaign. Synonymous with *payout*. See *break-even point*.

(2) *marketing:* the time, usually in years, from the point of full-scale market intro-duction of a new product until it has recov-ered its costs of development and market-ing. The market testing stage is usually considered a part of the evaluation proc-ess (and not in the payback period).

payback period: the period of time that passes before the incoming cash equals the outgoing cash on a specific project, or-der, or other effect.

payee: the person or organization to whom a check or draft or note is made payable. The payee's name follows the expression "pay to the order of."

payment guarantee: a guarantee to the supplier of merchandise that payment will follow if he or she performs his or her obligations.

payola: (slang) a gift or other valuable item offered to people who have the potential for using their influence in the promotion or sale of a product or service.

payout: synonymous with *payback*.

pay-per-view: an increasing service; indi-vidualized programming provided by a ca-ble television service.

peak: an exceptionally busy period in a business.

peak season: the period of days or months in which an item is in greatest customer demand (e.g., charcoal for barbecuing during the summer months).

pecuniary exchange: any trade that uses money.

peddler: (slang) a person who travels and sells small quantities of merchandise.

pegged price: an artificial price kept at a given level below which it cannot drop even if market forces indicate the need for a change. Government intervention, often in the form of subsidies, controls pegged prices.

peg point: the pay rate for a major task that becomes the base from which rates of pay for other related tasks are derived.

penetration: the degree of effectiveness of an advertisement on the general pub-lic (e.g., an ethnic food item such as kosher meat would have a high penetra-tion in large cities in the United States and a lower penetration in small towns or rural communities). Firms try to in-crease their penetration by applying ag-gressive marketing strategies, such as increased advertising, special promo-tions, and greater incentives for their salespeople or channel intermediaries. See *penetration strategies*.

penetration pricing:

(1) an approach in which the price of an item is set low to enter the market quickly.

(2) a pricing strategy in which the ini-tial price is set low to generate the great-est possible demand for the product.

penetration strategies: a reference to two forms of pricing and promotional strate-gies that are used when merchandise is first introduced:
(a) *rapid penetration*—setting a low product price and placing aside a large amount of money for promotion to get the fastest market penetration and the largest market share. This method is used where there is a low level of product awareness and the market is large.

(b) *slow penetration*—setting a low product price and allocating little money for promotion, thereby suggesting a rapid market acceptance of the item because of its low price and low initial costs; used when the market is large and product awareness is quite high. See *market penetration; penetration; skimming price.*

pennysaver: synonymous with *shopper.*

people meter: an instrument attached to a television set for measuring consumer broadcast preferences, viewer habits, and viewing frequencies.

people's capitalism: of interest to marketing analysts; the full range of income levels in the population of a community being represented in the ownership of the business.

per annum: by the year.

per capita income: used by marketing/advertising researchers; total income divided by the number of individuals. Per capita income can be adjusted to reflect changes in prices or purchasing power over a stated time period to show real per capita income.

per capita output: the gross national product of a nation divided by its population. This is often used to identify a country's standard of living, which is of special interest to both marketers and advertisers.

perceived equitable rewards: the rewards people feel they should receive as the result of their performance.

perceived risk: the hazards a customer believes to be related to the buying of a specific term (e.g., difficulty of obtaining servicing, cost of servicing, lifetime of the item, obsolescence of the item). Perceived risk can be socially based. Marketers try to understand reasons for perceived risk, and therefore they provide product information to assist people in their buying decisions. See *dissonance-reduction.*

perceived-value pricing: basing the price of an item or service on the purchaser's perception of its value and not on the seller's cost of production.

percentage of sales method: a method of setting a marketing budget based on a forecast of sales. A budget allocation approach for advertisers that is both simple and can relate advertising costs directly to sales. Two shortcomings of this technique include a failure to recognize that as conditions are altered, advertising costs must change with them; and this approach can falsely lead to excessive spending for large established brands and an inadequate budgeting for items that would profit from further advertising, such as new brands.

percentile: used by market researchers; one of the 99 point scores that divide a ranked distribution into groups or parts, each of which contains $1/100$ of the scores or persons. The points are located to coincide with the obtained score below which, in each division, $1/100$ of the cases fall. Scores are numbered from 1 to 99.

per centum: by the hundred.

perception: a process by which individuals attend to incoming stimuli and translate such stimuli into a message indicating the appropriate response; an major force in consumer behavior. See *product image; selective perception; symbol.*

perceptual defense: the subconscious screening out of stimuli that the individual chooses to reject because of a belief, value, etc.

perceptual gap: a gap that appears on a mapping of products where the positions of the products are determined by user opinions, not necessarily fact.

perceptual mapping: creating a graph of brand attributes, one product at a time, as noted by consumers on a scale of low to high. Helps to identify the positioning of all brands in a product category where consumer preferences are not being well provided for. See *multidimensional scaling; product positioning.*

per contra item: a balance in one account that is offset by a balance from another account.

perfect competition: a description for an industry or market unit consisting of a large number of purchasers and sellers, all involved in the buying and selling of a homogenous good, with awareness of prices and volume, no discrimination in buying and selling, and a mobility of resources. Cf. *imperfect competition; pure competition.*

perfect hedge: a hedge where the loss or gain on the commodity transaction equals the loss or gain on the finished items transactions.

perfect (pure) monopoly: a situation in which one person or organization has total control over the manufacture and marketing of an item. See *monopoly; oligopoly.*

performance analysis: a means to compare the actual performance of a marketing strategy with the expectations for the plan. It is used to upgrade the operations of the program, spot trouble areas, and correct shortcomings.

performance-based compensation: in advertising, the payment by firms to their agencies based on the agencies' performance, usually based on the sales of the item being advertised, instead of on a retainer or project basis.

performance budgeting: grouping of budget accounts into categories related to a specific product or service that is produced, and evolution of product-cost measurements of these activities.

performance label: a label affixed to a product describing the operating characteristics and features of performance for that item. See *label.*

performance standard: the measure of performance against which the actual performance is to be compared.

perimeter advertising: the collective term for posters, billboards, and signs placed in public structures to attract spectators. Often used at sporting events.

per-inquiry payment: payment based on the percentage of all funds received from an advertiser's inquiries or actual sales, instead of on published time or space rates. Per-inquiry arrangements are often carried out to introduce advertisers to new media.

period cost: synonymous with *fixed cost.*

period expense: an expenditure that cannot be associated with or assigned to a product and so is reported as an expense in the period in which it is incurred. Cf. *product costing.*

periodical: synonymous with *magazine.*

periodic stock control: a unit control system in which stock is identified and recorded periodically and sales for intervening time slots are calculated. See *inventory control; out-of-stock.*

peripheral service: an added service offered without charge to a basic item or service. These services, which add to operating costs, enhance an advertising agency's image and competitive advantage.

perishability of services: services that cannot be stored for future sale. The service supplier attempts to manage consumer usage so there is consistent demand throughout various periods of the week, month, and/or year.

perishable distinctiveness: a product having serious competition over the coming years, usually five. At first, the item may have an exclusive distinctiveness, but with the passing of time, as others capture a larger share of the market, the product passes into a stage of declining distinctiveness.

perishable goods: items that are subject to rapid decay unless given proper storage (e.g., meat, dairy products).

PERK: short for perquisites.

perpetual inventory: a book inventory identifying the stock on hand by means of a detailed record, enabling the firm to know the composition of its inventory at any point in time. See *inventory; perpetual inventory control.*

perpetual inventory control: a unit control system whereby orders, receipts, and sales are identified as they occur and inventory is computed. See *inventory; perpetual inventory.*

perquisites: additional compensation furnished by management, usually in goods or services, over and above the general payment of wages. Shortened to PERK.

perpetual inventory system: keeping a record of the firm's inventory by constantly noting the movement of merchandise into and out of the company. Usually involves the recording of orders and receipt quantities, and requisitions of sale quantities. See *perpetual merchandise control.*

perpetual merchandise control: synonymous with *perpetual inventory system,* but limited to retailing.

personal care items: hair dryers, electric shavers, toothbrushes, facial cosmetics, and the like.

personal consumption expenditures: the funds spent by households for consumer items. Disposable personal income minus savings equals personal consumption expenditures.

personal demographics: the basic identifiable characteristics of individual final consumers and organizational consumers and groups of final consumers and organizational consumers.

personal disposable income: synonymous with *disposable income.*

personal distribution of income: the distribution of natural income among individuals or households; used by advertisers in setting strategies.

personal income: used by marketers; national income less various kinds of income not actually received by individuals, not-for-profit institutions, and so on, plus certain receipts that do not arise from production. See *disposable income.*

personal influence: the power of people to sway or influence the purchasing decisions of others. For this reason, marketers attempt to identify those people who exert influence over others. See *bluefingers.*

personal interview: a survey technique in which respondents are questioned in a face-to-face setting, in homes, shopping malls, offices, etc. It is considered the preferred method, although costly, in the early stages of research when there is a lack of certainty as to the best questions to ask.

personality: in broadcasting, synonymous with *format (2)*.

personalized advertisement: a specially bound periodical insertion that features the individual subscriber's name.

personalizing shoppers: one of a four-way sociological classification of consumers who seek out retail outlets that they are most secure in, in particular those with salespeople they feel they can relate best with. For other categories, see *apathetic shoppers; economic shoppers; ethical shoppers.*

personal saving: of special importance to advertisers and marketers; the difference between disposable personal income and personal consumption expenditures, including the changes in cash and deposits, security holdings, indebtedness, reserves of life insurance companies and mutual savings institutions, the net investment of unincorporated enterprises, and the acquisition of real property net of depreciation.

personal selling:
(1) *general:* a promotion method involving interpersonal communication between individuals.
(2) *salesmanship:* verbal presentation to a prospective customer for the purpose of making a sale. As contrasted with advertising, personal selling is usually more effective.

persuasion: a primary objective of advertising, the act of influencing an individual or group to work for a desired objective.

persuasion vehicles: synonymous with *advertising media.*

persuasive impact: the impact of a message on a prospect.

persuasive label: a label whose primary objective is to attract the consumer to buy the item and not to inform.

persuasive pricing: psychological pricing that tends to convey a sense of extra-good value to the consumer. Cf. *odd pricing.*

PERT: see *program evaluation and review technique.*

PERT/COST: a modified PERT system that, in addition to time, deadlines, and schedules, includes all cost considerations.

phantom market: a market that when examined carefully does not exist at all or is too small to demand attention.

phantom shoppers: sellers' representatives who pose as customers to assess methods used by dealers in selling some items. They may receive prizes if preferred methods are being used.

phase zero: the preliminary evaluation or study preceding the decision to go ahead with a project or strategy.

phony list price: the list price presented to a prospect to indicate that the price has been discounted from list. At times, customers wind up paying more for the item or service than the actual market price. This practice is outlawed by the Wheeler-Lea Amendment. See *list price.*

physical distribution:
(1) the movement of merchandise from manufacturer to consumer.
(2) the movement of materials from sources of supply to producers. See *distribution.*

(3) all the activities that provide for the efficient flow of raw materials, in-process inventory, and finished goods from the point of procurement to the ultimate consumer.

physical distribution concept: a theory requiring all physical handling and the trade channel system be looked on as one total system.

physical distribution manager: the corporate person responsible for the flow of materials used in manufacturing and for the distribution of finished merchandise to the market; coordinates the work of corporate departments in the procurement of raw materials and, eventually, the delivery of finished items to channel intermediaries or end-users. Synonymous with *logistics manager.*

physical distribution strategy: the transportation form(s) and warehouse form(s) used, the inventory levels maintained, and the number and locations of plants, warehouses, and shopping facilities employed in moving goods from one place to another.

physical inventory: inventory calculation obtained by making an actual listing of stock on hand.

physical obsolescence:

(1) any worn-out, broken item resulting from normal wear and tear.

(2) obsolescence that results when products are built to last only a limited time.

physical product: the actual physical entity or service offered to consumers.

physiological motives: motives whose satisfaction is needed for survival. Cf. *psychological satisfaction.*

physiological needs: synonymous with *primary needs.*

pick-and-pack: goods shipment methods where merchandise is chosen from a warehouse based on what has been ordered by each customer, and then packed for shipment.

pickup: synonymous with *pickup materials.*

pickup materials: advertising materials that can be used again, in part or total, in a different advertisement. Synonymous with *pickup.*

piece goods: fabrics that are purchased in required lengths for home sewing.

piece rate (wage): the amount of money received for each unit of output. When wages are so determined, an incentive wage system is in operation.

piggyback: see *piggyback commercial.*

piggyback commercial: in broadcasting, two or more commercials aired one to follow each other, with different merchandise of the same sponsor. Advertisers like piggyback commercials to get two or more unrelated advertising messages into the time allocated for one, without the increase of commercial time. See *bookends.*

Pigou effect concept: the concept that a lowering of the overall price level creates higher consumption of time and services.

pilferage: the theft of property while such goods are in transit or being stored. See *inventory shortage; shoplifting.*

pilot film: a filmed television program produced to demonstrate to prospective sponsors and advertising agencies the format, talent, and quality of the entire series that is projected for future filming.

pilot marketing: a marketing method to test the feasibility of the proposed course of action; provides the firm with valuable marketing experience while forging ahead with manufacturing plans and demands of the market.

pilot plant scale production: production of a modest number of units in small facilities designed to prove methods that may be used in full-scale plants.

PIMS: see *profit impact of marketing strategy.*

pinch:

(1) a bind or tight situation.

(2) a sudden, unanticipated rise in prices. When money rates go up suddenly, it is called a *money pinch.*

pinochle season: (slang) in the garment industry, the off-season.

pioneering innovativeness: a strategy of trying to be the first to market new types of products. The highest order of innovativeness (others are adapting and imitating), it is often based on technical breakthroughs.

pioneering stage: the first stage in the product life cycle. Emphasis is placed on achieving a demand for sale of the item. Synonymous with *primary stage.* See *spiral stage.*

pipeline: a manufacturer's inventory purchased by wholesalers and retailers, but not as yet purchased by consumers.

pirate parts: replacement units made and sold by producers specializing in only making replacement parts. Traditionally, the makers are firms other than the makers of the machines that the pirate parts match.

pirating: the illicit use by a nonsubscriber of a subscriber's rating reports.

pitch:

(1) a presentation to a prospect by the salesperson to obtain an order or new business, as in a sales pitch.

(2) the presentation by one or more people from an advertising agency to a prospective account.

place: one of the 4 P's of marketing, dealing with strategies and distribution channels for making a product physically available to consumers; concerned with physical handling and distribution of items, such as warehousing, packaging for transportation, modes of transport, and the number of wholesale and/or retail outlets through which the item is available. See *P.*

place utility:

(1) the additional value in having a product where it is utilized or consumed.

(2) the satisfaction that buyers receive from having a product available at the appropriate place. See *utility.*

plan: a written document that specifies resource requirements, costs, expected benefits, and activities necessary to achieve a goal.

planned economy: a system whereby the government has a major influence in the control of economic resources by deciding what to manufacture, in what quantity, and often for whom.

planned gap:

(1) the difference between a forecast and a plan.

(2) the difference between what will occur assuming that no changes are made (forecast) and a projection of what the organization wants to accomplish (plan).

planned impulse buying: a form of impulse buying in which the customer uses the store's stock as a shopping list. Cf. *pure impulse buying; reminder impulse buying.* See *impulse buying.*

planned obsolescence: an approach of consciously making an item out of fashion in the eyes of the consumer by repeatedly bringing out new models or products featuring improvements that are promoted as being superior or beneficial. There is a question of the value to the consumer of these systematic changes. The weakest-link theory claims that the least durable component in a product will determine its useful life. Cf. *product obsolescence.* Synonymous with *managed obsolescence.* See *weakest-link theory.*

planned presentation: synonymous with *canned presentation.*

planned purchases:
(1) *retailing:* the means to determine the dollar value of merchandise to be drawn into stock during a given season or cycle; helps ensure having adequate stock on hand to fulfill increased demand.

(2) *marketing:* in the consumer purchasing process, decisions to buy that are made prior to the prospect's entry into the outlet and prior to the prospect having direct contact with the item.

planned shopping center: a retail location that consists of centrally owned or managed facilities. It is planned and operated as an entity, ringed by parking, and based on balanced tenancy. The three types of planned centers are regional, community, and neighborhood.

planning: an organizational activity that requires establishment of a predetermined course of action, beginning with a statement of goals. See *market planning; strategic planning; tactical planning.*

planogram: a computerized diagram used in merchandising to design the ideal display of merchandise on retail store shelves.

plans board: a group of advertising agency executives who meet regularly to discuss and plan the advertising and marketing strategies for the agency's clients.

plant:
(1) *general:* an establishment that manufactures or distributes items and services.

(2) *advertising:* a group of outdoor structures and display areas used for the presentation of advertising messages and consisting of poster panels, metal and wood bulletin boards, walls of buildings, and electric spectaculars and semispectaculars, located in a city or an area characterized by a great volume of traffic and owned and operated by an individual or firm.

plant operator: an individual or organization servicing advertisers by offering outdoor display facilities for the presentation of sales messages.

plant turnover ratio: the relationship between an organization's sales income and cost of operating its physical plant. It gives the sales volume generated for each dollar invested in physical facilities.

plasticity of demand: the degree to which consumer choices are influenced around a given point on the demand curve. See *price elasticity; promotional elasticity of demand.*

plateauing: the cessation of salespeople's sales efforts because of a variety of variables, including the lack of motivation.

PLC: see *product life cycle.*

pledging: the offering by a borrower of his or her assets as security for the repayment of a debt.

plow back:

(1) to put earnings from sales back into the business operation.

(2) to appropriate funds representing net profit received during an earlier period to the advertising budget; used by advertisers who wish to invest maximum dollars in their promotions.

plug:

(1) *general:* to work hard and steadily (verb).

(2) *packaging:* a type of closure made to be inserted into the opening of a container (noun).

(3) *advertising:* a testimonial that is received without charge (noun).

plunge method: synonymous with *task method.*

p.m. deal: a monetary payment made to retail salesclerks by a manufacturer for a specific item sold by the clerks under a special incentive plan. To induce clerks to push the product and to favor it over items of competitors, a manufacturer may offer a special payment or bonus for each unit sold during the life of the offer.

point of equilibrium: the point at which supply equals demand.

point of ideal proportion: in a production process, the point at which the most profitable relative amounts of the forces of production (land, labor, capital, and management) are used.

point of indifference: in production, the point at which the cost of an added increment of land, labor, capital, or management merely equals the money return of the additional item made because of that

increase. Cf. *diminishing returns; diseconomies of scale.*

point of origin: the location at which goods are received for transportation.

point-of-purchase (POP): synonymous with *point-of-sale.*

point-of-purchase advertising: see *POP advertising.*

point-of-sale (POS): in retailing, the location within the store where a sale is completed (e.g., cash register, merchandise pick-up counter). Synonymous with *point-of-purchase.*

point-of-sale terminal (POST): a communication and data-capture terminal located where payment is made for goods or services.

Poison Prevention Packaging Act of 1970: federal legislation requiring manufacturers to use safety packaging on items containing substances considered dangerous or harmful to children.

policy: a plan of action.

policy rights: in purchasing, the authority given managers to set procurement goals.

political marketing: marketing of ideas and opinions that relate to public or political issues or to specific candidates for office.

polybag: a bag employed by direct marketers for shipping multiple pieces of items of goods or sheets of promotional material. See *shrink wrapping.*

polycentricity: one of a three-way classification of the policies of a company involved with international marketing that concentrates on the legal, cultural, and demographic differences and similarities among markets, where each is looked on as different so that only local managers can understand and react to local conditions. Cf. *ethnocentricity; geocentricity.*

pony spread: print advertising composed of two junior page advertisements appearing on opposite pages in a magazine or periodical. The spread consists of two advertisements that use equal portions of the adjoining pages but are united visually to form one advertisement. Synonymous with *junior spread.*

pool:
(1) an agreement between two or more companies to curtail output, divide sales areas, or in any other way to avoid competition.

(2) a combination of resources of funds, for some common purpose or benefit.

pooled interdependence: the relationship between units of an organization such that their separate products can be added together to form the total final product.

pooled marketing: an agreement of two or more manufacturers to offer each other's products as a premium when customers purchase a certain number of units of the first company's product. Cf. *symbiotic marketing.*

pooled purchasing: a number of independent middlepeople who combine their orders to keep costs lower. Synonymous with *informal buying group.*

pooling: uniting several manufacturers' items without trying to keep separate the contribution from any one producer.

POP: point-of-purchase. See *point-of-sale.*

POP advertising: promotional material placed at the point of purchase, such as interior displays, printed material at store counters, or window displays. See *point-of-sale; position media.*

pop-in: a short paid announcement by a broadcast advertiser that is usually of special interest to the viewer or listener (e.g., a Christmas holiday greeting to the public during which the company does not mention any of its products available on the market). Synonymous with *image liner.*

population: in marketing research, the full group under study and for which the researcher will attempt predictions or forecasts, and draw conclusions. See *sampling.*

pop-up: a print advertising piece or magazine insert created to rise when the reader opens it.

Porter-Lawler model: an extension of the expectancy theory that draws together individual, job, and organizational characteristics to describe the motivational process.

portfolio: a set of things. Most often applied to that group of projects currently active in a research laboratory but may apply to all new projects under way.

portfolio analysis: a technique by which an organization individually assesses and positions every business unit and/ or product. Company efforts and resources are allocated and separate marketing mixes are aimed at their chosen target markets on the basis of these assessments.

POS: see *point-of-sale.*

POSDCORB: the seven functions of administration: planning, organizing, staffing, directing, coordinating, reporting, and budgeting.

position:
(1) the location of an advertisement or commercial in a given vehicle. Advertis-

ers often pay a premium for a preferred position. See *island position; positioning.*

(2) the space occupied by an advertisement in a publication in relation to its placement on the page and its proximity to the front, middle, or back of the publication.

positioning:

(1) *marketing:* the projection of an item as possessing a desired image, to make it attractive to a part of the market for that type of merchandise (e.g., a low-priced sports car that looks like an expensive model). See *market target; multidimensional scaling.*

(2) *marketing:* a process in which a marketer communicates with consumers to establish a distinct place for its product or brand in their minds. Cf. *repositioning.* Synonymous with *market positioning.*

(3) *advertising:* the place on the page where an advertisement appears.

(4) *broadcasting:* programs or time spots felt by advertisers to be particularly attractive.

positioning advertising: advertising that targets a segment of the market, and the item or service is then presented to appeal directly to that segment.

position media: outdoor and transit advertising media including nonstandardized signs and point-of-purchase advertising. See *point-of-sale; POP advertising.*

positive appeal: advertising copy method purporting to alleviate a person's anxiety about purchasing and using an item. Emphasis is given to the positive components of an item and the ensuing gains from purchasing the product. Cf. *negative appeal.*

positive concept of valuation: used in international marketing; an application of ad valorem duties holding that duties should be applied on the actual value of the transaction, as defined by the buyer and seller.

positive conversion: synonymous with *boomerang (2).*

positive file: an authorization system file that contains information about every account holder and is capable of providing a variety of data to be evaluated in responding to a request for authorization of credit, check cashing, or other privileges.

positive option selling: a direct-mail method where a consumer indicates whether or not he or she wishes to receive a regularly scheduled product shipment. With a positive option, there is less revenue per customer than a negative option, but the positive option usually attracts more purchasers. Cf. *negative option selling.*

positive reinforcement: the administration of positive rewards, contingent on good performance, that strengthens desired behavior in the future.

possession utility: synonymous with *ownership utility.*

POST: see *point-of-sale terminal.*

postage stamp pricing: synonymous with *freight allowed.*

poster: synonymous with *billboard.*

posterior analysis: in marketing research, data that lead to a change in marketing decisions and strategy because of new insights or new information. See *preposterior analysis; prior analysis.*

posting: the physical placing of an advertisement on an outdoor advertisement. See *posting date; posting period.*

posting date: the date on which a display of an outdoor advertisement commences; usually every fifth day, starting with the first of the month.

posting period: the amount of time remaining on a display, (e.g., a billboard's posting period is anywhere from 3 to 12 months).

postmark: an impression on letters and packages, showing the time, date, and post office or sectional center of origin.

postmark advertising: advertising printed by a postage-meter machine on an envelope as part of its postmark. Postmark advertising is required to fulfill certain U.S. Postal Service requirements; must be nonpolitical and noncontroversial and cannot confuse the public by having a design that appears as a regular postal marking.

postmortem: the analysis of an operation after its completion.

postponed obsolescence: obsolescence that occurs when technological improvements are available but are not introduced until the demand for existing products declines. See *obsolescence.*

postponement: to reduce risks in marketing by having the inventory location take place at the last possible moment. It may allow the greatest possible sorting while the item is relatively undifferentiated as it presently exists.

postpurchase anxiety: a customer's feeling of doubt following his or her purchase commitment. See *postpurchase behavior.*

postpurchase behavior: the final stage in the consumer adoption process, includes the continued evaluation of the item or service, maintenance, and if the item or service should be repurchased. See *postpurchase anxiety.*

postscript: a sentence or block of copy added to a direct-mail letter immediately beneath the advertiser's signature as a means of calling attention to an important point that should be impressed on the reader.

posttest: a procedure to the assessment of an advertisement or advertising campaign. Posttesting by advertisers is used to obtain insight into consumer responses to certain advertising methods and to minimize costly mistakes in the future; measures both the impact of an advertising message as well as its ultimate impact on product sales. See *pretest.*

potential competition: the possible entry into the market of new companies, substitute products, or materials of similar or superior quality and/or benefit, all perhaps introduced at equal or lower prices.

potential demand: demand that can be expected to become effective at a future date (e.g., when purchasing power is increased). Cf. *overall market capability.*

potential market saturation: the maximum number of potential users (or buyers) during a specified period.

potential need satisfier: any item, service, or consideration perceived by a prospect as a possible means of satisfying their need. See *risk reduction.*

poverty:

(1) the absence of most of the comforts of life and undersupply of the necessities.

(2) the point at which deprivation makes the level necessary for physical efficiency impossible.

poverty of time: a consumer life-style where the quest for financial security means less free time because of the alternatives competing for time expended.

power: in marketing, the ability of one member of a marketing channel to influence the trading behavior of another.

power of attorney: a written instrument, usually acknowledged before a public officer or witness, in which one person grants to another the rights of utilization, tenancy, transfer, or disposal of assets owned by the first person as though he or she were exercising these rights. A power of attorney has the force of law; it may be limited with respect to the assets listed in the power of attorney, or it may give full power over all assets owned.

practical capacity: the maximum level at which a plant or department can economically operate most efficiently.

praise method: the use of compliments by the salesperson to convince a prospect to purchase an item or service.

preapproach: the step in the sales process of finding critical data about a potential customer prior to contact. See *canvass.*

preaudit: the examination of a creditor's invoices, payrolls, claims, and expected reimbursements before actual payment, or the verification of sales transactions before delivery.

precautionary motive: a rationale used by firms and consumers for retaining a portion of their assets in cash, to ensure their ability to satisfy unexpected demands easily.

precedence: in product innovation, the order of market entry. A product is first to market, second, etc.

preclusive purchasing: buying materials with the expectation of denying their use to a competitor.

preclusive specification: a specification that only one or few suppliers qualify to bid on, placing the buyer at a disadvantage by having so few potential suppliers.

predatory pricing: cutting prices with the objective of harming one's competitors. The opposite of umbrella pricing. See *extinction price; rate war.*

predictive research: the category on the level-of-outcome dimension when the outcome of a research effort is to predict the future. Predictive research is the third level, preceded by the first level of descriptive research, which states that something does exist or has occurred in the past. Evaluative research is the second level and adds value judgments to data to form comparisons. Cf. *forecasting.*

predictor variable: synonymous with *independent variable.*

preempt: in broadcasting, removing a program from the air and replacing it with another. Cf. *preemption.* See *non-preemptible time.*

preemptible rate: in broadcasting, a discount rate to advertisers for the time that may have to be surrendered if another advertiser is willing to pay even more.

preemption: the prerogative of customs authorities to seize and sell items that an importer has deliberately undervalued to avoid the payment of duties. Cf. *preempt.*

preemptive marketing: advertising a service or product prior to its availability in the marketplace so as to forestall the purchasing of a competitor's product or service that is already available.

preemptive price: a price that is so low it makes the market unattractive to possible entrants who might eventually become strong competitors. Synonymous with *keep-out price; stay-out price.*

prefabricate: to manufacture standardized components of a larger unit in a factory, thus making possible the assembling of the item elsewhere (e.g., the buyer's home) without production facilities.

preference gap: an opportunity first discovered on determinant gap maps or perceptual gap maps and then evaluated using maps based on customer preferences; often coincides with an area of no preference.

preference item: a consumer's choice of a particular item even when similar items are less costly (e.g., insisting on Coca-Cola, although a chain grocery store's cola-type soft drink is less expensive).

preferences: in international sales, special trade advantages given by governments to trading partners to promote export growth and development. Licensing practices, quotas, or preferential application of other measures, including taxes, can also be granted in the nontariff areas.

preferential tariff: of importance to international marketers; a tariff that grants lower rates of duty on goods imported from certain "preferred" countries than on the same goods from other nations.

preferred position:
(1) any specifically requested advertisement position for which the advertiser pays a premium. It could be a right-hand page, top of a column, space surrounded by editorial materials, or a sports page. Publications often have a special higher rate for preferred position advertisements.

(2) the advertisement's placement in the section of the medium that is appropriate to the advertised merchandise or service. Cf. *split run.* See *fixed location/ position; premium; prime time; upfront selling period.*

preferred resource: a seller chosen by the consumer as his or her first choice source of supply for a particular time of good or service.

prejudice: a human characteristic of special importance to advertisers; a mental bias tending toward some preconceived judgment or opinion, thus affecting the person's attitude toward work or employees. See *bias; proactive inhibition.*

prelaunch: the first stage of the launch cycle. Involves preparations to launch the product, including getting distribution and building necessary field service capability.

preliminary expenses: expense incurred in the establishment of an advertising agency (e.g., costs for developing and circulating a prospectus).

preliminary market analysis: a type of market research that follows ideation and entry evaluation. Often used to gain greater knowledge of a particular market prior to setting up a concept test plan.

premarketing: synonymous with *prepricing.*

premarking: a service provided by some manufacturers of placing the purchaser's selling price on the items at the factory.

premium:
(1) *merchandising:* a product offered free or at less than the regular price to induce the consumer to buy another product.

(2) *retailing:* an offer of merchandise, at a minimal cost or at no charge, as an inducement to the customer to purchase a

given item. See *coupon; direct premium; referral premium.*

(3) *advertising:* the higher charge paid for special advertising, as with a preferred position. Synonymous with *premium pricing.* See *preferred position; trade premium.*

premium jobber: a wholesaler of incentive items who usually deals with a full range of merchandise. See *jobber.*

premium money: synonymous with *push money.*

premium offers: offers such as a (a) gift, (b) free send-away item (gift in exchange for proof of purchase), and (c) self-liquidating premium (consumer sends both money and proof of purchase to obtain the offer).

premium pricing: synonymous with *premium (3).*

premium representative:

(1) a manufacturer's representative working with premium users; offers factory price, support, experience, and personal attention.

(2) a commission salesperson serving a host of manufacturers on a direct-factory-price basis.

prepackaging:

(1) *general:* packaging of fresh foods (meat, vegetables, cheeses) in consumer units for self-service sales.

(2) *merchandising:* to avoid repackaging by the retailer, packaging of merchandise such as chinaware and furniture by the manufacturer so that it may be sold directly to the consumer without opening. Synonymous with *prepak.*

prepaid: indicating that shipping charges have already been paid or are to be paid at the point of delivery.

prepaid expense:

(1) payment for items not yet received.

(2) a charge deferred until the benefit for which payment has been made occurs.

prepak: synonymous with *prepackaging.*

prepay: to pay before or in advance of receipt of goods or services.

prepayment: payment of a debt before it actually becomes due.

prepayment clause: the privilege of repaying part or all of a loan in advance of date or dates stated in a contract.

preposterior analysis: in marketing research, the attempt to determine if further information is worth the cost of generating it. See *posterior analysis.*

prepricing: the printing of the retail or suggested price of an item directly on the packaging of the item at the time of manufacture. Although it saves the dealer the cost and time of pricing merchandise, it locks him or her into a situation where the items cannot be sold to a customer at a higher price. Synonymous with *premarketing; preticketing.*

preprint:

(1) a copy of an advertisement made before it is run in a print medium. Such advertisements are usually larger than they will actually appear when printed and are also mounted on a board for display purposes.

(2) materials printed ahead of the publication's regular printing time schedule (e.g., freestanding inserts, advertisements printed on special paper stock).

prepurchase activity: the stage after the buyer becomes aware of the assets in purchasing a product; involves seeking information, sources of supply, the lowering of uncertainty, with assessments each step of the way.

preretailing: assignment by the retailer of retail prices to goods at the time an order is made, thus allowing the determination of retail values of items on order. This practice also speeds up the checking and marking procedures when merchandise arrives.

prerogatives: the rights, powers, privileges of an individual that others do not possess.

prescreening: those evaluation steps that follow ideation and precede the full screen; involves entry evaluation, preliminary market analysis, and concept testing and development.

present value: the discounted value of a certain sum that is due and payable at a specified future date.

presold market: buyers waiting for the arrival of a new product or service.

press:
(1) the print news media.

(2) a casual expression for publicity received for a service, item, accomplishment, or other effect from a company/marketing activity. Synonymous with *press coverage.*

press coverage: synonymous with *press.*

press run:
(1) the number of copies printed.

(2) the actual printing of a specific job.

prestige advertising: advertising to enhance the prestige of a firm or a firm's services or products. See *corporate advertising.*

prestige pricing: increasing the price of an item to establish a quality image of the product or the seller.

pressure-sensitive label: a label with an adhesive back that can be readily removed from its original sheet and attached to a mailing envelope. It is assumed to be an incentive for recipients to respond to a mailing.

presumption: an assumed fact, which can serve as evidence until facts are obtained.

pretest:
(1) *general:* a test given to determine an individual's performance in some area in advance of training, education, or some other condition that is expected to improve performance. Cf. *posttest.*

(2) *marketing:* the measure of the acceptance of a concept, item, or service presented to prospects; usually accomplished with interviews and impacts on selling strategy.

preticketing: synonymous with *prepricing.*

prewrap: to wrap or package merchandise before it is placed on the floor for sale.

price:
(1) that which the buyer gives up in exchange for something that provides satisfaction.

(2) the amount of money a seller receives for goods or services at the factory or place of business. Price is not what the seller asks for the product or service but what is actually received. It is one of the four Ps of marketing, the only part that produces revenues. See *pricing.*

price agreement plan: a central purchasing accord where the purchaser for the stores arranges prices, colors, sizes, etc., in addition to the shipping terms. Synonymous with *catalog plan.*

price analysis: a purchaser's study of a supplier's costs to manufacture an item with the purpose of assisting the purchaser to negotiate a price similar to the supplier's cost.

price appeal: the practical approach to advertising, in which the promotion of an item or service is based on its price rather than on an emotional appeal.

price-based shopping products: products for which consumers believe the attributes of alternatives are relatively similar and thus seek the least expensive items or stores.

price ceiling: a government-established maximum price.

price competition: competition among firms that purport to differentiate their merchandise based on price alone. Items are marked as being preferred based on how much less they will cost. Cf. *nonprice competition.*

price control:

(1) *general:* regulation of the prices of goods and services to reduce increases in the cost of living; a government-imposed strategy that is rarely used.

(2) *merchandising:* the result of the demand by a manufacturer that the buyer for resale not be permitted to determine a resale price for the goods. See *fair-trade price.*

price cutting: a procedure used usually when firms have excess capacity and wish to generate additional business without increasing selling efforts, adding to the cost of advertising, or improving the item. Price cutting offers goods or services for sale at a price below that recognized as typical or appropriate by buyers and sellers. Coupons, rebates, larger packages at the same price, lowering of the retail price are approaches used in price cutting. Its negative side is that consumers may perceive that the quality of the item has been reduced. See *underselling.*

price discretion: the ability of a sales representative to alter the price of an item for purposes of making a sale.

price discrimination: the practice of charging different prices for the same quality and quantity of merchandise to different buyers. Should this practice result in reducing competition, it is illegal under the antitrust laws. Cf. *functional discount.* See *Robinson-Patman Act of 1936.*

priced out of the market: see *price out of the market.*

price elasticity: reflected in a reduction in sales when the price of an item is raised. Cf. *price inelasticity.* See *elastic demand; income elasticity of demand; plasticity of demand.*

price equalization: a competitive pricing policy leading to a company's delivered price to a customer; composed of the price of the item at the factory plus the freight cost to the customer as if the shipment began at the shipping point of the company's competitor nearest to the company's customer.

price escalation: advancement in the final price of an item or service because of unanticipated or miscalculated costs of distribution, transportation, tariffs, etc.

price fixing: an agreement by competing organizations to avoid competitive pricing by charging identical prices or by changing prices at the same time. Price fixing is in violation of the Sherman Antitrust Act. Cf. *conscious parallel action; price stabilization.* See *price negotiation.*

price floor: the lowest price at which a company can sell an item or service and still realize a profit.

price-floor pricing: a form of cost-based pricing whereby a firm determines the lowest price at which it is worthwhile to increase the amount of goods or services it makes available for sale.

price guaranty: a seller's agreement to make a proportionate refund to a customer on all items in the buyer's inventory at the time of a price reduction. It usually has a time limit following purchase. Synonymous with *guaranty against price decline; price protection.*

price index: a measure to illustrate the changes in the average level of prices. See *purchasing power of the dollar; wholesale price index.*

price inelasticity: a change in price that yields a disproportionately small change in demand. Cf. *price elasticity.*

price inflaters: charges placed on top of the list price of an item or service that increase its true selling price, such as credit charges, service contracts, handling fees, etc.

price leader: see *price leadership.*

price leadership:
(1) a situation in which prices can be determined by one major manufacturer in an industry, thus influencing others to accept the prices as determined. See *administered price.*

(2) merchandise whose price has been significantly dropped to enhance store traffic. See *loss leader.*

price level: the value of money in comparison with a specified base period.

price lining:
(1) *retailing:* placing several items of varying costs together and selling them all at the same price. This practice is used frequently in retailing. See *loss leader.*

(2) *marketing:* a pricing strategy in which prices are used to sort products into "lines" based on an attribute such as quality, prestige, or style.

price loco: the price at the place where a purchase occurs.

price-minus pricing: a method for determining the price of an item or service by initially estimating the price at which that item or service would find a share of the market, and then developing the item or service to be profitable at that found price.

price mix: a firm's strategy of raising and lowering prices to meet competition head on.

price negotiation: price fixing based on the belief that the purchaser is a price-maker than a price-taker. See *price fixing.*

price-off: a price reduction used to induce trial or increase usage of a product. The percentage reduction is traditionally noted on the product package. See *price leadership.*

price out of the market: items that have been made so expensive that they are no longer purchased in their usual market (e.g., vendors of $12 ice-cream cones would find themselves priced out of the juvenile market). Cf. *inelastic demand.*

price pack: items available at a lower price to consumers. Two forms of price packs are:
(a) *reduced-price packs*—two single packages sold together at a lowered rate, such as three for the price of two.

(b) *banded price packs*—two related items, bound together and sold at a price lower than the cost of buying them separately, such as shaving cream and a razor. See *economy pack.*

price planning: systematic decision making by an organization regarding all aspects of pricing.

price point: the standard retail price used by marketers for some items that vary slightly in wholesale cost but share a similar level of perceived value to the consumer (e.g., instead of selling five shirts on an absolute profit margin, resulting in prices such as $19.95, $18.75, $18.00, $17.50, and $17.00, the marketer could price all of them at $18.25). Small differences in price tend to have a disproportionate impact on sales.

price protection: synonymous with *price guaranty.*

price quality association: the belief that consumers equate high prices with higher quality and low prices with lower quality. See *prestige pricing.*

price reducers: methods for lowering the selling price (e.g., providing free services, rebates, discounts).

price repression: the deliberate reduction of domestic prices when imported items that are competitors are sold at significantly lower prices than the domestically produced items. Synonymous with *price suppression.*

price rigidity: a long-term lack of concern for prices of raw or produced items in relation to the inflationary aspects of a depression or recession.

price sensitive: the tendency of the demand for an item or service to vary based on the variations in price. Some items or services are more price sensitive than others because of the impact of demand and availability. Marketers of price-sensitive items often test new prices before implementing them, to assess the impact on demand. See *elasticity; price elasticity.*

price shading: where discounts are available to wholesalers, retailers, and consumers with the expectation that an increased demand will evolve.

price space: the distance between price points in the product line (e.g., the distance from one price to another).

price-specie flow theory: a theory stating that imports of precious metals increase the supply of funds and therefore advance the price level of items that use these metals.

price stabilization: keeping prices at a state level. This is primarily a government strategy, especially during wartime or periods of rapid inflation, but it is illegal when practiced by private companies. Cf. *price fixing.* See *Sherman Antitrust Act of 1890.*

price suppression: synonymous with *price repression.*

price system: the market system of resource allocation.

price takers: firms that have no market power over price. Therefore, the market dictates price for them.

price war: a combative competition between firms that lower prices in the attempt to undersell each other. A price war often results in the failure of one or more competitors.

price zone: price lines that appeal to a group of a store's customers. See *price lining.*

pricing: setting and/or changing the cost to the consumer for a service or item. See *price; pricing above the market.*

pricing above the market: establishing prices lower than those of the competitor so as to maximize the use of price as a competitive factor.

prima facie: (Latin) at first view. That which appears to be true, until contrary evidence is given.

primary advertising: used most by trade associations; advertising where the marketer tries to increase demand for a product category. Synonymous with *generic advertising.*

primary audience: in advertising, the target group for a particular advertising campaign. When a strategy is under discussion, the features and purchasing habits of a primary audience are to be evaluated carefully.

primary boycott: see *boycott.*

primary circulation: the number of households that purchase a particular publication. Cf. *pass-along circulation.* Synonymous with *primary readership.*

primary data:
(1) data collected specifically for use in a particular research project.

(2) information collected by a researcher from the original source. Cf. *secondary data.*

primary demand:
(1) demand for a product type.

(2) market demand for a product class rather than a particular brand.

primary demand advertising:
(1) advertising purporting to create primary buying motives with consumers. See *selective demand advertising.*

(2) advertising in which the marketer attempts to create awareness of and provide information about a type of product.

primary group:
(1) a reference unit to which a person belongs that provides a major influence on attitudes and behavior.

(2) a group that is small and intimate enough for all its members to communicate with one another face to face.

primary market: synonymous with *local market.*

primary market area: the major area of sale and distribution for an advertiser's goods or services (e.g., the primary market for bathing suits would be southern states or other warm climate areas). Synonymous with *heartland.*

primary needs: basic physiological needs. Based on Maslow's hierarchy of needs theory, these are hunger, thirst, shelter, sex. Synonymous with *biogenic needs; innate needs; physiological needs.*

primary processed items: lumber, stone, clay, and glass; blast furnace and steelwork products; nonferrous and other primary metals; fabricated metals; textiles; paper; chemicals; petroleum; and rubber. Cf. *primary product.*

primary product: any product of a farm, forest, or fishery, or any mineral, in its natural form or that has undergone such processing as is customarily needed to prepare it for marketing in substantial volume in international trade. Cf. *primary processed items.*

primary readership: synonymous with *primary circulation.*

primary research: gathering market data in the field by a firm or individual to examine a specific marketing problem or situation.

primary service area: the geographic area surrounding a radio or television station in which the ground waves are not subject to objectionable interference or fading.

primary stage: synonymous with *pioneering stage.*

primary trading area: the geographic area in which a marketing organization has dominance, and often control.

prime time: in broadcasting, the few hours during the day that attracts the largest audience, usually in the early evening. May differ for radio and television stations, and may be affected by the product described within the commercial (e.g., toys are best advertised on Sunday morning while children are watching television). Cf. *drive time.* See *day parts; preferred position.*

principal: the face value of an instrument, which becomes the obligation of the maker or drawee to pay to a holder in due course. Interest is charged on the principal amount.

principal markets: the chief places in the nation of exportation where the items are freely sold or offered for sale, not necessarily the place where they are manufactured or delivered.

Principal Register: a classification of trademarks established by the Trade-Mark Act of 1946 in which certain qualified trademarks may be included.

principle of diminishing utility: the principle stating that as ownership usage decreases the number of its units increases.

principle of marketing relativism: synonymous with *marketing relativism.*

principle of massed reserves: a concept of reducing the size of many inventories at the retail level while at the same time increasing the size of inventories carried by wholesalers, with the impact of lowering the total stock carried in the store.

principle of minimum total transactions: the inclusion of an intermediary between buyers and sellers that should reduce the number of transactions.

principle of postponement: see *postponement.*

principle of relative loss: a producer's failure to sell goods to a retailer thus retaining unused capacity and experiencing unrealized profit opportunities.

print media: printed materials, as contrasted with broadcast or electronically transmitted information.

print-run: the quantity of pieces, circulars, etc. that will be printed.

prior analysis: analysis that offers the reasons for selecting among alternative courses of action, all based on existing information. See *posterior analysis; preposterior analysis.*

prior donor file: computer listing of people who have already bought gifts from a marketer in a completed sale transaction. Prior donors are usually fine prospects for additional gift promotions.

prioritize: to set in order of preference or priority the attributes or needs of an organization. Assignments are made from this list of priorities.

priority practices: unfair trading acts that are or will become trade barriers to an exporting nation.

prior source: a source from a previous order from a client who has ordered again. It is important to know who these people are as they tend to become repeat buyers.

Privacy Act of 1974: federal legislation designed to protect citizens from invasion of privacy by the federal government and permitting individuals, for the first time, to inspect information about themselves contained in federal agency files and to challenge, correct, or amend the material. The act prohibits an agency from selling or renting an individual's name or address for mailing list use.

private brand:

(1) a middleperson-owned brand name or trademark (e.g., Sears Roebuck owns the Kenmore brand). Synonymous with *private label*.

(2) a brand sponsored by a wholesaler, retailer, dealer, or merchant (e.g., a supermarket item bearing a store label with an item's name, as contrasted with a brand having the name of a manufacturer or producer; usually priced lower than manufactured brands and appeals primarily to bargain-conscious customers).

private cost: the cost of a specific item to an individual.

private label: synonymous with *private brand*.

private rate of return: the financial rate of return anticipated by businesspeople prior to investing their monies.

private sector: the segment of the total economy composed of businesses and households but excluding government. Cf. *public sector*.

private warehouse: see *warehouse; private*.

prize broker: the person who arranges the exchange of an advertiser's goods for free broadcast time or radio or television "plugs." Synonymous with *barter broker*.

prizm: information used in segmenting a market based on a combination of geographic and demographic variables. The data defines areas by zip code, census tract, and block group. Such data are used in developing marketing mix variations and media planning to attempt to reach prospects most likely to purchase the sellers' merchandise.

proactive inhibition: an existing barrier resulting from a consumer's previous experience; an attitude that interferes with his or her learning of new relationship, concepts, etc. See *prejudice*.

probability: used by market and advertising researchers; the likelihood of the occurrence of an event, estimated as a ratio between the number of ways in which the event may occur and the number of ways in which alternative events may occur. See *probability sampling*.

probability chain: an informal communication chain in which information is passed on a random basis.

probability sampling: used by advertising analysts; a sampling technique in which each unit of the population has an equal chance of appearing in the sample. Cf. *random sample*. Synonymous with *random sampling*. See *probability*.

probability theory: see *probability*.

probable error: used in market research; a measure of dispersion, variation, or scatter on both sides of the arithmetic mean, yielding a space that includes one-half the total number of cases. It is computed by multiplying the standard deviation by 0.6745.

problem analysis: a part of the problem find/solve method of concept generation. It relates to finding the problems and involves study of users to learn their dissatisfactions and unmet needs.

problem awareness: the stage in the final consumer's decision process during which the consumer recognizes that the good, service, organization, person, place, or idea under consideration may solve a problem of shortage or unfulfilled desire.

problem child: (slang) a high-growth item that can only attract a low market share. If the situation is prolonged, the company either must abandon the item or invest more money into it to alter its appearance or for promotional activities.

problem definition: the first stage in marketing research, where a clear and detailed statement of the problem emerges.

problem detection analysis: a study focusing on the complaints or problems that consumers have with the item or service.

problem find/solve: a general method of concept generation, usually thought to be the best; requires finding problems faced by customers and other users and solving them. New product concepts are found in the solutions.

problem identification: the first stage of the problem analysis method of ideation. It involves finding, describing, and analyzing the problem(s) of target market participants.

problem-solution advertisement: an advertisement that concentrates on a consumer issue and provides a solution to the problem (e.g., a cigarette smoking kit for ending the habit will remind viewers and listeners of the health risks in smoking).

proceeds:

(1) the actual amount of funds given to a borrower, following deductions for interest charges, fees, and so on.

(2) the funds received by a seller after deductions for the payment of commissions (e.g., proceeds from a sale).

process analysis: the study of the approaches used for producing a part or a product for purposes of yielding the lowest cost and most efficient process that will produce items of adequate quality.

process average: in purchasing, noting the average percentage of defective parts found in a supplier's shipment. It helps in deciding the degree of inspection where it is to be determined by sample.

process control: a monitoring method to assure that the production system is functioning properly.

process costing: a method of product costing whereby costs are accumulated by process or work centers and averaged over all products manufactured in those centers for a specified period.

process departmentation: grouping jobs into subunits based on the sequential processes involved in an organization's operations. This is common in one-product plants, such as oil refineries.

processing in transit: synonymous with *transit privileges.*

process inspection: inspection at intervals during or between production operations. Cf. *quality control.*

process machinery: synonymous with *installations.*

process-related ethical issues: issues involving the unethical use of marketing strategies or tactics.

procurement: the purchase of goods for resale to a store's customers. Synonymous with *purchasing.* See *purchasing agent.*

produce exchange: a market for perishable agricultural products.

producer:

(1) *general:* an individual who manufactures goods and/or services.

(2) *advertising:* a person working on the staff of an advertising agency or an advertiser, or even on a free-lance basis who is responsible for the production of advertisements or commercials.

(3) *marketing:* creators of goods and services for consumers or for a particular target market.

producer commodity cartel: an organization of producers of a key raw material commodity in world trade (e.g., the Organization of Petroleum Exporting Countries).

producer-controlled brands: brands owned or controlled by firms that are primarily in the manufacturing business. Synonymous with *natural brands.*

producer cooperative: a member-owned wholesale operation that assembles farm products to sell in local markets.

producer goods: items intended to be used and worn out in the course of producing other items in the future (e.g., ink in newspaper printing).

producer market: a set of buyers that purchase goods and services and use them to make other products.

producer price index: synonymous with *wholesale price index.*

product:

(1) *general:* goods and services made available to consumers; the total of benefits offered. Cf. *goods.*

(2) *marketing:* one of the four P's of marketing; an offering that may satisfy a need or a want, that is offered to a target market for use. The item will project its benefits, styling, quality, brand name,

and packaging to give it its own unique image or distinguishing characteristics.

product adaptation: altering items to fulfill local or regional requirements (e.g., changing the current fixtures for items sold overseas).

product adoption process: the sequence of stages that individuals and firms go through in the process of accepting new products. The stages vary greatly in usage but tend to include (a) becoming aware of the new product, (b) seeking information about it, (c) developing favorable attitudes toward it, (d) trying it out in some direct or indirect way, (e) finding satisfaction in the trial, and (f) adopting the product into a standing usage or repurchase pattern.

product advertising: advertising whose goal is the attempt to create adequate demand for a product or service. Synonymous with *brand advertising.*

product assortment: the brands and types of items in a product class available to consumers.

product attributes: the characteristics by which products are identified and differentiated; usually comprises features and benefits.

product augmentation: a technique for maintaining sales of items marketed in their mature life cycle stage. The life may be extended by repackaging, reducing its selling price, etc.

product buy-back agreement: synonymous with *buy-back agreement.*

product champion: a person who takes an inordinate interest in seeing that a particular process or product is fully developed and marketed. The role varies from situations calling for little more than stimulating awareness of the item to extreme cases where the champion tries to force the item past the strongly entrenched internal resistance of company policy or that of objecting parties.

product characteristics: attributes that buyers and sellers use when deciding if a product or service meets a particular need.

product class: a group of items treated as natural substitutes and/or complements by most consumers.

product concept: the general belief that consumers are interested in purchasing quality items at fair and reasonable prices. Thus the manufacturer concentrates on means to fulfill these characteristics, such as improving the item's performance at minimal cost.

product costing: the assignment of manufacturing costs to products to determine the cost of finished goods. Cf. *period expense.* See *absorption costing; variable cost.*

product deletion: synonymous with *simplification.*

product depth: the number of items in each product line available for purchase.

product design model: in the new product development process, a concept to determine the most desirable characteristics for a net item by creating the ideal relationship between product features and attributes to advance its marketability. See *conjoint analysis; multidimensional scaling.*

product development: the generation of new ideas for new or improved goods to be added to or to replace existing items.

product differentiation: synonymous with *differentiation.*

product disfeature: a characteristic of a product that the consumer does not like—frequently, its price.

product driven: the manufacturer's strategy of concentrating on the production of items with minimal concern for the needs of the prospect, based on the assumption that if the item is a quality one or can create a need, people will purchase it.

product elimination: removing a product from a company's list of offered items, usually after the product has passed through the decline stage of the life cycle.

product feature approach: determining channels of distribution by assuming that size, unit value, perishability, etc. are used for fitting the item into a channel set to handle them.

product fit: the degree to which a product fulfills the needs of the marketplace.

product form: the physical shape or nature of a good or the sequential steps in a service. Form is provided by one or more technologies and yields benefits to the user; for example, many technologies go to make a front-wheel drive form of an automobile. Products of the same form make up a group within a product class (e.g., all front-wheel drive automobiles). Differences in form of service separate discount and full-service stockbrokers.

product hierarchy: an organizational chart-type array of the products offered in a given market, breaking first into class, then form, the variations on form, then brand. There are various options within these product hierarchy dimensions, so the array can be designed to fit the needs of the analyst. The hierarchy concept fits services as well as goods.

product image: how a prospect or user perceives one or more characteristics of an item. This image may be as important, or more important, to the specific real usage of the item. See *brand awareness; perception; product positioning.*

product improvement: activities for increasing sales by upgrading an item's attributes to attract either new customers or to encourage existing customers to buy the product more often. Product improvement is carried out by:

(a) *quality improvement*—increasing the function of the product, such as making it stronger to last longer.

(b) *feature improvement*—adding new features, such as accessories, to introduce versatility or convenience for people.

(c) *style improvement*—altering the item to enhance its physical or aesthetic appeal (e.g., a new design for a television set). Synonymous with *product modification.*

product innovation gap: the difference between a firm's projected sales/profit goals and what its current product line is expected to produce. The gap must be filled by some form of product innovation.

product innovation strategy: the decision by management to compete with another firm in the introduction of a new product, and not on the basis of price, promotion, etc.

product introduction: the first stage of the product life cycle, during which the new item is announced to the market and offered for sale. See *divest-and-exit strategy.*

production:

(1) any form of activity that adds value to goods and services, including creation, transportation, and warehousing until used.

(2) a criterion of effectiveness that refers to an organization's ability to provide the outputs demanded of it by the environment.

(3) usually, but not always, synonymous with *manufacturing.*

production costs: funds used in manufacturing an item for market consumption, either as fixed or variable.

production effect (of a tariff): the increase in domestic production of an item as a result of a protective tariff that hikes the price of the imported item.

production era: devotion to the physical distribution of products due to high demand and low competition. Consumer research, product modifications, and adapting to consumer needs are unnecessary.

production fit: the compatibility of a new product with established manufacturing equipment and processes.

production inventory: the stock of items consumed in manufacturing, such as raw materials, parts, supplies, etc.

production-oriented diversification: synonymous with *congruent production diversification.*

production sharing: a situation in which a product is manufactured in one country, assembled in another, and marketed in a third. Cf. *reexport.* Synonymous with *outward processing.*

product item: a specific model, brand, or size of a product that a company sells.

productive efficiency: a situation that exists when there is no possibility of increasing the yield of one item without decreasing the yield of another item.

productivity: a measurement of the efficiency of production; a ratio of output to input (e.g., 10 units per manhour).

product liability: liability imposed for damages caused by accident and arising out of goods or products manufactured, sold, handled, or distributed by the insured or by others trading under his or her name. The accident must have occurred after possession of goods had been relinquished to others and away from premises owned, rented, or controlled by the insured. In the case of food products, however, the accident does not have to occur away from the premises (e.g., in a restaurant). Cf. *warranty.* See *consumer protection legislation.*

product life cycle (PLC):
(1) a sequence of stages in the marketing of a product that begins with commercialization and ends with removal from the market.

(2) the six stages of market acceptance of any goods: pioneering, growth, maturity, saturation, decline, and abandonment. See *growth stage.*

product line: the assortment of items presented by a firm, or a group of items that are closely related because they either satisfy a need, are used with each other, are sold to the same consumer, are marketed within the same outlets, or are within similar price ranges. Cf. *service line.* See *line; product mix.*

product management: the business activities dealing with the evolution of new items or brands, their introduction to the market, and their management through the product life cycle.

product manager: an executive responsible for marketing approaches, such as promotion, pricing, distribution, and establishment of product characteristics. The product manager deals more with the planning aspects than with actual selling to the consumer. Cf. *sales manager.* Synonymous with *brand manager; program manager; project manager.* See *marketing management.*

product manager system: a product management organizational format under which a middle manager focuses on the performance of a single product (brand) or a small group of products (brands). This manager handles both new and existing products and is involved with everything from marketing research to package design to advertising.

product market: synonymous with *consumer market.*

product market grid: used primarily in developing market coverage strategies, a chart identifying market segments that are to be or have been targeted.

product/market opportunity matrix: identifies four alternative marketing strategies that may be used to maintain and/or increase sales of business units and products: market penetration, market development, product development, and diversification.

product markets: markets in which firms sell the outputs that they produce.

product/market segment: that portion of a product defined in terms of geographic area, end-use application, customer demographic characteristics, type of customer institution, and/or buyer behavior.

product mix: the composite of items offered for sale by one company. Some firms have a wide product mix geared for a diverse consumer group, whereas others maintain a narrow product mix geared toward a particular market segment. See *mix; product line.*

product modification: synonymous with *product improvement.*

product motives: the reasons people purchase a particular product.

product obsolescence: the effect on items that become less attractive to the consumer because of the introduction of newly improved items that do the job less expensively or better, or perhaps both. Cf. *planned obsolescence.*

product pattern: an organizational pattern whereby jobs and activities are grouped on the basis of types of products or services.

product planning: the process leading to the identification of goals and procedures as well as the precise nature of the merchandise to be marketed. See *marketing research.*

product-planning committee: a product management organizational format staff by high-level executives from various functional areas including marketing, production, engineering, finance, and research and development. It handles product approval, evaluation, and development on a part-time basis.

product portfolio:
(1) a group of products marketed by the same company.
(2) a company's product mix viewed from a strategic perspective; a set of products or brands that are at different stages in the product life cycle.

product positioning: the way in which a product is characterized to attract consumer interest and purchase. A product may be positioned in a variety of ways, such as economical, durable, stylish, safe, convenient, and so forth. See *perceptual mapping; positioning; product image; product space.*

product proliferation: an excess of products performing the same or similar function. Usually results from too many firms entering into the manufacture of competing products.

product protection: in advertising, separating advertisements of competing items so that either time or pages keep readers from seeing one item after the other. Synonymous with *commercial protection; separation.* See *competitive separation.*

product publicity: publicity used for promoting a new or existing item.

product quality:
(1) an objective measure of a product's conformance to requirements, to perform as intended and advertised. See *ISO; ISO 9000.*
(2) a subjective measure of a product's performance as determined by the user's reaction to the item's price, packaging, promotion, service, and channel of distribution.

product recall: calling back of an item because of imperfection, defect, or other problem. At times, a governmental agency demands that a product be recalled when violations of a law are determined. See *recall.*

product-related ethical issues: issues involving the ethical appropriateness of marketing certain products.

product relaunch: a product management strategy that focuses on finding new markets and untapped market segments, new product uses, and ways to stimulate increased use of a product by existing customers.

product reliability: the probability that a product will perform a stated function under specific conditions for a specified period without failure. See *guarantee.*

product reputation advertising: synonymous with *commercial advertising; promotional advertising.*

product research: synonymous with *qualitative market analysis.*

product screening: the process of eliminating proposed products from future consideration.

product segmentation: in industrial marketing, the subdivision of a market on the basis of product specifications that fulfill the needs of the purchaser.

product/service life cycle: the market phases for most products and services.

product shifting: the switch from the manufacture and export of one item to the manufacture and export of still another.

products-market equilibrium: a situation in which aggregate demand equals aggregate supply.

product space: the characteristics of a product, including those perceived by the human senses, such as touch and smell, but also including price and size. See *product positioning.*

product-specific buying factors: product-based variables that lead to either autonomous (independent) or joint decision making. These variables include perceived risk, purchase frequency, and time pressure.

product-specific investments: capital investments made for facilities, equipment, and personnel resources for use in stocking, selling, and servicing a specific product line.

product spotter: any eye- or ear-catching device, such as a colored spotlight, for attracting consumer's attention to a product or package. It is used most frequently in promoting a new item.

product-structured sales force: a sales force organization where sellers are assigned particular items or item lines. It is used most often by sellers of sophisticated or technical products enabling the sales force to have expertise in the workings of a specific product. Cf. *market-structured sales force; territory-structured sales force.* See *sales force.*

product testing: a system for testing and certifying products, calling for the mutual recognition of testing and certification so that a product approved by authorities in one country could be marketed anywhere else. See *market testing.*

product usage segmentation: one of a four-way classification of the strategies of segmentation that relates observed factors of use to the way in which consumers with specific characteristics respond to certain marketing mixes. See *benefit segmentation; state-of-being segmentation; state-of-mind segmentation.*

product use test: one of several key evaluation steps in the product development process. It involves giving some of the new product to persons or firms in the intended target market and asking them to use it for a time and report their reactions to it. The purposes of a product use test are to (a) see if the item developed by the organization has the attributes prescribed for it, (b) learn whether it satisfies the market needs identified during the ideation process, and (c) disclose information about how and by whom the item is used.

product width:

(1) the number of product lines that a company offers to the public.

(2) the availability of a large variety of different items within a classification.

professional advertising:

(1) advertising by professional people (e.g., doctors, lawyers).

(2) advertising by manufacturers or distributors whose message is pointed to a professional group seeking their support, approval, or at times their endorsement.

profile analysis: used by consumer and marketing analysts; a method for appraising individual uniqueness and characteristics that consists of a search for patterns of behavior displayed by an individual.

profile sheet: a form that displays the characteristics of a proposed product at the time of screening. Scores are plotted on a diagram for easier analysis.

profit:

(1) *general:* the reward to the entrepreneur for assuming the risks of establishing, operating, and managing of a given enterprise or undertaking. See *uncertainty theory.*

(2) *general:* the monies remaining after a business has paid all its bills.

(3) *marketing:* the excess of the selling price over all costs and expenses incurred in making a sale. See *profit-impact-of-marketing strategy.*

profitability: a firm's ability to earn a profit and its potential for future earnings.

profitability measures: the ratios of net profit to capital, to total assets, and to sales.

profit and loss statement: the summary listing of a firm's total revenues and ex-

penses within a specified time period. Synonymous with *income statement.*

profit-based pricing objectives: goals that orient a firm's pricing strategy toward some type of profit—profit maximization, satisfactory profit, return on investment, and/or early recovery of cash.

profit center: a segment of a business that is responsible for both revenues and expenses.

profit-impact-of-marketing strategy (PIMS): a program that provides individual companies with a database summarizing the financial and market performance of a few thousand business units representing several hundred firms. It focuses on the links between various factors and profitability/cash flow.

profit margin: sales less all operating expenses divided by the number of sales.

profit maximization: corporate strategy to fulfill maximum long-term profits from a marketing effort, as opposed to emphasis on capturing or market or fulfilling a social need of consumers, which may or may not be as profitable. Synonymous with *profit optimization.*

profit optimization: synonymous with *profit maximization.*

profit-oriented audit: assessing a marketing plan in relation to expenses and revenues generated by that plan.

profit-taking strategy: see *milking.*

profit target analysis: determining the volume of sales required to pay for all the costs of operation and still command a predetermined profit for the firm.

pro forma invoice: a preliminary invoice indicating the value of the items listed and informing the recipient that all have been sent. It is not a demand for money.

program evaluation and review technique (PERT): a method to facilitate planning and to give management tools for the control of specific programs. Original PERT programs were developed by the U.S. Navy. Cf. *critical path method; PERT/COST.*

program manager: synonymous with *product manager.*

program merchandising: combined efforts of a retailer and a key source to make merchandising and promotion plans for a store.

prohibited articles: in shipping, merchandise that cannot be handled.

project: a unit of activity in the product development process that usually deals with creating and marketing one new product. A project involves a multidisciplinary group of people and may often be part of a larger unit of work—a program—which delivers a stream of new products from several projects.

projection: synonymous with *forecasting.*

projective technique: a procedure for discovering a person's behavioral characteristics by observing how the individual acts in situations that do not demand a particular response.

projectization: the degree to which a group of people working on a new product project feel committed to the project as against being loyal to the departments where they work. On major innovations, a high degree of projectization is often essential to break through barriers.

project manager: synonymous with *product manager.*

project matrix: an organization in which the matrix leans toward the project. Participants have dual reporting relationships, but the project is intended to dominate their thinking and action.

promo: in broadcasting, a local or network spot offering a brief promotional message about a forthcoming program. Synonymous with *promotion spot.*

promotion:
(1) stimulating the demand for goods by advertising, publicity, and special events to attract attention and create interest among consumers. See *advertising; sales promotion.*

(2) any technique that persuasively communicates favorable information about a seller's product to potential buyers; includes advertising, personal selling, sales promotion, and public relations. One of the 4 P's of marketing. See *promotional mix; trade promotion.*

promotional advertising: advertising purporting to stimulate the rapid buying of a particular item or service. Cf. *institutional advertising; local advertising; national advertising; noncommercial advertising.* Synonymous with *product reputation advertising.*

promotional allowance: payment given to a middleperson by a manufacturer for the middleperson's promotion of goods. It is often in the form of gifts, discounts on merchandise, or free merchandise. Cf. *advertising allowance.* See *trade promotion.*

promotional department store: a discount outlet that has sufficient size and merchandise to qualify as a department store. It operates at lower gross margins because of minimal services and limited public services. Synonymous with *full-line discount store.*

promotional discount: a discount that is offered to intermediaries as compensation for carrying out promotional activities.

promotional elasticity of demand: holding other variables constant, the percentage change in quantity requested that may result from a percentage shift in promotional activity. Cf. *price elasticity.* See *plasticity of demand.*

promotional fit: the compatibility of a new product with existing advertising approaches.

promotional message: often shortened to promo. See *promo.*

promotional mix: the combined promotional efforts of advertising, publicity, sales promotion, and personal selling as they attempt to communicate with customers to sell a product. See *mix; promotools.*

promotional package: materials forwarded to the dealer to assist with the advertising campaign, such as inserts or banners.

promotional price: a lowered price offered on a temporary basis to promote particular items.

promotion mix: see *promotional mix.*

promotion planning: systematic decision making relating to all aspects of an organization's or individual's communications efforts.

promotion spot: synonymous with *promo.*

promotools: media used in the promotional mix, such as demonstrations, contests, giveaways, catalogs. See *promotional mix.*

proof of purchase: evidence that merchandise or a service has actually been bought. Programs that request users to retain a collection of multiple proofs of purchase over a time period are continuity programs.

propensity to consume: used by market researchers; the percentage of consumers' disposable income that they can be expected to spend.

proportional law: the relationship between factors of production and the results of production; the desirable relationship among production factors that will yield maximum results. Cf. *law of increasing costs.*

proposal: an oral or written statement or offer.

pro rata: (Latin) "according to the rate," in proportion to a total amount. For example, if a contract is terminated before the end of the period for which payment has been given, a pro rata return of the payment is made in proportion to the unused time remaining.

prorate:

(1) to allocate proportionally.

(2) to redistribute a portion of a cost to a department or product in accordance with an agreed-on formula.

prospect:

(1) a person who has never purchased the item or service before.

(2) a potential customer of a service or product. See *prospecting; qualified prospect.*

prospecting: the first phase of the selling process; searching for an individual or concern that needs a product or service and possesses the ability to purchase it. Two major methods of prospecting are: (a) *endless chain*—asking existing customers for the names of people they know who might be interested in the seller's product or service.

(b) *centers of influence*—asking influential and professional people for the names of potential customers. See *business cycle; hitlist; prospect; qualifying.*

prospect list: names of people qualified to purchase a product or service; held by marketers for promotional purpose in the expectation that the people can be reached and will become customers.

prosperity: the uppermost phase of a business cycle.

protected market: a market in which buyers and sellers avoid market fluctuations and disruptions by the use of voluntary export restraints (VERs) imposed on them by exporters of items to these markets. See *restrained exporter; voluntary restraint agreement.*

protection: the imposition of high (protective) tariffs on imports that are presumed to compete with domestic items, with the objective of giving the domestic manufacturer an advantage. See *protectionism.*

protection in transit: in shipping, the purpose of a product's package.

protectionism: the erection of barriers to trade in an attempt to protect domestic industries from foreign competition. See *protection.*

protectionists: people who favor high tariffs and other import restrictions to enable domestic items to compete more favorably with foreign items.

protective tariff: a tax on imported goods designed to give domestic manufacturers an economic shield against price competition from abroad.

protocol: a statement of the benefits (not features) a new product should have; prepared prior to the project being assigned to technical departments. The benefits statement is agreed to by all parties, thus the term protocol.

prototype: the first physical form or service description of a new product, still in rough or tentative mode. With complex products, there may be component prototypes as well as one finished prototype. For services, the prototype is simply the first full description of how the service will work. See *prototype concept test.*

prototype concept test: a test performed after technical work has produced a prototype. The prototype clarifies many aspects of the concept and leads to superior concept test reactions. It may precede technical work if the prototypes are inexpensive to prepare, such as food products. See *prototype.*

proximo: (Latin) in the following month.

pseudo sale: a category of market-testing methods wherein the customer does various things to indicate reaction to the product and to its marketing strategy but does not actually spend money.

psychic income: nonmonetary income regarded by an individual as desirable to fulfill needs, wants, and psychological demands. Power, control, independence, and actualization are examples of psychic income. Synonymous with *intangible rewards.*

psychographic market segmentation: in segmentation, choosing people who react in the identical fashion to a particular emotional appeal, or who share common behavioral patterns. Cf. *demographic segmentation.*

psychographic segmentation: see *psychographic market segmentation.*

psychographics: psychological profiles of prospects within a given market.

psychological discounting: offering an illusionary lowering of prices by providing artificial comparisons of present price with a supposedly earlier price, although it never existed. This tactic is illegal today. Synonymous with *was-is pricing.*

psychological moment: that point when the salesperson feels he or she is ready to attempt the trial close.

psychological pricing: synonymous with *odd pricing.*

psychological product: the physical product along with its warranties, services, and psychological overtones.

psychological satisfaction: the satisfaction received from the intangible benefits of a product, such as a feeling of self-worth. Cf. *physiological motives.*

psychometric: a technique used by market researchers; any quantitative measurement of an individual's psychological traits or assets.

publication: any material published in any format (e.g., magazines, newspapers).

publication-set: an advertisement set in type by the publication where it is to appear, ready for final publication. Often shortened to pub-set.

public consumption monopoly: a governmental monopoly created to regulate the consumption of specific items that are considered harmful. Cf. *sumptuary laws.*

public domain: federally owned land.

publicity:
(1) any message about an organization that is communicated through the mass media but is not paid for by the organization.

(2) any event or communication, through established media or otherwise, free or paid, solicited or not, that attracts attention to a product or service. Cf. *advertising; public relations.*

publicity agent: a person or organization responsible for disseminating news and information about clients through newspapers, magazines, radio stations, and other media, the use of which is not paid for by the clients.

public policy: any conduct that affects the public good.

public relations:
(1) *general:* any communication or activity created or performed primarily to enhance prestige or goodwill for an individual or an organization. Cf. *publicity.*

(2) *marketing:* a promotional activity that aims to communicate a favorable image of a product or its marketer and to promote goodwill. It differs from advertising and sales promotion, which disseminate marketing information through paid media.

public relations institutional advertising: advertising directed toward enhancing the image and reputation of a company. See *patronage institutional advertising; public service advertising.*

public responsibility: the responsibilities of individuals or groups that are presumed to reflect the broader and more pervasive needs of the entire community, state, or nation.

publics: groups, such as customers, shareholders, and government agencies, to which a firm markets its merchandise and services or that affect the firm's ability to succeed in achieving its goals.

public's demand: the characteristics and needs of employees, unions, stockholders, consumer groups, the general public, government agencies, and other internal and external forces that affect company operations.

public sector: the segment of the total economy that includes all levels of government and excludes businesses and households. Cf. *private sector.*

public service advertising:
(1) advertising with a central focus on the public welfare, usually sponsored by a not-for-profit organization, religious institutions, political group, or trade association.

(2) advertising related not to the marketing of products but to social betterment goals (e.g., preventing forest fires, promoting traffic safety, securing blood donations). Cf. *advocacy advertising; social marketing.* See *Advertising Council, Inc.; patronage institutional advertising; public relations institutional advertising.*

public warehouse: an organization offering storage space for a fee to any person who seeks out the service. See *warehouse.*

publisher's representative: an independent organization or person that sells advertising space for a publication.

pub-set: short for publication-set.

puff: (slang) a free promotion of a product or service.

puffery:
(1) *general:* a story or news release lacking news value or perceived to be overly self-serving.

(2) *advertising:* an exaggerated advertising campaign or promotion, often with words such as "the best," "the greatest," "the longest lasting." Deception can be the next step.

pull: the ability of an advertisement to enhance sales, as the "advertisement pulled well."

pull date: the date stamped on perishable products (e.g., bakery and dairy goods), after which the items should not be sold.

pulling power:
(1) *general:* the ability to draw an audience.

(2) *advertisement:* the power of an advertisement or of an advertising medium in which a sales message is placed to draw response from the advertiser's prospects and customers, usually measured by the number of orders or inquiries received after publication of the advertisement.

pull strategy: a promotional strategy in which each channel member attempts to persuade the next member in the system to handle and promote the product. Cf. *push-pull strategy.*

pulsation: using advertisements on a sporadic basis, with spacing so as not to saturate the market. Money is also saved. Synonymous with *wave scheduling; waving.* See *pulsing strategy.*

pulsing strategy: a media scheduling strategy in which a continuous campaign is combined with short bursts of heavier advertising. See *pulsation.*

purchase allowance: a lowering of the price of an item when the merchandise as requested does not meet the expectations as identified on the invoice. Cf. *on consignment.* See *returns to vendor.*

purchase contract: an agreement between a buyer and seller that itemizes items and services to be bought and sold, respectively.

purchase decision: the final stage in the buying process culminating in the choice to buy the item or service from a particular supplier.

purchase discount: a reduction in the price of an order that has been paid promptly.

purchase distribution: the percentage of all retail outlets that received a shipment of the product since a previous audit, whether or not they were in stock then or at the current audit.

purchase history: a customer record of purchases over a time period.

purchase order: a statement permitting a vendor to deliver merchandise or materials at an agreed-on price.

purchase price: the amount for which an item or service is bought.

purchase privilege offer: synonymous with *semiliquidator; trade card.*

purchaser:
(1) a buyer.
(2) a person who obtains title to or an interest in property by the act of purchase.

purchase requisition: see *requisition.*

purchase research: synonymous with *value analysis.*

purchase returns and allowances: a contra-purchases account in which the returns or allowances for previously purchased merchandise are recorded.

purchasing: synonymous with *procurement.*

purchasing agent: an individual who buys products for store maintenance and daily operation, not for resale to customers. Some purchasing agents are employed as company staff; others are independent middlepeople who work for a company on a contractual basis and are paid on commission. Cf. *procurement.*

purchasing leverage: the impact of effective purchasing on profitability.

purchasing power:
(1) *general:* the value of money measured by the items it can buy. Cf. *real value of money.* Synonymous with *buying power.*
(2) *marketing:* the capacity to purchase possessed by an individual buyer, a group of buyers, or the aggregate of the buyers in an area or market.

purchasing power of the dollar: a measurement of the quantity of goods and services that a dollar will buy in a specified market, compared with the amount it could buy in some base period. It is obtained by taking the reciprocal of an appropriate price index.

pure competition: a situation in which there are many sellers and buyers of a standardized product or service with free entrance to the market and no collusion. The primary characteristics of pure competition are:
(a) a large degree of homogeneity between items.
(b) such a large number of sellers that the marketing mix variations by one seller do not affect market prices.

(c) the seller's lack of need for a price policy since the market will determine price, thus reflecting what consumers are actually willing to pay. Cf. *imperfect competition; perfect competition.*

Pure Food and Drug Act of 1906: federal legislation prohibiting manufacturers' mislabeling of the contents of food, liquor, and medicine containers.

pure impulse buying: purchases made by the customer because he or she becomes consumed with the uniqueness or worthiness of the offering. Cf. *planned impulse buying; reminder impulse buying.*

pure market economy: a competitive economic system of numerous buyers and sellers, in which prices are determined by the free interaction of supply and demand.

pure monopoly: see *perfect (pure) monopoly.*

pure premium: a premium, arrived at by dividing losses by exposure, to which no loading has been added for commissions, taxes, and expenses.

pure profit: synonymous with *economic profit.*

pure public item: an item consumed in equal amount by all people, even though the item may have different value to these people. No one can be excluded from being a customer of a pure public item (e.g., air, water, a sidewalk).

push incentive: some form of compensation, traditionally money, offered to a retail salesperson to push the sale of a particular item; offered by a manufacturer, the head of a chain store, or the executive of a larger department store. Synonymous with *spiff.*

pushing strategy: see *push-pull strategy.*

push money: synonymous with *spiff.*

push-or-pull distribution strategy: see *push-pull strategy.*

push-pull strategy:
(1) a promotional strategy in which the producer uses mass promotion to stimulate demand in the consumer market, thereby causing intermediaries to want to carry the product.

(2) the balance between a firm's attempts to stimulate the demand for its products by pushing them forward through the channels with efforts aimed at the middleperson and pulling the goods through the channels to the consumer with promotional efforts aimed directly at the market. Cf. *pull strategy.* Synonymous with *push strategy.*

push strategy: synonymous with *push-pull strategy.*

putting-out system: the second stage in the evolution of a materially productive civilization, initially characterized by an entrepreneur's agreement to take all the output an individual (or family) can produce at a fixed price. This stage eventually progresses to the stage at which the entrepreneur provides the workers with the raw materials and pays them on a piece-rate basis for finished goods.

pyramiding: see *pyramid selling.*

pyramid ratio: a tool used in the analysis of management and income to determine the relationship of profits and capital.

pyramid schemes: synonymous with *pyramid selling.*

pyramid selling: business opportunity frauds, usually promoted through advertisements for job opportunities guaranteed to yield enormous or quick profits, requiring little education or demanding a minimal personal invest-ment. There are government regulations against certain pyramid schemes. The pyramider induces many people to buy his or her products, which they are to resell at a higher price. For example, if 10 people buy 50 units each but can sell only 15 each, the pyramider is still ahead, because he or she has sold 500 units. See *fraud; roll-out.*

Q&A format: see *question-and-answer format.*

QERs (quantitative export restraints): see *quantitative restrictions.*

Q-rating: in research conducted on audi-ence behavior, the level of awareness peo-ple have about a broadcast program or personality; measures how many televi-sion viewers or radio listeners are famil-iar with a particular program and if they regard it as their favorite. Synonymous with *Q-score.*

QR inventory system: see *quick-response inventory system.*

QRs: see *quantitative restrictions.*

Q-score: synonymous with *Q-rating.*

Q-sort: a personality inventory in which the individual sorts a considerable num-ber of statements into piles that represent the degrees to which the statements ap-ply to him or her.

Q-system: an inventory control system that holds the reorder quantity constant and

shifts the reorder period. Synonymous with *reorder system.*

quadrangle: synonymous with *advertis-ing quadrangle.*

qualified lead:
(1) *retailing:* a person who shows inter-est, usually by making an inquiry from a retailer, in purchasing an item or service.
(2) *merchandising:* an individual pos-sessing the financial ability to purchase an item or service; a valid potential cus-tomer. See *qualifying.*

qualified prospect: a potential customer who is able to buy a product and has the authority to make a decision to purchase. This conclusion is often arrived at fol-lowing a check of the individual's credit.

qualifying: determining whether or not a sales prospect is a serious and potential customer, and therefore, worth following. Attempts are made to minimize lost time and to avoid involvement with people who are not interested in or able to make a pur-chase. Criteria used by the seller are:
(a) whether the prospect has the funds to purchase the item or service.
(b) whether the prospect has the author-ity for making the decision to buy.
(c) whether the prospect has a need to secure the product or service. See *prospecting.*

qualifying decisions: synonymous with *qualifying dimensions.*

qualifying dimensions: characteristics of people in a target market making them eligible to purchase a product or service. Synonymous with *qualifying decisions.*

qualifying (descriptive) variables: a set of variables that allow or qualify an individ-ual to be a member of a particular market segment.

qualitative factor: a factor that is significant but cannot be measured precisely and easily.

qualitative market analysis: the examination of the market with the goal of gathering data that can affect the product or service. Synonymous with *product research.*

qualitative research: in defining a group or situation, market research that is not statistical in nature; describes the nature, type, or components of a consumer group or market situation. Qualitative research generated cannot be extrapolated to larger populations. Cf. *quantitative research.*

quality: a product's or service's characteristic making it appropriate for its intended goal; a valid product or service.

quality control:
(1) the attempt to ensure the presence of qualitative factors in a product or standards of performance in a service. See *process inspection.*
(2) the traditional approach to quality in which problems are detected after manufacturing and an effort is made to remove substandard products before shipping them to customers.

quality creep: a new product that is better than it needs to be to fulfill needs of its target customers.

quality description: a message to the supplier of the type and features of the item required.

quality discount: a lowering of price offered by the seller as a way to get the purchaser to buy large quantities of the item.

quality market: a market in which quality is more important than price.

quantitative export restrictions (QERs): see *voluntary restraint agreements.* Cf. *quantitative restrictions.*

quantitative factor: a factor that affects decision making and can be measured numerically.

quantitative research: involves representative sampling of respondents; a market research technique of a statistical nature that involves the measurement of quantifiable amounts; entails collecting data, the result being statistics that are assigned specific characteristics or values as variables. Cf. *qualitative research.*

quantitative restrictions (QRs): of concern to global marketers; specific limits on the quantity or value of goods that can be imported or exported during a specific time period. Synonymous with *export quotas; quantity restrictions.*

quantity demanded: the amount that would be purchased at a particular price, at a moment of time. See *marginal propensity to invest.*

quantity discount: synonymous with *patronage discount.*

quantity restrictions: synonymous with *quantitative restrictions.*

quantum meruit: (Latin) "as much as is merited"; a principle of business law providing that when a service is given without a written estimate of price, there is an implied promise by the purchaser of the service to pay for the work as much as it is worth.

quarter showing: the display of car-card advertising in one fourth of the subway cars, buses, or other means of transportation included in the transit advertising service offered to advertisers.

quasi: as if; that which resembles.

quasi-chain: independently owned retail outlets that are affiliated with a form of central organization. See *voluntary chain.*

query: a customer or prospective customer's request for information on his or her account or about the item or service involved. See *customer service; inquiry.*

question-and-answer format (Q&A format): in advertising, a method for writing copy where the advertiser or a spokesperson for the advertiser responds to questions posed by the customer or prospective customer. Although Q&A format is primarily used in print media, at times it is also used in broadcast advertising.

question mark: a strategic-business unit that has a low relative market share and is in a high-growth market.

questionnaire: used by marketing and advertising researchers; a set of questions seeking objective data or subjective opinion on a given subject. The questions are intended not to test an individual's ability to answer the questions (e.g., to arrive at a score) but rather to elicit responses with respect to the subject at hand.

quick-response (QR) inventory system: a cooperative effort between retailers and their suppliers to reduce retail inventory while providing a merchandise supply that more closely addresses the actual buying patterns of consumers.

quid pro quo: (Latin) "something for something"; a mutual consideration; an advantage or a concession received in return for a similar favor.

quota:
(1) *general:* the amount of production expected from the average employee to receive the specified base pay. See *sales quota; trade quota.*

(2) *merchandising:* a specific limit on the number of items of a particular kind that may be imported.

quota cartel: an agreement among firms to a specific industry by which each participant is assigned a portion of market demand.

quota control sampling: synonymous with *quota sampling.*

quota sample: see *quota sampling.*

quota sampling: a sampling technique in which interviewers look for specific numbers of candidates with special characteristics. All units in the population do not have known or equal chances of being chosen. Cf. *area sample; nonprobability sampling.* Synonymous with *quota control sampling.* See *sampling.*

quotation: an offer to sell goods at a stated price and under specified conditions.

quoted price: the stated price for an item

rack: the floor stand for holding goods on shelves, hooks, or in pockets. See *rack jobber.*

rack jobber:
(1) a limited-service wholesaler that supplies nonfood products to supermarkets, grocery stores, and drug retailers.

(2) a wholesaler who maintains stocks of convenience-type merchandise, primarily in supermarkets, drugstores, and

other related retail operations. He or she delivers merchandise by vehicle, sets up the displays and makes frequent visits to stores and refills the inventory of display items. See *jobber; rack.*

Radiation Control for Health and Safety Act of 1968: federal legislation establishing performance standards and limits of radiation that may be emitted from consumer items (television sets, microwave ovens, etc.).

radiation selling: using a specific sale as a starting point for future related sales, based on the first sale as the example of need (e.g., selling the camera that will lead to sales of film and film processing services).

radio: a form of broadcast advertising medium. Its advantages include being able to control when an advertisement appears, creating advertisements best adapted to sound, and being less expensive than television.

radio network: a group of radio stations linked to each other by telephone wire and simultaneously broadcasting programs originating from one of the stations.

rag business (trade): (slang) the sentimental name given to the fashion apparel industry. See *rags.*

rags: (slang) garments made by the apparel industry. See *rag business.*

rain-lap posting: a method of posting outdoor advertising messages on panels in which one sheet or section is laid beginning at the bottom of the poster panel, the succeeding upper sections overlapping each other until the top of the panel is reached.

random demand: a change in market demand that has no pattern and cannot be forecasted.

random-digit dialing: a method for choosing household telephone numbers to be called during a research study; a sample method where numbers are randomly generated. In practice, the first three digits are retained, thus ensuring that all calls come from the same geographic area. Only the final four digits are chosen at random. Securing unlisted telephone numbers is the key to an accurate survey.

randomization: the process of choosing a sample on the basis of chance. See *random sample.*

random sample: a limited number of observations chosen by chance from an entire aggregate of a phenomenon. In this form of sampling, every item in the population has the same chance of being chosen as any other items. Cf. *probability sampling; quota sampling.* See *area sample; randomization.*

random sampling: synonymous with *probability sampling.*

range: a measure showing the approximate extent of total variability or dispersion, found by determining the difference between the lower limit of the lowest class interval and the upper limit of the highest class interval.

rate:

(1) *general:* the movement and handling of goods or persons, the determining factor used in arriving at the charge or fare for services rendered.

(2) *advertising:* the cost of advertising space or commercial broadcasting time in a medium, as set by owners of the

medium; based on the circulation of the publication or the size of the listening or viewing audience, the quality of the medium's recipients, etc. The rate can vary once the advertiser exceeds a certain minimum dollar volume, and/or when payment of advertising expenses is made within a given time period.

rate base: the circulation of a periodical guaranteed as the base for its rate structure. The advertiser usually receives a refund should circulation fall below the agreed-on rate base. See *rate protection.*

rate card: a brief printing of media owners providing charges (a price list) for units of advertising space or advertising times. The card provides the advertiser with all necessary relevant information for advertising with a particular medium.

rate differential: the separation between the higher rate charged by the advertising media to national as contrasted with local advertisers. Should the difference be extreme, management must decide on the wisdom and expense for national advertising. See *one-time rate.*

rate holder:

(1) *advertising:* an advertisement, usually the smallest space a publication will permit, that has been placed by an advertiser to "hold" a contracted discount rate offered by the publisher for a minimum number or insertions and/or lines.

(2) *broadcasting:* as in (1), where advertisers can purchase a 10-second spot for the same purpose.

rate protection: how long a time period the advertiser is guaranteed a specific rate base; usually from 3 to 12 months from the time of contract signing. See *rate base.*

rate war: a negative form of competition in which sellers drop their prices below their costs for purposes of putting the competition out of business. See *predatory pricing; underselling.*

rating:

(1) *general:* a traditional method of performance appraisal in which a judge evaluates performance in terms of a value or index that is used in some standard way. It traditionally involves global rating scales.

(2) *outdoor advertising:* an estimate of the number of people exposed to an outdoor advertisement. Each sign is rated in terms of the number of people who pass by it on a daily basis as compared with the total population in the community where the structure is found. The rating is used in determining the cost per thousand for outdoor advertising.

(3) *broadcasting:* the size of an actual listening or viewing audience for a specific program or commercial as contrasted with the size of the potential audience. Programs with high ratings deliver a large audience to advertisers for their commercials. See *audience measurement.*

rational appeals: messages for the industrial prospect designed to stimulate sales by promoting the item's economic and technical superiority instead of emphasizing emotional or behavioral factors.

rational buying motives: used by researchers of consumer behavior; all costs of money, use, labor, and profit that affect a purchaser. Cf. *motivation.*

rationality: the process of making decisions that serve to maximize the firm's goals.

rationalization: any approach that has the potential to increase efficiency or output.

rationing: a technique for limiting purchases or usages of an item when the demanded quantity of the item exceeds the quantity available at a specific price. This occurs most often during wartime and under extremes of natural conditions (e.g., drought).

ratio of finished goods inventory to the cost of goods sold: of importance to marketers; a ratio determined by dividing the cost of goods sold by the average finished-goods inventory. The resulting figure is the number of times the investment in the finished-goods inventory has turned over during the period under consideration. The present ratio is compared with a similar ratio for several previous periods, since it portrays the stability and trend of sales or a possibly overstated or expanded inventory.

ratio of notes payable to accounts payable: of importance to marketers; a ratio whose desirability is determined by consideration of three quantitative factors: (a) notes issued in payment of merchandise; (b) notes issued to banks and brokers; and (c) notes issued to others. If a relatively large number of the outstanding notes were issued to merchandise creditors, this might indicate that the firm is unable to take advantage of the cash discounts offered in the trade and that other lending agencies might consider the firm's credit unfavorably.

ratio of notes receivable to accounts receivable: of importance to marketers; a ratio that, if large as compared with other firms in a similar line of business, indicates that the firm with the high ratio may have a lax credit policy or may be extending credit to customers whose ability to pay promptly is dubious.

ratio of raw-materials inventory to cost of manufacture: of importance to marketers; a ratio determined by dividing the cost of goods manufactured by the average raw-materials inventory. The resulting figure is the number of times the investment in raw-materials inventory has turned over during the period under consideration. When the present ratio is compared with a similar ratio for the previous period, it portrays the trend and steadiness of production or indicates a possibly overstated or overexpanded inventory. See *raw-materials inventory.*

raw data: data that have not been processed or reduced.

raw material: nonprocessed resources utilized in producing an item. The act of production results in an alteration in the form of the original material. See *fabricated parts.*

raw-materials inventory: the items purchased by a manufacturing firm to be used in production. See *ratio of raw-materials inventory to cost of manufacture.*

reach:
(1) the percentage of total prospects exposed to a specific advertisement in a specified period.

(2) the total audience a medium reaches, without duplication. See *audience; coverage; exposure; frequency.* Synonymous with *media coverage.* See *cumulative audience.*

reach and frequency: components for determining the gross rating points obtained by a broadcast media schedule; indicate how many households can be exposed to the schedule, and how often each household will be exposed. Multiplied together, they show, by percentage, the total potential audience exposure in a particular market.

reactive management: a management style in which decision makers respond to problems rather than anticipating them.

reactive selling: the customer's seeking out of a particular vendor.

reader interest: readers' expression of interest in an advertisement found in a particular publication.

reader response: the measurement of advertising and editorial readership based on orders and requests resulting from the appearance of an advertisement or editorial copy.

readership:
(1) the total audience of a publication, including those who purchase the periodical or newspaper and those who secure it by other means. Cf. *circulation.* See *pass-along circulation.*

(2) in audience measurement, the percentage of an audience who can recall reading a print advertisement.

readership profile: a description of the people who read a particular magazine or newspaper including their lifestyle, income, and social relationships.

readers per copy: the number of people who read a particular issue of a magazine; determined by dividing the total audience of the publication by its circulation of an typical issue of the magazine or periodical.

reading-and-noting: a survey of actual readers of newspapers and magazines, indicating which pages or advertisement they read or studied.

reading notice: a printed advertisement appearing as editorial material. However, it should always be marked as an advertisement so as not to confuse the reader. See *advertorial.*

read-most: people or a grouping of people who read more than 50 percent of a particular advertisement.

real income:
(1) the sum total of the purchasing power of a nation or an individual.

(2) income that has been adjusted for the effect of inflation.

reallocation: synonymous with *reapportionment.*

real other: a consumer's perception of other people's views of his or her skills, personality, etc.

real price: the price of goods and services measured by the quantity of worker hours needed to earn sufficient money to purchase the goods or services.

real self-image: used in setting advertising strategies; our mental picture of ourselves as we think we really are.

real value of money: the price of money measured in terms of goods. Cf. *purchasing power.*

reapportionment: allocation of the costs of operating the service departments to the various production departments in proportion to the relative benefits or services received by each production unit. Synonymous with *reallocation.*

reason-why approach: synonymous with *factual approach.*

rebate:
(1) *general:* any refund of a payment.

(2) *sales:* any deduction made from a payment or charge. In contrast to a discount, a rebate is not deducted in advance but is returned to the consumer following payment of the full amount (e.g., a GE appliance costs $24, with a rebate of $5 after the consumer has mailed in a coupon from the appliance package). Cf. *discount.*

(3) *sales:* any refund given to a consumer for sending in proof-of-purchase following a sale. See *refund offer.*

rebate offer: synonymous with *refund offer.*

rebuild strategy: investment and marketing efforts designed to increase or exceed sales, profits, or market share levels that were held at an earlier time.

recall: in manufacturing, the return of a distributed production for purposes of adjustment, repair, or other necessary work. If found unsatisfactory, it may result in returning the cost of the item to the customer. See *product recall.*

recall testing: a means for determining advertising effectiveness; measures the degree that a person remembers aspects of an advertisement. In studies of recall, people describe the advertisement by responding to questions on its message, points made in the copy, and its campaign theme. The two forms of recall tests are:
(a) *aided recall*—the researcher presents the advertisement to the respondent and then asks questions about it.

(b) *unaided recall*—without showing the advertisement, the researcher merely asks the respondent questions about the advertisement. Cf. *recognition.*

receipt: written acknowledgment of value received.

receipt of goods dating: see *regular dating; ROG dating.*

receiver: the audience that is the target of a message.

receiving apron: in the receiving department of a store, a statement that contains all pertinent data concerning an incoming shipment. The form is used to identify the shipment for purposes of accounting and control. See *pro forma invoice.*

recency/frequency: the measure of the value of a customer or group of customers based on the number of purchases made and the length of time in between purchases as well as the time passed since the last purchase. The most valued customer has a high degree of recency and frequency. See *recency/frequency/monetary value.*

recency/frequency/monetary value: the measures for determining the value of a customer or group of customers based on time since the last purchase, the number of actual purchases, and the dollar value of the bought merchandise. See *recency/ frequency.*

receptivity to innovation: the extent to which a person or firm is willing to consider and perhaps purchase a new item or process.

recession: affects marketing and advertising activities; a phase of the business cycle that shows a downswing or contraction of the economy.

reciprocal demand: the situation created when one person offers what another person desires, and vice versa.

reciprocal trade agreement: an international agreement between two or more countries to establish mutual trade concessions that are expected to be of equal value.

reciprocity:

(1) *merchandising:* the purchasing of goods by one firm from another on a preferential basis, with the expectation that the second firm will preferentially buy the goods of the first.

(2) *international marketing:* a provision of a guarantee of similar or at least non-discriminatory opportunities for enterprises to operate in foreign markets on the same basis as local firms.

reclamation: the act of obtaining useful materials from waste products. Cf. *recyling.*

recognition:

(1) in advertising, acceptance of an agency by a medium. A recognized agency receives standard agency discounts.

(2) consumer awareness of having seen or heard an advertisement or commercial. If a high degree of recognition of the advertising message is found, then the advertiser believes that the advertisement is accomplishing its goals. See *aided recall; recall testing.*

recognized agency: the advertising agency that is acknowledged by the media as acceptable to receive a commisison or fee for the time or space it purchases for advertisers. It bills its clients at full rate.

recommendation: the transmittal to media members by a media association of the latter's evaluation of an applicant advertising agency's financial and related conditions including its qualifications to receive credit and agency commission from the association's members.

reconsignment: any alteration, including a route change, made in a consignment before the items have arrived at their billed destination.

recording delay: the delayed response effect indicating a time lag between the actual buying of merchandise and the manufacturer's knowledge of the purchase in his or her accounting records. It affects reorders, promotional needs, etc.

recovery:

(1) *general:* the period of the business cycle that follows a depression.

(2) *sales:* the difference between the purchasing price and the selling price of goods or services.

recruiting:

(1) *general:* personnel department activity involving the search for employees to meet the specific needs of an organization. In addition, the company may utilize the services of outside recruiting firms.

(2) *sales:* the activitiy of locating skilled salespeople and inducing them to apply for employment.

recycling: the conversion of waste products (e.g., empty beer cans) to usable material for the purpose of reducing pollution, saving money, and/or conserving resources. Cf. *reclamation.*

Red Book: see *Standard Advertising Register.*

red clause: a clause, printed in red, on a letter of credit, authorizing a negotiating banker to make advances to a beneficiary so that he or she can buy the items, and deliver them for shipment.

redemption: returning, usually to a retailer, coupons or proofs-of-purchase to receive a discount or premium. Firms follow these numbers to measure the effectiveness of a promotion. See *redemption center.*

redemption center: a store or outlet established by a trading-stamp firm where holders can redeem filled stamp booklets for goods. Synonymous with *redemption store.* See *redemption.*

redemption store: synonymous with *redemption center.*

red goods: food items and other consumer goods consumed and replaced at a rapid rate and having a low profit margin. Cf. *brown goods; orange goods; yellow goods.*

rediscount: to discount for the second time.

red label: a shipping label indicating flammable contents.

reduced-price pack: a package marked with a price that is less than regular retail.

reduced rate:
(1) see *allowance.*
(2) see *discount.*

reexport: of importance to global marketers; to export already imported items, without duty charges, in basically similar form to a third country. Cf. *production sharing.*

reference group:
(1) a sociological unit from which an individual takes his or her behavioral cues.
(2) any set of people influencing an individual's attitudes or behavior. Includes membership groups—where people actually belong; aspirational groups—where people would like to belong; and dissociative groups—where people have values the person rejects and therefore does not wish to belong. See *opinion leader.*

reference media: sources of statistical, commerical, or demographic information periodically printed for advertisers and other businesses.

referral: See *referral leads.*

referral leads: names of potential customers given to a sales representive, usually by satisfied customers. Referrals respond to promotions at a much higher rate than other prospects. See *friend-of-a-friend promotion; lead.*

referral premium: a reward offered to a satisfied customer when a prospect recommended by the customer purchases a product or service. See *premium.*

reflation: on recovering from a depression or a recession, the period during which prices are returned to the level they had attained during a period of prosperity by lowering the purchasing power of money.

refund: money returned by a seller of goods or services in exchange for the return of some part of an item or service, (e.g., the return of empty soda bottles).

refund check: a statement for a customer's purchase that is returned.

refund offer:
(1) a sales-promotion technique guaranteeing the purchaser a refund if not completely satisfied. See *trial offer.*
(2) a sales-promotion or manufacturer technique promising to refund part of the sales price to the consumer on receipt of proof of purchase. Synonymous with *rebate offer.*

refusal to sell: the right of a seller to choose the dealers that will handle his or her merchandise. Invoking this right, which is recognized by law, a seller may refuse to deal with firms that do not meet certain standards or qualifications. See *franchise.*

regiocentrism: a marketing strategy where the marketing effort targets regions instead of individual nations, or the entire global marketplace. Such regions can be composed of nations that possess any or all of the following characteristics: (a) they are contiguous to each other; (b) they share a common language; (c) they are at similar levels of economic and technical development; and (d) they belong to the same economic community or trading zone. Cf. *geocentricity.*

regional edition: a national publication with a particular advertising section aimed at a specific geographic location, enabling local advertisers to participate, without having to pay the rate for national advertising. Their distribution is limited to the specific geographic area involved in the advertising. Synonymous with *sectional edition.*

regional store: a branch store, usually located far from the central store, that functions under the name of the parent store. In most cases, a regional store operates an an autonomous unit. Cf. *branch store.*

regional wholesaler: synonymous with *sectional wholesaler.*

register:
(1) *general:* to record a trademark, patent, copyright, etc., with a governmental unit so as to claim exclusivity.
(2) *sales:* a unit or machine for temporarily storing information while or until it is used (e.g., a store's cash register).

regression: a means of coping with anxiety by reverting to a typically immature act; a form of returning to an earlier behavior stage.

regression analysis: used by consumer and marketing analysts; a method for predicting the values of a quantitative variable from scores of a correlated variable.

regular dating: terms of a sale under which the period for discount and the date on which payment is required are determined from the date of the invoice. Cf. *ROG dating.*

regularly unsought items: products that are regularly required by consumers, but which they will not go out of their way to purchase. (e.g., reference books for their children, insurance coverage). These items are often heavily promoted to increase consumer awareness and sales. Cf. *new unsought items; unsought goods.*

regular wholesaler: synonymous with *service wholesaler.*

rehypothecate: to pledge a second time.

reinforcement: the extent to which satisfaction is derived from a response to an aroused need.

reinforcement advertising: advertising that guarantees the buyer of a product or service that he or she has made a wise decision and suggests forms of satisfaction that are to be realized following purchase.

reinforcement schedule: the timing or scheduling of rewards.

reinforcement theory: a motivation approach that examines factors that energize, direct, and sustain behavior.

reinforcer: a stimulus that follows an act and (a) reduces the need motivating the act and (b) strengthens the habit that led to the act in the first place.

reinstatement:

(1) *general:* restoration of a worker to a former position without the loss of seniority or benefits.

(2) *marketing:* placement of a customer's record back into active status after being suspended, canceled, or becoming inactive.

reinvoicing: in international marketing, a strategy employed by global firms where one of its national companies imports commodities through an offshore firm and following, dumps the profits made on the transaction in the offshore tax haven, thus lifting its apparent costs to reduce taxes on the mainland firm.

related-item display: synonymous with *cross-merchandising.*

relationship analysis: a category of fortuitous scan methods of ideation in which the essential element is bringing together things not normally so considered.

relationship marketing: exists when firms seek to develop and maintain continuous long-term ties with their suppliers, distribution intermediaries, and customers.

relative advantage: the potential market's perception of the amount of utility a replacement item has over the item it replaces or with which it will compete.

relative income concept: the hypothesis that spending is a function of a family's relative place in the income distribution of similar family units (people who earn the same amount tend to spend the same amount of money).

relative market share:

(1) the market share held by a company or service or item compared with the market shares of competitors.

(2) an organization or strategic-business unit's market share divided by that of its largest competitor.

relative product failure: occurs if a firm makes a profit on an item but the product does not reach profit objectives and/or adversely affects the firm's image.

relaunch: the reintroduction of a product, service, or promotional program after a period of inactivity. Usually, it follows a discontinuance of the item or service. Relaunching will proceed by creating a change in the item or service, or a new promotional approach prior to its beginning.

release:

(1) *general:* the cancellation or resolution of a claim against another person.

(2) *advertising:* a legal instrument authorizing an advertiser to utilize the name of a person or his or her photograph.

relevant range: the band of activity in which budgeted sales and expense relationships will be valid.

reliability:

(1) *general:* accuracy and dependability.

(2) *market research:* the quality of data when repetition of the same research produces essentially the same results.

(3) *retailing:* the consistency of performance of goods (e.g., a hairdryer is guaranteed to continue to work the same way over and over again until the warranty date passes). Cf. *validity.* See *product reliability.*

remainder:

(1) *merchandising:* goods unsold at the original price because of a lack of demand that are then sold at a lower price.

(2) *publishing:* an unsold book that has never been retailed. Remainders are often

offered by the publisher to special stores for sale at reduced prices.

(3) Synonymous with *overstock*.

remarketing: a technique for reviving the demand for an item or service that has been experiencing decline.

reminder impulse buying: buying stimulated by reminders to the customer within the store of the value in purchasing the merchandise. Cf. *planned impulse buying; pure impulse buying*.

remit rate: that part of a subscription sales price remitted to the publisher by a subscription agent following the deduction of the agent's commission. Short for remittance rate.

remittance: funds forwarded from one person to another as payment for purchased items or services.

remittance rate: see *remit rate*.

remote delivery: sending goods from a central warehouse to customers by truck or via area delivery stations located in the suburbs.

renege: to go back on a promise; to pull out of an agreement.

renewal promotion: sending by mail a reminder of the expiration of a periodical to subscribers hoping that it will encourage a renewal of the subscription. The mailing is often carried out three to six months prior to the expiration date.

rented-goods service: involves the leasing of a good for a specified time period.

reorder system: synonymous with *Q-system*.

rep: short for representative. In advertising, the person who sells space or time for an advertising medium. Synonymous with *sales representative*.

repeat demand: the demand created for items that are frequently requested and bought.

repeating technique: synonymous with *mirror response technique*.

repeat purchasing: purchasing the same item or service from the same source of supply over a given time period.

repeat rate: the number of times an item or service is bought by a consumer within a time frame. When the repeat rate is low, it can indicate that the item or service could use more advertising; if that fails, the item or service might be redesigned or even dropped from the market.

repeat sales: sales perpetuated by going back to the same store or retailer to make a purchase.

repetition: the repeated frequency of an advertising message, slogan, or concept so as to reinforce it with consumers.

replacement demand: capital goods or consumer items that are in demand because of depreciation or obsolescence.

replacement potential: as measured in unit or dollars, the sales potential of merchandise to present consumers who will require replacing the item within a fixed time period.

replacement rate: the frequency with which merchandise is bought by consumers.

reply envelope: used primarily in direct-mail packages, a self-addressed envelope from a direct marketer for the return on orders and other types of responses. As an incentive to the consumer, most reply envelopes are postage-paid. Studies show that postage-paid reply envelopes lead to a higher response return rate.

repositioning: by changing a product's target market, a strategy for increasing sales of an already existing item. It requires altering the original positioning strategy, especially when a competing product starts to dominate and a new or revised strategy is required, or when the decline stage of the product life cycle begins. Cf. *positioning*.

repossession: the reclaiming or taking back of items bought on an installment sales contract on which the buyer has become delinquent.

reprint: in advertising, the reproduction of an advertisement after it has been shown in a publication.

repurchase agreement: an agreement between a seller and a buyer that the seller will buy back the property at the expiration of a stated period or on completion of certain conditions, or both.

required rate of return: a financial hurdle that is a firm's cost of capital adjusted for the risk of the project. Most new product projects have more risk than ongoing operations, so most required rates are well above costs of capital. See *risk premium*.

requisition: a written demand from a department to its purchasing department to release on a specific date materials to be used in a production process or other activity of consumption within an organization. See *stores requisition*.

resale: the selling of goods or services that have been bought by the seller from another person in essentially the same form.

resale price maintenance:
(1) the practice by a supplier of prescribing, and taking action to enforce, retail or wholesale prices for the resale of items.
(2) a supplier's control over the selling price of his or her goods at various stages of distribution by means of contractual arrangement under fair trade laws or other means. See *fair-trade price*.

rescale: synonymous with *resizing*.

rescind: see *right of rescission*.

rescission: the process of making void or annulling. See *right of rescission*.

research and development (R&D): application of the findings of science and technology in creating a firm's products or services.

research design: an overall plan for conducting a research project, including the choice of the method that will be used to achieve the goals of the research.

research study: an activity to gather market research information on a particular market problem or situation.

reseller: synonymous with *jobber*.

reseller markets: firms and individuals who buy products in order to resell them to others. Most products are sold through such intermediaries.

reserve stock: synonymous with *backup merchandise; buffer stock*.

reserve stock control: a technique for earmarking appropriate stock for the maintenance of business until new merchandise is purchased.

reshipper: a shipping container for receiving empty containers (e.g., soda bottles) intended for reuse.

resident buyer: any person or firm located in a market area who aids retailers in making market contracts and assists in their purchasing. Cf. *merchandise mart.*

resident salesperson: a supplier's salesperson located within the structure of one of the supplier's primary accounts. He or she provides full attention to the customer's needs.

residual: a fee paid to an individual for repeated transmission (e.g., on radio or television) of a performance in which he or she originally participated. The residual can be paid for by the television or radio station or advertiser. Synonymous with *reuse fee.*

resister: a person who has a history of not replying to direct-mail promotions.

resize: see *resizing.*

resizing: the production of the means of running an advertisement in several sizes to fit different units of space. Synonymous with *rescale.*

resource:

(1) *general:* anything a country uses to produce goods and services (manpower, minerals, oil, etc.).

(2) *merchandising:* a producer or wholesaler from whom a merchant buys goods for resale. See *merchandise resource.*

respondent:

(1) the person who provides information in an inquiry or on a questionnaire.

(2) a person who participates as a subject and provides information in a poll, study, or other research-gathering service.

response:

(1) whatever occurs as a reaction to an aroused need.

(2) replies and reactions to a stimuli. See *response analysis; response rate.*

response analysis: a statistical treatment of the reply to a direct-mail promotion indicating the performance of the varying elements of the promotion.

response function: in marketing, the impact of any shift in the four P's and the result it produces on sales and profits. It is usually plotted as a curve on a graph showing the effects of changes in the component marketing mix elements.

response projection: forecasting of a response to a promotion based on the number of responses received to date or based on earlier experience with the promotion, product, or service.

response rate: usually less than 5 percent, the gross or net responses received as a percentage of total promotions mailed.

response variable: synonymous with *dependent variable.*

restrained exporter: a nation that uses voluntary export restraints to slow down the export of particular items to identified markets. See *protected market.*

restraint of trade: of critical importance to marketers; the effect of any contract, combination, or agreement (e.g., a monopoly) that impedes free competition. See *Robinson-Patman Act of 1936; Sherman Antitrust Act of 1890.*

restricted articles: articles that are handled only under certain conditions.

restrictive business practices: acts of enterprises, public or private, that limit access to markets or indirectly restrain competition.

restrictive license: an agreement under whose terms an owner of a patented item allows a licensee to sell the patented good under certain limited conditions.

retail advertising: the dissemination of sales messages by retail store operators through local media such as newspapers and nonnetwork radio and television radio directed toward those consumers living within the trading area of the advertiser. See *local advertising.*

retail catalog showroom: a discount retail establishment at which consumers select merchandise from a catalog and shop at a warehouse-style location. Customers typically write up their own orders, products are usually stocked in a back room, and there are limited displays.

retail chain: involves the common ownership of multiple units. See *factory outlet.*

retail cooperative: a voluntary association of independent retailers who jointly own and operate their own wholesale facilities and often serve together as a buying club to achieve the economies of large-scale purchasing.

retail display allowance: a decrease in the funds paid by the retailer to the manufacturer in exchange for a more favorable display of the item in the store or on the shelf.

retailer:

(1) a merchant whose primary activity is to sell directly to consumers.

(2) an intermediary that sells products primarily to ultimate consumers. There are store retailers—operators of department stores, outlets, supermarkets, boutiques, etc.; and nonstore retailers—firms that sell through mail-order catalogs, have direct-selling procedures, or operate vending machines.

retail franchising: a contractual agreement between a franchisor (a manufacturer, wholesaler, or service sponsor) and a retail franchise that allows the franchisee to conduct a certain form of business under an establishment name and according to a specific set of rules.

retailing:

(1) the activity of purchasing for resale to a customer.

(2) all activities undertaken by intermediaries whose primary function is to sell goods and services to ultimate consumers. The four functions of retailing are (a) buying and storing merchandise; (b) transferring title of those items; (c) providing information on the nature and uses of those goods; and (d) in some situations, extending credit to buyers. Cf. *wholesaling.*

retailing mix: the retail store's combination of controllable variables giving it a unique image and position in the market. Variables include product, price, promotions, place, operating policy, purchasing, personnel, service, etc. Synonymous with *trade marketing mix.*

retailing the invoice: indicating retail prices on the seller's invoice as approval for the markers in a receiving area. See *preretailing.*

retail installment credit account: synonymous with *all-purpose revolving account.*

retail marketing: setting sales objectives based on market potential with heightened attention to the consumer's behavior; concerned with who is purchasing what and the underlying reasons for this action.

retail method of inventory: an accounting technique for recording all inventory inputs, including sales, purchases, markdowns, and so on, at their retail values. Purchased items are recorded at cost. See *markdown; markdown cancellation; markup; markup cancellation.*

retail outlet: a store that sells directly to the customer.

retail price: the price at which goods are identified for sale or are sold.

retail price maintenance: a manufacturer's right, under protection of state law, to set retail prices for his or her products. This is in accord with the terms of the fair-trade acts. See *fair-trade acts.*

retail rate: synonymous with *local rate.*

retail salesperson: an individual who works inside a store, where customers come to him or her.

retail store cooperative: a store that is owned and operated by a number of people as a source of supply for at least a certain kind of product.

retail store strategy mix: an integrated combination of hours, location, assortment, service, advertising, prices, and other factors retailers employ.

retainer: a method of compensating an advertising agency or other organization for services rendered. Usually it involves providing a standard monthly fee to be paid by the company to the client. Out-of-pocket expenses (e.g., travel) are billed to the client separately from a retainer's fee.

retention cycle: the time an inactive customer's record is retained.

retentive stage: a product's stage when its acceptance of a particular brand is so broad that the advertiser need only keep reminders before his or her customers, accomplished with little effort and expense. Throughout, loyalty is preserved. See *spiral stage.*

return: see *returns.*

return card: see *return postcard.*

return on investment: see *ROI.*

return percentage: see *response rate.*

return postcard: a self-addressed card used in direct-mail packages to offer recipients an easy way to request information or order goods or service. The postcard is traditionally paid for by the advertiser.

returns:

(1) any response to a direct-mail campaign.

(2) goods returned to a supplier for credit, and sometimes, refunds. See *returns and allowances.*

returns and allowances: in retailing, the total dollar amounts of items that were returned to the seller by dissatisfied customers (returns), and the total price reductions/discounts that were granted to consumers by the seller (allowances). The monetary amount of returns and allowances deducted from the outlet's gross sales to arrive at total net sales. See *returns.*

returns to vendor: goods sent back to the vendor by a store for various reasons (e.g., damaged merchandise, lateness of delivery). Cf. *purchase allowance.* See *vendor chargebacks.*

reusable packaging: containers that have another use subsequent to their service as merchandise containers.

reuse fee: synonymous with *residual.*

revenue: the grant total of all resources received from the sale of a firm's product or service during a stated period; not to be confused with general revenue.

reverse distribution: synonymous with *backward channel.*

reverse elasticity: a brief increase for a product or service that triggers an increase in purchasing and a decrease in price along with a decrease in buying. This is caused by buyer anticipation that the initial act will be followed by other price cuts.

reverse-order perception: the rate occurrence when consumers prefer to purchase the more expensive item because of the perception that the price is a better bargain. For example, an item marked $19.95 may be thought to be a better buy than the same good were it marked $16.50.

revolving account: synonymous with *revolving charge account.*

revolving charge account: a credit system permitting the customer to have repeated purchases on account as long as the charge balance does not exceed a set amount and the customer make agreed-on payments on time. Synonymous with *all-purpose revolving account; revolving account.* See *Truth-in-Lending Act of 1968.*

revolving credit: a regular 30-day charge account that is paid in full or in monthly installments. Paid in full within 30 days of the statement date will not commence any finance charge.

rhochrematics: a way of managing the material flow process that has an integrated system for making and marketing an item.

rifle technique:
(1) the sales practice of concentrating on selling only a few items, using a carefully prepared style of presentation that will lead to a rapid decision. Cf. *shotgun approach.*

(2) the distribution of publicity materials to select news media instead of mass-mailing them to numerous different media.

rigged market: the situation that exists when purchases and sales are manipulated to distort a normal supply-and-demand price.

right of rescission: the privilege, guaranteed by the Truth in Lending Act, of canceling a contract under certain circumstances within three business days, without penalty and with full refund of all deposits that have been submitted. See *Truth in Lending Act of 1968; voidable contract.*

rights of consumers: a doctrine enunciated by President John F. Kennedy, stating that consumers have the right to be safe, to be informed, to choose, and to be heard.

risk: any chance of loss. Marketers try to comprehend the forces that create risk in consumers' minds and take appropriate actions to lower it. See *marketing risks.*

risk analysis: a strategic planning activity to identify the external threats of the marketplace and evaluate them in terms of their potential impact on the organization and the chances of occurrence.

risk matrix: a matrix of the risks at any particular point in a new product's evaluation process. It shows the risk of rejecting a product idea that would ultimately succeed and the risk of going ahead with a project that would ultimately fail.

risk premium: the amount by which cost of capital is raised to reflect added risks of any particular new product proposal. Such addition yields the required rate of return. See *required rate of return.*

risk reduction: the effort by a customer to solve a problem and make a purchase while cutting down on the uncertainties linked with a product or service. The customer is provided with a host of materials, information brochures, etc., to reduce this risk. See *potential need satisfier.*

risk taker: one who is willing to take chances and may aggressively seek out chancy situations that offer the possibility of significant payoffs or profits. See *risk taking.*

risk taking: a marketing function that accepts the possibility of failure or loss in the selling of a product or service. See *risk taker.*

risky shift phenomenon: the concept that the action of people as individuals is often radically different from their group behavior and thus that the shift away from conformity can be risky.

roadblocking: early in a program, the advertiser's engaging of the same time period on all the major networks to provide for maximum exposure with the public.

Robinson-Patman Act of 1936: federal legislation, amending the Clayton Antitrust Act of 1914, in which price discrimination practices are more clearly identified. Quantity discounts in excess of the cost savings realized by selling in such quantities are declared illegal, as are false brokerage deals. Promotional allowances must be made to all buyers on a proportionately equal basis, and price discrimination is acceptable if it is done to meet a proper low price of a competitor and if the price does not restrict competition. Synonymous with *chain store law.* See *price discrimination; restraint of trade; unique user; volume bonus.*

rock bottom: (slang) the lowest level that will be entertained in a business transaction (the lowest price at which a seller will agree to sell his or her goods).

ROG dating: receipt-of-goods dating. Under this condition of sales, the date for payment and the discount period are determined from the date the buyer obtains shipment, rather than from the invoice date. This procedure is primarily employed when great shipping distances are involved. Cf. *regular dating.*

ROI: return on investment; the amount earned in direct proportion to the capital invested.

role: behavior patterns expected from people in various economic, social, or other status positions.

role expectations: the rights, privileges, duties, and responsibilities associated with a particular role.

role of marketing: the purpose and functions of marketing, as determined by top management, which notes its importance, outlines its activities, and integrates it into the firm's overall operation.

role theory: an approach to the study of group influence that recognizes people conduct their lives by playing many roles, each of which is accompanied by a certain range of acceptable behaviors.

roll-out:

(1) *general:* the expansion of a new item into previously unknown markets from a local introduction.

(2) *merchandising:* an approach to new-product introduction in which the product is launched in a series of geographic areas over an extended period.

(3) *direct mail:* the largest mailing in a campaign. See *pyramid selling.*

ROP: see *run-of-paper.*

Rorabaugh reports: quarterly statements on spot advertising expenditures in television that are released by a private advertising consultant every three months.

ROS: see *run-of-schedule.*

rotated merchandise control: counting a retailer's inventory on a rotated or staggered basis by scheduling counts on specific days.

rotation: advertisements repeated in sequences after the entire series has been run.

rough: a preliminary, sketchily drawn layout of an advertisement designed to indicate the relative size and placement of the various units composing the advertisement, usually as a prelude to a more carefully drawn layout.

round turn: the execution at different time periods for the same principal of a purchase transaction and a sale transaction that offset each other. Synonymous with *turn.*

routine: in broadcasting, the opening of a broadcast program. See *billboard.*

routine consumer decision making: in consumer behavior, a decision requiring minimal discussion and planning because of the routine nature of the purchase. Such items are usually inexpensive carrying little consumer risk.

routing: the selection of a path and steps in the operation performed on materials during the manufacturing process. Salespeople use routing in the hope of ensuring adequate coverage of a territory at the lowest possible cost to the selling organization. Cf. *traffic.*

ROW: see *run-of-week.*

rubricated account: see *flagging an account.*

rule line: the straight line used as a border or dividing line in an advertisement; used for decoration or to clearly define a panel by creating a boundary, or other aspect of the advertisement.

rule of reason: the Supreme Court decision in 1911 that only unreasonable restraint of trade was illegal, thereby permitting companies to become as large as they wished, under the argument that the law did not outlaw mere size. This interpretation has largely been reversed since World War II.

rules of content: see *rules of origin.*

rules of origin: critical in international marketing and sales; products that are treated differently in international commerce according to their country of origin. Shifting the percentages of content rules inevitably stirs criticism. Most accords set 50 to 60 percent as a minimum of parts that must come from one of the nations involved.

Rules of origin remain a set of criteria by which to determine what country a given product is made in; that a product's country of origin is to be the last country where assembly or processing operations "substantially transformed" the inputs or components into a new product. Strong rules of origin provisions assist customs inspectors to make determinations of what passes free of tariffs or duty while not unduly inhibiting and impeding trade. See *dumping.*

running: in merchandising, a best-selling item, especially one that is continually kept in stock because of its heavy sales volume. Cf. *sleeper.* See *fill-ins.*

running costs: direct or indirect costs that result from keeping an operation and/or machinery functioning. These costs include wages, rent, and taxes.

run-of-paper (ROP): a media buyer's ordering instruction thereby controlling the use and placement of an advertisement. The advertiser presents an advertisement to the publisher, and the publisher decides where it shall appear. Should the advertiser have a preferred position, the advertiser will negotiate the cost to have the advertisement run in a specific location. Cf. *run-of-schedule.* Synonymous with *run-of-press.* See *run-of-week.*

run-of-press: synonymous with *run-of-paper.*

run-of-schedule (ROS): in broadcasting, the equivalent of run-of-paper; the situation where the advertiser provides a television commercial and its air time is set by the station management, with possible negotiation occurring for a preferred position with an agreed-on revised rate. Cf. *run-of-paper.*

run-of-week (ROW): a media buyer's ordering instruction, where the adver-

tisement appears in whatever newspaper, magazine, etc., the media owner selects. Cf. *run-of-schedule.*

run sizes: the number of items manufactured at one time in a given lot.

sacrifice: to make a sale at a loss for purposes of raising cash, with the awareness that it will reduce the profit.

safety: in magazine advertising, the space between the perimeter of the advertisement and the edge of the page, thus allowing binding of pages without losing the boundaries of the advertisement.

safety stock: a minimum inventory that provides a cushion against reasonably expected maximum demand and against variations in lead time. See *cushion.*

sag sale: see *residual.*

sale:

(1) the transfer of title to an item or items.

(2) the agreement to perform a service in return for cash or the expectation of cash payment.

sale-below-cost laws: synonymous with *unfair practices acts.*

sales:

(1) revenue received from the sale of goods.

(2) final sales plus producer item sales. See *net sales; selling.*

sales agent: a middleperson who undertakes to sell the entire output of items of a business that he or she represents. As controlled by the manufacturer's contract, sales agents can or cannot exercise control over setting prices and other terms of the exchange between purchaser and seller. Cf. *selling agent.*

sales allowance: a lowering of the price of an item when merchandise delivered is not exactly what was ordered by a buyer.

sales analysis: an aspect of market research involving the systematic study and comparison of sales information; carried out for specific territories, products, or salespeople, quarterly, monthly, or annually. Cf. *cost analysis.* See *systems selling.*

sales anchors: concepts and statements used by sales representatives when attempting to overcome customer resistance.

sales aptitude: the capability to achieve success in the sales field, as acknowledged by a sales department and measured by means of interviews and recommendations.

sales audit: an audit that is a comprehensive assessment of sales strategy of fulfilling sales objectives with the aim to improve the overall effectiveness of the salespeople. This audit purports to determine whether or not the objectives set are realistic, appropriate, and reachable. It can also determine the firm's sales plans and policies. Usually, a sales audit is carried out by an independent consulting organization.

sales-based pricing objectives: goals that orient a company's pricing strategy toward high sales volume and/or expanding its share of sales relative to competitors.

sales branch: a producer's outlet that maintains inventory and delivers to buyers from that stock.

sales broker: an agent who, though not physically handling merchandise that he or she deals with nor having little control over the terms of a contract between principal and third party, serves a critical phase in the relationship between parties in the production and distribution process.

sales budget: a budget based on forecasted sales for a coming period; usually includes all marketing expenditures of which selling is only a part. It will have an impact on the funds provided to the sales department over a set time period.

sales call pattern: a pattern of effort where salespeople in the field call on prospective customers. The pattern evolves by (a) the universe of target customers and their geographic distribution; (b) the frequency of calls required by each customer; (c) the cost-effectiveness of calling; and (d) the selling culture of, and competitive sales pattern in, the particular universe of customers.

sales clerk: an individual in a retail store who records the customers' purchases, who usually is responsible for maintaining stock, and who at times helps the customer in making a selection from the available stock. A minimum amount of salesmanship need be employed by a sales clerk.

sales closing: see *close (1).*

sales company: a corporate entity established in a foreign country by the parent firm to sell goods or services imported from the parent firm and other foreign affiliates.

sales compensation: money paid to sales-people in the form of straight compensation, salary, or a combination. The three primary forms of sales compensation are: (a) *straight salary*—paying a salesperson a fixed annual amount.

(b) *commission basis*—basing compensation on the salesperson's performance (e.g., as a percentage of sales that he or she generates).

(c) *combination compensation*—mixing a straight salary arrangement with a commission.

sales contest: a sponsored competition, usually by a dealer or manufacturer of an item, where outstanding sales efforts and results are rewarded.

sales control: a system of supervision involving the use of such devices as records, statistical analyses, correspondence, and personal contact for the purpose of carrying out or adjusting marketing policies and plans.

sales decline stage: in the cycle of a product, the period when sales fall and will continue in that direction unless remedies are taken.

sales demonstration: the depicting of an item's functions and potential. Synonymous with *demonstration*.

sales discount: synonymous with *cash discount*.

sales effectiveness test: a means for determining the ability of an advertising program or communications medium to sell a product or service.

sales efficiency: the correlation between sales volume or value and individual and total selling expenses.

sales engineer: a person who sells products that require technical knowledge and training. Synonymous with *technical salesperson*.

sales era: the hiring of a sales force and sometimes the use of advertising to sell inventory, after production is maximized. The role of the sales force and advertising is to make the desires of consumers fit the attributes of the products being manufactured.

sales exception reporting: the documentation of products as either slow- or fast-selling merchandise.

sales expense budget: a budget allocating expenditures relating to personal selling efforts. Affects budget setting.

sales fertility: the amount of marketing effort needed to achieve a stated sales volume.

sales finance company: a financial organization that purchases installment contracts from dealers and finances dealers' inventories.

sales force: canvassers and sales representatives who contact potential purchasers of goods and attempt to persuade them to buy items. These people are organized by geographic territory, type of merchandise, the market, or any combination of these factors. See *market-structured sales force; product-structured sales force; territory-structured sales force*.

sales forecast: a dollar or unit sales estimate made for a specified period in a marketing campaign. See *forecasting; sales forecast opportunity variance*.

sales forecast opportunity variance: a measure of the differential between scheduled capacity and the master budget sales forecast capacity, usually expressed in dollars. See *forecasting.*

sales incentive: traditionally, money offered by the manufacturer to a salesperson for exceeding some preset sales goal. Other perks include free trips and special prizes.

sales invoice: the main written, typed, or computer-generated source of sales analysis data.

sales journal: a book in which records of sales are entered.

sales lead: information or a contact provided to the salesperson to assist in his or her selling efforts.

sales letter: correspondence from a selling firm sent to prospective or existing customers providing information on the product or service, with reasons for a quick reaction from the reader.

sales management: management activities in the development of a skilled sales force. It involves recruiting, selecting, and training, plus follow-up activities of supervision and motivation. See *sales analysis; sales audit; sales manager.*

sales manager: an executive responsible for planning, directing, and controlling the activities of sales personnel. The manager plans the firm's sales objectives and strategies for achieving these objectives. He or she also organizes and directs efforts of the sales force, develops sales programs, and monitors overall sales performance in relation to stated sales goals. Cf. *product manager.* See *sales management.*

salesmanship: the art of selling goods or services by creating a demand or need

for a particular item or service and realizing an actual order. Cf. *conmanship.* See *creative selling; hard sell; low-pressure selling; service selling.*

sales manual: a book describing the product, merchandise, or service to be sold and suggesting approaches for selling to a customer.

sales mix: a combination of the various company products leading to a firm's total sales.

sales objective: synonymous with *sales quota.*

sales office: a facility for taking orders and handling adjustments that serves as a contact point for suppliers and customers. No inventory is maintained at the office. Cf. *merchandise mart.*

sales penetration: the degree to which a firm is achieving its sales potential as measured by:

$$\text{sales penetration} = \frac{\text{actual sales}}{\text{sales potential}}$$

salesperson: a person who practices salesmanship. Synonymous with *sales representative.*

sales pitch: a strong statement aimed at persuading a potential customer to buy the salesperson's product or service.

sales plan: a merchandise budget that contains a detailed projection of sales for a given period, specifying the purchases, inventory, and so on, needed to achieve this goal.

sales potential: fulfillment of the identified market share or market objective with consumers. See *market potential; market share.*

sales potential forecast: a forecast of total potential sales for the firm for a specific time period.

sales presentation: the total selling process of describing to a potential customer the product or service, including the attempt to plan an order. See *trial close.*

sales promotion: the array of techniques that marketers use to stimulate immediate purchase, including using coupons, rebates, continuity programs, price packs, premiums, samples, contests, sweepstakes, incentives, point-of-purchase advertising, and events marketing. Synonymous with *demand creation; demand stimulation.* See *promotion.*

sales promotion agency: a firm specializing in supplying broad sales promotion services to clients. See *advertising agency.*

sales promotion conditions: requirements that channel members or consumers must meet to be eligible for a specific sales promotion.

sales promotion orientation: the focus of sales promotion—channeling of members or consumers—and its theme.

sales quota: a projected goal for sales of a product. Usually the quota is established as part of a marketing campaign. Assessing a salesperson's performance is frequently based on the actual sales generated contrasted with a sales quota. Cf. *activity quota.* Synonymous with *sales objective.* See *quota; trade quota.*

sales reports: written reports summarizing to management results of sales performance and salespersons' activities. These reports can detail customers' reactions to items, services, or company procedures, in addition to competitors' efforts.

sales representative: synonymous with *manufacturer's representative; rep; salesperson.*

sales results test: an effort to measure the impact on sales of a specific advertisement or campaign.

sales returns and allowances: a contrasales account in which the returns or allowances for previously sold merchandise are recorded.

sales revenue: total income derived from sales for a stated time period.

sales tax: a tax levied by a state on items at the time of their purchase. It may be a tax on the sale of an item every time it changes hands or only on its transfer of ownership at one specific time. The sales of manufacturers are taxed when the items are considered to be completed goods; the sales of wholesalers are taxed when their goods are sold to retailers; and retail sales are taxed when the goods are purchased by consumers.

sales terms: synonymous with *terms of sale.*

sales territory: the segment of a firm's total market; defined by prospect, customer, or by geographic boundaries. In sales, synonymous with *territory.*

sales trainee: a recently hired sales representative who is learning the basic concepts of selling. Usually the trainee receives a small salary during this period.

sales training: a firm's program for training sales personnel; may be carried out external to the institution, by hiring consultants or sending candidates to specialized programs or classes, or within the organization itself.

sales variance analysis: a method of data analysis in which data on actual sales are compared with quantitative sales objectives.

sales volume analysis: a method for assessing performance in the marketplace by measuring the target market's reaction to the firm's offering of items.

sales wave method: a measure in market testing where an item is placed in the prospect's home on a trial basis and made available for purchasing.

salon: a shop within a store for the selling of high-price apparel and accessories. Cf. *boutique.*

salting: in direct-mail, inserting fictional names and addresses into a mailing list to uncover any unauthorized usage of the list.

salutory item: a high-priced item or service held in low esteem by the consumer because the high-priced item or service has yet to provide the satisfaction or benefit to the consumer.

salvage:
(1) *general:* equipment or property that is no longer used for its initial purpose.
(2) *merchandising:* goods soiled beyond reclamation for purposes of sale and thus usually disposed of by other means. See *salvage value.*

salvage value: the expected worth of a depreciable item at the end of its service life.

sample:
(1) *general:* an item selected to represent the entirety.
(2) *merchandising:* an item of a product that is a proper representative of all the units of that product.

(3) *retailing:* a portion of an item provided free to a prospective consumer.

(4) *market research:* a subset of a population drawn for testing activities under the assumption that the results will forecast the results or behavior of the entire population. See *sampling.*

sample buyer: a person who buys at a special introductory rate or obtains at no cost a product sample. See *trial size.*

sample package: see *trial size.*

sampling:
(1) *general:* choosing a representative portion of a population to characterize a larger population. See *Monte Carlo method.*

(2) *salesmanship:* exposing a market to a new item, package, or package size by providing prospects with a miniature or actual unit of the item, hoping successful usage will lead to future purchases.

(3) *marketing:* in marketing research, providing information about a large population from data gathered about a few units from that population. With probability sampling, every member of the total universe of respondents has an equal and known chance of being chosen; nonprobability sampling is based on criteria to ensure that some members of the population have a greater probability of being chosen than others. See *cluster sample; convenience sampling; judgment sampling; population; quota sampling; sample; simple random sampling; stratified random sampling.*

sampling accuracy: the degree to which the parameter of the population characteristic is properly estimated by the chosen sample. See *sampling error.*

sampling buying: in industrial buying, purchasing an item after studying a portion of the potential shipment for quality.

sampling error: an error that occurs when the sample used is not representative of the population it was designed to represent. Sampling error points to the difference among figures generated in repeated measurements of the population and will decrease as the size of the sample increases. Cf. *standard error.*

sampling frame: the sampling units from which a sample is taken, such as a listing of firms, people, or geographic location. See *universe.*

sampling unit: the segment of the total population to be sampled in marketing research.

sanction: a penalty for the breach of a rule of law.

sandwich board: an old-fashioned, but still used form of advertising, with two boards, one hung in front of the person, the other behind. Announcements or advertisements are usually placed on both sides.

satisfaction:
(1) a criterion of effectiveness that refers to an organization's ability to gratify the needs of its employees. Synonymous with *morale; voluntarism.*

(2) an enjoyed purchase.

satisfaction of demand: customer satisfaction based on product availability, actual performance after purchase, perceptions of safety, after-sale service, and other factors.

satisficing: decision-making behavior in which the manager selects an alternative that is good enough (one that will yield a satisfactory return to the organization).

saturated market: a situation occurring when there is a greater supply of a particular item than there is demand for it. A company's item can gain market share at this point, only at the expense of another item.

saturation: the phase of the product life cycle in which an item is no longer able to be sold because most consumers who are likely to be interested in it have already purchased it. Synonymous with *horizontal saturation.* See *burst advertising; life cycle of product; product life cycle; saturation campaign.*

saturation campaign: intensive use of radio or television advertising to promote or sell a product in a market. There are usually special low rates for saturation-level advertising. See *flight saturation; saturation.*

saving: the amount of existing income not spent on consumption.

Say's law: used by market analysts; a concept developed by Jean Baptiste Say in the late eighteenth century that the supply of all economic items must always equal the full demand for them. Therefore, any increase in output is an increase in demand, and overproduction is an impossibility. See *overproduction; underconsumption theory.*

SBUs: see *strategic business units.*

scaling method: in marketing research, a method of measuring the nature and strength of an individual's attitudes or opinions toward a specific object, concept, or idea.

scanner: in merchandising and retailing, an electronic instrument that reads bar codes and other graphic information on product packages, coupons, and mailing envelopes. See *scanner market; universal product code.*

scanner market: a type of controlled market testing where products are offered for sale in stores where scanners have been installed, and special arrangements made to gather all relevant information about the products and their buyers. See *scanner.*

scarcity value: an increase in value caused by a demand for an item whose supply cannot be increased (e.g., works of art from the nineteenth century).

scare purchasing:
(1) purchasing to hoard.
(2) unusually heavy buying of items in short supply.

scatter plan:
(1) the purchase of a number of specially selected spots on television.
(2) a broadcast media plan that schedules an advertising announcement to run during a program, giving the advertiser a wider audience for his or her money than would be achieved by being a single program sponsor.

scenario: the sequence of events that may occur in the future. Useful to the firm in planning product strategies of the future. See *scenario analysis.*

scenario analysis: a forecasting technique in which market researchers develop a subjective picture of several possible futures by identifying cause-and-effect relationships and following them to their logical conclusions. See *scenario.*

schedule:
(1) *general:* a systematic plan for future operation over a given period.
(2) *advertising:* a list of advertisements, by stated media, giving dates of appearance, space, time, and so on.

scheduled production: the rate of activity assigned for the production of a given item in a specified period.

schedule of variance: the difference between actual production and scheduled production.

scheduling: the organization and control of the time needed to carry out a sales effort.

schlock (shlock): (slang) cheap, inferior items or services.

scientific method: a philosophy for marketing research based on objectivity, accuracy, and thoroughness.

scientific tariff: a duty to cover foreign and domestic manufacturing costs.

scintilla of evidence: a small amount of evidence that assists in the proof of an allegation.

scoop:
(1) to beat out a rival (verb).
(2) a considerable profit following a transaction that is likely to involve advance notice over or exclusion of competitors (noun).

scoring model: a weighted-factor checklist used to screen new-product proposals. Factors are scored, and the scorings are weighted and then totaled to yield a judgment on the concept.

scrambled merchandise:
(1) the practice of carrying any product line, however dissimilar from other lines carried, if it yields a profit.

(2) an approach by retail outlets of maintaining types of goods not normally found in those stores (e.g., clothing and large appliances sold in a drugstore).

scrap: equipment or material that has not be used and therefore has been discarded. Synonymous with *excess*. Cf. *waste*.

scrap value: see *salvage value*.

scratch and sniff: a device for advertising an area impregnated with a fragrance that is released by scratching its surface. See *action device*.

scratch-off: found in sales promotions materials, a card with a section the consumer scratches with a coin to reveal a message, usually indicating whether the person is an instant winner of a contest and what the prize is.

screening stage: in new product development, the assessment of new concepts to determine which of them have the potential for development.

screwdriver duties: a means of reducing costs to global marketers; a reference to the vulnerability to antidumping duties of imported components of foreign products made within a national country or member of an international trade agreement unless an adequate proportion of the final unit is made outside the foreign nation.

scruff: (slang) to earn sufficient monies for the basic necessities of life.

*s***-curve effect:** the situation that occurs if sales of a product rise sharply after it is introduced because of heavy initial promotion effort (advertisements, coupons, samples, etc.), drop slightly as promotional support is reduced, and then rise again a positive word-of-mouth communication takes place.

SEA: see *Single European Act.*

sealed bid pricing: a pricing technique in a competitive bid situation; the firm bases its price on what it anticipates its competitors will charge, what the competitors will bid as contrasted with the company's own costs or demands. Sealed-bid pricing requires the submission of confidential bids, all within a stated time of a particular day, with a contract usually going to the lowest bidder.

sealing:
(1) *advertising:* reducing or enlarging an illustration or advertisement.

(2) *packaging:* holding a closed box or package adequately by cord, tape, glue, or other means.

seal of approval: an award in the form of insignia made by a consumer magazine or an association to a manufacturer whose product specifications have met the standards set up by the magazine's testing bureau or by the association's committee. Such seals are valued by advertisers.

search: the process whereby buyers gather and interpret information enabling them to decide whether or not to purchase an item or service, including consideration for alternative items or services.

search goods: items the qualities of which are easily determined prior to purchase. See *experience items.*

seasonal dating: synonymous with *advance dating.*

seasonal demand: synonymous with *seasonality.*

seasonal discount:
(1) a discount offered to customers who purchase a product or service during a

season when the demand for that product or service is low.

(2) a price reduction given for purchases made out of season (e.g., ski equipment bought at a discount in the spring). Cf. *static inventory problem.*

seasonal employee: a worker employed for limited periods of activity (e.g., for working in a department store during the Christmas season).

seasonal fluctuations: regular and predictable shifts in business activity created by changes in the season (e.g., housing construction increases during spring).

seasonal forecast: changes in market demand that depend primarily on the time of year.

seasonal industry: an industry that has high peaks of employment at specified times of the year and down periods during other seasons.

seasonality: a time, the changing of the seasons, characterizing a market, product, or promotional campaign that indicates some variation in sales (e.g., trying to sell ski equipment in the summer may fail unless other incentives, such as bargain prices, are introduced). Cf. *erratic demand.* Synonymous with *seasonal demand.* See *demand states.*

season dating: synonymous with *advance dating.*

secondary data: information not received by a user from its original source, but coming instead from references gathered earlier. Cf. *primary data.*

secondary group: a large group whose members have a shared goal but do not engage in face-to-face communication.

secondary research: in marketing research, using data from already available published sources (e.g., U.S. Census reports) as contrasted with primary research information gleaned from original field research. Secondary research differs from primary research in that the latter is for a particular firm and the information gathered is often proprietary, not for free circulation.

secondary shopping district: a series of stores outside the urban center, but within the city limits, that services a fairly large population. Convenience items are particularly important in these stores.

secondary source: a source providing data collected for a purpose other than the research project in question.

second cover: synonymous with *inside front cover.*

secondhand:

(1) not new.

(2) descriptive of merchandise offered for sale that has already been used.

seconds: goods bearing defects that have possible effects on wearability and appearance. See *bargain store.* Cf. *thirds.*

second sale:

(1) a sale achieved by building on a customer's receptive mood following an initial purchase.

(2) an additional sale to the same person.

sectional edition: synonymous with *regional edition.*

sectional wholesaler: a wholesaler who limits his or her activities to a fixed and small number of geographic areas or states. Cf. *local wholesaler; national wholesaler.* Synonymous with *regional wholesaler.*

secular inflation: the most serious economic problem of the 1970s. In contrast to cyclical inflation, which moves in and out of the economic system roughly every two years, secular inflation is primarily a long-term social phenomenon, impacting sales and advertising investments.

secular stagnation: a low level of economic movement measured over an extended time period that impacts sales and advertising investments.

secured distribution: a field-warehousing technique where carload lots are shipped to a distributor's premises for release based on the bonded warehouse's arrangement as the distributor requires the items.

security agreement: the agreement between a seller and a buyer that the seller shall have an interest in the goods. The security agreement must be signed by the buyer and must describe the goods.

seed trends: current trends used to spot possible scenarios. See *scenario*.

segment:

(1) *general:* a portion of a message.

(2) *marketing:* a subgroup of people found within a market. See *market segmentation*.

(3) *broadcasting:* television or radio advertising time within which there is no variation in the unit charge.

segmentation: the division of a market into subunits with similar motivations and needs. It is used to increase product or service acceptance by recognizing item appeals. Demographics, geographics, personality, attitudes, values, and preferences, are the most popular base for segmenting a market. Cf. *fragmentation*. Synonymous with *market cleavage*.

See *demographic segmentation; market segmentation*.

segmentation pricing: the setting of prices at different levels for different segments of the population (e.g., the airline industry has different prices for different classes of service).

segmentation research: a form of marketing research that uncovers new bases for market segmentation. See *market segmentation*.

segmentation strategy: synonymous with *differentiation*.

segmenter: a marketing organization that uses the single-target market approach or the multiple-target market approach in the evolution of a strategy. See *imaginative segmenter; innovative segmenter*.

selection criteria: the basis for choosing a subset from a group.

selective demand: the demand for a particular brand. See *primary demand; selective demand advertising*.

selective demand advertising: advertising purporting to determine selective buying motives within a particular audience. See *primary demand advertising*.

selective distribution:

(1) an approach to distribution that involves the use of a limited set of outlets in a given territory.

(2) the choice of retail outlets that will be permitted to receive a manufacturer's merchandise for sale; traditionally used with hard goods, such as appliances, VCRs, refrigerators, and furniture. It permits manufacturers to maintain greater control over the way their merchandise is sold and reduces price competition among

sellers of the items. See *exclusive distribution; intensive distribution; open distribution.* Synonymous with *limited distribution; selective selling.*

selective headline: a headline directed to the interest of a specific market segment.

selective perception: people's cognitive ability to shield themselves from the onslaught of external stimuli to which they have been exposed so as to create order and reduce psychological disruption. The three aspects of selective perception used by consumers and of importance to marketers are:

(a) *selective exposure*—the likelihood that consumers will choose only some communications from the mass of external stimuli that have been presented to them.

(b) *selective distortion*—the probability that people who are confronted with general, limited, or dissonant data will unconsciously supplement the information with their own perception to create a message that is comprehendible and consistent with their feelings and beliefs.

(c) *selective retention*—people's tendency to recall external stimuli that are similar to their preconceived notions and beliefs, and to forget other stimuli that are not. See *consumer behavior; perception.*

selective selling: synonymous with *selective distribution.*

selective stage: synonymous with *competitive stage.*

selective stocking: balancing the cost of service with the expense of maintaining inventory to determine what merchandise should be stocked at every distribution center.

selectivity index: in media planning, a measurement method that compares print advertising media in a stated geographic area; determined by dividing a medium's audience size by the percentage of the target market potential population. See *cost per thousand.*

self-concept: synonymous with *self-image.*

self-concept theory: the notion that two factors influencing an individual's purchasing behavior are how the person perceives himself or herself and how he or she wishes to be perceived by others. Cf. *motivation.*

self-fulfilling forecast: a forecast encouraging behavior that causes itself to be realized.

self-fulfilling prophecy: a situation in which a firm predicts sales will decline and ensures this by reducing or removing marketing support.

self-image: people's concepts of themselves and their roles in relation to others. Synonymous with *self-concept.* See *ideal self-image; self-concept theory.*

self-liquidating: an asset that can be converted into cash or is subject to total recovery of invested money over a period of time.

self-liquidating offer: see *self-liquidating premium.*

self-liquidating premium: a premium for which the buyer pays all or part of the cost, where the advertiser offers something of value that enhances the item's image without incurring any cost. Cf. *semiliquidator.* See *trade card.*

self-liquidator: see *self-liquidating premium.*

self-mailer: in direct mail advertising, a piece structured so that it can be addressed directly on the piece; it is then folded or mailed without being enclosed in an envelope.

self-reference criterion: a firm's conclusion that if a product prospers in the domestic market it should do equally as well or better in an overseas market. Therefore, the firm concludes that no new market research effort is required.

self-selection selling: a merchandising approach that allows customers to make their choices without the initial assistance of sales help.

self-service: a sales outlet or store in which the customer chooses the items to be purchased, removes them from the shelves, carries them to a checkout counter for completion of the transaction, and carries or sends them to the place of use.

seller concentration: the number of sellers found in a single industry. As the number of sellers increases, there is less chance that one firm can influence prices.

seller's lien: the seller's privilege of holding onto certain items until the buyer has delivered payment. Cf. *vendor's lien.* See *lien.*

seller's market: a market in which demand is greater than supply, resulting in sellers setting the prices and terms of sale. It is a market characterized by rising or high prices. Cf. *buyer's market.* Synonymous with *tight market.*

seller's surplus: the difference between the price a seller actually receives and the lowest price that he or she would accept.

sell-in: the manufacturer's attempts to convince retailers to distribute and stock his or her merchandise. Cf. *sell-through.*

selling: the process of assisting and/or persuading a potential customer to buy merchandise or services, or to act favorably on an idea. See *sales.*

selling against the brand: the artificial inflation of prices on some items to increase sales on other items.

selling agent: an agent who handles the entire marketing function for a manufacturer. These agents usually work on an extended contractual basis with the manufacturer and traditionally have full authority for setting prices. They differ from sales agents, in that sales agents do not have control or influence over prices and terms of sales and rarely get involved in advertising and promotional activities. Cf. *sales agent.*

selling calendar: a schedule for promotions identifying specific dates for each intended special selling event.

selling costs: marketing costs (e.g., advertising, sales promotion) necessary to attract a potential buyer to an item or service.

selling error: the use of inappropriate, error-filled selling methods which often lead to markdowns of merchandise. Cf. *buying error.*

selling formula approach: a selling method that assumes all consumers are alike or at least will respond in a predictable way to a set sales presentation.

selling price: the cash price a customer must pay for purchased items or services.

selling process: the process of prospecting for customer leads, approaching customers, determining customer wants, giving a sales presentation, answering questions, closing the sale, and following up.

selling short: synonymous with *short selling.*

sell off: to resell advertising space and time that have already been contracted for to another advertiser.

sell out:

(1) *general:* to betray a person, organization, or cause, usually for profit or special treatment.

(2) *merchandising:* to dispose of an entire stock or set of products.

sell-through: the manufacturer's attempt to increase sales of merchandise at the retail level. Cf. *sell-in.*

semantic differential scale: a method to determine consumer attitudes. It is a scale of opposite pairs of words separated by a line divided into seven parts. By connecting the checks, the market researcher is left with a picture of consumers' attitudes.

semidirect channel: a channel of distribution with a limited number, often only one, middleperson between the producer and consumer. Cf. *indirect channel.*

semifinished items: synonymous with *fabricated parts.*

semijobbing: the making of wholesale sales by the retailer or retail sales by the wholesaler. See *split-function wholesaler.*

semiliquidator: a premium offer paid in part by the consumer. Synonymous with *purchase-privilege offer; semi-self-liquidator.* See *self-liquidating premium.*

semimanufactured items: raw materials that have passed several stages of production but still have other processes to pass into before the items can be used. Synonymous with *fabricated parts.*

semi-self-liquidator: synonymous with *semiliquidator.*

semispectacular: an outdoor advertising message hand painted on a panel of wood or metal placed adjacent to a highway or railroad line or in a metropolitan district containing heavy traffic and making use of an electrical, mechanical, or three-dimensional device or animated copy or figures.

semivariable costs: synonymous with *mixed costs.*

sensitive market: a market characterized by fluctuations determined by the announcement of favorable or unfavorable news.

sensitive products: products in sectors that are deemed highly vulnerable to injurious import competition.

sensory thresholds: the upper and lower limits on the ability of human sensory processes to perceive increases or decreases in the intensity of a stimulus.

separation: synonymous with *product protection.*

sequential interdependence: the relationship between units of an organization such that the product of one is passed along to the next in order, after which the final product results.

serendipity: the ability to gain knowledge from accidental events. Many famous new products have been discovered accidentally, but many potential discoveries were overlooked because the observer was not serendipitous (having a prepared mind).

serpents in the garden: inducements and displays placed near the doors of a store to attract customers' immediate attention.

serrated edge: a sawtooth edge, as around the mouth of a paper bag.

service: a deed, act, or performance.

service area: synonymous with *accommodation area.*

service blueprint: a visual portrayal of the service plan by a firm. It is essentially a detailed map or flowchart.

service costs: the operating costs of service departments that are usually allocated to production departments.

service department: an organizational unit that does not directly produce goods but serves other departments.

service charge: a payment by a financial institution against an individual or organization for services rendered.

service fee: funds paid to the advertising agency by the advertiser. Usually, the agency is paid a retainer for a wide variety of services. Other extraordinary services are compensated at special rates.

service line: the offering of a sales organization that may be called on by a client when marketing its products or services. Cf. *product line.*

service mark:

(1) a trademark for a service.

(2) a mark used in the sale or advertising of services to identify the services of one person and distinguish them from the services of others, such as the names, symbols, titles, designations, slogans, character names, and distinctive features of radio or other advertising used in commerce.

service marketing:

(1) efforts to raise the sale or delivery of a service.

(2) efforts that encompass the rental of goods, the alteration or maintenance or repair of goods owned by consumers, and personal services.

services:

(1) work offered by people or organizations for others without transferring goods or commodities (e.g., insurance companies, banks).

(2) privileges for customers of a firm beyond the items themselves, such as credit, assortment, home delivery, gift wrapping.

service salesperson: usually, a person who interacts with customers after sales are completed and undertakes delivery, installation, or other follow-up tasks.

service selling: efforts by a salesperson who satisfies a consumer's needs and thus retains goodwill.

services marketing: see *service marketing.*

service wholesaler: the merchant selling to retailers, industrial users, and wholesalers. Complete services are provided including credit, delivery, and variety of items. Synonymous with *regular wholesaler.*

setback: a reversal or partial loss in an activity.

setup: the time or costs needed before production of an item can commence.

shading: (slang) giving a small reduction in a price or terms of sale.

shadow boxes: boxes that can display small items in retail stores; usually a framed box with tiny shelves.

share:

(1) *general:* stock that names the holder and indicates ownership in a corporation.

(2) *broadcasting:* the percentage of households in a specific geographic location with television sets tuned to a particular program as compared with the total percentage of households tuned on. See *audience share; brand share.*

shared services: common carriers, a combined captive sales force, or public warehousing shared by several marketers at any one time.

share of advertising method: a method of setting the advertising budget based on a share of the total advertising expenditures in a specific field.

share of audience: the percentage of radio or television sets in use or households watching a particular program. Cf. *audience flow; Hooperating; Nielsen rating.*

share of the market: synonymous with *market share.*

share of voice: the level of advertising by a brand in a particular product category compared with others within the same category. The greater the brand's share of voice, the greater the number of advertising messages being offered to consumers. Companies that advertise most frequently usually gain a greater level of market share in the product category.

sharpening: a cognitive process in which the information retained becomes more vivid and important than the event itself.

shelf life: the time identified on the package or label that a certain item can remain in stock or on the shelf before significant deterioration occurs. When that date arrives, the product should not be sold to the consumer. See *stock rotation.*

shelf miser: synonymous with *space miser.*

shelf stock: items available to store customers who remove what they desire from the shelves on which the merchandise is placed. See *floor stock; forward stock.*

shelf talker: printed advertisement hung from the shelf in a retail store, supermarket, or a variety store.

shell firm: an organization that is incorporated but does not function or produce any goods or services.

Sheridan stuffer: synonymous with *newspaper stuffer.*

Sherman Antitrust Act of 1890: federal legislation aimed at preventing business monopoly. Some courts, however, applied the sanctions of the law against strikes, and unions were fined triple damages for acts that were considered to be in restraint of trade. See *price stabilization; restraint of trade.*

shipment:

(1) *general:* delivery and transport of items by a carrier.

(2) *distribution:* a collection of items that are transported as a unit.

(3) *merchandising:* merchandise sent to a manufacturer to be processed, or items sent from the manufacturer to a wholesaler or retailer. See *drop shipper; middleperson.*

shipper's agent: an international service facilitating intermediary who buys cargo capacity on transport modes and then resells this to shippers.

shipper's cooperative:
(1) a group of shippers that pool shipments of similar items to benefit from lower freight rates.

(2) an incorporated firm, owned by shippers of goods and run on a not-for-profit basis, that performs the functions of a foreign freight forwarder.

shipping order: instructions of shippers to carriers for forwarding all goods; usually the duplicate copy of the bill of lading.

shipping permit: authority issued by a transportation line permitting the acceptance and forwarding of goods against the movement of which an embargo has been placed.

shirt-board advertising: an advertising medium in which a sales message is printed in full color on a specially processed shirt board inserted in each shirt sent out to customers by laundries.

shoehorn: (slang) to add copy or visuals (e.g., last-minute changes) to an already existing advertisement.

shoplifting: thievery of a store's items by a customer or employee. Cf. *pilferage.* See *inventory shortage; shrinkage.*

shop merchandising: establishing certain locations in a store for serving buyers with special interests (e.g., tennis shop, teen-age corner).

shopper: the individual engaged in a search for goods or services. Synonymous with *pennysaver.*

shopping center:
(1) a cluster of stores and other related facilities (restaurants, rest rooms) planned and built to service a trading area.

(2) a group of retail stores at a single location that is planned, developed, and controlled by one organization. Cf. *superstore.*

shopping goods: consumer goods that are purchased only after the buyer compares the offerings of more than one store. See *convenience goods; specialty merchandise.*

shopping mall: synonymous with *mall.*

shopping mall intercept: a form of personal interview in which respondents are approached or intercepted as they pass a particular spot in a shopping mall.

shopping plaza: synonymous with *mall.*

shopping products: goods and services about which consumers will seek information before making a purchase.

shopping radius: the area around the store from which it usually attracts customers.

shopping store: a retail outlet favored by consumers who are shopping for a certain type of product.

shortage:
(1) an excess of quantity demanded over quantity supplied, indicating that the price is below equilibrium. See *short merchandise.*

(2) a deficiency in quantity shipped.

shortage advertising: the advertising run when an item or service is in short supply resulting from production problems. Rather than attempt to influence the customer to purchase more of the item or service, the advertisement turns to education or other forms of influence while stock is replenished.

short-hour: descriptive of part-time workers who work during peak store hours.

short merchandise:

(1) *general:* goods bought in small quantities, usually in extreme sizes, to complete an assortment.

(2) *merchandising:* purchased goods that were not included in a shipment. See *over, short, and damaged.*

short of destination: prior to reaching the final port, warehouse, or destination.

short rate: the higher rate an advertiser pays when he or she fails to use the space or time contracted for.

short run:

(1) a one-time job.

(2) the time during which a firm can alter the price or output of its goods but not change the size of its plant or close down operations.

short selling: selling items and purchasing them at a lower price to receive a profit. Synonymous with *selling short.*

short term: see *short run.*

shotgun approach:

(1) a disorganized approach to selling or advertising, aimed at reaching a large number of potential customers without expecting to make sales to all. Cf. *rifle technique.*

(2) in publicity, the mailing of news releases to different media outlets.

showing: the number of outdoor advertising displays bought for the placing of advertisements. For example, a 100 showing indicates that the entire combination of units bought will be exposed to the entire population of a market at least once during any given day. A 50 showing indicates that half the population will pass by the advertising at least once during any given day, etc.

shrinkage: the gradual loss of inventory over time due to damage, misplacement, or theft. Shoplifting is a major cause of shrinkage. See *inventory shortage; shoplifting.*

shrink wrapping: a plastic coating applied over a package. When subjected to heat, the coating conforms to the shape of the package; used in mailing multicomponent promotion packages, such as catalogs and fliers. See *polybag.*

SIC: see *Standard Industrial Classification System.*

sideline stores: stores whose primary interest is other than retailing (e.g., a wholesaler who also sells to the consumer as an accommodation).

signature:

(1) *advertising:* the advertiser's name as mentioned in the advertisement.

(2) *broadcasting:* the sound effect or music used to identify a commercial or program.

significance: statistical importance; the degree of probability that in an infinite series of measurements of the type in question, the value actually obtained will not occur with meaningful frequency by chance alone and hence can be attributed to something other than chance.

silent salesperson: a POP display, direct mail item, or money used in a vending machine.

similitude: the practice of customs authorities when an imported article does not conveniently fit into any existing classification within the customs tariff. Articles are then compared with similar articles listed in the tariff for justification.

simple random sampling: used by market researchers; probability sampling in which respondents are chosen at random from a complete list of the members of the population. See *sampling.*

simple regression analysis: see *regression analysis.*

simple trend analysis: used by market researchers; a forecasting technique in which managers review historical data and use the rates of change to project future trends.

simplification: cutting down on the different products in a company's lines. Cf. *diversification.* Synonymous with *product deletion.*

simulated test market: a type of market testing where consumers are presented with a simulated purchase situation to determine their reactions and feelings toward the merchandise, advertising campaign, or marketing mix combinations.

simulation:
(1) the representation of certain features of the behavior of a physical or abstract system by means of the behavior of another system.

(2) a method of reviewing an operation or problem that overcomes the difficulty of not being able to study it in real-life form. A model of the system or process is subjected to a series of assumptions and manipulations in an effort to find one or more acceptable solutions.

simulcast: a program broadcast simultaneously over radio and television.

singing commercial: a radio or television advertising message delivered in the form of a song, usually accompanied by one or more musical instruments.

single customs document: for international marketers, a document that replaces some 70 different forms once used in trade across the European Union's internal borders. Effective 1988, this document attempts to harmonize and simplify trade procedures and alleviate the long delays at Europe's border crossings.

Single European Act (SEA): of importance to international marketers; this amendment to the original Treaty set new objectives for the European Union with the completion of the internal market "an area without internal frontiers in which the free movement of goods, persons, services and capital is ensured in accordance with provisions of this Treaty." It took effect on January 1, 1993, with fiscal and trade barriers eliminated among the 12 nations.

single-item pricing: synonymous with *unit pricing.*

single-line store: a store that carries a wide variety of one type of goods.

single-line wholesaler: a full-service wholesaler that carries only one or two product lines but offers considerable depth in each.

single market: see *Single European Act.*

single-price policy: the setting of a fixed price for the entire assortment of a given category of items so that the purchaser can concentrate only on the items offered (e.g., all gloves are $10.00). Cf. *one-price policy.*

single-product strategy: the policy of manufacturing only one item or a single item with a limited number of options.

single rate: a radio or television station's charge that does not differentiate between local and national advertisers. Cf. *local rate; one-time rate.*

single-source data collection: a technique that allows research firms to tract the activities of individual consumer households from the programs they watch on television to the products they purchase at a store.

single-sourcing: purchasing all the firm's requirements for a specific product or service from one source of supply.

single-stage sampling: synonymous with *cluster sampling.*

single-target market method: a marketing segmentation approach where one homogeneous group is chosen as the target market and one marketing mix is employed to market the item.

single-variable segmentation: the simplest form of market segmentation where only a single factor (e.g., a person's age) is used to segment the population.

singularity: the number of other products against which a new item will be tested. If one, singularity is monadic. If two, the singularity is paired comparison.

sister-store concept: synonymous with *equal-store concept.*

situational analysis: an assessment of the marketing environment, a key part of the marketing plan. The firm's strengths and weaknesses are assessed as well as its products; the analysis may also include data on market characteristics, consumer needs, buying patterns, and other factors that influence the outcome of the marketing effort. Synonymous with *market review.*

situational factors: factors that can interrupt the organizational consumer's decision process and the actual selection of a supplier or brand. They include strikes, machine breakdowns, organizational changes, and so on.

six C's: in preparation for making marketing decisions, the careful examination of the following areas: commodity, company, competitors, channel members, consumers, community.

six-sheet poster: a printed sheet of outdoor advertising material measuring 4 feet 4 inches high and 9 feet 10 inches wide adopted as a standard of outdoor advertising service.

60: the designation for a 60-second television or radio commercial, as shown on the broadcast script.

skewness: used by consumer and marketing researchers; the property of a nonsymmetrical distribution curve. See *kurtosis.*

skimming: see *skimming price.*

skimming price: use of a high introductory price followed by a series of price reductions, designed to get all the trade the market will bear at one price level before lowering the price and also to appeal to the more price-conscious consumer. Synonymous with *skim-the-cream price.* See *penetration strategies.*

skim-the-cream price: synonymous with *skimming price.*

skip: a customer who moves from a known address without paying the bill of a business or utility.

skip loss: see *skip.*

skywriting: an out-of-the-home advertising medium that uses an airplane to write a short message in the sky. Small puffs of smoke, from a chemical mixture, form letters telling a message for a few seconds, and then disappear.

slack:

(1) the time in which a minor operation can be completed in advance of the next major operation that depends on it.

(2) a dull or inactive business period (a slack season).

slack filling: employing deceptively oversized boxes or other packages. An unlawful practice as regulated by the Federal Trade Commission.

sleeper: a fast-selling item that has the potential to become a runner. Cf. *running.*

slice-of-life:

(1) *broadcasting:* a commercial indicating how a person overcomes a barrier by utilizing the advertised item or service. These commercials often take the form of a minidrama where a common problem is solved by using the advertised item.

(2) *advertising:* advertising that portrays consumers in realistic situations that are consistent with consumers' perception of their own life-styles.

sliding scale: a reason for increasing or decreasing charges to a customer in relation to the volume of activity or usage over a stated time (e.g., a gas company may charge for gas on a sliding scale, with lower rates for greater consumption).

sliding scale tariff: a customs tariff in which rates of duty vary according to the price of a given import. Usually, as the price of the merchandise falls, the duty is lowered.

slippage:

(1) *general:* lost time.

(2) *merchandising:* people who purchase an item intending to redeem a coupon, request a rebate, or send in for a premium, and then fail to do so.

slogan: verbal material in an advertisement that is repeated and recalled precisely as presented. Highly memorable slogans ultimately define the features of the advertised product or service. Slogans can be printed or verbal.

slug: in advertising, the signature of the advertiser on the print advertisement. Either a logo, trademark, or just the name of the advertiser is given for purposes of identification.

slump: a short-lived decline in the activity of a business or economy.

small order: small orders for merchandise. See *small-order problem.*

small-order problem: purchase orders which are so small that the transaction may not produce a profit.

smorgasbord plan: a sales compensation method allowing the person to choose among salary, commissions, bonuses, and other fringe benefits that he or she prefers as a means to fulfilling individual needs.

smuggling: removing from or putting in goods or persons without permission. Smuggling can be done across the borders of countries or other political entities (e.g., cigarette smuggling across state lines).

snapper: an added incentive used to encourage prospects to buy a heavily promoted item or service.

sniffer: a display that provides an aroma or odor to attract prospects or to enhance the appeal of an item.

snob impact: the degree to which demand for an item is discounted because too many other people use it.

snowballing method: a means for evolving media advertising schedules where the climax of a campaign is looked on as important and therefore receives the greatest proportion of the budget. Synonymous with *crescendo method.*

social benefit: the value to society resulting from a specific act or action (e.g., the discovery of penicillin, the invention of the automobile).

social channel: others familiar with the prospect who share information and attitudes about products and services. Cf. *social classes.*

social classes: employed in marketing research and market segmentation; categories of status and position that are often overlapping and impossible to define adequately. These social stratifications are upper-upper (social register), lower-upper (nouveau riche), upper-middle, lower-middle, upper-lower, lower-lower. Cf. *social channel.* See *social mobility.*

social contract: a model conceptualizing the relationship between a firm and society as a whole, whereby the organization is granted freedom to exist and is obligated to function in the public interest.

social cost: the price paid by people for the side effects of economic performance (e.g., pollution, destruction of forests). See *comparative advantage.*

socialization: a formal and informal process of training, guidance, indoctrination, influence, or even coercion, whereby a new or potential organization member is made to internalize the norms, values, attitudes, or behavior patterns of the organization.

social marketing: the use of marketing philosophy and techniques in the dissemination of societally useful ideas. The concept was propounded by Phillip Kotler and Gerald Zaltman in the 1970s. Synonymous with *societal marketing.* See *advocacy advertising; public service advertising.*

social mobility: the movement from one social class or stratification into another. See *social classes.*

social responsibility: the expectation that companies, including marketing and advertising firms, should act in the public interest and contribute to the solution of social and ecological problems.

social styles model: a classification system for segmenting organizational consumers in terms of a broad range of demographic and life-style factors. The model divides the personnel representing those consumers into various life-style categories.

societal marketing: synonymous with *social marketing.*

socioecological view of marketing: examines all the stages in a product's life span from raw materials to the junkpile. It incorporates the interests of all consumers influenced by the use of a good or service. See *eco-audit.*

socioeconomic segmentation: market segmentation based on age, income, occupation, education, etc. Usually, a variety of these variables are used together to help identify potential purchasers of specific items or services.

sociogram: a means of describing the preferences people have in being with others. The sociogram is used in choosing teams, work partners, etc.

sociographics: a means to describe group influences on consumer behavior.

soft goods: ready-to-wear clothing, piece goods, linens, towels, and small fashion accessories. Cf. *capital goods.* Synonymous with *nondurable goods.*

soft market: synonymous with *buyer's market.*

soft sell: a selling technique that is convincing, subtle, and indirect. Cf. *hard sell.* See *consultative selling.*

soft technologies: a way to industrialize services by substituting preplanned systems, such as prepackaged vacation tours, for individual services.

SOH: stock on hand.

solo mail: a direct-mail promotion used for an item or service.

sort: to segregate items into groups according to some definite rules, such as grade and quality. Cf. *assorting.*

sort and count: gathering of results from people who respond to an advertiser's request to respond to the advertisement. Responses are usually coded for future usage by an advertiser in breaking down the information into useful information.

sorting: a process in which products are brought together at one location and then divided up and moved in smaller quantities to locations closer to the ultimate buyers.

sorting out: see *sort.*

source:

(1) *general:* the originator of a message.

(2) *marketing:* the channel of sale generating an order or customer. See *source evaluation.*

(3) the individual who communicates an advertising message. See *message development.*

source effect: the public's reaction to an advertisement as dictated by their perception of the source of the message.

source evaluation: a critical part of direct marketing enabling marketers to concentrate their promotion resources on the best sources. See *source (2).*

source marking: the pricing of merchandise by vendors before shipment.

source migration: a customer's order pattern over a time period in response to varying promotions.

space: the area of medium in which an advertisement is placed.

space allocation: the quantity of shelf space in a retail store set aside for the display of merchandise.

space buyer: an advertising agency executive who assists in the planning of printed media campaigns and chooses and purchases space in the media. Cf. *time buyer.*

space contract: an agreement between a publisher and advertiser on the rate structure for the publication.

space miser: a point-of-purchase display created to hold items that can be readily removed, as well as carry a promotional message. It is frequently placed on a shelf where the item is available. Synonymous with *shelf miser.*

space position value: a measurement of the effectiveness of outdoor advertising based on four factors: the distance from where the advertisement is seen, the speed of traffic approach, the angle seen, and the number of competing outdoor advertisements in the area; expressed as a percentage from 0 to 100, with zero indicating zero visibility.

space spots: newspaper advertisements of small size that are volume bought by national advertisers.

span of control: the extent of a supervisor's responsibility, usually identified in the organizational chart by lines of authority. Synonymous with *span of supervision.* See *evoked set.*

span of recall: the number of brands a person can name when asked to do so. See *evoked set.*

span of supervision: synonymous with *span of control.*

special event pricing: promotional pricing where a sale is advertised, frequently linked with an event or holiday. The goal is to bring inventories into line with consumer demand or to raise cash.

special events: see *events marketing.*

special features: regularly run broadcasts of continuing interest to the public (e.g., weather reports; sports). Traditionally, it is sold to advertisers at a higher rate than other programs.

specialization: reducing an operation or task into separate simplified, individual activities.

special order: an order that may be priced below the normal price to utilize excess capacity and thereby contribute to company profits.

special-line retailer: synonymous with *specialty store.*

special position: the particular location of an advertisement in a newspaper, magazine, or other periodical.

specialties: synonymous with *advertising specialty.*

specialty: synonymous with *advertising specialty.*

specialty advertising counselor: synonymous with *specialty distributor.*

specialty advertising field: the utilization of advertising novelties as the advertising medium. See *Specialty Advertising Information Bureau.*

Specialty Advertising Information Bureau: an organization within the specialty advertising field that fosters interest in the subject by sharing information and educating users about the advantages of the medium. See *specialty advertising field.*

specialty discount store: an outlet that carries a single item category and sells it at below regular retail prices.

specialty distributor: a wholesaler in the specialty advertising field; handles a variety of advertising novelties and assists in advertising campaigns of these items. Synonymous with *advertising specialty distributor; specialty advertising counselor.* See *direct selling house.*

specialty goods: synonymous with *specialty merchandise.*

specialty-line market research firm: a research organization that provides data gathering or analysis to other researcher or company marketing research units. Cf. *syndicated service.*

specialty line retailer: a limited-line retailer that carries only one or two product lines but offers substantial depth and expertise in those lines.

specialty line supplier: a research firm that specializes in a single aspect of the marketing research process.

specialty merchandise: consumer goods that have special features for which buyers are willing to make a major purchasing effort (e.g., imported foods, hi-fi equipment, cameras). Synonymous with *specialty goods.*

specialty-merchandise wholesalers: full-service merchant wholesalers that concentrate their efforts on a relatively narrow range of products and have an extensive assortment within that range. Synonymous with *limited-line wholesalers.*

specialty products: goods and services for which there are no acceptable substitutes in the consumer's mind (e.g., some luxury cars, consumer electronics equipment, designer fashions).

specialty salesperson: a salesperson, other than retail, who specializes in the sale of one product or a few products of a line of one or more manufacturers or producers.

specialty selling: usually, the sale of products or services at a person's home or place of work (e.g., the selling of insurance, encyclopedias, vacuum cleaners).

specialty shop: synonymous with *specialty store.*

specialty store: a retail outlet that maintains a large selection in a limited line of merchandise (e.g., men's apparel store). Synonymous with *specialty-line retailer; specialty shop.* See *store.*

specialty supplier: a company that processes advertising novelties for sale through a host of outlets. See *direct selling house; specialty advertising counselor; specialty distributor.*

specialty wholesaler: see *specialty distributor.*

specification: a written identification of the work to be done and materials to be used in the completion of a task or product. Shortened to specs.

specific identification: a method of valuing inventory and determining the cost of goods sold whereby the actual costs of specific inventory items are assigned to those items of inventory on hand and to those that have been sold.

specific tariff: a tariff based on a fixed amount charged per unit of the goods imported.

specs: see *specification.*

spectacular: an outdoor advertising display characterized by the use of electric or neon lights and lavish color, and sometimes by such special effects as flashing lights, laser beams, billowing smoke, and animation.

speculation: the employment of funds by a speculator. Safety of principal is a factor secondary to increasing capital. See *speculator.*

speculative pitch: synonymous with *speculative presentation.*

speculative presentation: an expensive demonstration by an advertising agency to a prospect indicating what the agency can do should it be awarded the contract; involving considerable and expensive time for the agency and therefore usually done for large accounts. Synonymous with *speculative pitch.*

speculative purchasing: buying items when prices appear lowest, with the expectation of realizing a profit from a future price increase.

speculator: one who is willing to assume a relatively large risk in the hope of gain. The speculator's principal concern is to increase capital rather than dividend income. Speculators may buy and sell the same day or may invest in enterprises that they do not expect to become profitable for years. See *speculation.*

spendable earnings: considered by market analysts; net earnings after deductions for taxes, or the amount available for spending. Synonymous with *take-home pay.*

spiff: synonymous with *push incentive; push money.*

spillovers: synonymous with *externalities.*

spin-out: a form of new product team organization in which the team is broken out from the ongoing organization. It is the ultimate in projectization and used only in cases where the project will have major barriers to overcome.

spiral stage: in advertising, varying points of development for a product or service, as determined by consumer acceptance. See *competitive stage; pioneering stage; retentive stage.*

split-function wholesaler: a merchant wholesaler who is vertically integrated to operate on two or more levels of the channel of distribution. See *semijobbing.*

split item: merchandise that a firm both produces and purchases simultaneously.

split-off point: see *joint production costs.*

split order: a large order that is separated into smaller units to be sold over a period of time. When purchasing or selling goods, a very large transaction could cause substantial price fluctuation, and the splitting is supposed to prevent this.

split run: two or more advertisements of equal size with the identical position in different copies of the same publication issue. This affords a means of determining the impact of differing versions of an advertisement, and it allows an advertiser to feature different products in regional printings of a national publication. Cf. *preferred position.* See *copy testing.*

spoilage: merchandise found to be defective.

spokesperson:
(1) *general:* a manager's role in speaking for the unit and representing it to others. A key concept of the spokesperson role is that of representation; the manager must act as an advocate for subordinates.

(2) *advertising:* the person who delivers the message in a testimonial. See *celebrity testimonial.*

sponsor: a radio or television advertiser who runs one or more advertisements during a program. Usually, sponsoring a program requires the advertiser to buy the majority of commercial announcements made on the program. Cf. *sustaining program.* See *sponsorship.*

sponsor identification: the association of a radio or television program with the name of the sponsor or the brand name of his or her product, as elicited from listeners or viewers during or after the broadcast.

sponsorship: financial backing of an advertisement. See *alternate sponsorship; sponsor.*

sports marketing: sponsorship in sporting programs or events. See *events marketing.*

spot: in broadcasting, a place or position in a listing or schedule (e.g., having a spot on television). Synonymous with *occasion; time slot.*

spot advertising: a campaign wherein advertisers choose specific stations to be used. This contrasts with network or local advertising. See *flight saturation.*

spot announcement: a brief commercial, usually one minute long or less, inserted between portions of a radio or television program. Cf. *spot broadcasting.*

spot broadcasting: the use of a local radio or television station in a specified market by a national advertiser; permits an advertiser to select individual markets closely matching his or her areas of distribution, and those trading zones in which special sales or distributive problems must be solved. Cf. *spot announcement.*

spot campaign: an advertising campaign using spots.

spot delivery: immediate delivery.

spot display: items set down along store aisles with an attention-getting device attached.

spot market:
(1) a market in which commodities are sold for cash and delivered quickly.

(2) a market in which transactions between buyers and sellers take place at spot prices, which fluctuate daily and, sometimes, hourly to reflect supply-and-demand conditions.

spread:
(1) *general:* the differences between the bid and asked prices of an item.

(2) *retailing:* the difference between two prices.

(3) *broadcasting:* stretching a live broadcast to fill the entire time slot allotted it.

(4) *advertising:* an advertisement appearing on two facing pages in a periodical or magazine. Should it appear in the center of the magazine, the piece is called a *center spread.* See *center spread.*

SRDS: Standard Rate and Data Service, Inc.; an organization that releases up-to-date data on advertising rates, standards, and so on, of various media. SRDS is considered to be the prime source of advertising media information.

SRO method: in sales, a closing approach that warns the prospect to make a purchase immediately because the chances are small that the item will be available at a later time. It is considered by most to be an unethical practice.

stability: the objective of creating a sense of predictability, control, and certainty in an organization.

stable environment: an environment characterized by relatively small changes in technology and customers who have a minimal impact on the internal operation of the organization.

stable market: a market with few short-term price fluctuations, where purchasers are able to do little to influence prices. Cf. *unstable market.*

stacker: a freight handler who loads a vehicle.

staff: employees who advise and assist line managers and employees but are not directly engaged in the production of the final good or service.

staff department: a department that provides assistance and support to line departments in attaining basic objectives of the organization. In a manufacturing firm, purchasing and accounting would be staff departments.

stagflation: affects marketing and advertising revenues; inflation coexisting with economic stagnation. Prices for goods and services continue to increase during a period of minimal capital investment in equipment, research and development, etc.

staging: planning the location, and actions to be executed for a commercial.

stagnation: affects marketing and advertising revenues; conditions of minimal growth rate, or growth that is increasing at a lower rate than expected.

stake: the degree of dependency one channel member has over another for its success or failure.

Standard Advertising Register: the *Standard Directory of Advertising Agencies* and the *Standard Directory of Advertisers* are the two companion directories in the field; referred to as the Red Books, because of their red cover. The former provides information on advertising agencies, and the latter lists the 17,000 firms that advertise throughout the country,

with their agencies and annual advertising budgets.

standard advertising units: the standard sizes of advertising space set by newspapers for all national advertisers; unit sizes of differing columns and inches simplify the buying of advertising space by these advertisers. See *column inch.*

Standard Container Acts of 1916 and 1928: federal legislation that fixed the standard sizes for baskets and containers for fruits and vegetables.

standard costs: an estimate of what actual costs should be under projected conditions.

standard deviation: used by market researchers; the square root of the arithmetic mean of the squares of the deviations from the mean of the series.

Standard Directory of Advertisers: see *Standard Advertising Register.*

Standard Directory of Advertising Agencies: see *Standard Advertising Register.*

standard error:

(1) used by consumer and market researchers; a measure or an estimate of the sampling errors affecting a statistic.

(2) a measure of the amount a statistic may be expected to differ by chance from the true value of the statistic. Cf. *sampling error.*

Standard Industrial Classification System (SIC): a numerical system developed by the U.S. Bureau of the Budget to classify establishments by type of activity for purposes of facilitating the collection, tabulation, presentation, and analysis of data relating to such establishments and for promoting uniformity within U.S. agencies.

standardization:

(1) *general:* the determination of basic limits or grade ranges in the form of specifications to which produced items should conform. Greater standards compatibility removes structural barriers to markets and increases the competitiveness of firms. Standards define certain technical specifications that products must meet to establish an acceptable level of safety. See *grade labeling; Pan-European marketing; standards.*

(2) *manufacturing:* establishing specific criteria levels (size, quality, weight, etc.). Industrial standardization is achieved by an elaboration of standards throughout nations that trade with each other. See *ISO; ISO 9000.*

standardized approach: an international marketing strategy in which a firm uses a common marketing plan for all nations in which it operates. Synonymous with *global approach.*

standard of living: a consideration for marketers when planning strategies; the level of material affluence of a nation as measured by per capita output.

standard package: the quantity of an item usually shipped in one carton.

Standard Rate and Data Service, Inc.: see *SRDS.*

standards: regulations whose mutual recognition removes technical barriers to trade, irrespective of whether these involve technical rules, standards, tests, or certificates. See *standardization.*

standard volume: the expected sales over any given business cycle reduced to an annual basis.

standing details: in advertising, elements that appear in each advertisement (e.g., logo, trademark, photograph of item).

standing order: an authority to a vendor to ship specific products as available, or on a fixed-quantity basis per time interval.

standstill: in international marketing of goods, where participants agree not to take any restrictive or distorting measures inconsistent with global trade agreements, such as GATT.

staple items: see *staple stock.*

staples: see *staple stock.*

staple stock: goods on hand that are in continuous demand, such as milk, bread, sugar. Staple stock items are marketed primarily on the basis of price. Synonymous with *commodity products.*

star:

(1) a product line with a high growth rate and a significant share of the market.

(2) a strategic-business unit that has a high growth rate and a high relative market share.

state: one of the 50 geographic and governmental units of the United States, as well as Washington, DC, and all U.S. territories.

state-bonded warehouse: see *warehouse, state-bonded.*

statement: a summary of transactions between a creditor and his or her debts or a presentation of names and amounts of accounts to show a financial condition (e.g., an IRS statement).

state-of-being segmentation: one of a four-way classification of the strategies of segmentation. It refers to the physical, demographic, or geographic features of a population. See *benefit segmentation; product usage segmentation; state-of-mind segmentation.*

state-of-mind segmentation: one of a four-way classification of the strategies of segmentation. It refers to the psychological features of the population, especially the relationship between attitudes and behavior. See *benefit segmentation; product usage segmentation; state-of-being segmentation.*

static analysis: the determination of an equilibrium at a single point in time without considering the impact of the passage of time.

static inventory problem: the tendency of items bought for a specific selling season to lose value, either partly or completely, because of changes in the market at the season's end. Cf. *seasonal discount.*

station break: time allotted for giving the call letters or identification of a radio or television station; an advertising message or announcement also may be delivered during that interval.

station option time: time over which a network affiliate station has priority on first sales.

station poster: advertising billboards displayed in bus depots, train stations, airline terminals, and subway stations.

statistical demand analysis: an investigation of the direct relationship between sales and real demand factors. This analysis, based on multiple regression analysis, assists in overcoming forecasting problems.

statistical process control: the use of statistical analysis (usually by line employees) to measure and manage specific work processes. It is commonly used in total quality programs designed by marketers.

statistics: the mathematics of gathering data and the approaches used in describing and analyzing numerical information.

status:
(1) an individual's relative social or power position in a group. Cf. *social classes.*
(2) the position of an organization in a broad social context.

status consensus: the agreement of group members about the relative status of members of the group. Synonymous with *status consequence.*

status consequence: synonymous with *status consensus.*

status float occurrence: an attempt to explain the influence of fashion on different levels of social class. Numerous contradictions appear as to dress and code of dressing. See *trickle-down theory.*

status quo: the existing state of affairs.

status quo pricing: keeping prices at the level charged in the mature stage of the product life cycle to minimize chances of a price war with competitors.

status quo pricing objectives: orientation of a firm's pricing strategy toward maintenance of a prevailing favorable business climate for its operations or stability.

status symbol: an item or service purchased in the hope that it will communicate one's desired or real status to others.

stay-out price: synonymous with *preemptive price.*

stepped costs: costs that climb by increments with increased volumes of activity.

step-up: see *upgrading.*

stereotypes: preconceived notions, often based on superficial characteristics, that can distort communication between people. See *bias.*

stickers: items that have not been purchased after a reasonable time and occupy space needed for better-selling items. See *dead stock.*

stimulation marketing: efforts purporting to bring the affected market segment from a lack of interest in buying to the recognition of the value in the product and a reasonable level of positive demand.

stimulus: any change that interacts with a sense organ—vision, hearing, taste, smell, and touch.

stimulus-response: the basic unit of learning (habit) in both the classical and instrumental conditioning models.

stock:

(1) merchandise held for sale (e.g., inventory).

(2) material in inventory.

stock ahead: to maintain sufficient quantities of goods in inventory to cover an anticipated surge in future demand for the items.

stock control: regulating inventory levels so that stock on hand is balanced between demand and production ability.

stock cover: the ratio of current average weekly sales to current stock, providing information on the quantity remaining in stock before new items need to be ordered.

stock depth: merchandise determined to be needed to maintain assortments without too many lost sales because of an out-of-stock situation. See *stockout.*

stocking allowance: a special allowance by a manufacturer to encourage distributor organizations to carry a particular product.

stocking representative: a manufacturer's representative carrying an inventory for his or her principal, which is then shipped for the principal from that inventory.

stock in trade: the business activity usually carried on by a firm.

stockless purchasing: purchasing where financial responsibility for stock lies with the vendor. See *systems contracting.*

stock levels: the inventory carried by a business firm.

stockout: a condition that occurs when all inventory has been used or sold. Stockouts are very costly, as other inputs must then be utilized. See *stock depth.*

stockroom supervisor: synonymous with *materials controller; tool-crib supervisor.*

stock rotation: putting new incoming products behind those of the same kind already on the shelf, so that inventory remains fresh. See *shelf life.*

stock-sales ratio: the inventory retail value at the beginning of a given month, divided by sales for that month. This relationship is used to control the sales and inventory balance.

stock shortage: a condition that occurs when the dollar value of the real inventory in stock is less than that shown on the inventory books.

stock spotting: in warehousing, where items are warehoused close to the customer instead of near the factory of production so as to lower delivery time and transportation expenses.

stock-to-sale method: the determination of inventory levels from planned sales for a given month. The ratio of stock to sales of the same month in the prior year is used as a guide for the plan in the following year.

stock-turn: in retailing, synonymous with *turnover.*

stop and hold: the record status of an inactive customer; used when merchandise is undeliverable or when a cessation of service to the customer is needed.

storage: the holding of goods for future use.

store: any place where merchandise, goods, or services can be purchased, or placed for storage. See *department store; specialty store.*

store audit: a count of the merchandise carried and sold in a retail outlet.

store brand: a brand whose copyright is owned by the retailer, though the item may have been prepared for the store by a supplier. Usually the latter applies and a store label is affixed to the item.

storecast: a radio broadcast appearing in a store. Retailers using a storecast place loudspeakers around their store to receive musical programs as well as merchandise-related messages.

store check: a study of items in a store by nonsales personnel whose primary responsibilities and duties include running in-field examinations to determine how effectively merchandise is displayed, how

the sales force sells items, and how well the merchandise is indeed selling.

store count distribution: a measure of distribution based on the number of stores. A product sold in 90 percent of all grocery stores would have 90 percent store count distribution.

store image: the image of a store as perceived by customers or prospects.

store redeemable coupon: a merchandise discount certificate that is redeemed in any retail outlet where the item is sold, as contrasted with a certificate that can only be redeemed through the mail.

stores: plural of store.

stores requisition: the form for securing materials that are held in normal stock. It goes directly to the stores department from which materials are then supplied for use. See *requisition.*

store traffic: the number of customers coming and going in a store.

storyboard: see *storyline format.*

storyline format: a form of advertising where a story begins and presents the product or in some fashion relates its history to some present-day useful activity.

straight commission: compensation for sales that is limited to a fixed percentage of the salesperson's total sales. Cf. *straight salary.*

straight extension: an international product-planning strategy in which a company makes and markets the same products for domestic and foreign sales.

straight rebuy:
(1) a purchasing situation in which the organization has bought the item or

service before and is likely to reorder from the same vendor.

(2) an undramatic repurchase of an item previously bought. See *modified rebuy; new-task purchasing.*

straight-rebuy purchase process: see *straight rebuy.*

straight salary: compensation for a salesperson based on a fixed rate and at regular intervals, independent of performance considerations. Cf. *straight commission.*

strategic alliance: synonymous with *joint venture.*

strategic business units (SBUs):
(1) divisions composed of key businesses within multiproduct companies, with specific managers, resources, objectives, and competitors. SBUs may encompass a division, a product line, or a single product.

(2) one or more products, brands, divisions, or market segments that have something in common, such as the same distribution system. Each SBU has its own mission, it own set of competitors, and its own strategic plan.

strategic clusters: a means of identifying competitors by the grouping of international firms of overlapping activities within geographic proximity to their primary customers and to their supply networks.

strategic information scanning system: a formal structure of people, equipment, and procedures to obtain and manage information to support strategic decision making.

strategic marketing: a method for improving the customer orientation of a store or company. The correlation between marketing activities and strategic planning activities is measured, thus indicating the percentage of a firm's budget.

strategic plan: a long-term plan covering 3, 5, or sometimes 10 years. See *strategic planning.*

strategic planning:
(1) a basic type of planning by which a firm formulates its long-range goals and selects activities for achieving those goals. Decisions include whether to enter a new untapped market, to grow an existing market, to dominate an existing market, or to dominate a small segment of an existing market by replacing competitors or by satisfying an unmet desire.

(2) the process of developing a long-range plan designed to match the organization's strengths and weaknesses with the threats and opportunities in its environment. See *planning.*

strategic planning gap: the difference between the present position of a company and its desired future position.

strategic resource monopoly: an organization that has a monopoly by virtue of controlling a vital input to a production process (e.g., DeBeers of South Africa owns most of the world's diamond mines).

strategic window: the time period (when the window is open) when a firm's abilities to produce items in demand by the public are matched with sales. When the firm waits too long to act appropriately (when the window closes), the firm may have lost its marketing opportunity.

strategy: guidelines for making directional decisions that influence an organization's long-run performance. See *market strategy.*

stratified random sampling: probability sampling in which the total population is divided into subgroups, or strata, and a random sample is chosen from each subgroup. See *sampling*.

stratified sample: see *stratified random sampling*.

stratifying the market: determining the number of consumers who may purchase the item or service at various price levels.

strict liability: an extreme variant of product liability (in common practice today) in which the producer is held responsible for not putting a defective product on the market. Under strict liability, there need be no negligence, the sale no longer has to be direct from producer to user (privity of contract), and no disclaimer statement relieves the producer of this responsibility.

strip center: an uncovered shopping center as contrasted with an enclosed mall.

stripped-down price: an item offered for sale at a low price because it has no extra features. On visiting the store, the customer finds that the item contains fewer features than he or she originally thought (e.g., a stripped-down car has no air-conditioning or stereo).

strip programming: synonymous with *across-the-board*.

strong market: a market that has a greater demand for purchasing than for selling.

structural inflation: increasing prices caused by an uneven upward demand or cost pressures in a key industry, even when total demand remains in balance with total supply for the economy as a whole.

structured question: a question that limits respondents to a specific set of replies.

stuff: (slang) to sell goods that are not genuine or have been stolen.

stuffer: synonymous with *newspaper stuffer*.

stuffing: loading cargo or goods into a container or envelope.

style:
(1) a characteristic or distinctive method of expression, presentation, or conception in the field of some art.

(2) a particular design.

style modification: the alteration of a product to present a new image or to differentiate it from other brands that perform a similar activity or service.

style obsolescence: obsolescence that occurs when the physical appearance of a product is changed to make existing versions seem out of date.

style-out: to identify the characteristics of specific items that attract customers by separating the fast-moving products from the slow-moving products; the researcher then studies the fast-moving products to uncover the common features that may explain the greater sales.

subcaption: synonymous with *subheadline*.

subculture: a small cultural group within a society that reflects geographic, religious, or ethnic differences; important in analyzing consumer behavior since subculture members tend to display similar preferences for a variety of items and services, such as food, art, recreation, and politics. Subcultures represent a distinct market segment. However, stereotyping creates a bias as dissimilar features also exist. See *market segmentation; target marketing.*

subhead: see *subheadline.*

subheadline: a restatement of the idea of interest to a newspaper reader in a different and direct fashion than appears within the headline. Usually a subheadline is set in a smaller type than the headline but is larger in type than the type used in the text of the body. Synonymous with *subcaption.*

subject bid: a bid that is negotiable, rather than firm.

subjective method: used by consumer and marketing analysts; a forecasting method based on the subjective opinions of people who are knowledgeable about the field for which the forecast is being made.

subjective price: a consumer's perception of the price of a good or service as being high, fair, or low.

subliminal advertising: the delivery of a message below a receiver's awareness level, to be registered subconsciously. The receivers do not realize that they have seen or heard these messages, by which advertisers attempt to promote sales of a product or service. Since the 1960s, subliminal advertising has not been used on television as it has been declared illegal. See *hidden persuader; supraliminal awareness.*

subliminal awareness: see *subliminal advertising.*

submarginal: yielding less than enough to cover the cost of production.

submarket: a portion of the market separated on the basis of common motivations. See *segmentation.*

suboptimization: operating at a less-than-optimal level in one segment of a firm to optimize the functioning of the organization as a whole.

subordinate product advertising: advertising carried out to encourage consumer demand for the producer of a product that has utility, in part or whole, as a component of another item (e.g., shoelaces for shoes). Synonymous with *end-product advertising.*

subscriber: one who agrees in writing to purchase a certain offering.

subscription: a contractual agreement between a buyer and a seller to provide the buyers with a service or item to be delivered as stated in a contract or agreement at the total price based on the length of the service to be rendered. Discounts are often employed with new or long-term subscribers, but not for renewed customers.

subset: used by market analysts; a group of items that is contained in a larger grouping of items.

subsidiary: an organization whose voting stock is more than 50 percent owned by another firm.

subsidies: see *subsidy.*

subsidy:

(1) *United States:* impacts cost to marketers; federal payments to an individual or organization for which the government receives no products or services. The primary objective of a subsidy is to allow for production of the goods at prices that will attract buyers.

(2) *international:* financial encouragements provided, usually by a government to support businesses. Such subsidies can take the form of lower taxes, tax rebates, or direct payments. There are two general types:

(a) *export subsidy*—a benefit conferred on a firm by the government that is contingent on exports.

(b) *domestic subsidy*—a benefit not linked to exports, conferred by the government on a specific industry or enterprise, or group of industries or enterprises; it affects the profits of marketers.

substandard: conditions that make a risk less desirable than normal for its class.

substantiation: a consumer-protection legal concept that requires a firm to prove all the claims it makes in promotion messages. This means thorough testing and evidence of performance are needed prior to making claims.

substitute goods: items that can easily replace one another either in production or in consumption (e.g., natural and synthetic fibers, strawberries and raspberries). An increase in the price of one substitute good encourages purchase of the other(s).

substitution law: the economic statement that if one product or service can be a replacement of another, the prices of the two must be very close.

suggested retail price: though not mandatory, the list price of merchandise as stated by the manufacturer as a fair price to be charged by the retailer. Manufacturers hope and expect that stores maintain a price close to their suggested retail price. Cf. *discount.*

suggestion selling: see *suggestive selling.*

suggestive selling: the strategy of suggesting to a potential purchaser that he or she might have an additional need related to what has already been purchased (e.g., suggesting that a women who has bought a dress also select appropriate shoes or a sweater). Cf. *derived demand.* See *complementary products.*

sumptuary laws: laws that attempt to minimize the consumption of items believed to be harmful to individuals or to society in general. Cf. *public consumption monopoly.*

sunk cost:

(1) *general:* a cost that has already been incurred and is now irrelevant to the decision-making process.

(2) *marketing:* a cost that represents expenses already incurred in the development of a new product; they have been written off, involve no capital asset, and have no anticipated salvage value. For purposes of net present value, sunk costs are ignored. After the project is over, an overall recap will include all costs, whenever spent.

superior goods: products and services that are demanded in larger quantities as incomes rise (e.g., expensive cars, caviar, fur coats).

superdeductive method:

(1) a U.S. Customs procedure in determining the deductive value of merchandise for assessment of ad valorem duties.

(2) affecting marketers' costs; an alternative valuation method that allows a deduction from the value of the items for duty purposes of the cost of further processing within the United States prior to

sale to the ultimate buyer. Synonymous with *further processing method.*

superette: synonymous with *bantam store.*

superior good: synonymous with *normal good.*

supermarket: a retail operation, having at least eight employees, occupying approximately 25,000 square feet, that sells food and nonfood items. Cf. *bantam store.* See *superstore.*

superstore: a combination of a general-merchandise discount operation and a supermarket; usually ranges in size from 50,000 square feet to 200,000 square feet. Established to fulfill all consumer needs for every type of food and nonfood-household item purchased on a regular basis. Cf. *shopping center.* See *supermarket.*

supplement: an added newspaper section that enhances the content and prestige of a newspaper and allows advertisers in the supplement the ability of reaching a mass audience, especially if the newspaper is national.

Supplemental Register: a classification of trademarks established by the Trade-Mark Act of 1946 that includes certain qualified marks.

supplier: a firm that provides goods used in the manufacturing process but not incorporated into the item itself.

supplier-active: a new product development process. The manufacturer studies customers to obtain information that is then analyzed and eventually developed into a new product.

supplier/distribution intermediary contract: a contract that focuses on price policies, conditions of sale, territorial rights, the services/responsibility mix, and contract length and conditions of termination.

supply: the quantity of items available for sale. See *Say's law.*

supply and demand: a theory relating to the amount of product to be placed on the market over a time period (supply) and the number of the product units to be sold within that same time frame (demand). It is used by marketers in setting a marketing strategy, since supply and demand patterns affect product pricing (e.g., when supply of an item is low and demand for it is high, prices can be set at higher levels, and vice versa). See *demand states.*

supply curve: a graphic representation of the quantity of output supplied as a function of price. See *excess supply curve.*

supply price: the lowest price needed to produce a specified output. It is the lowest price a seller will accept for the act of supplying a given quantity of a commodity.

supply schedule: a table of prices and corresponding quantities offered for sale in a given period.

supporting the market: placing purchasing orders at or somewhat below the prevailing market level to maintain and balance existing prices and to encourage a price rise.

supportive service: in marketing; a benefit or service (e.g., extending credit) that contributes to an item's attractiveness to a consumer.

support level: the point at which demand for a product or service is reached. It is the moment when the resistance level is overcome.

supraliminal awareness: the detection of stimuli by a person on the conscious level. See *subliminal advertising*.

supramarginal: yielding more than the cost of production.

surcharge: a charge above the usual or customary charge.

surface changes: shifts in consumer preferences and interests that direct spending patterns from one activity to another without signaling a basic change in fundamental cultural values.

surplus: anything remaining or left over.

surrogate positioning: product positioning that eschews a product's features and benefits, turning instead to 1 of perhaps 8 or 10 substitutes, or surrogates. The two most popular surrogates are *nonpareil* (our product is simply the best available, no features or benefits cited) and *parentage* (our product is good because it was designed by the designers or producers of product *X*). Cf. *surrogate question*.

surrogate question: any question to which the answer can yield an answer to another question that cannot be answered at this time, if ever. For example, if the key question is "What retaliation will our chief competitor offer to our new product?" a surrogate question that can be answered would be "What retaliation did that competitor offer to its most recent serious competitive threat?" Cf. *surrogate positioning*.

survey: a unique inquiry using a sample as a database for each new study.

survey approach: a research method in which researchers use personal interviews, telephone interviews, or mailed questionnaires to question a group of people directly.

survey area: the geographic area represented by a sample group or that found in a radio/television market.

survey-feedback activities: activities that focus on collecting survey data and designing a plan of action based on the interpretation of the data.

survey of buying power: a detailed demographic, geographic statistical study of consumer power to purchase goods of various types.

survey research: research to provide descriptive data about a marketing problem or situation, often by purporting to gain insight into buying behavior of prospects and existing customers.

suspend: see *stop and hold*.

sustainer: see *sustaining program*.

sustaining program: an unsponsored broadcast program on radio or television, where the station or network covers the cost of preparing and broadcasting the program. Cf. *sponsor*.

swap: to exchange or barter. Cf. *exchange (3)*.

sweeps: the month-long time period when the audience size of network television time slots is determined. Its results set advertising rates for local stations. Consequently, networks air popular shows and films to attract the widest possible audience because the larger the viewing audience, the higher the rates that can be charged.

sweepstake: a sales promotion method where participants compete for awards by merely entering the contest. No skill or strategy on the part of the participant is required. A contestant merely submits an entry form with his or her name and address. Cf. *contest.*

swell allowance: a reduction from invoice cost to provide for the loss of item value due to damage in shipping.

switching customers: bringing in a sales specialist when the salesperson who originally served a customer is unable to close a sale.

switch selling: an unethical practice of using high-pressure tactics to sell an item that is more expensive than one advertised at a lower price. See *bait-and-switch advertising.*

SWOT analysis: *s*trengths, *w*eakness, *o*pportunities, and *t*hreats that are part of strategic marketing planning; used for forecasting by comparing present and future information.

symbiotic marketing: a form of marketing in which a company sells and promotes a product made or controlled by another firm. Cf. *pooled marketing.*

symbol:
(1) a representation of characteristics or transformations of ideas or things. See *perception.*
(2) the single capital letter or combination of letters acquired by a corporation listed on an exchange (e.g., IBM for International Business Machines).

symbolic pricing: using price to create an impression about a product or a brand in the minds of consumers.

symmetrical balance: synonymous with *formal balance.*

syndicate:
(1) *general:* the association of two or more individuals, established to carry out a business activity. Members share in all profits or losses in proportion to their contribution to the resources of the syndicate.

(2) *broadcasting:* to sell or distribute a program to one or more local stations.

(3) *advertising:* a group of newspapers forming a chain, owned or managed by the same person or organization.

(4) *newspapers:* a group of newspapers owned by the same company. See *syndication.*

syndicated research: research based on samples or from panels of people, where all or part of the same results are supplied to different users.

syndicated service: a research firm that periodically compiles specific types of data for sale to marketers. Cf. *specialty-line market research firm.*

syndication: the sale or distribution of radio and television programming to local stations by the owner of that programming. Broadcast syndication falls into two categories:
(a) *first-run syndication*—the distribution of original programs that were produced specifically for the syndication market, such as films and specials.

(b) *off-network syndication*—the distribution to local stations of shows that previously aired in prime time on network television (e.g., *I Love Lucy* reruns). See *syndicate.*

syndicator:
(1) a company that supplies products and associated brochures, envelopes, and other materials.

(2) people who sell merchandise via the mail. See *bangtail.*

synectics: like brainstorming, an idea-generating method where discussion evolves from an idea related to a problem, rather than the problem by itself. Used by advertisers and advertising agencies when preparing a campaign. Four concepts are used: (a) the identification of a particular leader; (b) knowledge of a common understanding of the situation, issue, or problem; (c) a common acceptance that all ideas contain some merit; and (d) the importance of equality from participants in the sharing of ideas and suggestions. Cf. *brainstorming.* See *idea generation.*

synergy: the feature of a system whereby, when the parts are properly interrelated and functioning, an output is achieved that is greater than or superior to the effects obtained when the parts function independently.

system:
(1) any purposeful organization of resources.

(2) an assembly of methods, procedures, or techniques united by regulated interaction to form an organized whole.

systematic error: the result of a relatively predictable tendency toward error when making a judgment.

systems analysis: the analysis of business activity to determine precisely what must be accomplished and how to accomplish it.

systems buying/selling:
(1) purchasing or selling of a multifaceted product or service. Firms that participate in systems buying do not choose to make different buying decisions when purchasing a complex item, such as a telecommunications network. Instead of coordinating their efforts with multiple groups or vendors, they prefer to deal with one contractor who is fully responsible for the bidding and assembling of subcontractors to provide the complete package.

(2) firms that provide systems selling market the capability to assemble all the items and services required by the purchaser.

systems completing product: a product that makes available to a large population an already accepted and used technology.

systems contracting: buying that permits little or no stock to be handled by the purchaser. The purchase agreement is based on a catalog furnished by the supplier for the agreed-on item. This method can benefit both the supplier and the purchaser. Cf. *systems selling.* See *blanket order; stockless purchasing.*

systems design: the formulation and graphic outlining of the nature and content of input, files, procedures, and output to display the necessary connection processes and procedures.

systems selling: the merchandising of a group of items with some functional relationship to one another as a package, rather than as single items (e.g., matching tie-and-handkerchief sets). Cf. *systems contracting.* See *sales analysis; systems buying/selling.*

table: in marketing research; a statement of factual information, usually assembled for reference purposes.

tabloid: a publication that resembles a magazine, but is actually a newspaper with a page size smaller than that of the standard newspaper.

tabloid inserts: separate, preprinted supplements of advertisements found inside newspapers, usually on weekend editions.

tactical planning: a short-term plan that specifies the activities necessary to carry out a strategic plan. See *planning.*

tactical product-line adjustment: the determination of the number of variations of any given item that is offered.

tactics: efforts to execute the strategies outlined within a marketing plan; steps for manipulating the context in which an item is sold.

tag:

(1) *merchandising:* see *Kimball tags.*

(2) *broadcasting:* an addition to a commercial broadcast (e.g., a voiceover message following a transcribed statement, an announcement or insertion of music serving as a conclusion).

tag line: see *tag (2).*

tailor-made:

(1) just right.

(2) made according to individual specifications.

take: (slang) in retailing, the funds in the cash register of a retail store at the close of a business day.

take-and-pay contract: a guarantee to purchase an agreed amount of a product or service, provided it is delivered. Cf. *tale-or-pay contract.*

take-home pay: synonymous with *spendable earnings.*

take-one: a print advertisement featuring coupons, refund blanks, or contest entry forms in a pad or pocket affixed to the advertisement. It carries an extra charge to the advertiser for maintenance services.

takeover time: the time required in marketing for a superior new product to go from 10 to 90 percent displacement of an inferior older product.

take stock: to make an inventory of items on hand.

take-withs: synonymous with *carryouts.*

taking inventory: the procedure of counting all stock on hand at a time set aside for this purpose. Cf. *unit control.*

tale-or-pay contract: an unconditional guarantee to purchase an agreed amount of the product or service whether or not it is delivered. Cf. *take-and-pay contract.*

talon: a special coupon (e.g., a voucher stub).

tame cat distributor: a wholesaler owned and controlled by a manufacturer.

tamperproof container: a container designed so that it cannot be opened and resealed without leaving evidence of tampering.

tangible assets: physical and material (perceptible to touch) assets (e.g., cash, land, buildings), as distinguished from intangible assets, which are imperceptible to touch.

tangible product: a basic physical entity, service, or idea; with precise specifications and offered under a given description or model number.

tape plan: a promotional strategy, usually run by supermarkets, offering premiums in return for cash register tapes totaling a specified amount. Synonymous with *cash-register-tape redemption plan.*

tare: an unproductive weight; an amount that is part of the gross weight of an article (e.g., the weight of a truck, a package, or any other container or vehicle). Net weight is gross weight less the tare.

target:
(1) the one to whom a selling message is addressed.
(2) a market where a selling effort is made. See *target audience.*
(3) the marketing goal toward which organizational resources are directed.

target audience: that portion of the population to which marketing efforts and advertising are directed; defined in terms of geographic, demographic, and/or psychographic factors. Used by marketers to develop promotional activities. Cf. *market target.* Synonymous with *audience (2); target market.* See *market segmentation; target marketing.*

target customers: the people who are the objects of a store's total efforts to attract business. Cf. *market target.*

target market: synonymous with *target audience.*

target marketing: a process in which the marketer evaluates a number of market segments, decides which one or ones to serve, and develops and implements a unique marketing mix for the targeted segment(s). The three target marketing steps are:
(a) market segmentation—the firm defines its market segments based on factors of geography, demographics, etc.
(b) market targeting—the firm decides which of the market segments to follow by assessing the potential profit for each segment, then setting a market coverage tactic.
(c) positioning—the firm makes decisions on how to present the merchandise offerings so as to make them more attractive to consumers than those of competitors. See *subculture; target audience.*

target marketing strategy: see *target marketing.*

target population: the population from which a sample is taken.

target pricing: a technique of establishing prices to reach a profit objective.

target return on investment: an amount of income equivalent to a certain percentage of the firm's investment; this amount is set as a goal to be achieved through pricing. See *target return pricing.*

target return pricing: setting a product's price to yield a specific return on investment using the formula:

$$\frac{\text{target return}}{\text{price}} = \frac{\text{unit}}{\text{cost}} + \frac{\text{desired} \times \text{invested}}{\text{return} \quad \text{capital}}{\text{unit sales}}$$

See *target return on investment.*

tariff:
(1) any list of prices, charges, duties, etc.

(2) a schedule of taxes on items imported or exported. In the United States, tariffs are imposed on imported goods only.

tariff bindings: of importance to global marketers; the agreement by contracting parties to maintain the duty rates on specified goods at negotiated levels or below.

tariff escalation: the common situation whereby raw materials and less processed goods generally have lower duties than more processed versions of the same or derivative goods. For instance, the import duty in most countries is generally higher for petrochemicals than for the petroleum and other raw materials necessary for their production. It is argued by primary commodity exporting nations that this situation confers a higher degree of protection for the processing industries of importing countries than nominal tariff rates would suggest.

tariffication: of importance to global marketers; to convert quotas and other restrictions to tariffs that would be reduced over time. For example, nations with strict import controls would start with prohibitive tariffs of several hundred percent. Tariffication includes provisions to guarantee a minimum level of imports at reduced tariff rates. Its intent is to permit high tariffs to shrink over a period of time and thus have a minimum tariff quota expanded. Synonymous with *tariffy.*

tariff rate: the charge rate or schedule established by the rating organization that has jurisdiction over a given class and territory (e.g., a schedule of freight rates for transporting different items to various cities).

tariff war: a form of competition between nations as evidenced by tariff discrimination of various forms.

tariffy: synonymous with *tariffication.*

task force: a team of individuals, often representing various departments or interests, with responsibility for coordinating a study or other efforts that involve a number of organizational units.

task interdependency: the extent to which two or more groups or individuals rely on each other for services, information, and goods to accomplish their own goals.

task method: a means of arriving at an advertising budget by setting a sales objective and then deciding the cost of reaching that objective through advertising. Synonymous with *plunge method.*

tastemakers: those who are the first to adopt product innovations, recognizing their influence on followers.

tax-and-board: charges included in premiums (almost always percentages of the paid premium) for state or local taxes and for the support of various rating offices, bureaus, and boards.

taxpayer:

(1) a small building or store.

(2) a person who pays taxes.

(3) an owner of property who pays taxes.

team: that group of persons serving as on-site managers for a new products program. Each team member represents a function, department, or specialty, and together they form the management for that product. Team members may work full-time or part-time, and persons may move on and off a team depending on the continuing need for their specialty.

team selling: a selling technique using several salespeople, especially with highly technical or complex products since no one person could be expert in all the features of the offering. See *systems buying/selling.*

tear sheet: a page bearing an advertisement to appear in a publication that is sent to the advertiser for purposes of proofing. Usually the tear sheet accompanies an invoice for the advertisement, as many advertisers will not pay their bill without evidence that the advertisement ran as ordered. See *checking copy.*

teaser advertisement: an advertisement that purports to increase curiosity by holding back the name of the advertiser or the product but pledging additional data in future statements. These advertisements are the front-running of an advertising program.

teaser ad: see *teaser advertisement.*

technical approval: a favorable technical assessment of a product's fitness for use for a particular purpose, based on its meeting the specific requirements.

technical barrier to trade: a specification that sets forth characteristics a product must meet (such as levels of quality, performance, safety, or dimensions) to be imported.

technical level: a low organizational level that is concerned primarily with the production and distribution of goods and services.

technical managers: low-level managers who are concerned with turning out goods and services as economically as possible. These managers tend to have an engineering point of view.

technical regulation: a document that lays down goods characteristics or their related processes and production methods, or services characteristics or their related operating methods, including the applicable administrative provisions, with which compliance is mandatory. It may also include or deal exclusively with terminology, symbols, packaging, marking, or labeling requirements as they apply to a good, process, or production or operating method. Cf. *technical specification.*

technical salesperson: synonymous with *sales engineer.*

technical specification: a written statement of a good's characteristics or their related processes and production methods, or services characteristics or their related operating methods, including the applicable administrative provisions. It may also include or deal exclusively with terminology, symbols, packaging, marking or labeling requirements as they apply to a good, process, or production or operating method. Cf. *technical regulation.*

technological obsolescence: obsolescence that results when technological improvements are made in a product.

technology driven: a new products strategy or operation based on the strength of a technology; yields new products, which are then offered to the market. Market driven is the alternative form of thrust. Dual drive uses both at the same time and is the preferred form today. See *dual drive.*

telemarketing:
(1) product and services sales using the telephone; carried out at both consumer and industrial levels of the marketplace. Such calls interrupt the consumer by

requesting immediate attention and are not identifiable as a promotion before the consumer has been interrupted, thereby sometimes leading to an antagonized prospect. Cf. *teleshopping*.

(2) sales of items and services via an interactive system or two-way television. Prospects are often preselected (e.g., current or prior customers or likely prospects selected from a rented list).

(3) synonymous with *teleselling*.

telephone agency: a firm that makes and/or receives telemarketing calls for another organization or person.

telephone coincidental method: a preselected sample of people who are called during the running of a television program and asked questions about their reaction to the program, how many people are watching it, etc.; the most popular form of audience research.

telephone interview: a survey technique in which respondents are questioned by telephone.

telephone retailing: selling by telephone at the retail level, usually to the consumer. See *telemarketing; teleshopping*.

teleselling: synonymous with *telemarketing*.

teleshopping: using a telephone to purchase products or services that have been seen in advertisements, or on radio and television. Toll-free 800-numbers are frequently employed to encourage responses. Cf. *telemarketing*.

television home: a home with one or more television sets; becomes the basic unit of measurement in determining the size of a program's audience. Synonymous with *television household*.

television household: synonymous with *television home*.

television ratings: see *rating (3)*.

television support: a television advertisement that plays a secondary role in a multimedia promotion, such as by informing the viewer that a supplement will appear in tomorrow's newspaper.

temporary employees: nonpermanent members of an organization's work force, often hired to do clerical or sales work. Such employment is often used during busy retail store seasons.

tender: to offer money in satisfaction of a debt by producing the money and stating to the creditor a desire to pay.

tension concept: a theory of consumer behavior stating that when a need has not been satisfied adequately, a condition of stress develops leading the person to seek equilibrium by searching for and finding an appropriate satisfaction.

tent card: a card used for the display of an advertisement; imprinted and folded to be read on either side of the fold that stands freely.

term:
(1) the prescribed time a person has to make installment or other payments as identified in a loan or credit contract.

(2) the duration of an agreement, subscription, etc.

terms of sale: identification of a vendor's given time to pay an invoice, any discounts offered, and other conditions of the sale. Synonymous with *sales terms*.

terms of trade: the number of units of items that must be surrendered for one unit of goods obtained by a group or nation that is a party to a transaction.

territorial departmentalization: organization of a department according to geographic location (e.g., a company with four major divisions: eastern, midwestern, western, and foreign).

territorial franchise: see *territorial rights*.

territorial potential: the full potential demand for a particular item within a defined area of territory.

territorial rights: an agreement between a supplier and a distributor that grants the distributor the exclusive right to develop the potential demand in a geographic area.

territory: synonymous with *sales territory*.

territory screening: synonymous with *canvass (2)*.

territory-structured sales force: a sales force organization that assigns each person an exclusive geographic area. It provides the salesperson with a clear knowledge of his or her responsibility; it increases the salesperson's chances for evolving closer relationships with prospects, customers, and local businesspeople; and it saves on travel costs. Cf. *market-structured sales force; product-structured sales force*. See *sales force*.

test:

(1) *general:* any instrument to identify a person's behavior or skills in a host of areas.

(2) *advertising:* the introduction of a new product or campaign on a small scale to determine consumer response; it includes decisions regarding where to test, how long to test, and what to do in response to test results.

testimonial:

(1) *general:* a statement by a satisfied customer praising a product or service that is used in advertising or sales promotion to influence others. Cf. *blurb*.

(2) *advertising:* an advertising message that is presented by someone who is viewed as an expert on the subject.

testimonial advertising: see *celebrity testimonial; testimonial (2)*.

testing:

(1) the determination at relatively low cost, before insertion of an advertisement or the running of a campaign, of the probable performance of a product, copy, appeal, price, proposition, illustration, medium, or other element.

(2) the determination of the success or effectiveness of an advertisement or campaign after it has been run.

test instrument: any approach used for eliciting data for hypothesis testing in marketing research (e.g., a questionnaire, psychological test).

test market: see *test marketing*.

test marketing:

(1) trial distribution of a new product in a small market to determine its likely acceptance in the total market. Cf. *market fit*.

(2) the controlled introduction of a new product to carefully selected markets for the purpose of testing market acceptance and predicting future sales of the product in that region. See *market fit; market testing; product testing*.

test panel: synonymous with *panel (1)*.

text: in advertising, synonymous with *body copy.*

Textile Products Identification Act: federal legislation requiring that sellers of yarns and fabrics and household items made from natural or synthetic fibers other than wool, attach labels to the items indicating the percentage by weight of each fiber they contain and to list the fibers by generic name set by the Federal Trade Commission.

TF: see *till forbid.*

theme: the major idea of an advertising campaign.

thin market: a market in which there are comparatively few bids to buy or offers to sell, or both. The term may apply to a single item or to multiple items.

third cover: synonymous with *inside back cover.*

third-party sale: a sale by an agency serving as the intermediary between a buyer and a seller.

thirds: goods of extremely poor quality, lower in grade than seconds. Cf. *seconds.*

thirty: a symbol used in the news field to indicate the end of a broadcast or article; written as -30-.

thirty-three: (slang) a potential customer who refuses to make a purchase from one salesperson and is then turned over to another.

three B's: see *Better Business Bureau.*

three C's of credit: used to determine whether a person's credit is acceptable; character—indicates determination to pay; capacity—measures ability to pay; and capital—represents a person's financial resources or net worth.

three-level channel: a marketing channel where there are three distinct levels of distribution between the manufacturer and the consumer (e.g., an agent, a distributor, and a retailer).

three-sheet: an advertising circular, brochure, or handbill.

threshold companies: firms on the threshold of corporate maturity in that they are not yet managed by professionals but are run intuitively by a handful of entrepreneurs.

threshold level of expenditures: the lowest amount a company must spend to participate in a market and receive sales from that market.

throughput: the distribution of merchandise via dealers and on to the consumer.

throughput agreement: an agreement to put a stated amount of merchandise through a production facility in an agreed time period, or if not, to pay for the availability of the facility.

throwaways: synonymous with *handbill.*

thumbnail: synonymous with *esquisse.*

tickler file: a follow-up diary or folder containing memos, letters, and so on, ordered by future dates and pulled periodically for review and action.

tie-in advertisement: an advertisement paid for by the retailer who sponsors it, relating to other forms of advertising, such as an ad carried by a retail store in conjunction with the manufacturer's advertisement for an item carried in that store. It can also be for several different items, from different manufacturers, that tie in with a local sales promotion. See *cross-promote; tie-in sales.*

tie-in promotion: marketing displays and approaches that connect with an active advertising campaign to create immediate sales, assist in introducing merchandise, or enhance the advertising program. Synonymous with *cross-promotion.*

tie-in sales: sales that are limited so a buyer cannot purchase one product or service without purchasing something else from the same manufacturer. The Clayton Antitrust Act of 1914 made this practice illegal in interstate commerce. See *tie-in advertisement; tying agreement.*

tight market: synonymous with *seller's market.*

till forbid (TF):

(1) instructions to continue using an advertisement until told otherwise.

(2) a standing order for goods or services, such as a request to run an advertisement in a time period, until told to stop running it.

time budgeting of purchase: the purchase of small units of items over short periods to even out changes in prices of merchandise. This will assure that the firm's average price for each product will approximate the true average for the period. However, it tends to increase the total cost of purchasing.

time buyer: an executive in an advertising agency who assists in the planning of media campaigns, and chooses and buys radio and television time. Cf. *media buyer; space buyer.*

time clearance: in broadcasting, setting aside a specific time period.

time discount: a reduction in an advertising rate determined by the frequency of appearance of an advertisement. Cf. *transient rate.*

time expenditures: the time a person allocates for participation in various activities.

time order: an order that becomes a market or limited price order at a specified time.

time rate of demand: the quantity of an item that the market can absorb at a given price over a specified time.

time-series forecast: a method of forecasting in which historical trends are projected into the future.

time slot: in broadcasting, synonymous with *spot.*

time utility:

(1) the satisfaction that buyers receive from having a product or service available at the appropriate time.

(2) a feature of an item making it feasible to satisfy a desire or want based on time preference. Storage creates time utility. See *utility.*

tinge: (slang) a salesperson who specializes in the sale of undesirable merchandise to earn bonus payments.

tip-in: an insert placed within a publication, such as an extra page of advertising. A tip-in, as contrasted with a tip-on, becomes an integral part of the bound product, requiring more complex application devices. Cf. *tip-on.*

tip-on: an item attached with glue or a glue stripping, to a promotional piece or advertisement in a printed publication. A tip-on is not considered an integral part of the bound material. Cf. *tip-in.*

tipping: the process of attaching a tip-on or tip-in to printed material.

tire kickers: (slang) inspectors or troubleshooters who are assigned to closely examine a project, item, or service for defects, flaws, or inadequacies.

title: proper and rightful ownership.

title flows: the path of the title to or ownership of products as they flow through channels of distribution.

token order:

(1) a small order placed to assess the desirability of an item.

(2) a small order placed as a means of getting rid of a bothersome salesperson.

tombstone advertisement:

(1) a solemn-appearing advertisement, often only listing the item with the names of sources of supply. Such an advertisement is used in financial announcements, including major securities offerings.

(2) a casual reference to an advertisement for a professional or organization that meets legal requirements and regulations imposed on the industry represented in the advertising.

tool-crib supervisor: synonymous with *materials controller.*

top credit: ready credit.

top-down method: in retailing, a budget method where the budgeter commences with a gross amount and follows with specific amounts to designated classifications of merchandise. See *bottom-up technique.*

top management: the top level of an administrative hierarchy. Managers at this level coordinate the work of other managers but do not report to a manager.

top of mind: a description of the brand or product name, or advertising promotion that a respondent recalls in response to a research question.

top out: the peak period of demand for a product or service, after which demand decreases.

total audience: people 12 years of age or older who are targeted for most broadcast advertising. See *audience share.*

total audience plan: synonymous with *package plan.*

total cost: the sum of a firm's total fixed costs and total variable costs.

total-cost approach: an approach that determines the distribution service level with the lowest total costs, including freight (shipping), warehousing, and the cost of lost business. An idea system seeks a balance between low expenditures on distribution and high opportunities for sales.

total fixed costs: the costs that do not change with an organization's output (e.g., payments on rent, property taxes).

total loss: items that have been so badly damaged that they are not worth repairing (e.g., a car that has suffered a head-on collision with a truck, merchandise that has been partially destroyed by fire).

total market approach: synonymous with *undifferentiated marketing.*

total net paid: synonymous with *total paid circulation.*

total paid circulation: the number of people who actually pay for a magazine or other periodical, as opposed to those who see it by other means, such as in a doctor's office or from a friend. Synonymous with *total net paid.* See *controlled circulation.*

total product: the marketing mix of a firm.

total-quality program: the most common rubric for Japanese-inspired efforts to build quality into a product or service as it is produced or performed. Total-quality programs require the active involvement of the line workers themselves, which generally is best achieved via a radical change in corporate culture led by the chief executive.

total revenue: total receipts of a company. It is equal to the price per unit times the number of units sold.

total variable costs: costs that change directly with the firm's output, increasing as output rises over the total range of production (e.g., labor, fuel).

Toxic Substances Control Act of 1976: federal legislation requiring chemical manufacturers to give the Environmental Protection Agency at least three months' notice before beginning commercial production of a new chemical or before marketing an existing chemical for new use. If the EPA sees no risks, the firm may proceed.

traceable costs: common costs that can be assigned to two or more specific functional areas.

tracer: a request to trace a shipment to determine its location, alter instructions, or affect its status.

tracking:
(1) *marketing:* the follow-up to a promotional campaign, either through direct marketing or from an advertisement. It involves the analysis of various elements of the promotion by examining the four stages in the life cycle of a promotion: the early response, halfway-point response, final response, and long-term results.

(2) *merchandising:* monitoring inventory received, ordered, and bought, to maintain optimum levels for future purchases.

tracking variable: a specific variable used to track a specific phenomenon. Distribution can be tracked, for example, by measuring the percentage of outlets that have stocked at least one package.

trade: transactions involving goods and/ or services from profit between legal entities.

trade advertising:
(1) advertising directed at wholesalers or retailers.

(2) consumer-product advertising used for stimulating wholesalers and retailers to buy merchandise for resale to their customers. Cf. *business-to-business advertising; consumer advertising.*

trade allowances: incentives provided by the manufacturer to retailers and other channel intermediaries to stock, display, or promote the manufacturer's goods. See *trade promotion.*

trade association: a nonprofit organization that purports to serve the common interest of its membership. Usually, members of trade associations work in closely related industries.

trade barrier: an artificial restraint on the free exchange of goods and services between countries, usually in the form of tariffs, subsidies, quotas, or exchange controls. See *barriers to competition; barriers to entry.*

trade card: a card used by a retailer to punch in the amount spent by a consumer until a total is reached qualifying the buyer to purchase a premium at a self-liquidating price. Synonymous with *purchase-privilege offer.*

trade channel: synonymous with *channel of distribution.*

trade character: people, objects, animals, or characteristics of animals, etc. used in advertising a brand. Trade characters come to be identified with that brand.

trade creation: the formation of commercial transactions because of the displacement of domestic production by cheaper imports.

trade credit: credit from producers and wholesalers to their customers on a short-term basis.

trade deal: synonymous with *deal (2).*

trade deficit: a negative trade balance. It occurs when a nation's imports are greater in value than its exports. Cf. *trade surplus.*

trade deflection: the entrance of imports into nations that offer the lowest tariffs to avoid the higher tariffs of other member nations in international trade agreements.

trade discount: a deduction from the agreed price, usually expressed as a percentage or a series of percentages. It is used in commerce to encourage prompt payment of bills. Trade discount should not be entered in the books of account, nor should it be considered to be a type of earnings. Synonymous with *functional discount.*

trade down: see *trading down.*

Trade Expansion Act of 1962: federal legislation permitting the President to nego-

tiate additional tariff reductions, eliminate or reduce tariffs on items of the European Union, reduce tariffs on the basis of reciprocal trade agreements, and grant technical and financial assistance to employers whose business is adversely affected by tariff reductions.

trade in: to surrender an old product for a new one, accompanied by additional payment to make up for depreciation of the item traded in.

trade industry: in industrial marketing, wholesalers and retailers, who purchase for resale to others or for use in conducting their own business.

trade magazine: a magazine with editorial content of interest to people engaged in a specific industry, profession, or occupation; provides advertisers with an opportunity to reach highly defined business audiences in both print and by way of the acquisition of mailing lists for direct marketing. Synonymous with *business publication.*

trademark:

(1) a brand that is given legal protection because it has been appropriated exclusively by one marketer.

(2) a distinctive identification of a manufactured product or a service in the form of a name, logo, motto, etc. A trademarked brand has legal protection, and only the owner can use the mark. Organizations that file an application at the U.S. Patent Office and use the brand for five years may be granted a trademark. A firm may lose a trademark that has become generic. Generic names are those that consumers use to identify the product, rather than to specify a particular brand (e.g., escalator, aspirin, nylon). See *Lanham Act of 1947.*

Trade-Mark Act of 1946: federal legislation, known as the Lanham Act, governing the registration of trademarks used in commerce.

trade marketing mix: synonymous with *retailing mix.*

trade name: the name under which an organization conducts business or by which the business or its goods and services are identified. It may or may not be registered as a trademark.

tradeoff: the side effect of an activity that presents disadvantages as well as benefits.

trade paper advertising: the dissemination of sales messages by a manufacturer to retail store owners, distributors, and others engaged in the resale of an advertised product directly to ultimate consumers.

trade preferences: trade concessions, usually preferential tariff treatment, granted by a country to a certain nations but not to others.

trade premium: an incentive, such as vacations, prizes, free merchandise, etc., from a manufacturer to a retailer or wholesaler who achieves a specific level of sales of the manufacturer's merchandise. See *premium.*

trade price: the manufacturer's price to a middleperson.

trade promotion: sales promotion efforts directed toward retailers and wholesalers offering incentives, such as gifts, price-off discounts, trips, merchandise, etc., to middlepeople who will carry the manufacturer's items or will increase their inventory of the manufacturer. See *advertising allowance; promotion.*

trade quota: a form of trade restriction that sets limits on the amount of goods that can be imported into a country. See *quota.*

trader: anyone engaged in trade or commerce.

trade rate: a special price given to retailers by wholesalers, distributors, or manufacturers.

trade reference: a person or firm to which a seller is referred for credit data on a potential customer.

trade salesperson: a salesperson whose primary duties are promotional, by assisting customers to promote a firm's items or services. They write orders but spend most of their time dealing with established customers.

trade secret: in contrast to getting a patent on an invention, the inventor or firm can simply attempt to keep secret the new aspect of the product. The Coca-Cola formula, for example, is a famous trade secret.

trade show: a meeting of manufacturers and/or wholesalers from a specific industry for the purpose of showing their merchandise; serves to generate new sales leads and to maintain existing customer relations.

trade specialty house: an industrial distributor who serves a specific type of customer, with a full line of items requested by him or her (e.g., barber shop supplies, shoe repair supplies).

trade style: the unique manner in which a firm displays its name in print in advertising and on letterheads.

trade surplus: a positive trade balance. It occurs when the value of a country's exports exceeds the value of its imports. Cf. *trade deficit.*

trade up: see *trading up.*

trading across: altering a store's marketing strategy to try to appeal to a different market segment. Shifting can be very difficult and expensive.

trading area: the region or shopping district whose limits are determined by the costs of delivering merchandise to the area.

trading companies: firms that develop international trade and serve as intermediaries between foreign buyers and domestic sellers, and vice versa.

trading down: attempting to increase the market of a store or item with an established reputation by lowering price or quality or by changing promotional strategy to appeal to a larger potential market, which is frequently in a lower socioeconomic level. By trading down, the image of the item is often sacrificed for gains in profit. Cf. *trading up.* See *social classes; wheel of retailing.*

trading house: a business that specializes in the import and export of items from overseas nations or regions.

trading stamp: a promotional device; a stamp given to customers that is worth a small percentage of the total amount paid for purchases. When a large number of stamps have been accumulated, they can be redeemed at the store or at a warehouse for merchandise. See *box-top offer.*

trading up: attempting to improve the image of a store or item by increasing prices or quality or by altering advertisement approaches, usually to appeal to a market in a higher socioeconomic

level. Cf. *trading down.* See *social classes; wheel of retailing.*

traditional break-even analysis: an assessment to determine the sales quantity in units or dollars needed for total revenues to equal total costs at a given price:

$$\text{break-even point (units)} = \frac{\text{total fixed costs}}{\text{price} - \text{variable costs (per unit)}}$$

$$\text{break-even point (sales dollars)} = \frac{\text{total fixed costs}}{1 - \text{variable costs (per unit) price}}$$

traditional department store: a department store that has a great assortment of goods and services, provides many customer services, is a fashion leader, and often serves as an anchor store in a shopping district or shopping center. See *department store.*

traffic:

(1) *general:* business done by a transportation or communications company.

(2) *merchandising:* the flow of people exposed to a store's goods. Measurement of traffic (counting the people) is usually done as customers enter and leave the store's premises. Cf. *routing.*

traffic appliances: portable appliances, such as toasters, blenders, irons.

traffic builder:

(1) a low-cost premium offered as an inducement to enter a store for a demonstration of a product.

(2) a popular item whose price has been lowered to attract customers to the store or outlet.

traffic count: the estimating of exposure to poster advertising by monitoring the poster as people walk by it.

traffic department: the department that schedules the work responsibilities of other units in an advertising agency and has primary responsibility for ensuring that deadlines are met.

traffic items: consumer products that have a limited life and will in time attract consumers back into a store to purchase new replacement items.

traffic management: the planning, selection, and direction of all means of transportation involved in the movement of goods in the marketing process.

traffic system: a method of advertising agency office management designed to route work from department to department according to a predetermined schedule and to permit the agency to maintain control over the progress of the work at any time.

transaction: any agreement between two or more parties that establishes a legal obligation. Cf. *exchange (3)*.

transactions motive: the holding, by consumers and businesspeople, of some of their assets in liquid form to make possible participation in day-to-day spending activities.

transfer costs: the costs that a department accepts for items supplied by other departments.

transfer impact: a feature of an offering making it possible for that item or service to force a transfer of a consumer's allegiance to the offering source.

transfer price:

(1) raising the price of a product shipped to a foreign affiliate to increase the amount of profit transferred from the affiliate to the parent firm.

(2) the price charged by one segment of an organization for a product or service it supplies to another part of the same firm. See *transfer costs.*

transfer pricing: see *transfer price.*

transient rate:

(1) the fee paid for a single nonrepeated advertisement.

(2) the one-time rate for an advertisement, without quantity or frequency reductions. Cf. *time discount.*

transit advertising: advertising for an audience enroute from one point to another using public transportation, usually a bus or train. It serves a large number of people, within a well-defined geography, and has a high rate of repetition. Synonymous with *transportation advertising.* See *one-sheet poster.*

transition time: synonymous with *fringe time.*

transit privileges: the privilege offered a shipper by a shipping company of unloading merchandise in transit for a future processing, then reloaded and delivered to their destination without additional costs. Synonymous with *milling in transit; processing in transit.*

transportation advertising: synonymous with *transit advertising.*

transportation service companies: marketing specialists that predominantly handle the shipments of small and moderate-sized packages. The three major kinds of service companies are government parcel post, private parcel, and express.

transshipping:

(1) *general:* the transfer of items from one carrier to another.

(2) *salesmanship:* the shipment of merchandise by a dealer or distributor to another dealer or distributor beyond the usual selling area.

traveling sales representative: a salesperson who travels considerably to obtain orders.

tray pack: a point-of-purchase display where the top of the case of goods can be opened and folded back so that the case actually becomes a display tray that is readily placed on a shelf or counter in the store.

trend extension: used by market researchers; the forecasting of sales for an existing item based on previous data information and projecting that information to the future.

Trendex: a research firm that issues statements on the relative popularity of network television programs. Most of the Trendex data are gathered by using the coincidental-telephone approach. See *coincidental telephone method.*

trend forecast: the long-term changes in market demand.

trial: within the adoption process of a consumer, the period when a product is first used. This is a critical point in determining the continued acceptance of the item by consumers.

trial-and-error pricing: selling an item at varying prices in different locations and then assessing the response to each of the prices.

trial buyer: see *trial offer.*

trial close: an attempt, based on perpetual clues, to zero in on the close of a sale before the natural termination of the sales presentation. See *check question; sales presentation.*

trial offer: a soft-sell method permitting a first-time purchaser to examine, use, or test an item for a short period before deciding whether to buy the item; may also include a special reduced rate. Synonymous with *free examination offer; free trial offer.* See *refund offer; soft offer; trial subscriber.*

trial sampling: in sales promotion, encouraging a consumer to try an item, usually by providing a free sample. See *trial size.*

trial size: a package that is smaller than the usual manufactured package; often used as a giveaway or sample. It can be free or sold at a low price to attract buyers. Trial-size packages are traditionally delivered by mail or are available in retail outlets.

trial subscriber: a first-time buyer of a subscription at a reduced rate and/or for a short time period. See *trial offer.*

trickle-down theory: the process by which federal funds flowing into the national economy stimulate growth by being distributed into organizations, as opposed to stimulating growth by direct payments. See *status float occurrence.*

trigger price: the world price for a commodity or product, set by an international organization.

trio of needs: three basic motivations that make consumers purchase an item or service—power, affiliation, and achievement. See *motivation.*

triple spotting: in broadcasting, running three commercials in succession without intervening news or programming. See *back-to-back commercials.*

troubleshoot: the activity of an individual who is engaged in locating and eliminating the source of trouble in a task or operation.

trough: the lowest point of economic activity.

truck distributor: synonymous with *truck jobber.*

truck jobber: a middleperson who delivers at the time of sale (e.g., vendors of ice cream, lunch specialties, and other items that must be sold fresh). Synonymous with *truck distributor; truck wholesaler; truck/wagon wholesaler.* See *cash-and-carry wholesaler; desk jobber; jobber.*

truck/wagon wholesaler: a limited-service merchant wholesaler who generally has a regular sales route, offers items from the truck or wagon, and delivers goods at the time of sale.

truck wholesaler: synonymous with *truck jobber.*

true panel: a panel that measures respondents repeatedly with respect to the same group of variables.

true prospect: a lead who can benefit from the use of the product, can afford to buy it, and has the authority to do so.

trunk show: the display of a vendor's total line of merchandise before an audience gathered for the purpose of inspecting the wares.

truth in advertising: the requirement of a firm to truthfully explain the attributes and benefits of products within its advertising. Firms that do not engage in truthful advertising can be cited for disciplinary action by the Federal Trade Commission. See *Truth in Lending Act of 1968.*

Truth in Lending Act of 1968: officially, the Consumer Credit Protection Act of 1968; requires that most categories of lenders disclose the true annual interest rate on virtually all types of loans and credit sales as well as the total dollar cost and other terms of a loan. See *Fair Credit Billing Act; right of rescission; truth in advertising.*

Truth in Packaging Act: synonymous with *Fair Packaging and Labeling Act of 1966.*

turbulence: a stage in a product's evolution representing the critical survival period for marginal producers.

turn: in merchandising, turnover of items within an inventory. Synonymous with *round turn.*

turn-and-earn concept: profit levels determined in terms of inventory turnover as the major variable.

turnaround: the movement by a freight carrier in which the driver returns to the point of origin following the unloading and reloading of cargo.

turnkey: a contractual agreement between a customer and an organization to provide full services or a complete product.

turnover: in retailing, the frequency with which an inventory is sold and replaced over a stated period, usually determined by dividing the net sales for the period by the average retail value of the inventory during that period. See *demand sensitivity.* Synonymous with *stock-turn.*

twenty-four-sheet poster: a printed sheet of outdoor advertising matter measuring 8 feet 8 inches high, and 19 feet 6 inches long, posted on an outdoor, steel-faced panel in an area of great traffic volume.

twin pack: a retail product package of two containers of the same product bound under the same wrapping or in the same holder and traditionally sold at a lower cost. See *bonus pack*.

twin streams of innovation activity: the innovation process as seen in building a product and also developing a marketing plan. The two processes go on simultaneously, and in fact, the marketing plan may originate first if the firm's strategy is to develop new products for specific target markets.

two-dimensional matrix: a simple form of relationship analysis using only two dimensions. Contrasts with the morphological matrix of several dimensions.

two-for-one sale: a consumer offer of two units of merchandise for the regular price of one, made by a seller to encourage sampling of the product and to unload dealers' shelves.

two-level channel: a marketing channel with two levels of distribution between the manufacturer/producer and consumer.

two-sheet poster: a printed sheet of advertising matter pasted on a display panel on subway and elevated platforms as a form of transportation advertising.

two-sided messages: communication in which a firm discusses both the benefits and limitations of a good, service, or idea.

two-step flow of communication: a theory stating that a message goes from the company to opinion leaders and then to the target market.

tying agreement:
(1) a method of control over distribution in which the producer forces the dealer to buy additional products to secure one highly desired product.
(2) an agreement between the manufacturer and dealer (or middleperson) requiring the dealer to buy certain items in order to purchase certain other items, or to not sell competing items. In turn, the dealer often receives exclusive rights to sales of the manufacturer's items in a specified territory. See *tie-in sales*.

UBD: see *undeliverable billing document*.

ultimate consumer: the individual who actually uses the bought merchandise. Synonymous with *final consumer*. See *consumer; industrial user*.

ultimo: the month prior to the present one.

umbrella brand: synonymous with *family brand*.

umbrella pricing: a large firm's strategy of maintaining the prices of its products at a level higher than needed so as to protect smaller competitors from overwhelming competition. The opposite of predatory pricing.

unaided recall: a means of determining a consumer's ability to remember an advertisement as a way of determining the effectiveness of the advertisement. Respondents are asked questions such as "What program did you watch this morning?" or "What commercials do you remember seeing yesterday?" In this method, respondents are not prompted in their replies as they are in aided recall. Cf. *aided recall.*

unbilled revenue: fees earned in a given period for which bills have not yet been sent to the customers.

unbundled prices: a pricing method that allows customers to select specific services on an optimal basis. Unbundling of prices is based on the concept that the seller will no longer quote one price for a product or service package.

uncertainty theory: the theory that profit arises from uncertainties due to innovations, changes in taste, price fluctuations, and the vagaries of competition. See *profit.*

unchanging list price: list prices that do not change over a determined time period, even when discounts from other competitors are offered. See *list price.*

uncontrollable factors: factors beyond the direct control of the manager (e.g., competitors' activities, international developments, economic conditions).

undeliverable billing document (UBD): an invoice that is undeliverable as addressed and will be returned to the sender by the Post Office.

underapplied overhead: the excess of factory overhead incurred over factory overhead applied. In practice, this means that the actual cost of overhead incurred was more than the amount charged to the manufacturing process during the year.

undercharge: to charge less than the proper amount.

underconsumption theory: a concept presented by the English economist J. A. Hobson that prosperity must always be brought to an end because consumption lags behind expanding output. Cf. *overproduction theory; Say's law.*

underground economy: of use to marketers in setting strategies; the part of a nation's income that, underreported or unreported, is not measured by official statistics.

underpackaging: the use of inadequate packaging methods for the level of protection needed.

underpayment: an invoice payment that is less than the billed amount. As a result, the seller may bill again for the remaining funds, accept the amount received as if full payment, or proportionately lower the service or items to be delivered.

underrun: the printing of fewer pieces of a publication or advertisement than originally planned. Cf. *overrun.*

underselling: selling at a price lower than that listed by a competitor. See *price cutting; rate war.*

undifferentiated marketing: a marketing technique offering one or more items for sale to the total market; no effort is made to be concerned with individual market segments. It is an easier and less expensive strategy to execute than differentiated marketing. Synonymous with *market aggregation; total market approach.* Cf. *differentiated marketing.*

undiscounted: goods or services sold at the full price without discounts or any allowances. Such items or services are usually stable in demand and have little price elasticity.

undisplay advertising: synonymous with *classified advertising.*

undistributed profits: the profits of a partnership, syndicate, or joint venture prior to division among the individuals concerned.

undo: to reverse a transaction.

unduplicated audience: synonymous with *cumulative audience.*

unearned discount: interest that is received but not yet earned.

unearned revenues: amounts that are received before they have been earned.

unfair competition: practices employed by a seller to increase profit by means of misleading advertising, selling below cost or dumping, obtaining rebates from suppliers, or utilizing other devices that unfairly take advantage of a competing firm.

unfair goods: products or items that are not produced by members of a union.

unfair practices: the discriminatory commercial exchange activities of goods that are either unfairly subsidized or dumped, or are otherwise illegitimate, as with counterfeit items.

unfair practices acts: state regulations establishing minimum resale prices. Such laws stipulate that goods must be sold for cost plus some nominal percentage. In practice, there is little enforcement of these rulings. Cf. *fair-trade acts.* Synonymous with *minimum markup laws; sale-below-cost laws; unfair sales acts; unfair trade practices acts.* See *tie-in sales.*

unfair sales acts: synonymous with *minimum markup laws; unfair practices acts.*

unfair trade practices acts: synonymous with *minimum markup laws; unfair practices acts.*

uniform delivered price: a pricing method whereby all the products are sold at the same delivery price in a stated area, without regard for delivery costs.

unique selling proposition (USP): differentiating the quality of an item on which an advertising strategy has been based. The three characteristics of an effective USP are:

(a) it should propose to the consumer that purchasing the merchandise will offer a particular benefit.

(b) the proposition should be one that a competitor cannot make, therefore making the brand or the advertising claim unique.

(c) the proposition must be strong enough to attract a large number of new customers. See *competitive advantage; message development.*

unique user: in altering the specifications of materials or other products, a company may be the only one to use it that way, thereby avoiding the issue posed by the Robinson-Patman Act concerning "like kind." See *Robinson-Patman Act of 1936.*

unit:

(1) *general:* a basic element; a standard of measurements; a single person or group.

(2) *marketing:* a standard package size or quantity where an item is sold, such as a case of beer or one page in a print advertising medium.

unitary demand: a situation in which a percentage change in price brings about an equal percentage change in quantity sold.

unitary elasticity: the concept that a change in price will be compensated by a corresponding change in demand, so that total income will remain the same.

unitary falloff: a percentage drop in response or sales volume equal to the percentage increase in the price of a good or service.

unit billing: a list of all purchases by a customer, prepared on a single statement.

unit contribution margin: the excess of the sales price of one unit over its variable costs.

unit control: an approach for listing the quantity of goods bought, sold, in stock, and on order, with additional breakdowns as needed. Cf. *taking inventory.*

unit cost: the cost of producing or distributing one unit of a processed item.

united load: a load in which all the containers are bound together in one or more units.

unitize: to combine a number of freight pieces into one large piece by banding, placing in a container, stacking, or any other means of assembling into a unit.

unit pricing:
(1) the quotation of prices in terms of a standard of measurement (by weight, length, count, etc.).
(2) the practice of pricing each product so that the price tag displays the price per unit of weight or volume in the package. Cf. *multiple-unit pricing.* Synonymous with *dual pricing; single-item pricing.*

unit-small batch technology: custom manufacturing of individual items.

unit store:
(1) an establishment of a company having but one place of business.
(2) a single store of a chain.

unit train: a train that ships only one cargo, nonstop between two locations.

unity: in advertising, the combination of all the factors in an advertisement to form a single impression that supports the one principle idea suggested by the advertisement.

unity of command: the concept in classical management that a subordinate must be responsible to only one superior.

universal product code (UPC): adopted by the food industry in 1973; a categorization where each item is given a 10-digit number, premarked on the package by the producer in the form of a bar code over 10 corresponding numbers. The bar code is easily read by an optical scanner at the checkout counter, which is controlled by a computer. The first 6 digits are the same for all the manufacturer's items and represent the name of the maker. The remaining digits refer to the item itself and are used by the maker to identify the product. Retailers use this portion of the code to set prices on computers. The correct price is automatically pulled from the table and recorded on the register. The last digit of the UPC code is a check digit. See *bar code; scanner.*

universe: the total population or market. Units of study to be examined in a marketing research effort are drawn from the universe through sampling. Therefore, the sample is a subset of the universe. See *sampling frame.*

unloading:
(1) selling merchandise at a relatively low price. Slang for dumping.
(2) stimulating the movement of consumer goods across retail counters by offering consumers inducements to pur-

chase merchandise through such techniques as premium offers, contests, and two-for-one sales.

unpaid balance: on a credit purchase, the difference between the purchase price and the down payment or the value of a trade-in; on a cash loan, the difference between the total loan and the amount that is still owed.

unplanned business district: a retail location that exists where two or more stores are located close to one another without the use of prior planning as to the number and composition of stores. There are four kinds of unplanned districts: central business district, secondary business district, neighborhood business district, and string.

unprotected consumers: people—usually children, the elderly, the sick and the poor—who are unable to argue for their legal rights in the market. State and federal legislation has been written to assist these consumers.

unselfish display: a form of altruistic display that also carries items not sold by the store.

unsought goods: products whose values are not yet recognized in the market. People may even be unaware of the existence of such products. Cf. *new unsought items; regularly unsought items.*

unstable market: a market in which forces of disequilibrium are reinforced so that movements away from equilibrium are not reversible. Cf. *stable market.*

unstructured question: used by consumer behavior researchers; a question that allows respondents to answer as they wish and does not limit the length of responses.

unstuffing: unloading cargo from a container.

unsystematic freight equalization: meeting competitors' locational discount and delivered prices so as to retain market share. This is an unfair pricing practice if used with predatory intent. A company with high fixed costs and significant capacity can have no other price-setting choices.

unwholesome demand state: a demand situation where a harmful item yields marketing activities that attempt to discourage consumers from buying it, such as tobacco products and alcoholic beverages. See *demand states.*

UPC: see *universal product code.*

upfront selling period: the season, usually in May and June, when television networks negotiate with advertisers on the cost of commercial time for forthcoming fall shows. See *preferred position.*

upgrade: see *upgrading.*

upgrading:
(1) *retailing:* offering superior goods and a greater assortment to customers.
(2) *merchandising:* increasing the value of an order either at the time of the order or purchase, or when a credit order is paid or a second order is requested.

upper turning point: a short period during which an upswing ends and a downswing begins.

upscale: people and households of well-above-average income and education. For advertisers and manufacturers, such people are the best prospects for purchasing expensive items, such as luxury cars, jewelry, cruise tickets. Cf. *downscale.*

upset price: the minimal price at which a seller is willing to sell; the beginning price asked at an auction prior to public bidding. Cf. *negotiated price.* See *marginal seller.*

upstream pricing: forming a market value for commodities from which other items are derived or other by-products are produced.

upturn: see *business cycle.*

upwardly mobile: descriptive of people within a market who are striving for and, to some extent, achieve a higher socioeconomic position. Numerous products are geared for these people.

urge line: in advertising, synonymous with *close.*

urgent consignments: merchandise that, because of its character, requires expeditious release by customs officials (e.g., perishable goods).

usage rate segmentation: a method of market segmentation based on the rate at which consumers purchase and utilize specific items; separates the market into heavy, light, and nonusers.

U.S. Customs bonded warehouse: see *warehouse, U.S. Customs bonded.*

U.S. Internal Revenue warehouse: see *warehouse, U.S. Internal Revenue.*

useless quality: goods created with quality, dependability, and/or performance that is superior to that demanded by the public.

user: anyone who requires the services of a system or product or who employs a service.

user-active: in new industrial product development, where the customer (a) develops the concept for the new item; (b) chooses a supplier able to make the item; (c) takes the initiative to purchase the item from the supplier, thereby assisting the diffusion of that new item.

user calls: callbacks made by a sales representative to a customer who has already made a purchase from him or her or from the organization. Cf. *callback.*

user expectation: a sales forecast construed after a consumer survey or some other form of consumer research has been conducted.

use tax: a tax levied on the initial use of an item rather than on the merchandise when it is sold. Cf. *value-added tax.*

USP: see *unique selling proposition.*

utility: the capability or power of an item to satisfy a need, as determined by the satisfaction the person receives from consuming something. See *form utility; place utility; time utility.*

vacuumize: to remove air from a filled container before closing it.

vacuum packaging: packaging in containers from which almost all air has been removed before the container is sealed.

valance: an identification strip or advertisement placed along the upper edge of a window, wall, counter, or shelf.

valence: a person's preference for a first-level outcome.

validated export license: a required document for global marketers; issued by the U.S. government authorizing the export of specific commodities. This license is for a specific transaction or time period in which the exporting is to take place. See *export license.*

validation: a process undertaken to assure the quality of research data; the quality of being truthful and or factual. It presupposes that the antecedent reasoning process is formal and correct. This quality is also a reflection on the quality of those researchers carrying out the research.

validity:

(1) used in the setting of marketing hypotheses; the degree to which a statistical technique accurately measures or predicts some value.

(2) the quality of being truthful and/or factual. It presupposes that the antecedent reasoning process is formal and correct. Cf. *reliability.*

valorization: government action leading to the establishment of a price or value for an item or service.

VALS: market information based on consumer's *values* and *lifestyles.* VALS data can be used to understand a buyer's decision making. VALS data group consumers into three categories:

(a) *need directed*—consumers who buy strictly on need.

(b) *outer directed*—consumers whose buying practices are influenced by how they believe other people will perceive them.

(c) *inner directed*—consumers whose buying practices are based primarily on satisfying their own psychological needs.

valuation: setting a value for anything.

value:

(1) purchasing power.

(2) the worth of property, goods, services, and so on.

value added: the part of the value of produced goods developed in a company. It is determined by subtracting from sales the costs of materials and supplies, energy, contract work, etc., as well as labor expenses, administrative and sales costs, and all other operating profits.

value-added reseller (VAR): a reseller that purchases goods from a primary producer and adds value through product assembly, modification, and/or customization.

value-added tax (VAT):

(1) a government tax on the value added; a tax on the selling price of manufactured items less the cost of the materials and expenses used in their production.

(2) a tax levied every time a product is sold to another member of the distribution channel. Cf. *domestic value-added; use tax.*

value analysis: a purchasing strategy of asking the buyer's engineers to project the costs of goods in an attempt to keep the vendor's prices low. Synonymous with *purchase research; value control.* See *value engineering.*

value control: synonymous with *value analysis.*

value engineering: synonymous with *value analysis,* but applied at the item's design stage.

value in use: the value of goods to the individual who uses them.

value judgment: in merchandising, the result of a consumer's comparison of the attractiveness of two or more alternative items or services.

value marketing: a concept integrating marketing, design, and communications into a mix created for a specific situation.

value of a customer: the total revenue coming from a buyer minus all expenditures associated with obtaining that total revenue excluding the cost of advertising which is associated with securing the customer.

values and lifestyles: see *VALS*.

vampire video: attention-getting devices in a television commercial that are more powerful in securing customers than the sponsor's comments about the product.

van container: a standard trailer used to carry general cargo.

VAR: see *value-added reseller.*

variability in service quality: differing service performance from one purchase experience to another. Variations may be due to the service firm's difficulty in diagnosing a problem (for repairs), the inability of a customer to verbalize service needs, and the lack of standardization and mass production for many services.

variable:
(1) a quantity that may assume any of a given set of values.

(2) a value that shifts as a result of direct intervention (independent variable) or a shift in another variable (dependent variable). See *dependent variable; independent variable.*

variable budget: a budget that divides expenses into fixed costs and variable costs.

The latter are allowed to vary on a predetermined basis with differing levels of output.

variable cost: a cost that is uniform per unit but changes in total in direct proportion to changes in the related total activity or volume. Cf. *fixed cost.* See *product costing.*

variable expenses: expenses that vary with the level of factory output or plant capacity (e.g., the expenses of power, oils, and lubricants vary with the number of machines in operation). Generally, variable expenses are considered controllable.

variable inspection: a method of quality control that uses measurements to determine the deviation from standards.

variable leader pricing: a strategy of offering specific products to consumers at prices so low that they produce little or no profit; frequently, these prices are changed each week.

variable markup policy: a form of cost-based markup pricing whereby separate categories of goods and services receive different percentage markups. It recognizes that some items require greater personal selling efforts, customer service, alterations, and end-of-season markdown than others. See *markup.*

variable presentation: in retailing, an approach to setting prices by examining customer services, salesperson's knowledge of the product, store image, assortment and variety, competition factors, and the prospect's satisfaction. The perfect combination gives the price the customer anticipates and is prepared to pay. Synonymous with *variable sales presentation.*

variable pricing: a marketing method permitting a different price to be charged to differing prospects or at differing times; used especially at outdoor flea markets, antique stalls, street vendors, and the like. Its shortcoming is that at various times customers may learn others have paid less for the same item. In addition, federal and state regulations protect competing retailers from discriminatory pricing that gives competitors an unfair advantage. Cf. *flat rate.* Synonymous with *flexible price policy.* See *market-minus prices.*

variable sales presentation: synonymous with *variable presentation.*

variable slot location system: the utilization of computers to keep track of where merchandise is kept. Items are placed in a warehouse by assigning newly brought merchandise to whatever place appears to be empty at that time.

variance:

(1) a disagreement between two sets of figures or facts.

(2) the measure of dispersion within a distribution of events.

(3) the difference between expected and actual production costs. See *management by exception.*

variance analysis: the difference between the actual and standard costs.

variety: different types of merchandise sold to consumers. See *assortment.*

variety store: a retail operation that carries limited quantities of apparel and accessories for the family as well as other goods, with prices set somewhat lower than in retail stores.

VAT: see *value-added tax.*

Veblen effect: an economic theory of Thorstein Veblen (1857–1929) where a higher price will increase the demand for products that, because of conspicuous consumption, have status attached to that higher price. See *law of demand.*

vehicle: an advertising medium within a media category (e.g., *Time* is a vehicle in the media category of magazines). Advertisers create a media mix tactic for an advertising campaign that details general media categories and the target vehicles within them.

vend: to offer to sell something.

vendee: the party who purchases or agrees to purchase something owned by another.

vending machine: selling merchandise with coin-operated equipment.

vendor: a manufacturer, wholesaler, or importer from whom goods or services are purchased.

vendor analysis: the assessment of the strengths and weaknesses of current or new suppliers in terms of such factors as merchandise quality, customer service, reliability, and price.

vendor chargebacks: the return of goods or services to a vendor, accompanied by an adjusted invoice. Proof of delivery to the vendor is usually provided. See *returns to vendor.*

vendor reliability: the capability of the seller to meet the conditions of the contract.

vendor's lien: an unpaid seller's right to take possession of property until the purchasing price has been recovered. Cf. *seller's lien.*

vent for surplus: the hypothesis that economic progress spreads from developing industrial locations to less developed geographic locations by means of the increasing demand for items in former areas.

venture: a business activity or undertaking that involves some or considerable risk.

venture capital: funds invested in enterprises that do not usually have access to conventional sources of capital (banks, stock market, etc.).

venture team concept: the new product development process, commencing with the creation of an idea or concept, through commercialization and sale to consumers.

VER (voluntary export restraint): see *voluntary restraint agreement.*

vertical audit: an in-depth analysis of one aspect of a firm's marketing strategy.

vertical channel system: a channel of distribution having centralization in management to coordinate efforts at all levels according to a set goal. See *voluntary chain.*

vertical conflict: conflict that occurs between channel members at different levels of the distribution system.

vertical cooperative advertising: synonymous with *cooperative advertising.*

vertical discount: a special lower rate for the buying of several broadcast time periods to be broadcast at intervals with a set time frame such as a day. The time slots are listed with hours vertically, and days horizontally.

vertical half page: a magazine advertising space dividing the page in equal halves vertically instead of horizontally. Space is then sold at the half-page rate. Cf. *vertical third page.*

vertical industrial market: a thin market for industrial products where nearly every industrial consumer is a possible customer.

vertically combined: a business firm that performs all the various stages of production of a single finished item. Synonymous with *vertically integrated.*

vertically integrated: synonymous with *vertically combined.*

vertical market: a market condition where the manufacturer's product is sold to buyers in only a single or a few industries. Cf. *horizontal market.*

vertical marketing system (VMS): establishments that deal with the manufacture and distribution of a particular item or related group of items. It often leads to vertical integration. VMSs were created to help firms control channel behavior (e.g., by reducing conflicts between channel intermediaries following their own financial goals).

vertical merger: the joining of firms responsible for different production stages of a particular product so that more of the entire process, from raw material to retail sales, is under the control of a single management.

vertical price fixing: a form of price fixing in which marketers at different levels of the distribution system get together to set retail prices.

vertical publication: in industrial advertising, a publication that reaches only people in one industry. Cf. *horizontal publication.*

vertical saturation: in broadcasting, numerous commercials from one sponsor who attempts to reach many people to build traffic for a sale to be held on the following day. See *saturation.*

vertical third page: print advertising space equal to one- third of the page, separated vertically into three units. Cf. *vertical half page.*

very profitable item (VPI): merchandise that a retailer believes will be quite easy to convince consumers to purchase from it as the preferred source of supply.

vest pocket supermarket: synonymous with *bantam store.*

video commercial: a commercial that appears at the beginning of a videotape film that has either been rented or bought.

Videodex: a research firm that supplies indexes of television program popularity, employing the diary technique to obtain information. See *diary method.*

video-shopping services: services that allow retailers to efficiently, conveniently, and promptly present information, receive orders, and process customer transactions. Its two basic categories are merchandise catalogs on videodiscs and videocassettes, and in-store and in-home ordering systems.

VIE: see *voluntary import expansion.*

viewer: a person who watches a television broadcast.

viewer impression: a person's reaction to a commercial or television program.

viewers per viewing household (VPVH): the estimated number of people in the viewing audience of any household where the television is tuned to a specific program or station, or during a stated time period.

vignette: a display that stimulates a product in actual use.

vintage capital: a measure of capital stock that assumes newly produced capital goods are more productive than older ones.

visible items of trade: see *visible trade.*

visible supply: stock in distribution centers that has been brought there from production areas. Cf. *invisible supply.*

visible trade: the portion of commerce between nations shown by records of transactions involving the exchange of tangible items.

visual: in advertising, one of the first rough layouts prepared for an advertisement; a sketch showing the relative placement of the elements in the advertisement.

visualizing: in advertising, interpreting and presenting a concept in pictorial format. It is usually followed with a headline. When presented in a layout, it can induce the reader to pause and examine, leading to the advertisement's great impact.

visual merchandise: in retailing, displaying items to be most pronounced and placed to their greatest advantage.

vital statistics: data on individuals having to do with dates of birth and death, ownership of a house, marriages, divorces, and so on. See *demographics.*

VMS: see *vertical marketing system.*

VO: see *voice-over.*

vocational advertising: advertising used in such diverse areas as farming, trade, industry, and the professions.

voice-over (VO): in broadcasting, narration with the speaker out of sight of the television audience. Synonymous with *announcer voice-over.*

void: that which has no legal effect.

voidable contract: an agreement that can be rescinded by either of the parties in the event of fraud, incompetence, or other sufficient cause. See *fraud; right of rescission.*

volume: a quantity, bulk, or amount.

volume bonus: a purchase incentive for customers who may be offered a discount on large purchases. See *Robinson-Patman Act of 1936.*

volume discount: synonymous with *bulk discount; patronage discount.*

volume merchandise allowance: a manufacturer's discount offered to a wholesaler or retailer for purchasing large volumes of goods.

volume of trade transacted: the sum of all sales of all business activities in a nation's economy.

voluntary chain: a wholesaling organization established by independent retailers or wholesalers to gather increased purchasing power. Synonymous with *wholesale-sponsored voluntary chain.* See *affiliated wholesaler; voluntary wholesaler.*

voluntary export quota: a quantitative restriction that a country places on the export of certain marketed items to another nation. Usually evolves from complaints from an importing nation that its domestic industry is being injured by continuing exports of the item from its trading partner.

voluntary export restraint (VER): see *voluntary restraint agreement.*

voluntary import expansion (VIE): a policy under which a nation replies to another's threats of trade sanctions by agreeing to buy more of certain marketed items from that country.

voluntary restraint agreement (VRA): a bilateral arrangement whereby an exporting country agrees to reduce or restrict exports without the importing country having to impose quotas, tariffs, or other import controls. Such agreements are generally undertaken to avoid action by the importing country against imports that may injure or in some way threaten the positions of domestic firms in the industry in question. See *protected market.*

voluntary simplicity: a consumer lifestyle in which people have an ecological awareness, seek material simplicity and durability, strive for self-reliance, and purchase more inexpensive products.

voluntary wholesaler: a wholesaler who sponsors a voluntary chain that is active in supplying numerous members. See *voluntary chain.*

volunteerism: synonymous with *satisfaction (1).*

voucher: a written statement that bears witness or vouches for something (e.g., a voucher showing that services have been rendered or goods bought).

VPI: see *very profitable item.*

VPVH: see *viewers per viewing household.*

VRA: see *voluntary restraint agreement.*

wagon distributor: synonymous with *truck jobber.*

wagon jobber: synonymous with *truck jobber.*

wagon retailer: a merchant middleperson engaged in selling anything for a profit. He or she conducts huckstering.

waiting line theory: an approach to maximizing the efficient servicing of arrivals at a service facility by balancing the costs associated with waiting time and idle time.

wait order: a request to a medium to hold an advertisement and not release it until a specified future date; used especially in newspapers.

waiver: the release signed by an inventor who wishes to get consideration of a non-patented idea or product.

waiver of restoration premium: a provision in many contracts whereby the company agrees not to charge an additional premium for reinstating the amount of the contract after loss has occurred.

walk: (slang) a customer who fails to purchase something and walks out of the store.

walk-out: see *walk.*

want slip: written statements submitted to buyers by salespersons indicating customer-requested items not in stock.

warehouse: a structure where goods are stored prior to distribution (see the following warehouse terms). See *bonded warehouse; public warehouse.*

warehouse, bulk: a warehouse for the tank storage of liquids and open, dry products (e.g., coal, sand, stone).

warehouse, captive: synonymous with *warehouse, private.*

warehouse, commodity: a warehouse that stores commodity goods (cotton, wool, tobacco, and other grown items). See *godown.*

warehouse, company: synonymous with *warehouse, private.*

warehouse, private: a warehouse operated by an owner, which holds his or her goods. Synonymous with *warehouse, captive; warehouse, company.*

warehouse, state-bonded: a public warehouse, under government supervision, that has been licensed by a state prior to operation. Merchandise is stored there without payment of duties or taxes until it is withdrawn.

warehouse, U.S. Customs bonded: a federal warehouse where goods remain until duty has been collected from the importer. Goods under bond are also kept there.

warehouse, U.S. Internal Revenue: a public warehouse in which the owner of goods has posted a bond guaranteeing payment of internal revenue tax on U.S.-produced items.

warehouse club: a no-frills, cash-and-carry discount store that operates in a poor location. To shop there, the customer must become a member and pay dues.

warehouse receipt: an instrument listing the goods or commodities deposited in a warehouse. It is a receipt for the commodities listed, for which the warehouse is the bailee. Warehouse receipts may be either nonnegotiable or negotiable.

warehouse replenishment time: the speed at which products sold from a warehouse are replaced by the factory.

warehouse retailing: high-volume, low-overhead mass merchandising with few customer services.

warehouse showroom: a discount store that follows a strategy based on low overhead and high turnover; customers pay cash and must transport the merchandise themselves.

warehouse stock: goods held in quantity in a warehouse for reasons of economy.

warehouse store:

(1) a no-frills supermarket that stocks a wide variety of food and nonfood items and sells them at lower prices than the typical supermarket price.

(2) a simply furnished retail outlet that offers a limited assortment of items at discount prices as a result of special arrangements made with a producer. Synonymous with *box store.*

warehousing: involving the physical facilities used primarily for the storage of goods held in anticipation of sales and transfers within a distribution channel.

wares: items or commodities offered for sale.

warranty:

(1) *general:* a statement, either written, expressed, or implied, that a certain statement identified in a contract is true or will be true.

(2) *sales:* a promise by a seller that the product or property being sold is as he or she has represented it. Usually a warranty is presented with the sold goods. Cf. *guarantee; product liability.* See *caveat emptor; express warranty; implied warranty.*

warranty price: the price established for an item that is deemed fair and just by both seller and buyer.

wash sale: a spurious sale in which the seller becomes the purchaser of what he or she sells. The purpose is to create activity in the item or to establish a market price. A wash sale is prohibited by law.

was-is pricing: synonymous with *psychological discounting.*

wastage:

(1) *general:* wear of property; loss because of usage, deterioration, etc.

(2) *marketing:* people of no specific value to an advertiser because they are not part of the designated target market.

waste: material or supplies considered unfit for its original use that results from poor handling, errors in production, mishandling, etc. Cf. *scrap.*

waste circulation:

(1) advertising done in a location where there is no distribution for the advertised product.

(2) the number of people in an audience who are not prospects (e.g., infants).

watermark: a distinctive mark or design produced in paper to identify the manufacturer.

wave scheduling: synonymous with *pulsation.*

waving: synonymous with *pulsation.*

weakest-link theory: the concept that the least durable component in a product will control its useful life. According to this theory, all components should be built so that their life span will be equal in all units of similar function and price. See *functional obsolescence; planned obsolescence.*

weak market: a situation characterized by a greater demand for selling than for purchasing.

wearout:

(1) the tendency of consumer response to a sales promotion to diminish over time.

(2) the point when an advertisement or advertising campaign is no longer effective; based on frequency of presentation, the target market, the quality of the advertisement, its novelty, etc. The length of deterioration varies from weeks to years.

Webb-Pomerene Act of 1918: federal legislation exempting exporters' associations from antitrust regulations.

Weber's Law: a marketing concept used in the understanding of people's perception of brands; suggests that consumers determine a product's value not on its separate characteristics but instead on their perceived differences between it and alternative brands. See *just noticeable difference.*

weekly: a periodical published weekly. Cf. *daily.*

week's supply technique: one of the four primary methods of retailers for stock planning. When sales shift considerably, this approach is not very helpful because it provides for the stock level to vary directly with sales, a situation that may not occur.

weight:
(1) *general:* the amount or quantity of heaviness or mass.
(2) *general:* the thickness of paper stock.
(3) *advertising:* the number of exposures of an advertising message.
(4) *advertising:* the number of gross rating points an advertiser wishes to place in a market. See *gross weight; media weight.*

weighted average: a periodic inventory cost flow assumption whereby the cost of goods sold and the ending inventory are determined to be a weighted-average cost of all merchandise available for sale during the period.

weighted-point method: determining sources of supply by setting evaluation factors to which numbers can be assigned as relative weights.

weighting: in market research, the statistical method applied when units drawn with unequal probabilities to form a sample are assigned weights to make them comparable for analytical purposes. As there is a great difference in population size between locations, people have different probability levels of being chosen for a sample. Weights are assigned to the units from each area to make the entire combined sample representative of the geographic population from which it was drawn.

wet goods: liquids.

Wheeler-Lea Amendment of 1938: federal legislation, amending the Federal Trade Commission Act of 1914, to protect the consumer against unfair trade practices in interstate commerce and against false or misleading advertising of foods, drugs, and cosmetics. See *phony list price.*

wheel of retailing: the theory that, when entering the market, new forms of retailing first emphasize lower prices; as time passes, the prices rise, making the merchandise subject to competition from newer organizations, which commence operations with lower prices. See *trading down; trading up.*

whiplash impact: shifts in the demand for items causing excessive or inadequate inventories at differing points in the channel of distribution because of inadequate controls and data. See *derived demand.*

whip shot: synonymous with *zip pan.*

white-coat ruling: a ruling from the Federal Trade Commission claiming that it is deceptive advertising to use actors attired in white laboratory smocks so they will look like doctors when speaking in support of any product or service in an advertisement or commercial.

white goods:
(1) appliances of substantial size and cost (e.g., refrigerators, freezers, washing machines, stoves). The name comes from the white enamel finish often used.

(2) sheets, pillowcases, and linens. The name comes from the early tradition of manufacturing these items in only white. Cf. *brown goods; orange goods; red goods; yellow goods.*

white mail: customer correspondence received in an envelope other than the one provided by the marketer; contains customer inquiries, complaints, or changes of address.

white space: open space in a print advertisement; usually found in advertisements for luxury goods as advertisers believe empty space gives an appearance of elegance. Conversely, inexpensive items are often crowded together when advertised.

whiz: synonymous with *zip pan.*

whole market approach: an approach that deals with the full range of customers; does not recognize nor make an effort to appeal to the differences between various segments. See *market segmentation.*

wholesale: to sell goods in gross to retailers, who then sell the merchandise to customers.

wholesale cooperatives: full-service merchant wholesalers owned by member firms to economize functions and offer broad support. There are producer-owned and retailer-owned wholesale cooperatives.

wholesale price: the price for goods paid by retailers to suppliers.

wholesale price index (WPI): a measure used by marketers, compiled by the U.S. Bureau of Labor Statistics, showing the average change in the price of approximately 2,200 commodities at the primary market level (usually the level at which the commodity is first sold commercially in substantial volume) compared with the average level in selected base years. Synonymous with *producer price index.* See *price index.*

wholesaler:
(1) an intermediary that distributes products primarily to commercial or professional users.

(2) an individual who buys and sells goods to retailers and other users but does not sell in significant amounts to the consumer. There are:

(a) full-service wholesalers—those who provide services such as carrying stock, maintaining sales forces, and offering management and credit assistance to purchasers.

(b) limited-service wholesalers—those who offer some, but not all, the services provided by full-service wholesalers. Cf. *jobber; merchant wholesaler.* Synonymous with *distributor.* See *cash-and-carry wholesaler; rack jobber; truck jobber.*

wholesale-sponsored voluntary chain: synonymous with *voluntary chain.*

wholesaling:
(1) all the activities provided by wholesaling intermediaries involved in selling merchandise to retailers; to industrial, institutional, farm, and professional businesses; or to other types of wholesaling intermediaries.

(2) selling merchandise to firms that purchase for reasons other than consumption, usually to resell the item for profit. Cf. *re-*

tailing. See *merchandise mart; wholesaling intermediary.*

wholesaling intermediary: any firm that engages primarily in wholesaling activities. See *wholesaling.*

wholly-owned subsidiary: a separate organization, owned and completely controlled by a parent firm.

width of a product mix: the number of different product lines a company offers.

windfall profit: an unexpected profit arising from causes that were not controlled by the recipient.

window dressing:
(1) a statement that appears to be more positive than warranted.

(2) a statement that makes something appear better than it is. See *painting the bus.*

window streamer: an advertising banner hanging in a store window. Synonymous with *window strip.*

window strip: synonymous with *window streamer.*

win-win situation: a completed transaction that pleases both the purchaser and seller.

withdrawals: items sold or bought out of a consignment. Usually the consignee reports on and pays for these items on a periodic schedule.

without recourse: in sales, an agreement that the purchaser accepts all risks in the transaction and gives up all rights of recourse. Cf. *with recourse.* See *caveat emptor.*

with-pack premium: a gift or other item placed inside or outside another product. See *in-pack; on-pack.*

with recourse: an agreement that if the seller is unable to meet his or her obligations, the purchaser has the right to endorse a claim against the seller for sustained damages. Cf. *without recourse.*

Wool Products Labeling Act: federal legislation, passed in 1939 and made effective in 1941, requiring that items containing wool, with certain exceptions such as carpets and upholstery, must show labels on the merchandise indicating the percentage of new wool, reused or reprocessed wool, and other fibers or fillers that are used.

word association: synonymous with *free association.*

word-of-mouth advertising: a promotion not paid for, where one satisfied customer of an item or service communicates his or her feelings to others who may in turn become buyers of the same item or service. In fact, it is not advertising as it is not paid for by an advertiser. See *nationally advertised brand.*

work flow: the sequence of jobs in an organization needed to produce the firm's goods or services.

working capital: the excess of current assets over current liabilities, representing the capital immediately available for the continued operation of a business.

working capital turnover: a measure of the amount of working capital used in sustaining the sales of a period, computed by dividing net sales by average working capital.

work-in-process inventory: all products that have begun the manufacturing process but have not been completed. Work-in-process inventory is the cost of partially completed production. Cf. *finished-goods inventory.*

workload analysis:

(1) the estimation of sales activities needed to fulfill the potential of a sales territory.

(2) an approach to sales force design in which the size of the sales force is determined by dividing the total workload in hours by the number of selling hours available from each salesperson.

work unit: the smallest subdivision of a job or operation.

world price: the price at which a given item is selling internationally under market conditions in effect at the time of the seale.

worldwide firms: organizations that are global, multinational, or transnational.

WPI: see *wholesale price index.*

wraparound: a decorative banner draped about or circling an in-store merchandise display. Wraparounds are an example of point-of-purchase advertising.

wrapper:

(1) a label.

(2) the sheet of flexible material (paper, foil, etc.) or lamination used to cover a product for storage, sale, or shipment.

wrap-up: (slang) a customer who buys readily.

write-off: an asset that has been determined to be uncollectible and therefore has been charged off as a loss. Sometimes it is the debt itself.

write-up: in sales, documentation of the making of a sale.

xenophobia: affects global marketing and consumer activities; the fear of foreigners. It can express itself in unfair and illegal trade practices around the world, especially for people living and working within the borders of competing nations.

yearly order: synonymous with *blanket order.*

yellow goods: nonconsumable household items with a high profit margin, such as refrigerators, dishwashers, and ovens, that are costly and replaced after many years of service. At times, they are also called white goods. Cf. *brown goods; orange goods; red goods; white goods.*

yellow pages advertising: advertisements placed in a telephone yellow pages directory. Yellow pages display advertisements have copy providing the advertiser's address and telephone number, product/service offerings, brands carried, and hours of operation. Sometimes there are illustrations. Cf. *directory advertising.*

"yes, but" technique: a sales approach to deal with objections, where the salesperson first sympathizes with the prospect, and then attempts to alter that person's point of view. Synonymous with *agree-and-counterattack technique; agreeing-and-neutralizing technique.*

yes-no controls: controls that allow for a screening process point at which specific approval is needed to permit the activity to continue.

yield:
(1) to give up possession.

(2) to pay.

yield management pricing: a form of demand-based pricing whereby a firm determines the mix of price-quantity combinations that generates the highest level of revenue for a given period.

YOU attitude: in advertising, the concept that all advertisements must appeal to individuals, not groups, for greatest impact and value.

youth market: people under 25 years of age, who are often interested in goods and services that are different, unusual, or suggest values other than those held by older people.

yuppie: a creation of the 1980s, *y*oung *u*rban *p*rofessionals with money. Usually, they are in their mid-30s and represent a target audience for some advertisers.

zapping: of great concern to marketers and advertisers, using a television remote control to change stations during a program's commercial breaks to avoid watching advertisements.

ZBB: see *zero-based budgeting.*

zero-based budgeting (ZBB):
(1) an approach to budgeting in which each part of the organization must justify each item in its budget before it will be granted the funds it needs.

(2) a financial management technique to redirect funds from lower-priority current programs to higher ones to pinpoint opportunities for improved efficiency and effectiveness, to reduce budgets while raising operating performance, and to improve profitability.

zero-based media planning: a media selection process that involves (a) listing and ranking media objectives in order of importance; (b) examining and ranking possible media components in terms of their compatibility with the stated media objectives; (c) forming decision packages (plans consisting of one or more of these components); (d) comparing the decision packages with other packages that are retained and compatible with objectives; and (e) reviewing, making tradeoffs, and arriving at resolution of the plan.

zero defects: a production function that is discharged with no mistakes and without wasted resources, a rare occurrence. At times, workers are rewarded when the zero defects are found.

zero haven: a tax-haven nation that levies no taxes (or practically none) on income.

zip advertisement: synonymous with *outsert.*

zip code: the U.S. Postal Service's system of designating geographic areas for mail sorting and delivery. Short for zoning improvement plan. See *zip code analysis.*